PEACE MAKER

ピースメーカー

Peace Maker Volume 2
Created By Nanae Chrono

Translation - Ryan Flake
English Adaptation - Christine Boylan
Retouch and Lettering - Star Print Brokers
Production Artist - Gavin Hignight
Cover Designers - Al-Insan Lashley & Chelsea Windlinger

Editor - Hope Donovan
Digital Imaging Manager - Chris Buford
Pre-Production Supervisor - Erika Terriquez
Production Manager - Elisabeth Brizzi
Managing Editor - Vy Nguyen
Creative Director - Anne Marie Horne
Editor-in-Chief - Rob Tokar
Publisher - Mike Kiley
President and C.O.O. - John Parker
C.E.O. and Chief Creative Officer - Stuart Levy

A  Manga

TOKYOPOP and 🐸 are trademarks or registered trademarks of TOKYOPOP Inc.

TOKYOPOP Inc.
5900 Wilshire Blvd. Suite 2000
Los Angeles, CA 90036

E-mail: info@TOKYOPOP.com
Come visit us online at www.TOKYOPOP.com

ISBN: 978-1-4278-0076-3

First TOKYOPOP printing: December 2007

10 9 8 7 6 5 4 3 2 1

Printed in the USA

PEACE MAKER

ピースメーカー

Volume 2
by Nanae Chrono

HAMBURG // LONDON // LOS ANGELES // TOKYO

ICHIMURA TETSUNOSUKE

HIJIKATA'S PAGE

BRASH TETSU HAS JOINED THE SHINSENGUMI TO LEARN TO BECOME STRONG. HE WANTS TO GET REVENGE ON HIS PARENTS' MURDERERS, CHOUSHUU REBELS. ALTHOUGH HE JOINED THE SHINSENGUMI WITH ASPIRATIONS OF BECOMING A SWORDSMAN, HE'S BEEN ASSIGNED THE THANKLESS DUTY OF HIJIKATA'S PAGE.

OKITA SOUJI

CAPTAIN OF THE FIRST SQUAD

THE BEST SWORDSMAN IN THE SHINSENGUMI. HE'S GENERALLY CALM AND FRIENDLY, BUT WIELDING A BLADE CAN TRANSFORM HIM INTO A HEARTLESS KILLER.

HIJIKATA TOSHIZOU

VICE COMMANDER

BECAUSE OF HIS COLD DEMEANOR AND BRUTALITY, HE IS KNOWN AS THE "DEMON VICE COMMANDER."

MAIN CHARACTERS

YAMAZAKI SUSUMU

SHINSENGUMI NINJA

A SPY FOR THE SHINSENGUMI, HE REPORTS TO HIJIKATA. TACITURN AND COLD, HE HOLDS MANY SECRETS.

KONDOU ISAMI

DIRECTOR

A FOUNDING MEMBER OF THE SHINSENGUMI AND ALSO A MASTER AT THE SHIEIKAN DOJO IN EDO, THE MAIN DOJO OF THE TENNEN RISHIN STYLE.

HARADA SANOSUKE

CAPTAIN OF THE TENTH SQUAD

A GIANT AMONG MEN, HE'S A MASTER OF THE SPEAR IN THE HOZOIN SCHOOL STYLE. HE'S GOOD FRIENDS WITH SHINPACHI.

ICHIMURA TATSUNOSUKE

TETSU'S OLDER BOTHER AND GUARDIAN. HE'S ALWAYS WORRYING ABOUT TETSU. TATSU WANTS NOTHING TO DO WITH SWORDFIGHTING, AND IS A BOOKKEEPER FOR THE SHINSENGUMI.

NAGAKURA SHINPACHI

CAPTAIN OF THE SECOND SQUAD

SMALL BUT STRONG. A SWORDSMAN LIKE OKITA. HE FIGHTS IN THE SHINTO-MUNEN SCHOOL STYLE.

SAYA

TETSU SAVED HER FROM SOME RUFFIANS, AND NOW THE TWO ARE FRIENDS. SAYA CANNOT SPEAK, BUT COMMUNICATES THROUGH HAND GESTURES AND WRITING.

☐ SHINSENGUMI MEMBERS

☐ PERSONS OUTSIDE THE SHINSENGUMI

THE STORY OF PEACE MAKER

IN THE FIRST YEAR OF GENJI, 1864, JAPAN WAS IN GREAT TURMOIL. MILITANT AND XENOPHOBIC FORCES, WHICH HAD LONG OPPOSED THE TOKUGAWA SHOGUNATE, ADVOCATED EXPELLING WESTERN INFLUENCE AND RESTORING THE EMPEROR IN KYOTO TO POWER. TO PROTECT THE SHOGUNATE'S INTEREST IN KYOTO, A LEGENDARY PEACEKEEPING FORCE WAS FORMED FROM TWO HUNDRED-SOME RONIN. THEY WERE THE SHINSENGUMI. THIS IS THE STORY OF ICHIMURA TETSUNOSUKE, WHO SOUGHT TO JOIN THEM.

CONTENTS

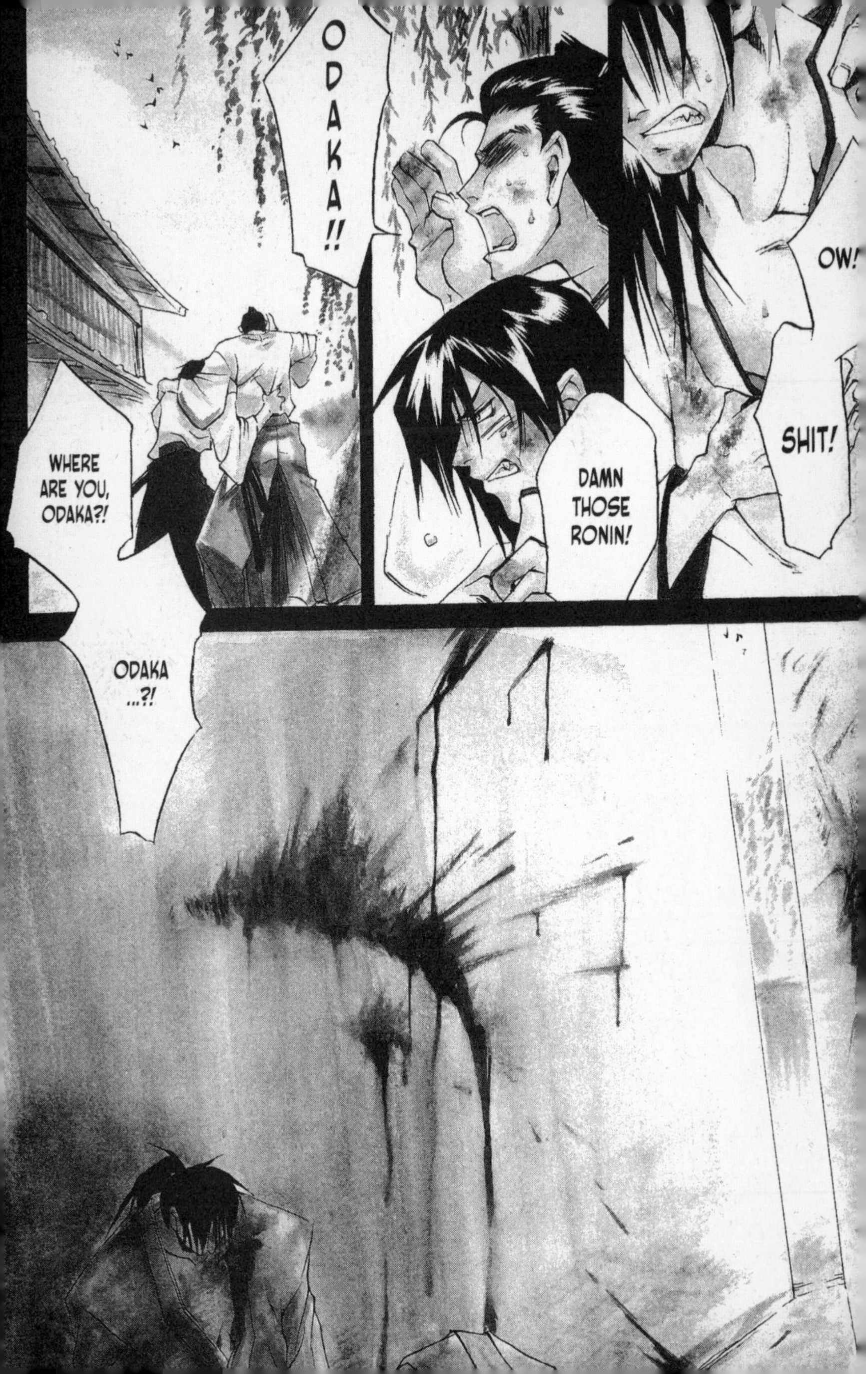
OW!
SHIT!
DAMN THOSE RONIN!
ODAKA!!
WHERE ARE YOU, ODAKA?!
ODAKA ...?!

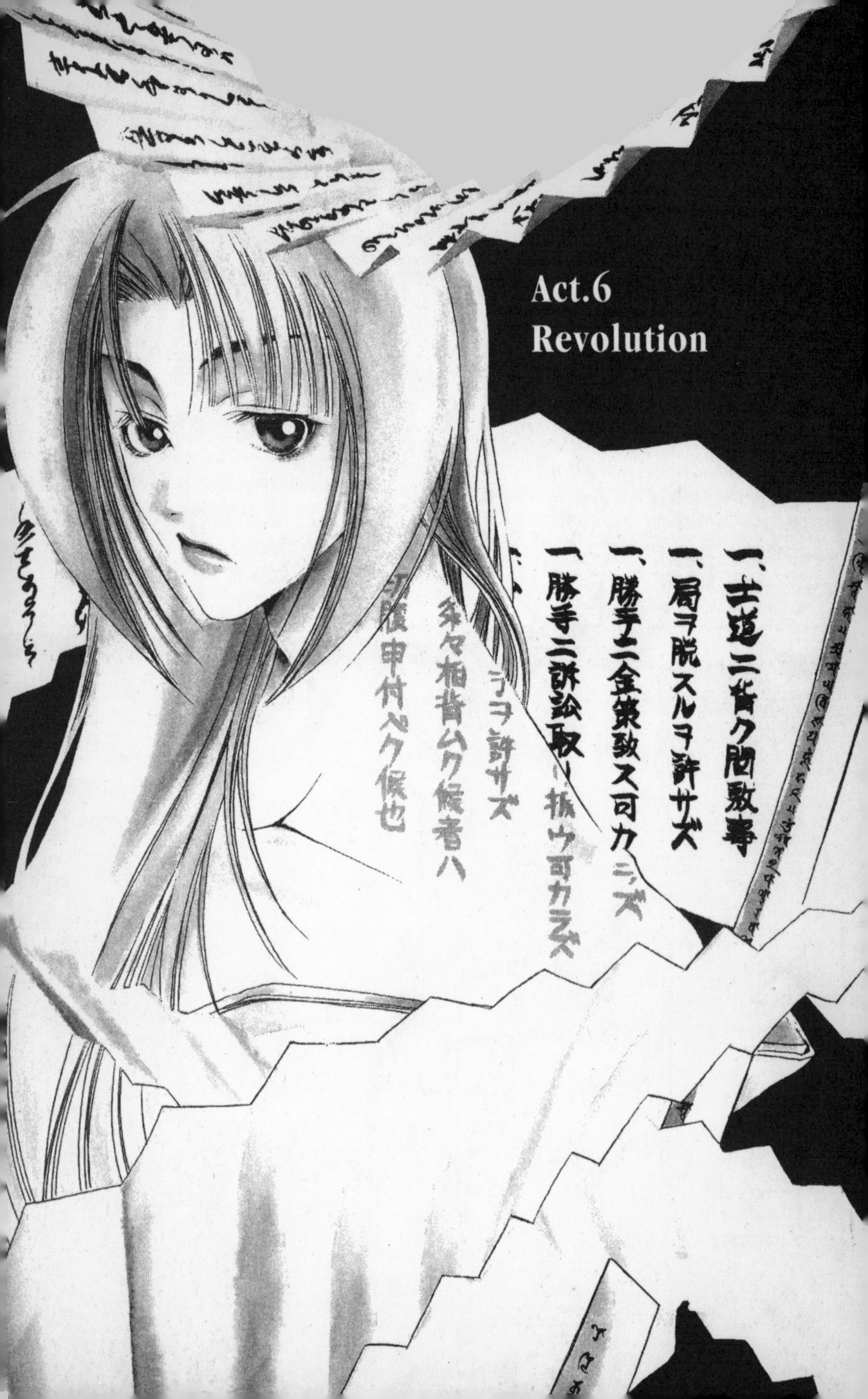
Act.6
Revolution
一、士道ニ背ク間敷事
一、局ヲ脱スルヲ許サズ
一、勝手ニ金策致ス可カラズ
一、勝手ニ訴訟取リ扱ウ可カラズ
ヲ許サズ
条々相背ムク候者ハ
切腹申付ベク候也

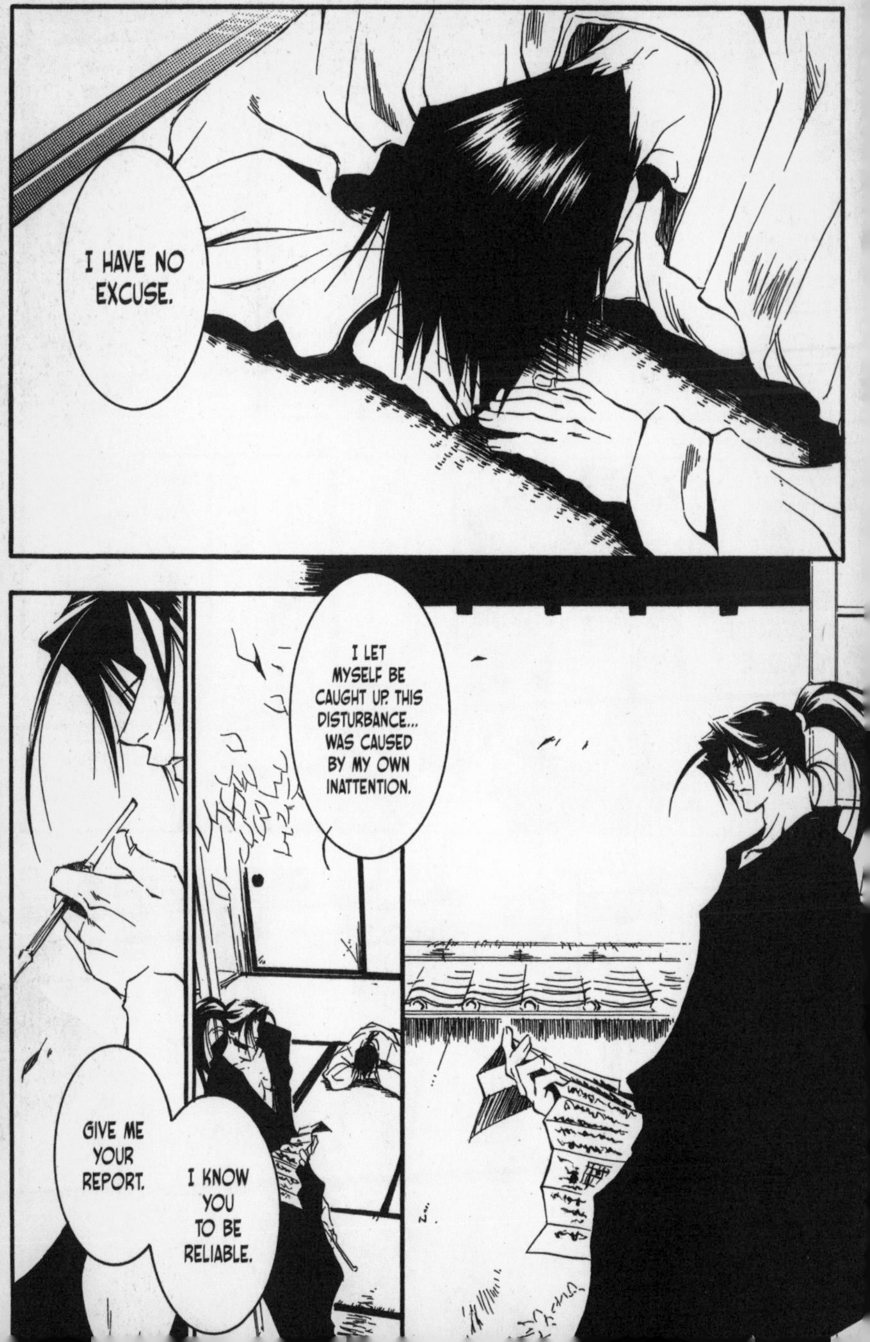
I HAVE NO EXCUSE.
I LET MYSELF BE CAUGHT UP. THIS DISTURBANCE... WAS CAUSED BY MY OWN INATTENTION.
GIVE ME YOUR REPORT.
I KNOW YOU TO BE RELIABLE.

* Roushi: Another name for ronin, or wandering samurai

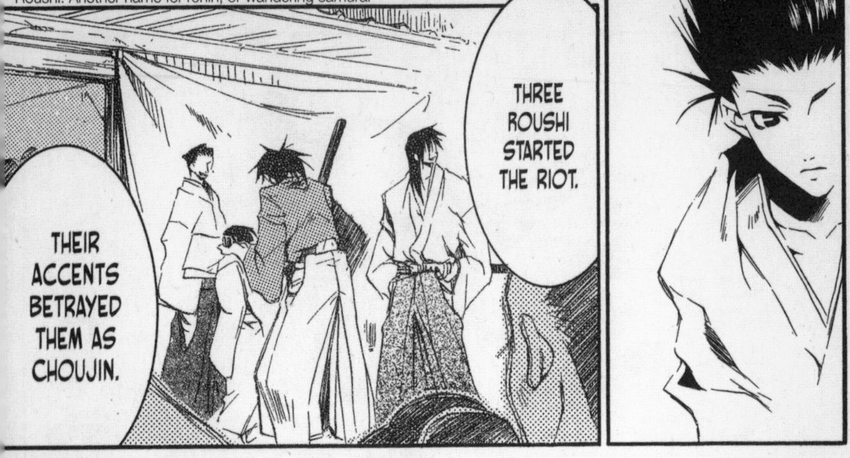
THREE ROUSHI STARTED THE RIOT.
THEIR ACCENTS BETRAYED THEM AS CHOUJIN.

* Choujin: People from the Choushuu province

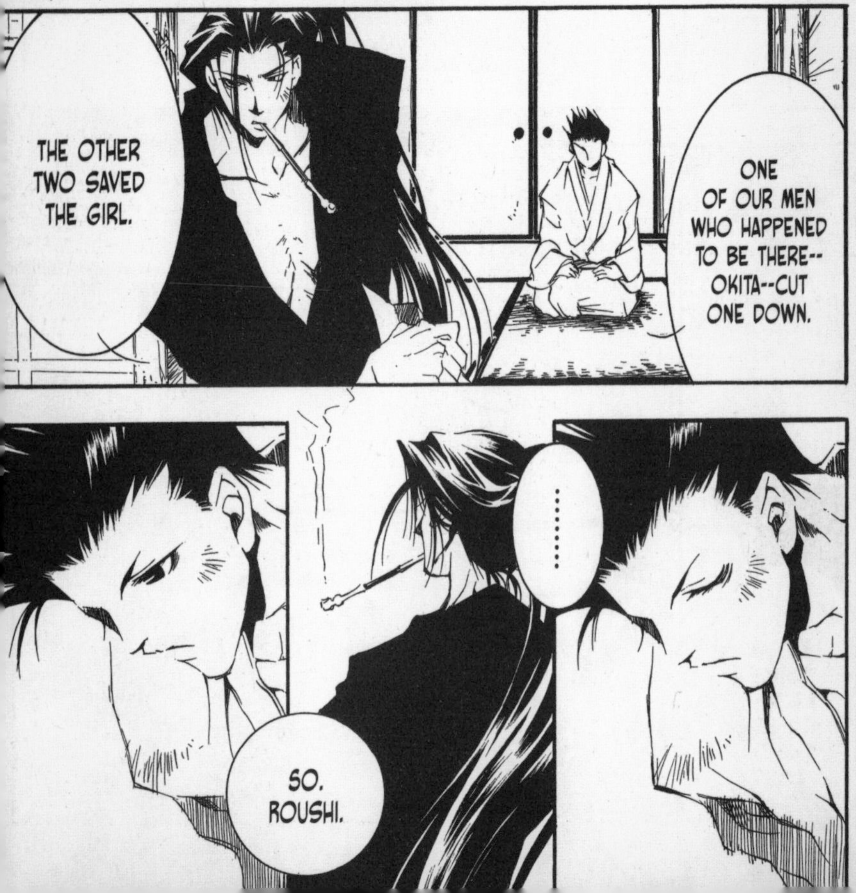
ONE OF OUR MEN WHO HAPPENED TO BE THERE--OKITA--CUT ONE DOWN.
THE OTHER TWO SAVED THE GIRL.
....
SO. ROUSHI.

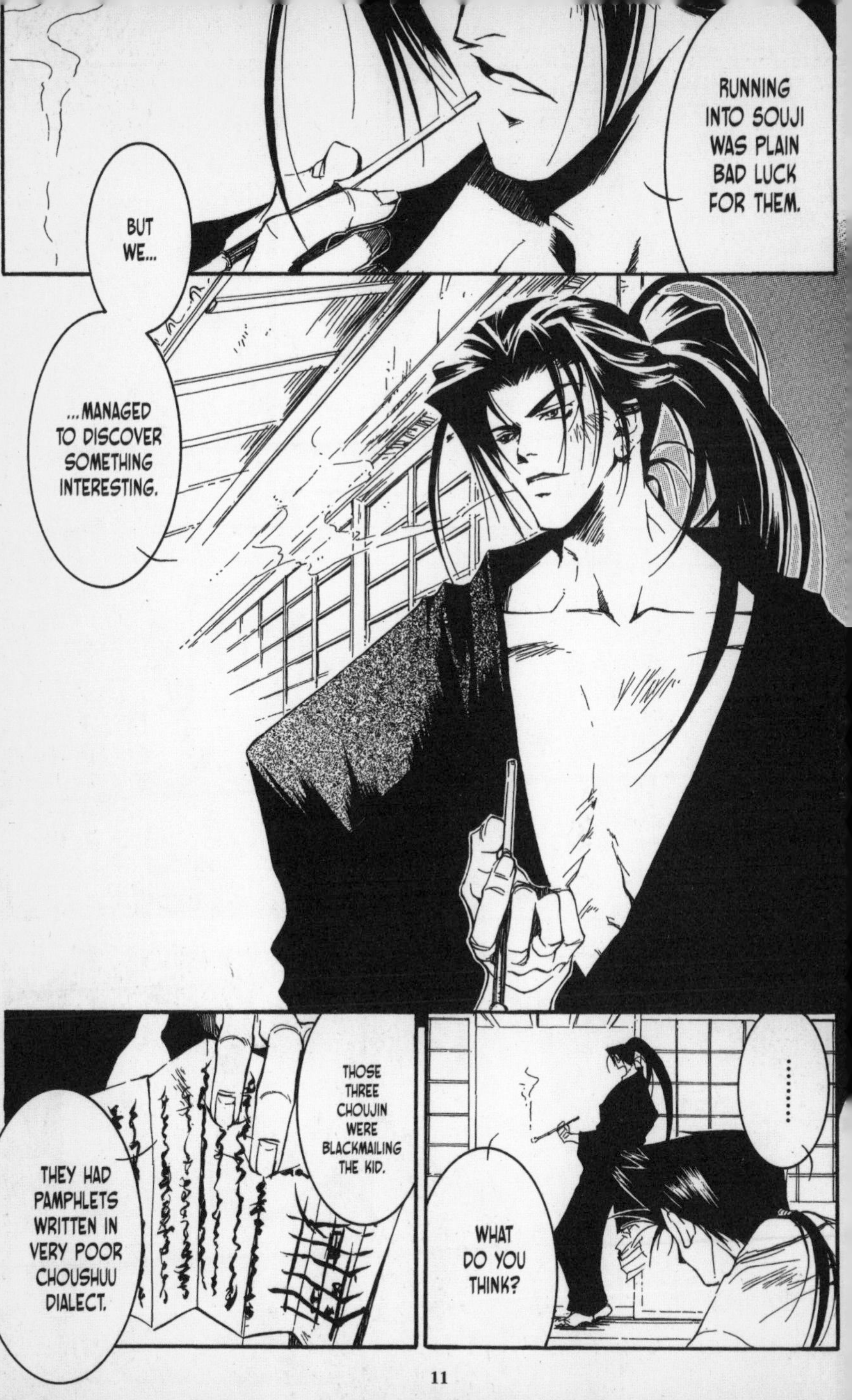
RUNNING INTO SOUJI WAS PLAIN BAD LUCK FOR THEM.
BUT WE...
...MANAGED TO DISCOVER SOMETHING INTERESTING.
....
WHAT DO YOU THINK?
THOSE THREE CHOUJIN WERE BLACKMAILING THE KID.
THEY HAD PAMPHLETS WRITTEN IN VERY POOR CHOUSHUU DIALECT.

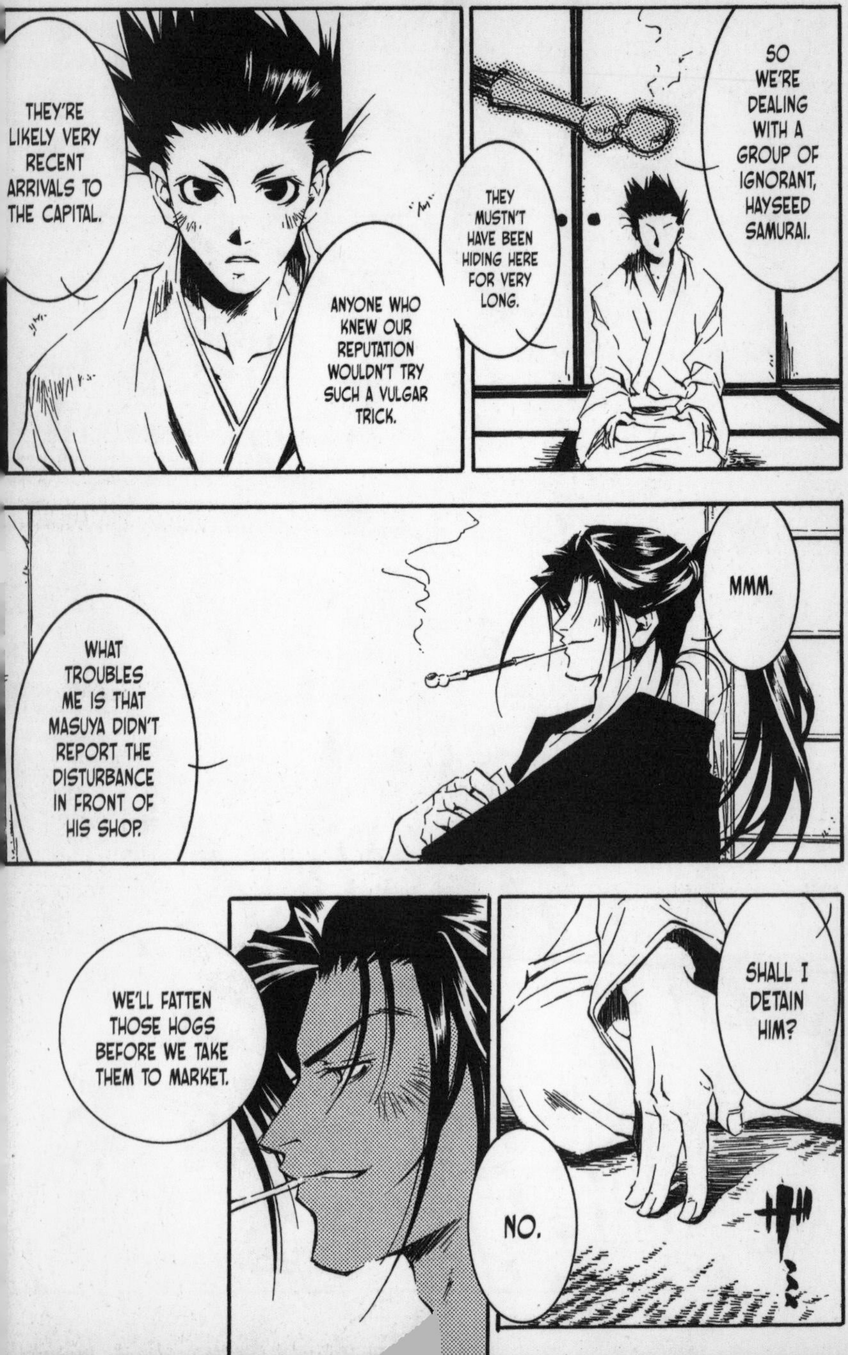
SO WE'RE DEALING WITH A GROUP OF IGNORANT, HAYSEED SAMURAI.
THEY MUSTN'T HAVE BEEN HIDING HERE FOR VERY LONG.
THEY'RE LIKELY VERY RECENT ARRIVALS TO THE CAPITAL.
ANYONE WHO KNEW OUR REPUTATION WOULDN'T TRY SUCH A VULGAR TRICK.
MMM.
WHAT TROUBLES ME IS THAT MASUYA DIDN'T REPORT THE DISTURBANCE IN FRONT OF HIS SHOP.
SHALL I DETAIN HIM?
NO.
WE'LL FATTEN THOSE HOGS BEFORE WE TAKE THEM TO MARKET.

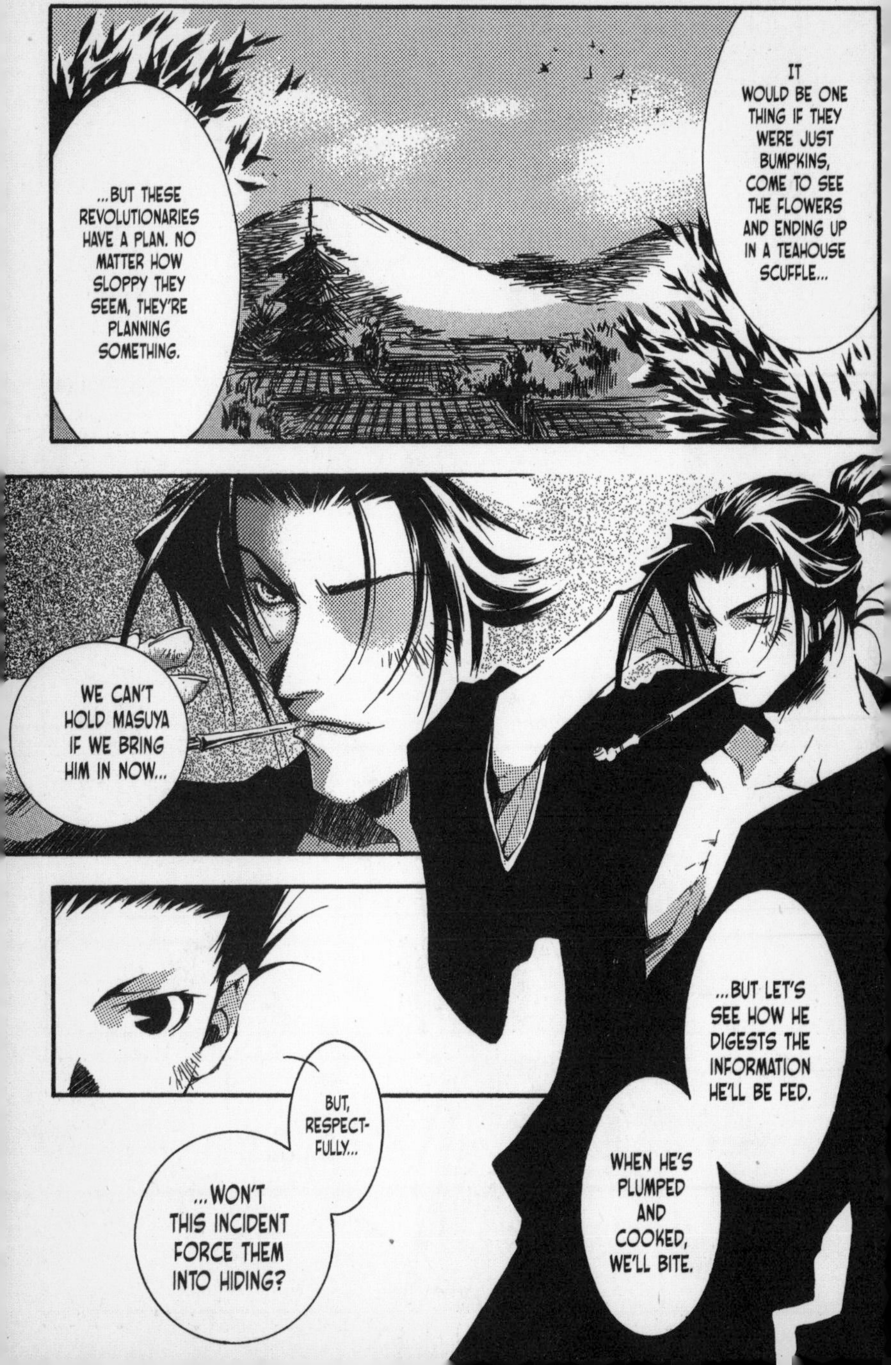
IT WOULD BE ONE THING IF THEY WERE JUST BUMPKINS, COME TO SEE THE FLOWERS AND ENDING UP IN A TEAHOUSE SCUFFLE...
...BUT THESE REVOLUTIONARIES HAVE A PLAN. NO MATTER HOW SLOPPY THEY SEEM, THEY'RE PLANNING SOMETHING.
WE CAN'T HOLD MASUYA IF WE BRING HIM IN NOW...
...BUT LET'S SEE HOW HE DIGESTS THE INFORMATION HE'LL BE FED.
WHEN HE'S PLUMPED AND COOKED, WE'LL BITE.
BUT, RESPECT-FULLY...
...WON'T THIS INCIDENT FORCE THEM INTO HIDING?

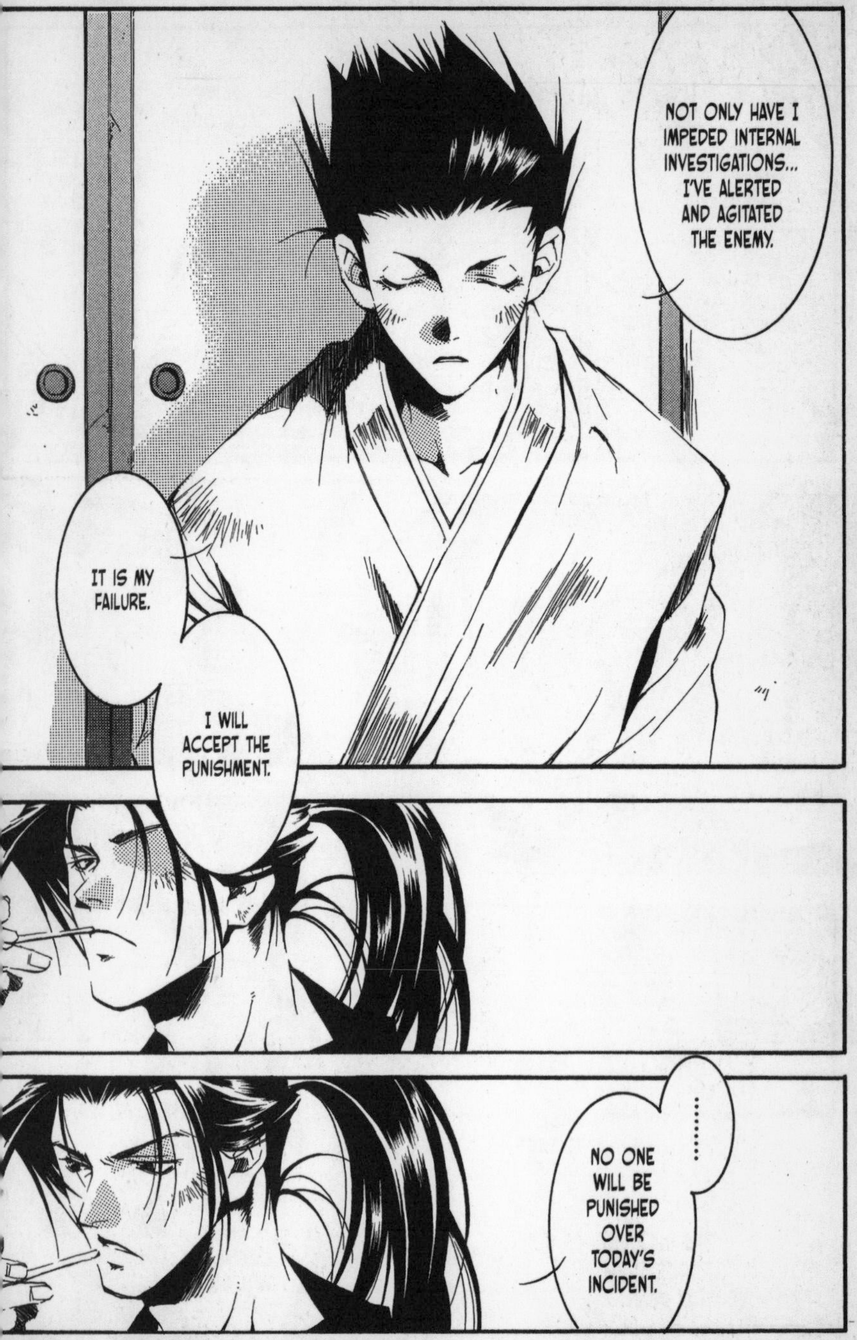
NOT ONLY HAVE I IMPEDED INTERNAL INVESTIGATIONS... I'VE ALERTED AND AGITATED THE ENEMY.
IT IS MY FAILURE.
I WILL ACCEPT THE PUNISHMENT.
......
NO ONE WILL BE PUNISHED OVER TODAY'S INCIDENT.

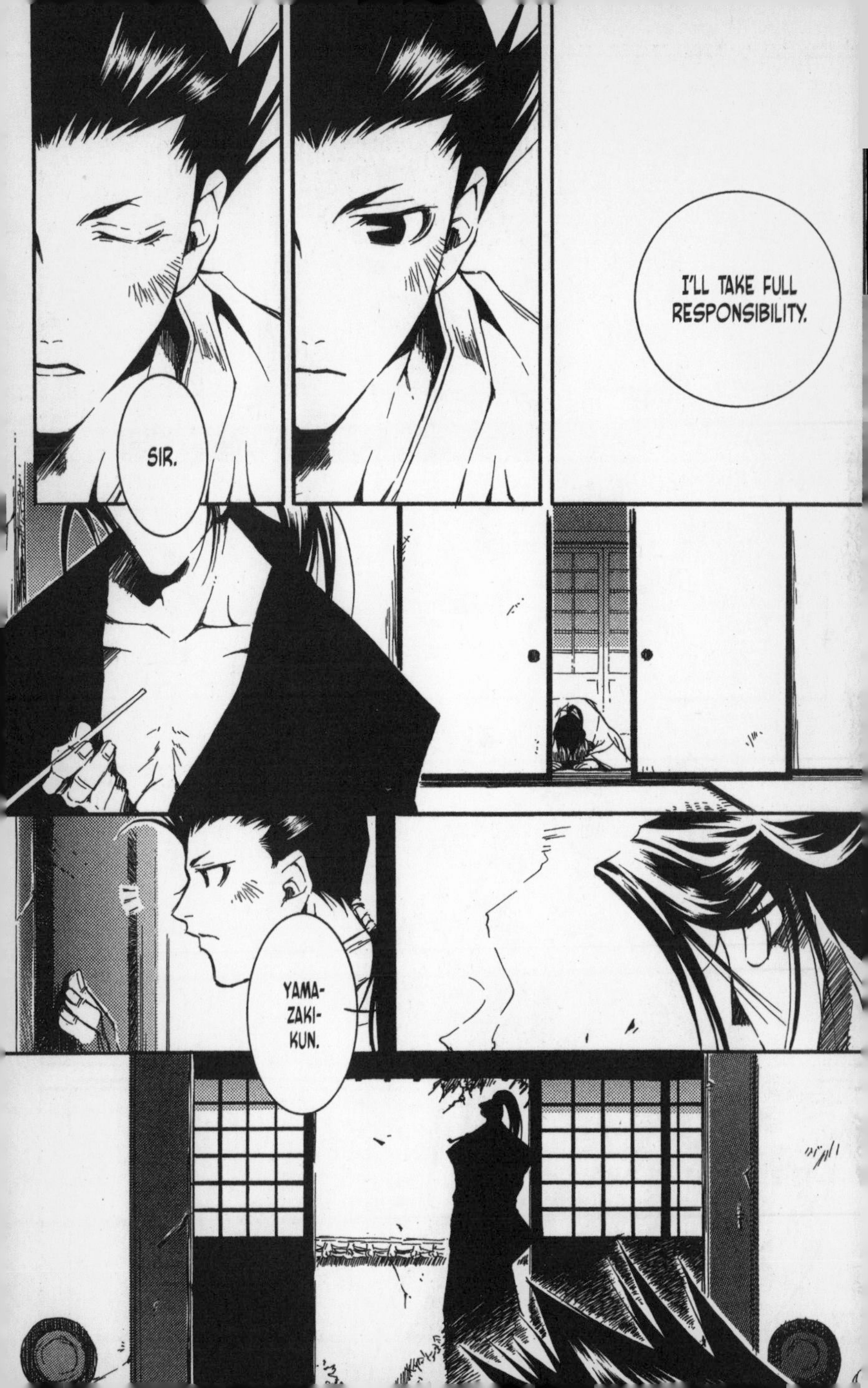
I'LL TAKE FULL RESPONSIBILITY.
SIR.
YAMA-ZAKI-KUN.

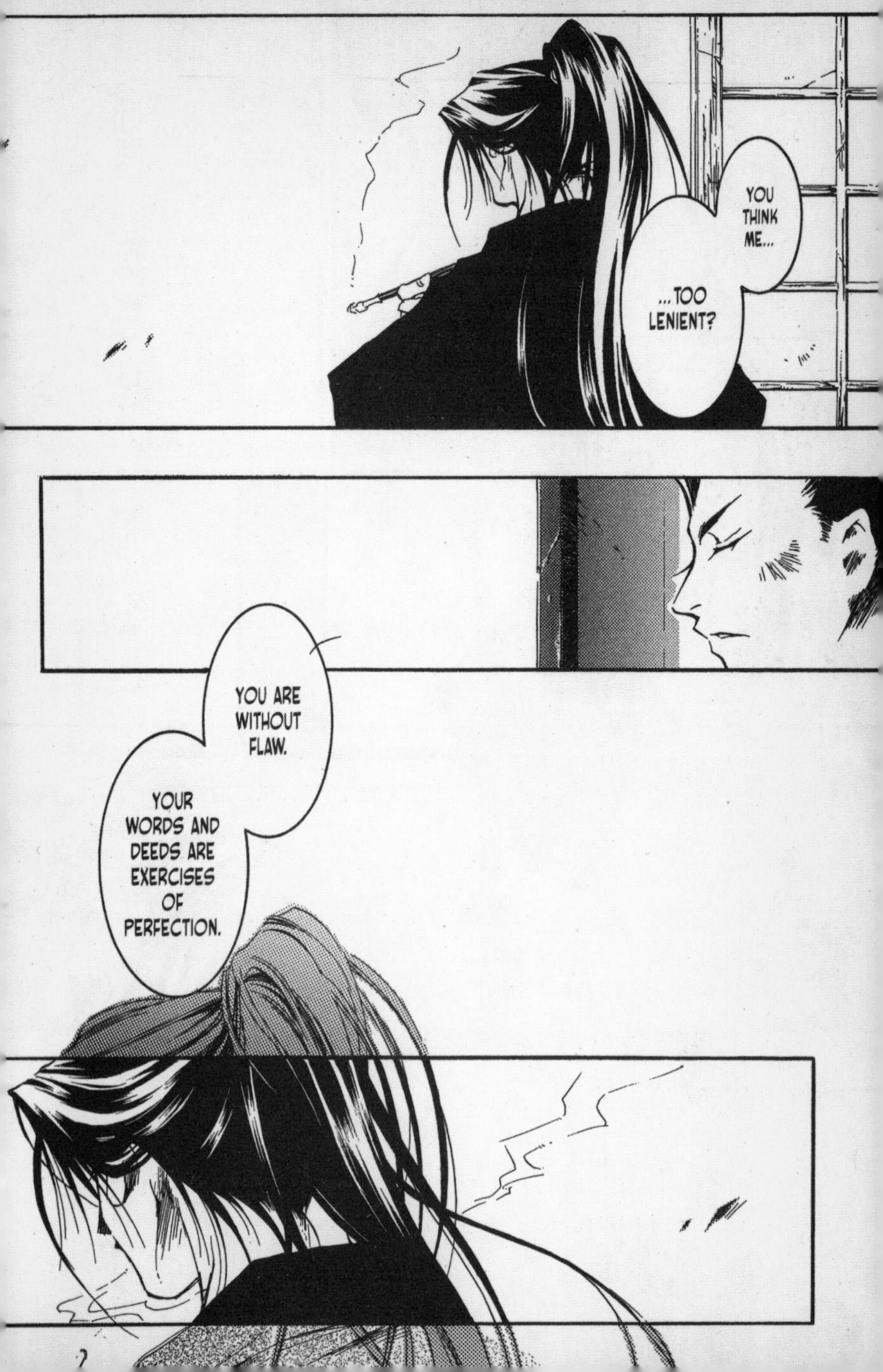
YOU THINK ME...
...TOO LENIENT?
YOU ARE WITHOUT FLAW.
YOUR WORDS AND DEEDS ARE EXERCISES OF PERFECTION.

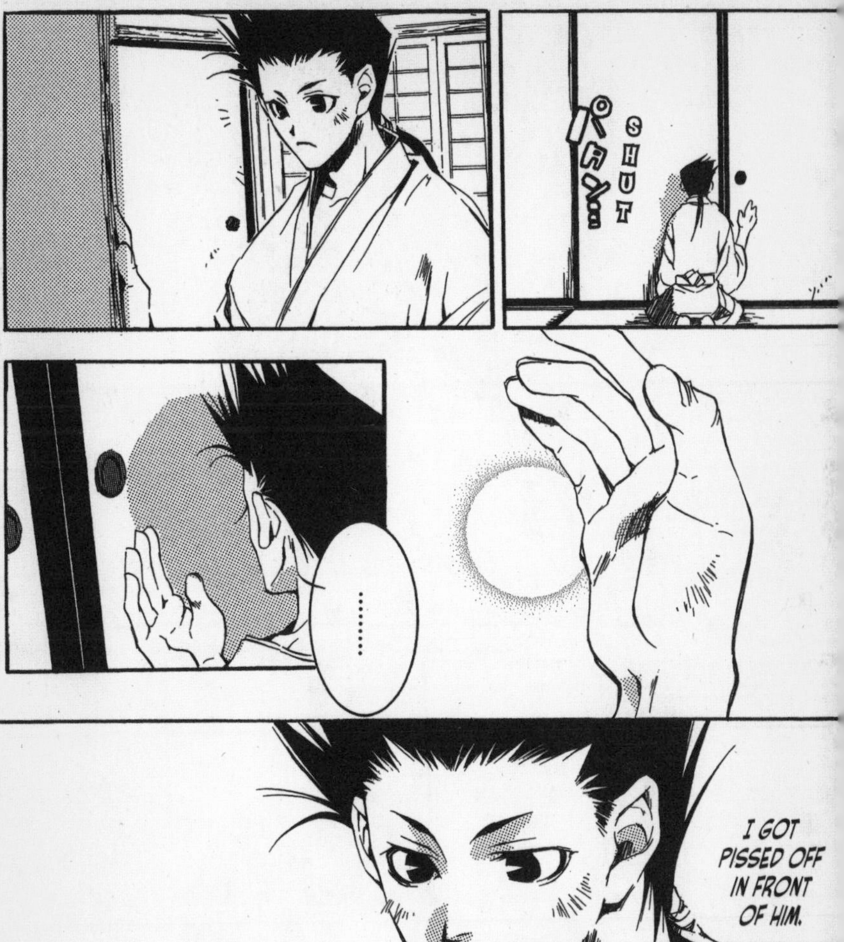
SHUT
......
I GOT PISSED OFF IN FRONT OF HIM.
THAT'S A FIRST.

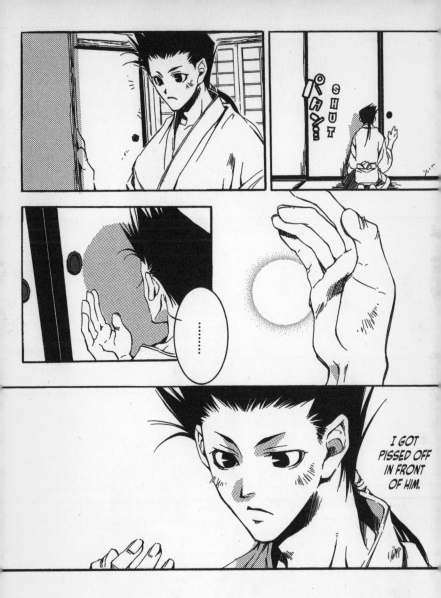

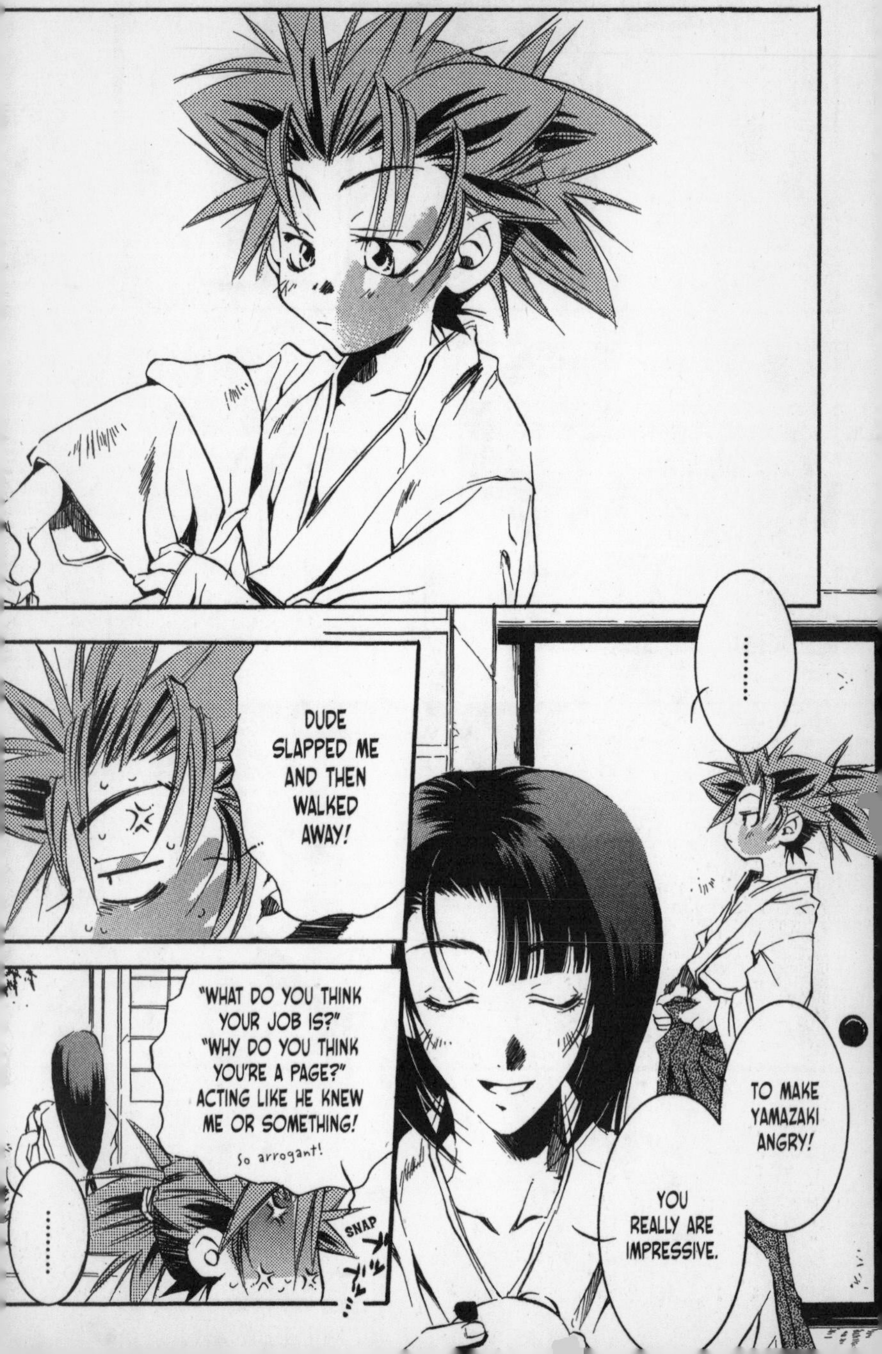
......
TO MAKE YAMAZAKI ANGRY!
YOU REALLY ARE IMPRESSIVE.
DUDE SLAPPED ME AND THEN WALKED AWAY!
"WHAT DO YOU THINK YOUR JOB IS?" "WHY DO YOU THINK YOU'RE A PAGE?" ACTING LIKE HE KNEW ME OR SOMETHING!
So arrogant!
SNAP
......

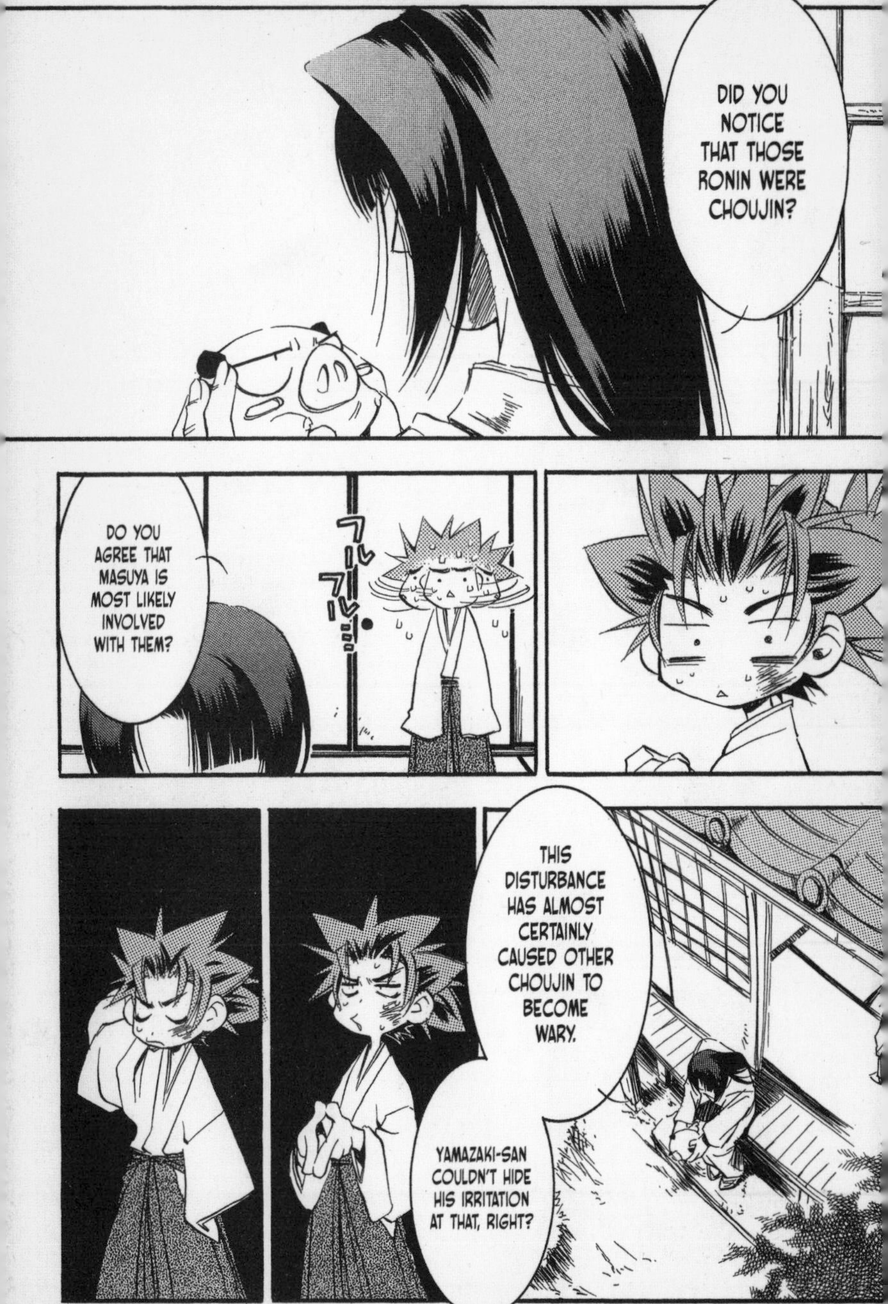
DID YOU NOTICE THAT THOSE RONIN WERE CHOUJIN?
DO YOU AGREE THAT MASUYA IS MOST LIKELY INVOLVED WITH THEM?
フルフル
THIS DISTURBANCE HAS ALMOST CERTAINLY CAUSED OTHER CHOUJIN TO BECOME WARY.
YAMAZAKI-SAN COULDN'T HIDE HIS IRRITATION AT THAT, RIGHT?

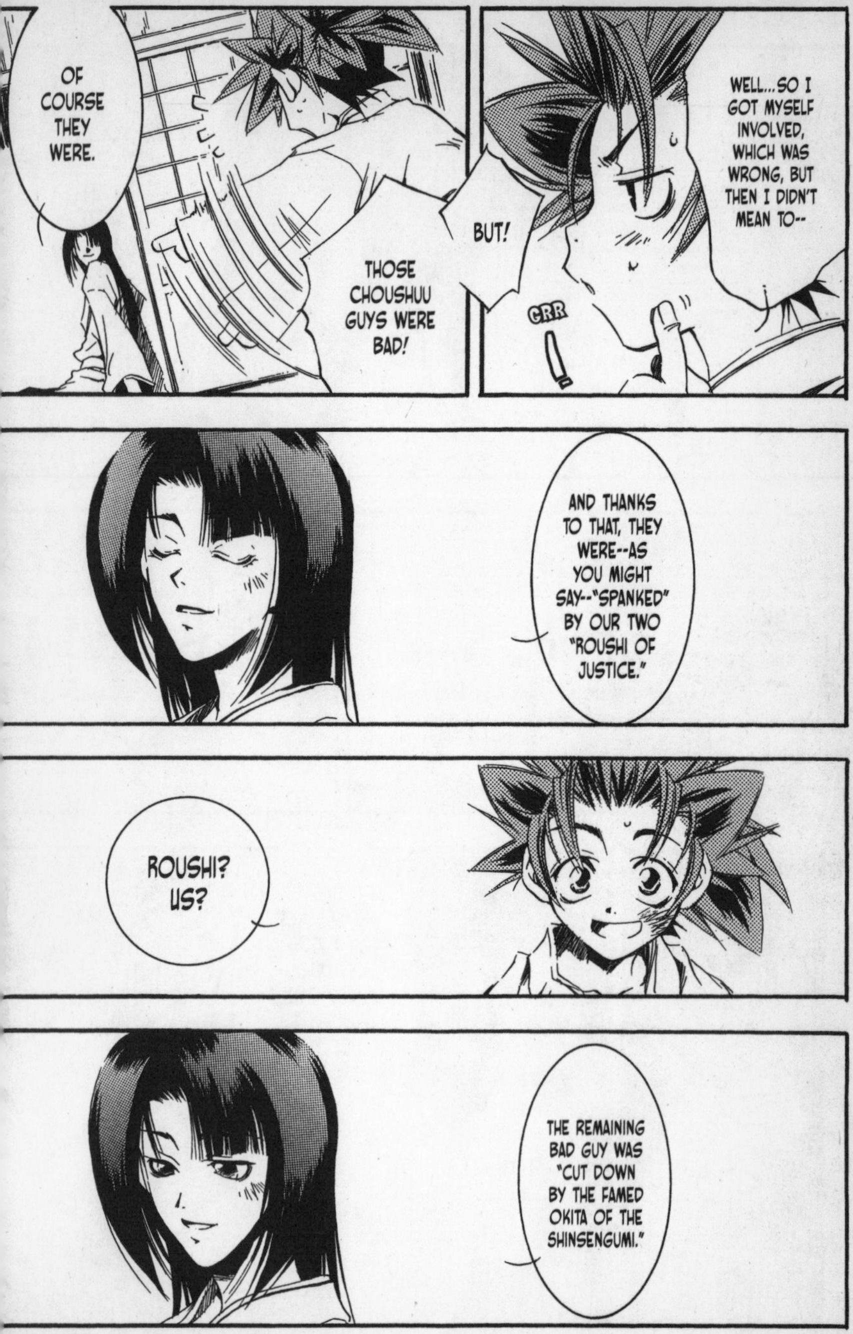
WELL...SO I GOT MYSELF INVOLVED, WHICH WAS WRONG, BUT THEN I DIDN'T MEAN TO--
GRR
BUT!
THOSE CHOUSHUU GUYS WERE BAD!
OF COURSE THEY WERE.
AND THANKS TO THAT, THEY WERE--AS YOU MIGHT SAY--"SPANKED" BY OUR TWO "ROUSHI OF JUSTICE."
ROUSHI? US?
THE REMAINING BAD GUY WAS "CUT DOWN BY THE FAMED OKITA OF THE SHINSENGUMI."

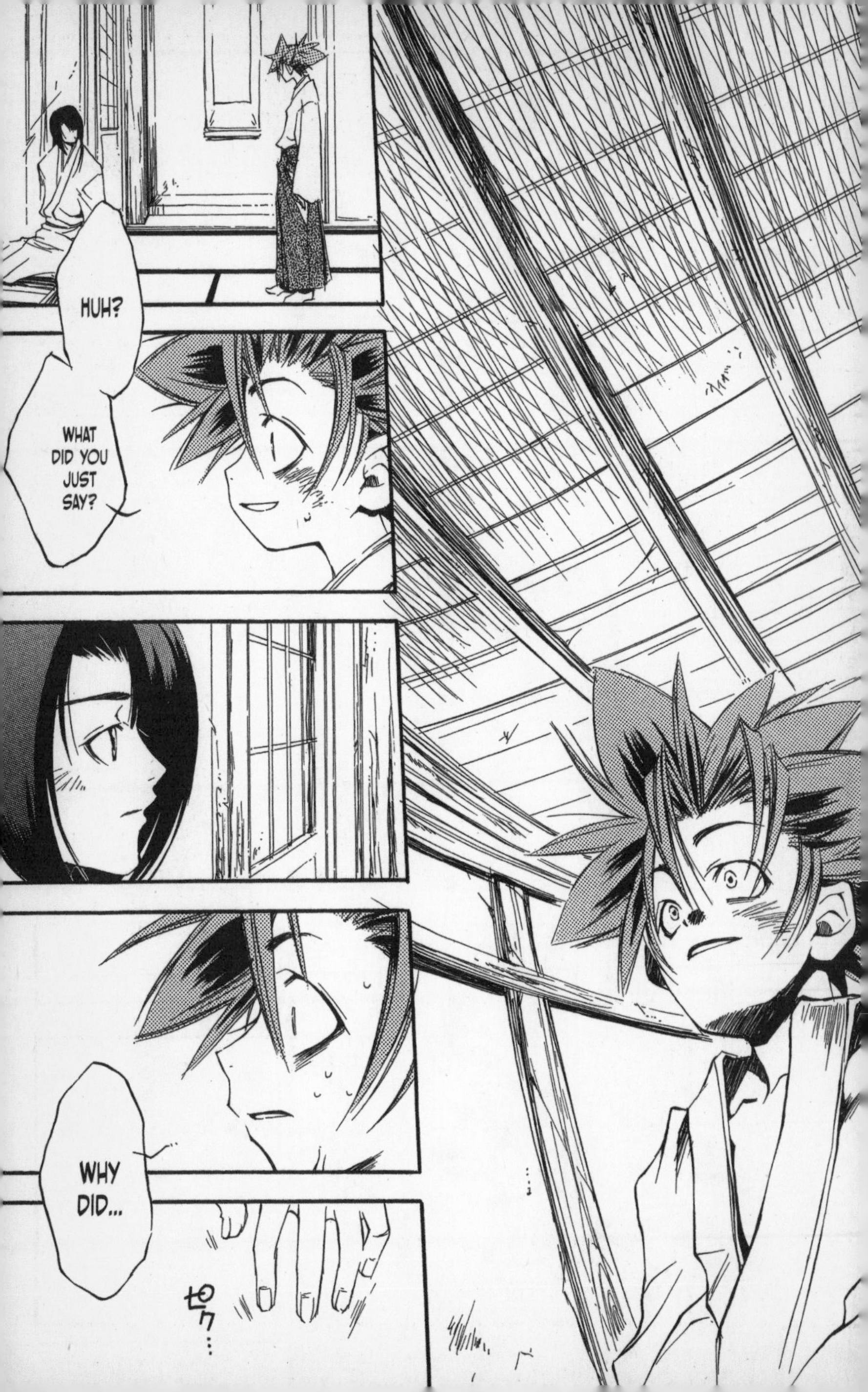
HUH?
WHAT DID YOU JUST SAY?
WHY DID...

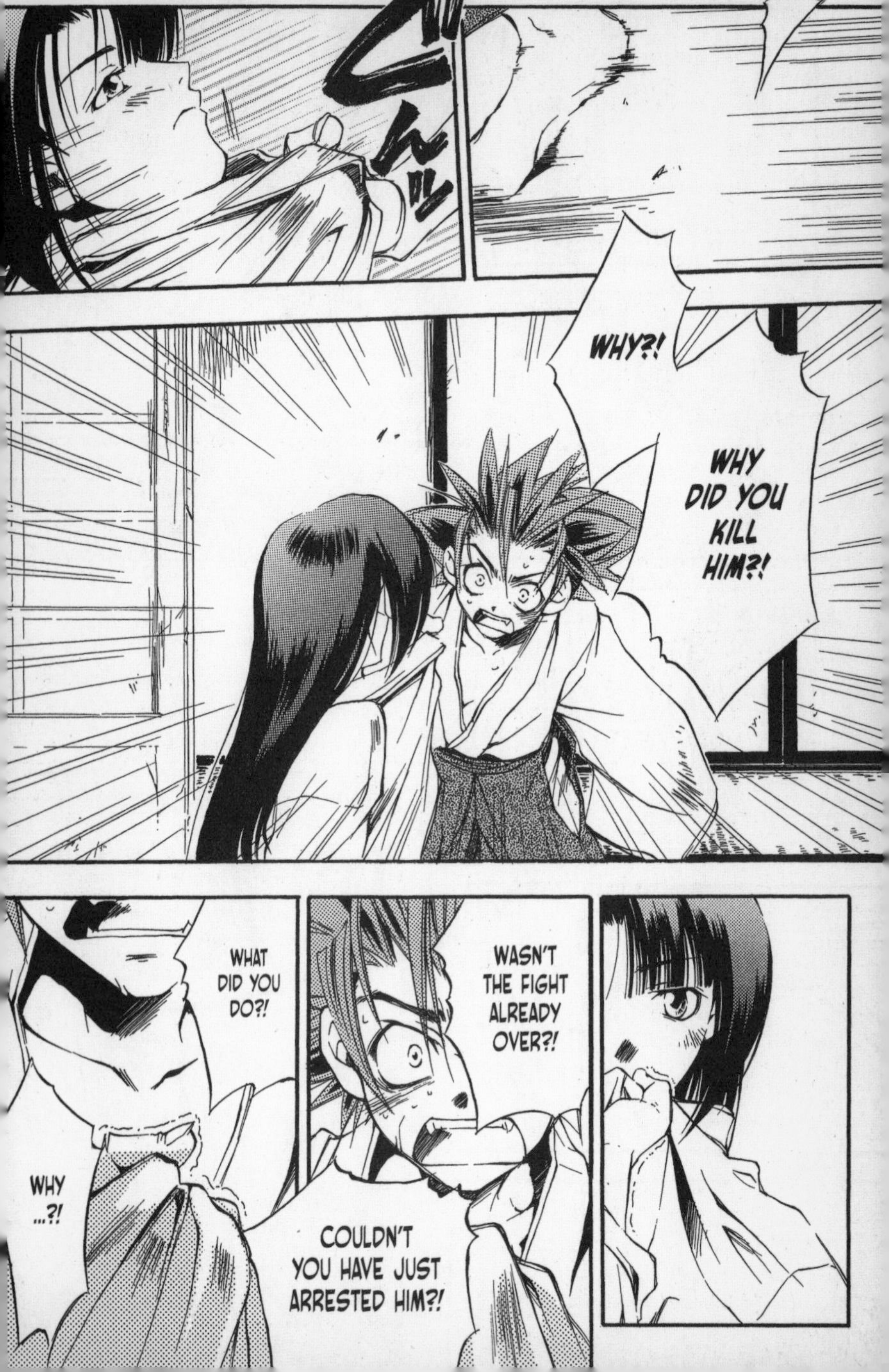
WHY?!
WHY DID YOU KILL HIM?!
WASN'T THE FIGHT ALREADY OVER?!
COULDN'T YOU HAVE JUST ARRESTED HIM?!
WHAT DID YOU DO?!
WHY ...?!

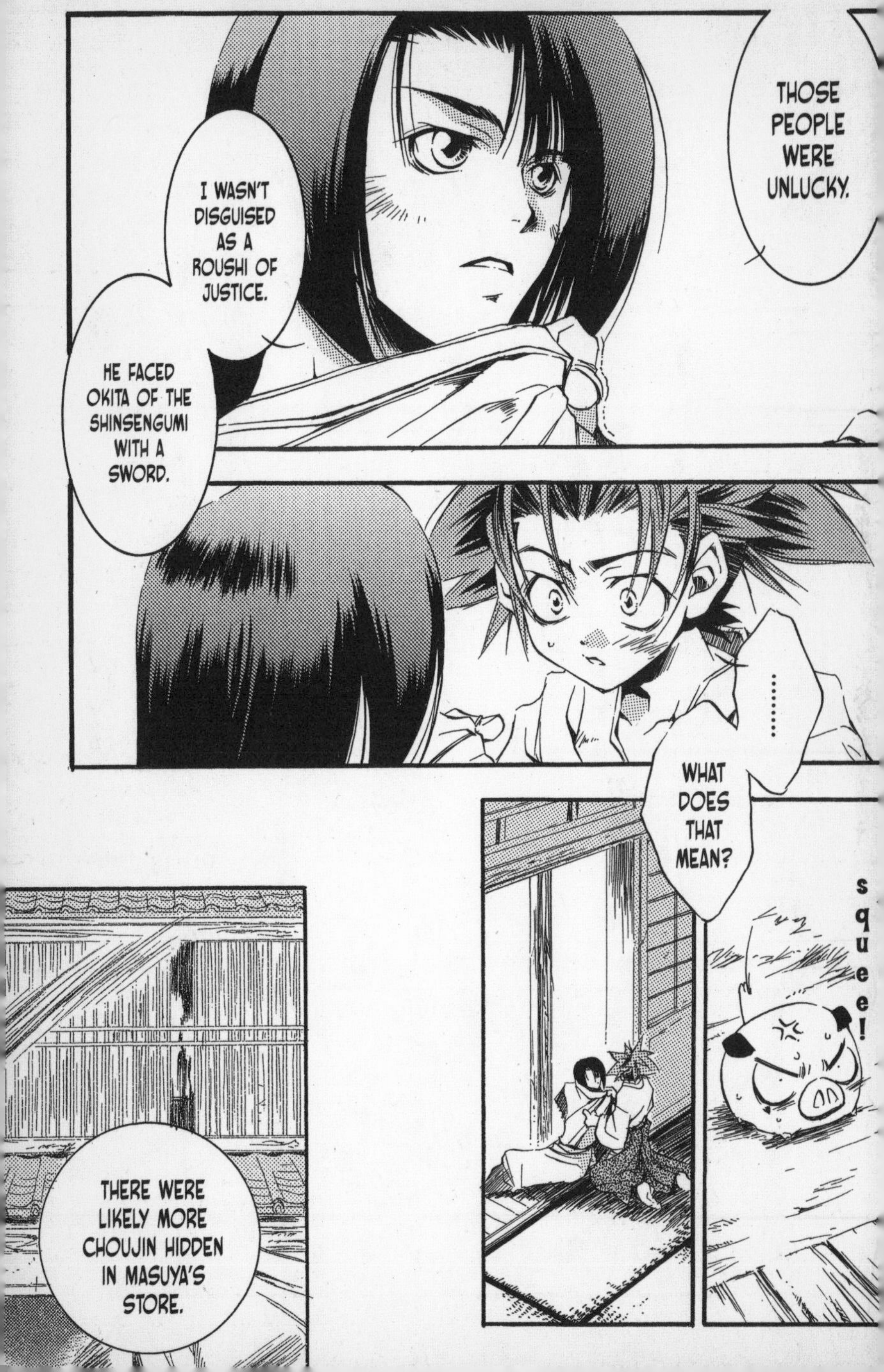
THOSE PEOPLE WERE UNLUCKY.
I WASN'T DISGUISED AS A ROUSHI OF JUSTICE.
HE FACED OKITA OF THE SHINSENGUMI WITH A SWORD.
......
WHAT DOES THAT MEAN?
squee!
THERE WERE LIKELY MORE CHOUJIN HIDDEN IN MASUYA'S STORE.

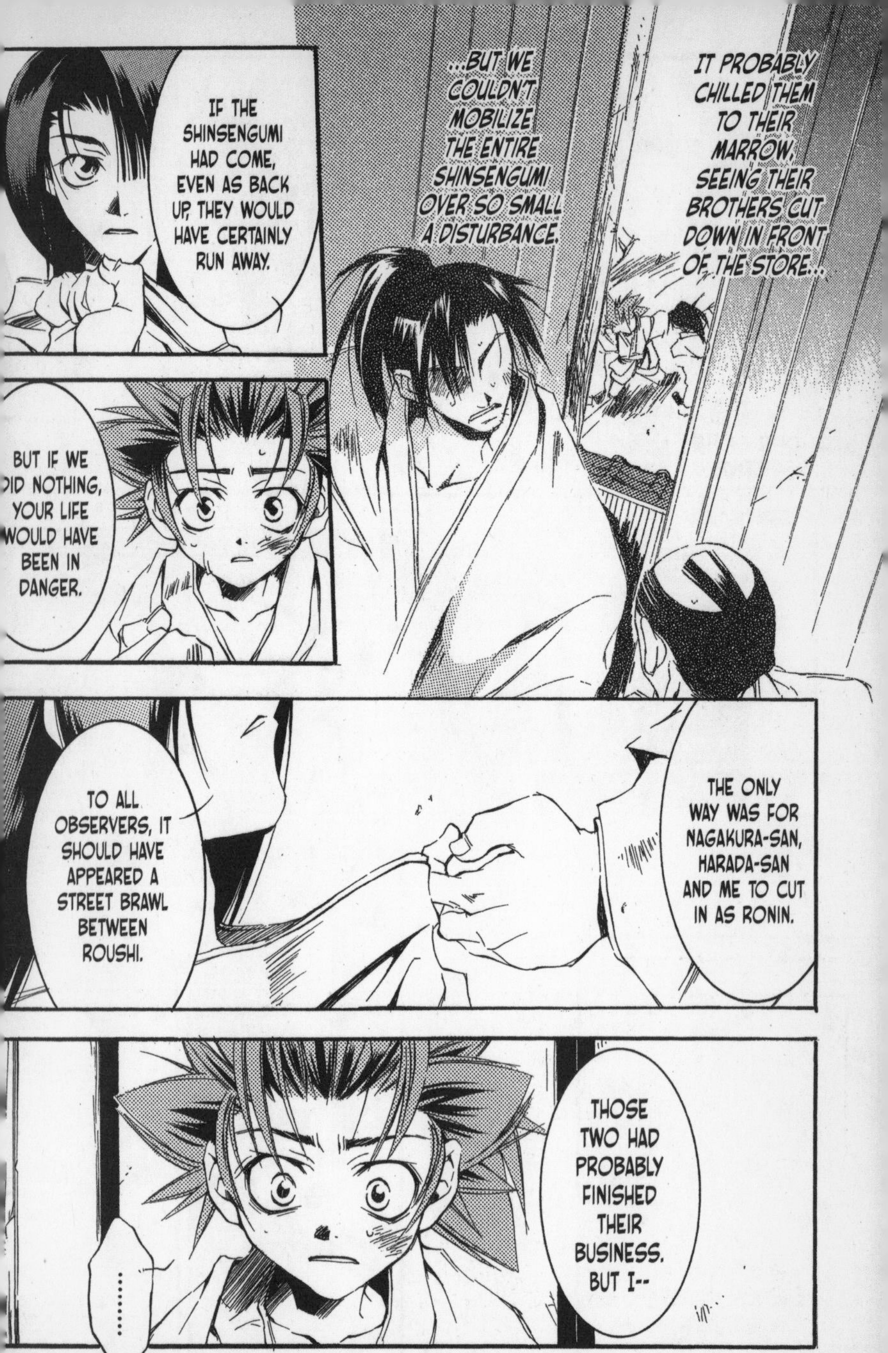
IT PROBABLY CHILLED THEM TO THEIR MARROW, SEEING THEIR BROTHERS CUT DOWN IN FRONT OF THE STORE...
...BUT WE COULDN'T MOBILIZE THE ENTIRE SHINSENGUMI OVER SO SMALL A DISTURBANCE.
IF THE SHINSENGUMI HAD COME, EVEN AS BACK UP, THEY WOULD HAVE CERTAINLY RUN AWAY.
BUT IF WE DID NOTHING, YOUR LIFE WOULD HAVE BEEN IN DANGER.
THE ONLY WAY WAS FOR NAGAKURA-SAN, HARADA-SAN AND ME TO CUT IN AS RONIN.
TO ALL OBSERVERS, IT SHOULD HAVE APPEARED A STREET BRAWL BETWEEN ROUSHI.
THOSE TWO HAD PROBABLY FINISHED THEIR BUSINESS. BUT I--
......

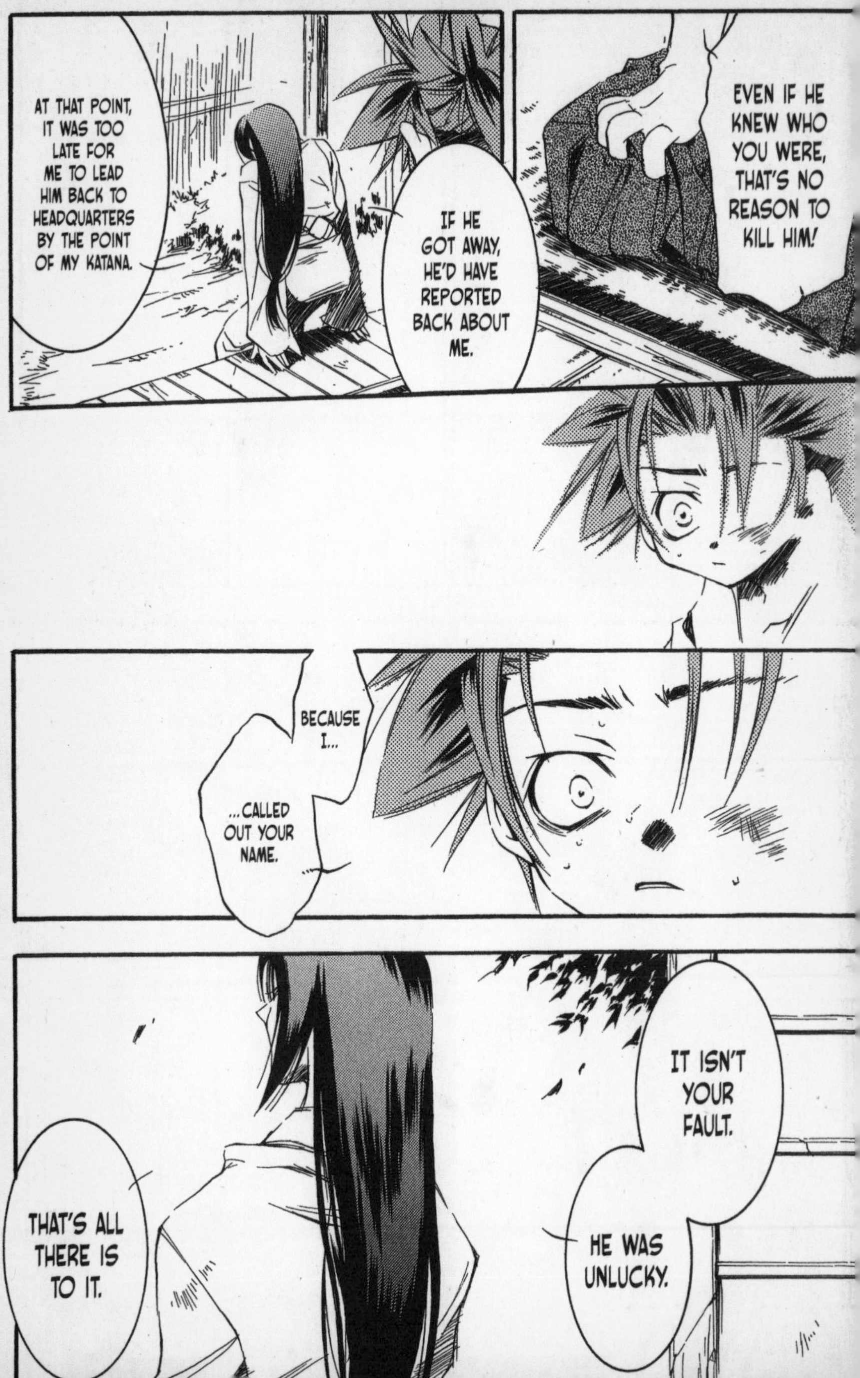
EVEN IF HE KNEW WHO YOU WERE, THAT'S NO REASON TO KILL HIM!
IF HE GOT AWAY, HE'D HAVE REPORTED BACK ABOUT ME.
AT THAT POINT, IT WAS TOO LATE FOR ME TO LEAD HIM BACK TO HEADQUARTERS BY THE POINT OF MY KATANA.
BECAUSE I...
...CALLED OUT YOUR NAME.
IT ISN'T YOUR FAULT.
HE WAS UNLUCKY.
THAT'S ALL THERE IS TO IT.

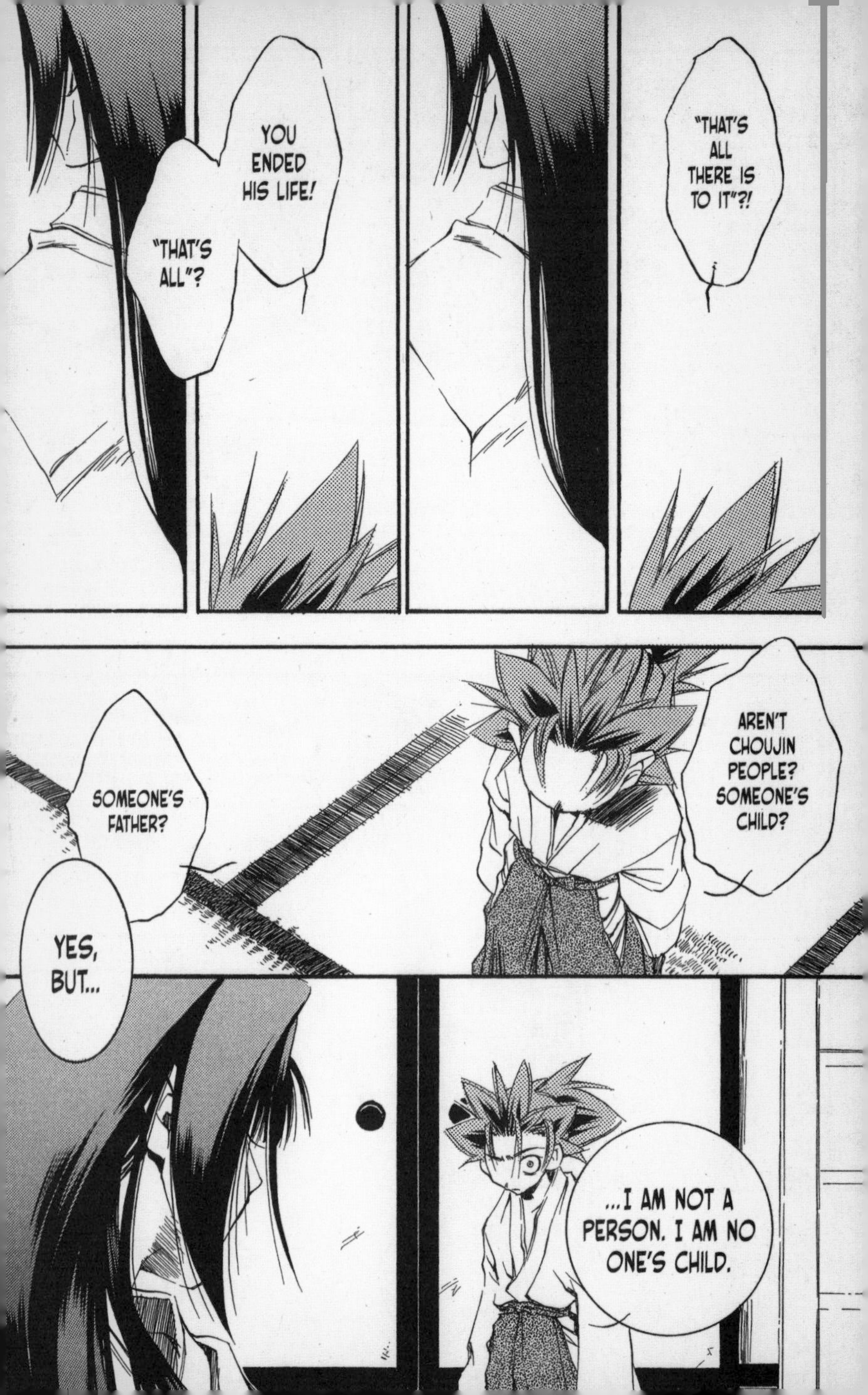

"THAT'S ALL THERE IS TO IT"?!
YOU ENDED HIS LIFE!
"THAT'S ALL"?
AREN'T CHOUJIN PEOPLE? SOMEONE'S CHILD?
SOMEONE'S FATHER?
YES, BUT...
...I AM NOT A PERSON. I AM NO ONE'S CHILD.

BECAUSE...

...I AM A DEMON'S CHILD.

TETSU-KUN.

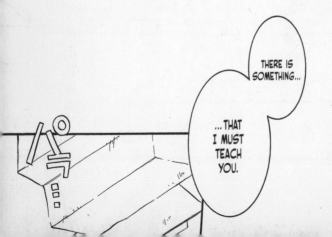

THERE IS SOMETHING...

...THAT I MUST TEACH YOU.

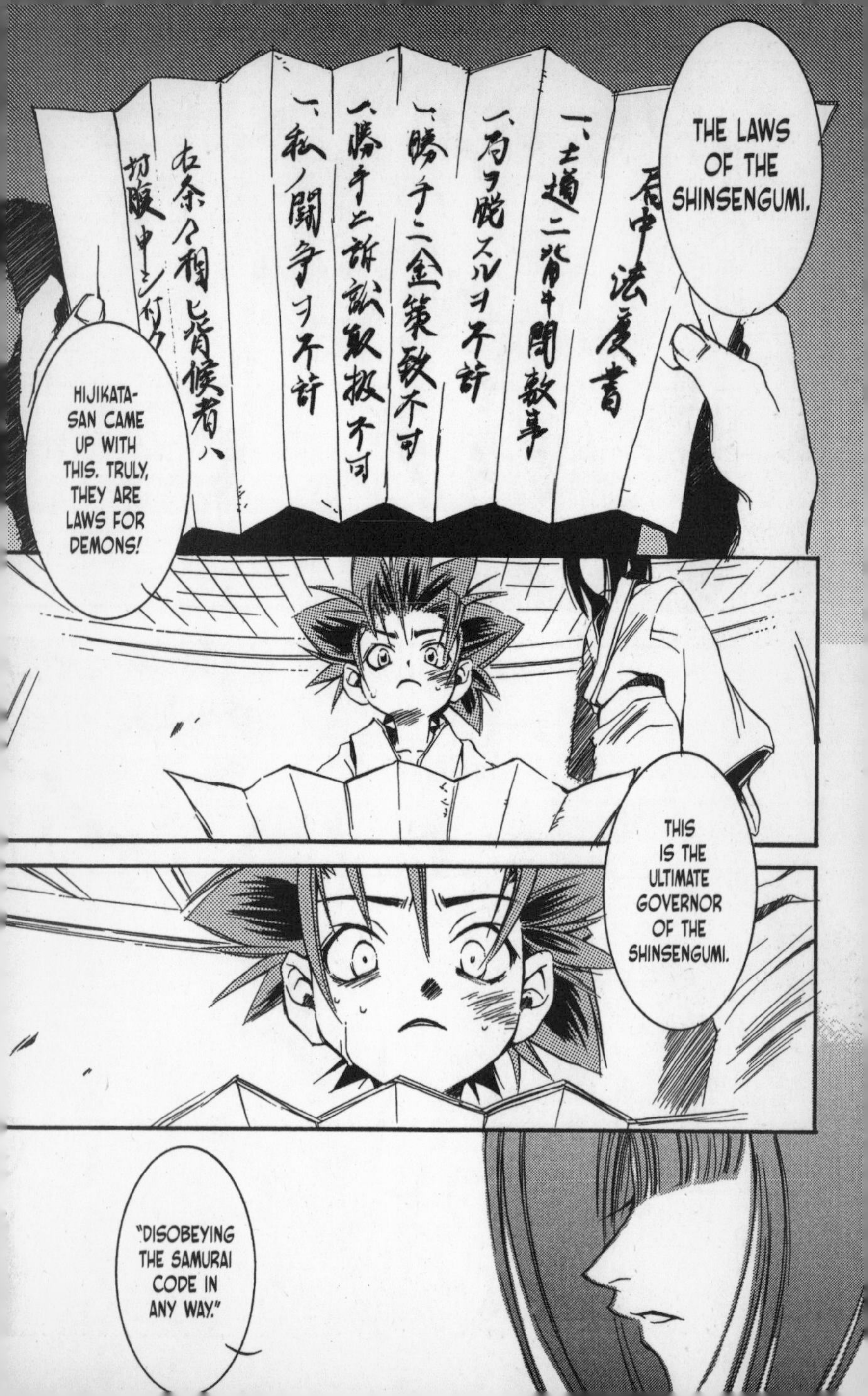
THE LAWS OF THE SHINSENGUMI.
局中法度書
一、士道ニ背キ間敷事
一、局ヲ脱スルヲ不許
一、勝手ニ金策致不可
一、勝手ニ訴訟取扱不可
一、私ノ闘争ヲ不許
右条々相背候者ハ
切腹申シ付ク
HIJIKATA-SAN CAME UP WITH THIS. TRULY, THEY ARE LAWS FOR DEMONS!
THIS IS THE ULTIMATE GOVERNOR OF THE SHINSENGUMI.
"DISOBEYING THE SAMURAI CODE IN ANY WAY."

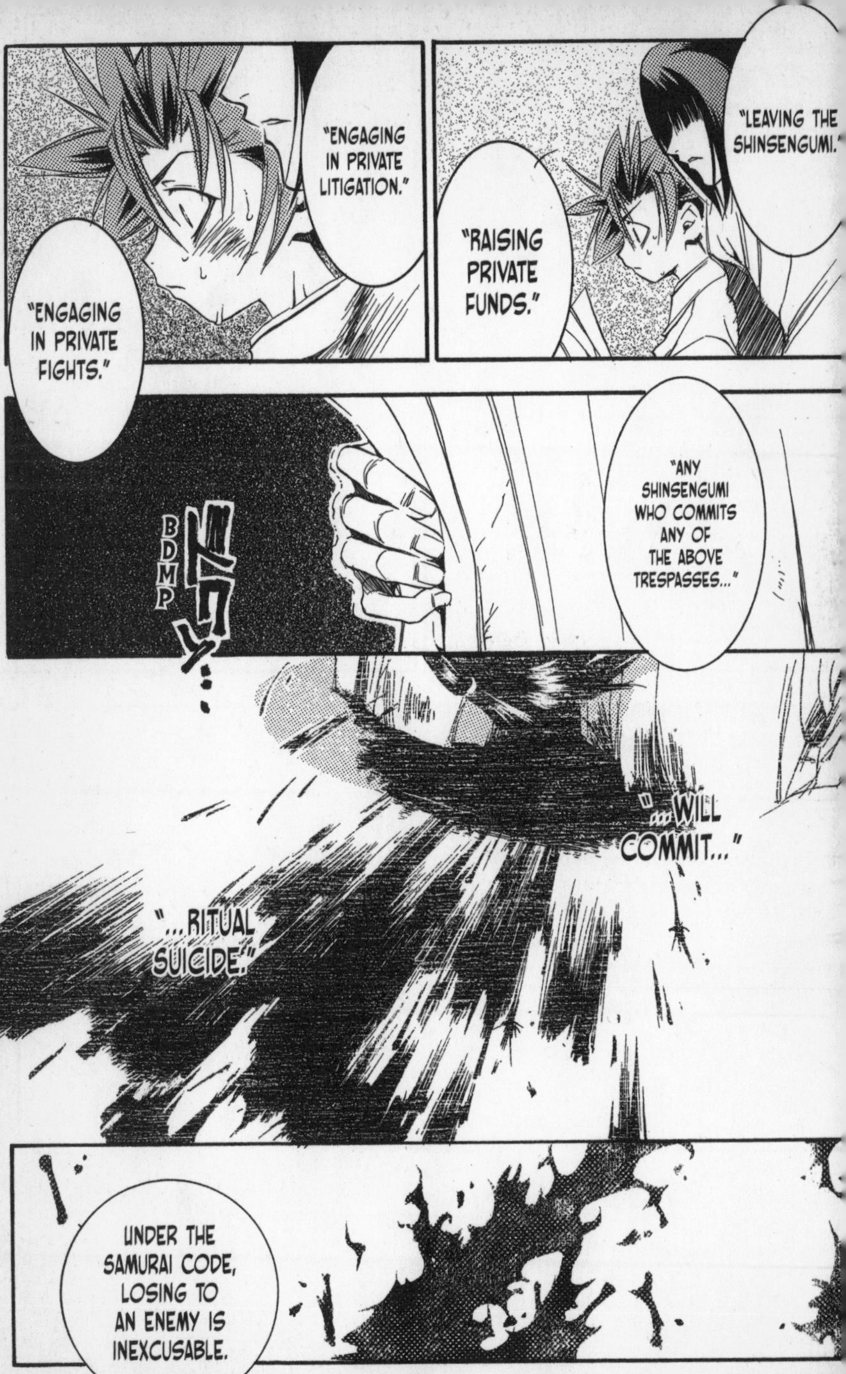
"LEAVING THE SHINSENGUMI."
"RAISING PRIVATE FUNDS."
"ENGAGING IN PRIVATE LITIGATION."
"ENGAGING IN PRIVATE FIGHTS."
"ANY SHINSENGUMI WHO COMMITS ANY OF THE ABOVE TRESPASSES..."
BDMP
"...WILL COMMIT..."
"...RITUAL SUICIDE."
UNDER THE SAMURAI CODE, LOSING TO AN ENEMY IS INEXCUSABLE.

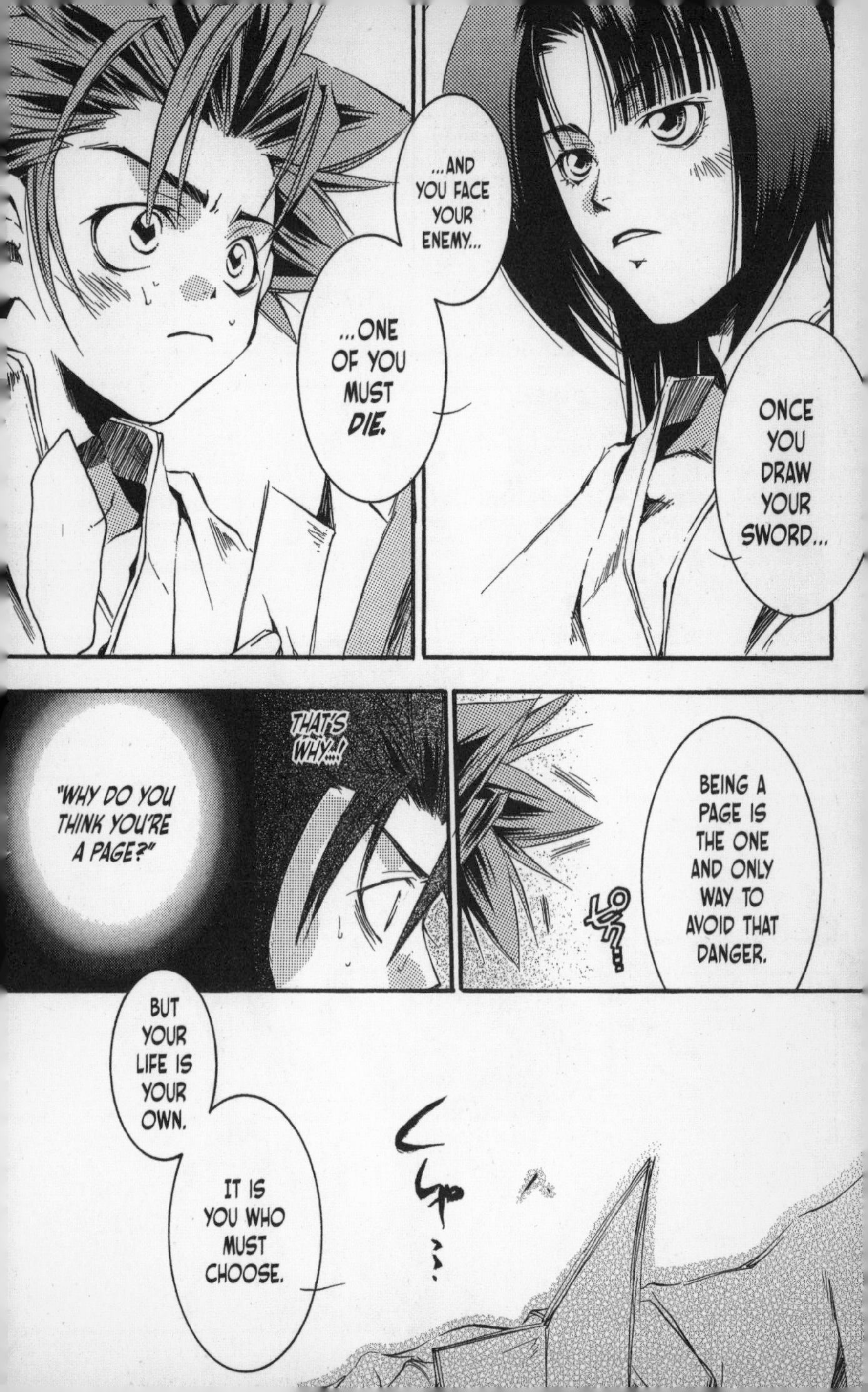
ONCE YOU DRAW YOUR SWORD...
...AND YOU FACE YOUR ENEMY...
...ONE OF YOU MUST DIE.
BEING A PAGE IS THE ONE AND ONLY WAY TO AVOID THAT DANGER.
THAT'S WHY...!
"WHY DO YOU THINK YOU'RE A PAGE?"
BUT YOUR LIFE IS YOUR OWN.
IT IS YOU WHO MUST CHOOSE.

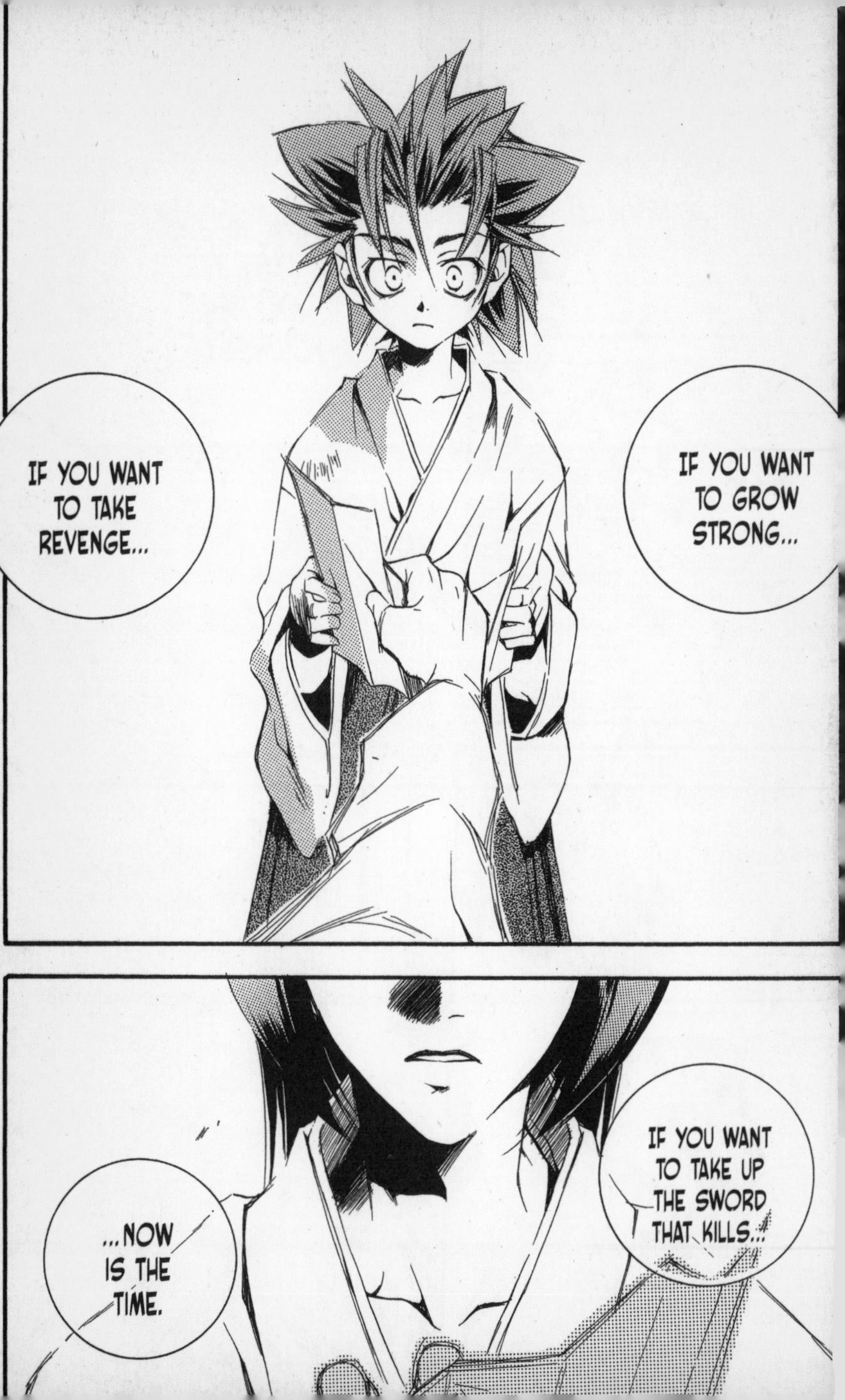
IF YOU WANT TO GROW STRONG...
IF YOU WANT TO TAKE REVENGE...
IF YOU WANT TO TAKE UP THE SWORD THAT KILLS...
...NOW IS THE TIME.

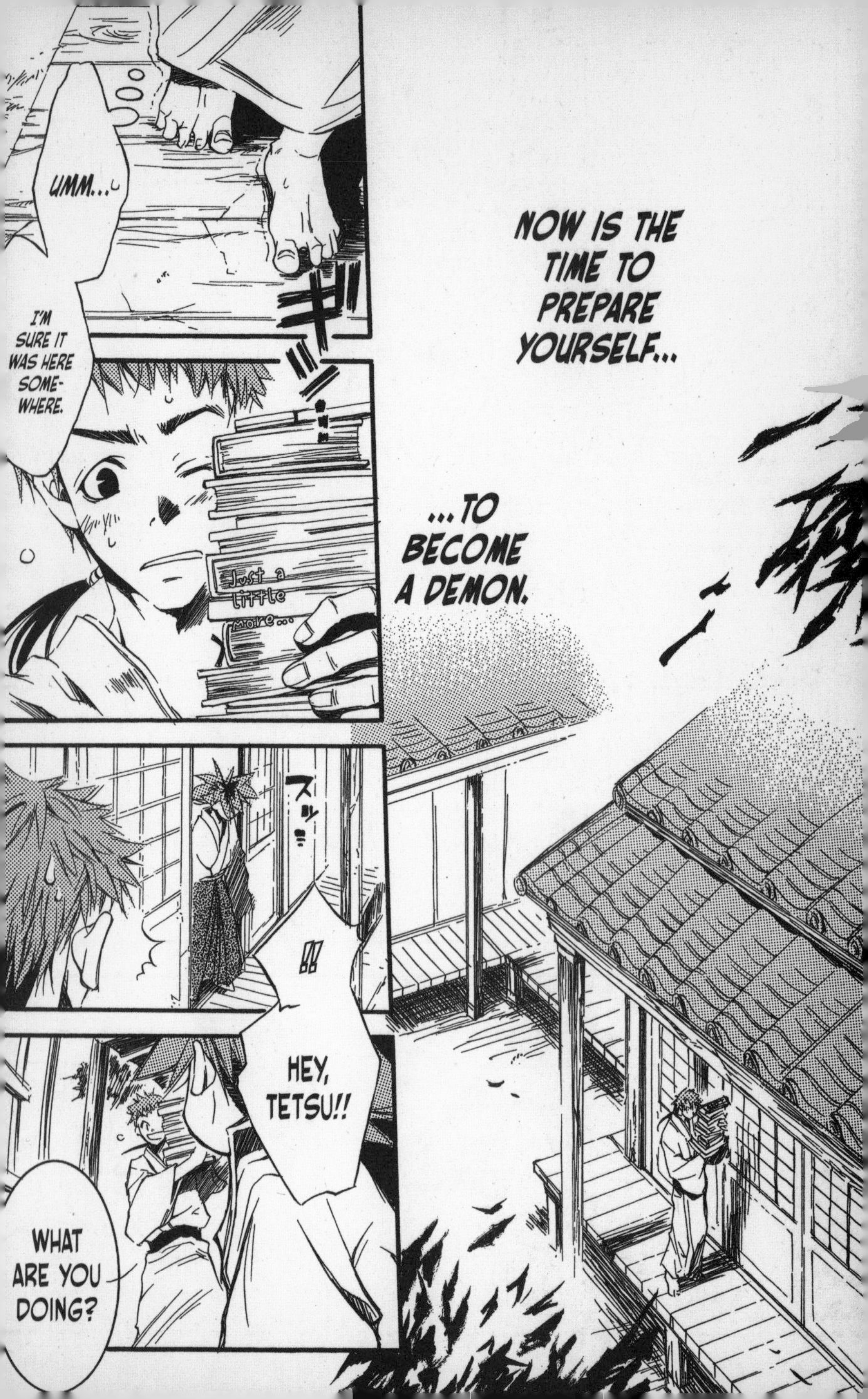
NOW IS THE TIME TO PREPARE YOURSELF...
...TO BECOME A DEMON.
UMM...
I'M SURE IT WAS HERE SOME-WHERE.
Just a little more...
!!
HEY, TETSU!!
WHAT ARE YOU DOING?

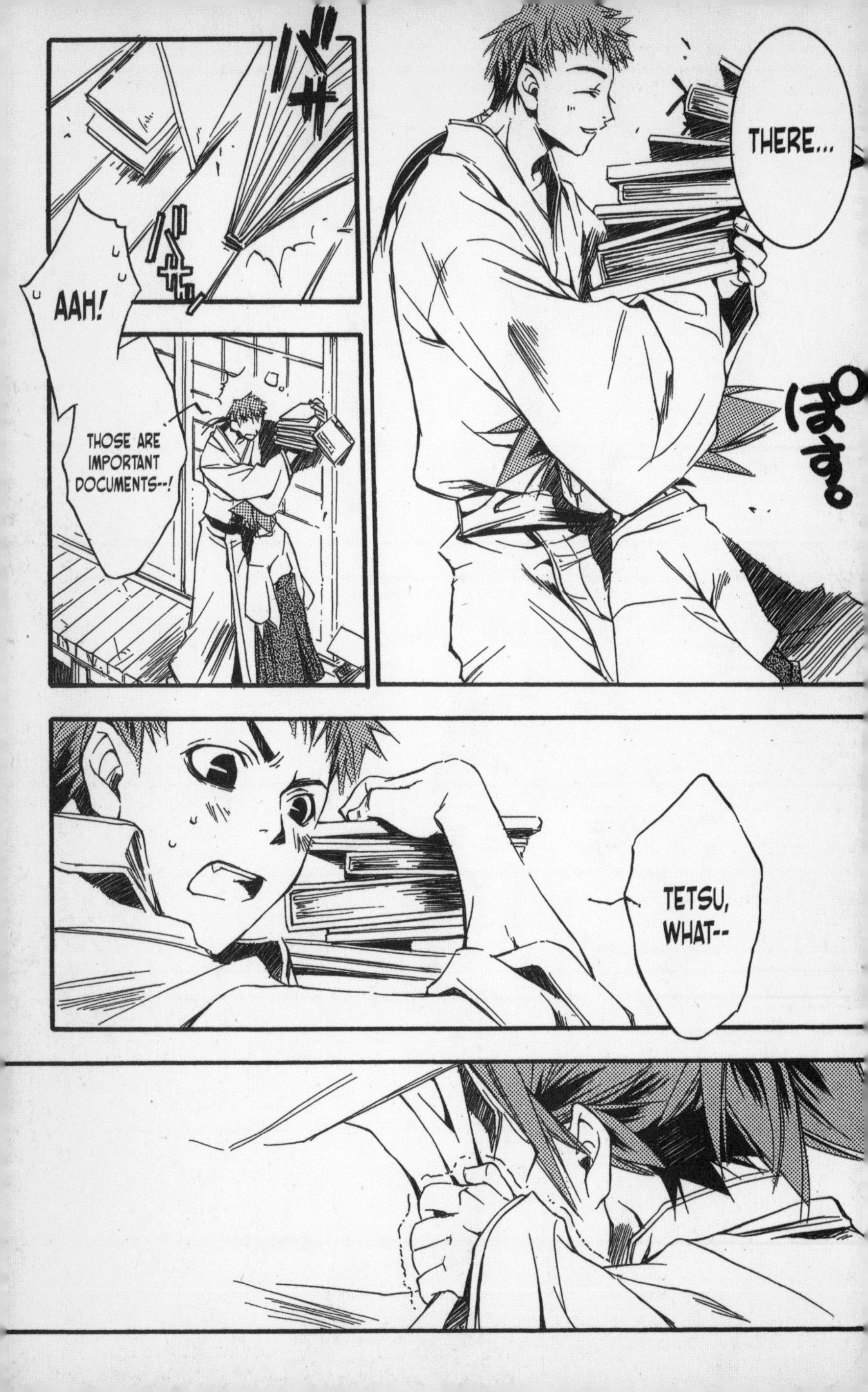
THERE...
ぽす。
AAH!
THOSE ARE IMPORTANT DOCUMENTS--!
TETSU, WHAT--

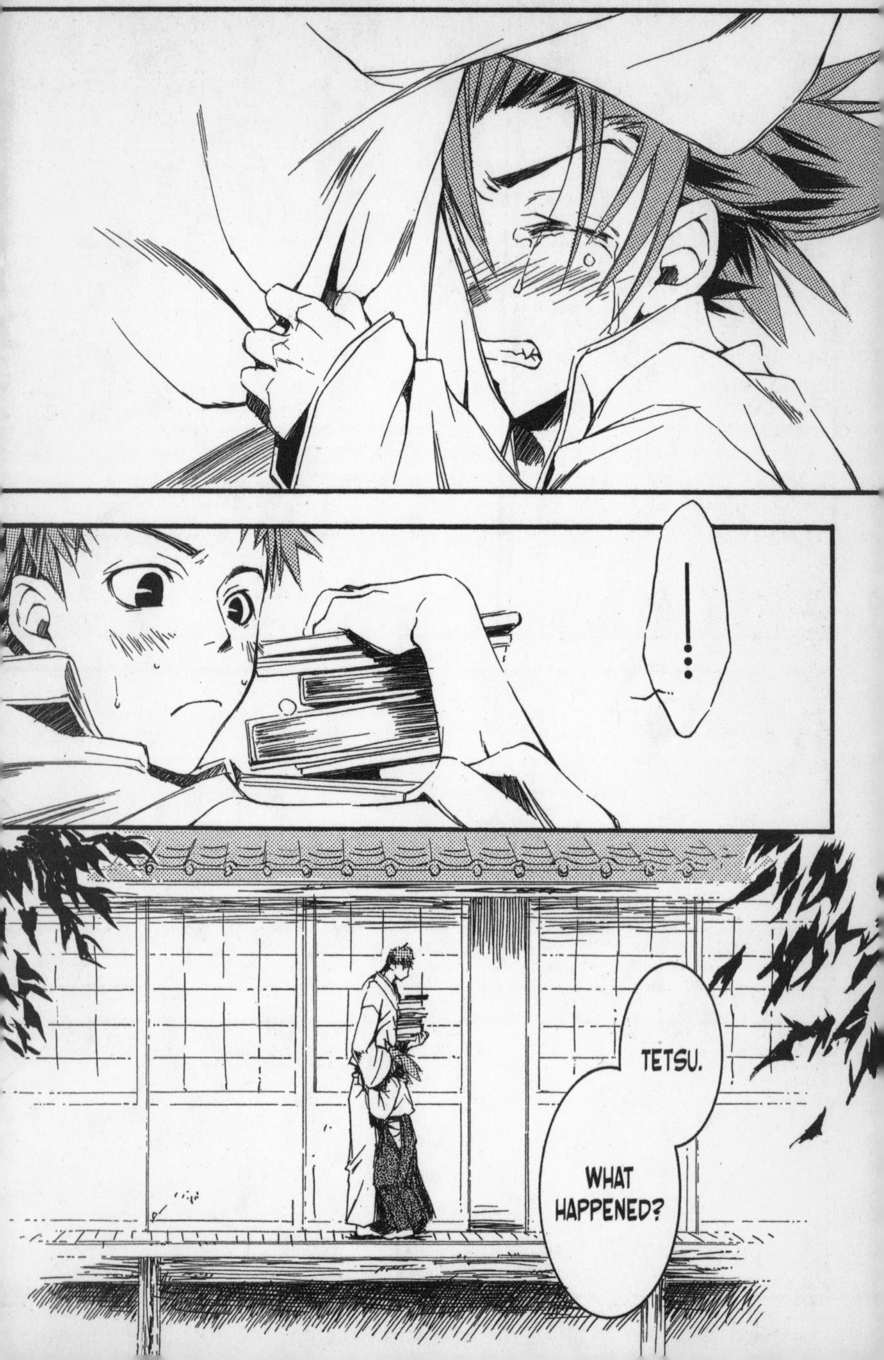
!......
TETSU.
WHAT HAPPENED?

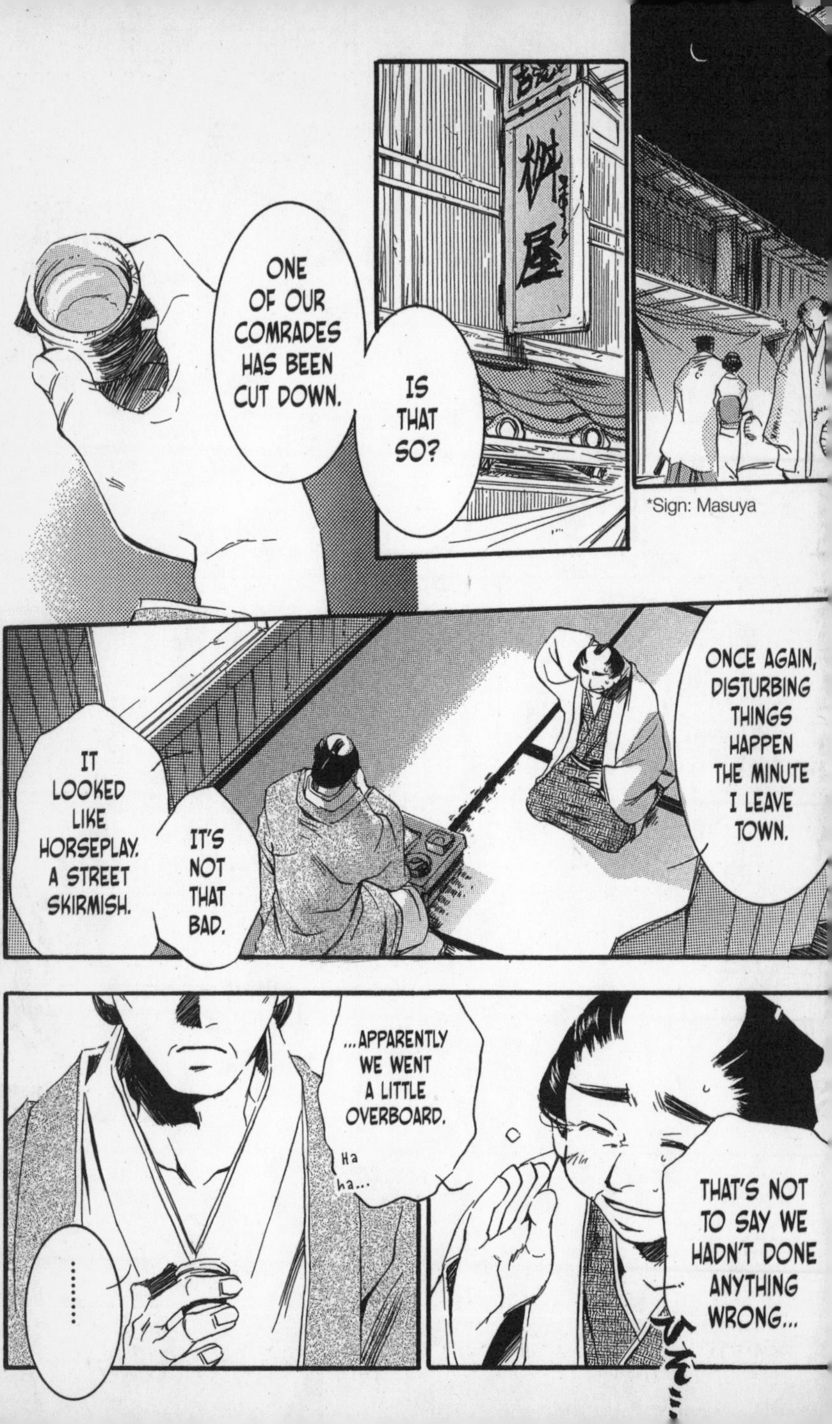
*Sign: Masuya
ONE OF OUR COMRADES HAS BEEN CUT DOWN.
IS THAT SO?
ONCE AGAIN, DISTURBING THINGS HAPPEN THE MINUTE I LEAVE TOWN.
IT'S NOT THAT BAD.
IT LOOKED LIKE HORSEPLAY. A STREET SKIRMISH.
THAT'S NOT TO SAY WE HADN'T DONE ANYTHING WRONG...
...APPARENTLY WE WENT A LITTLE OVERBOARD.
Ha ha...
....

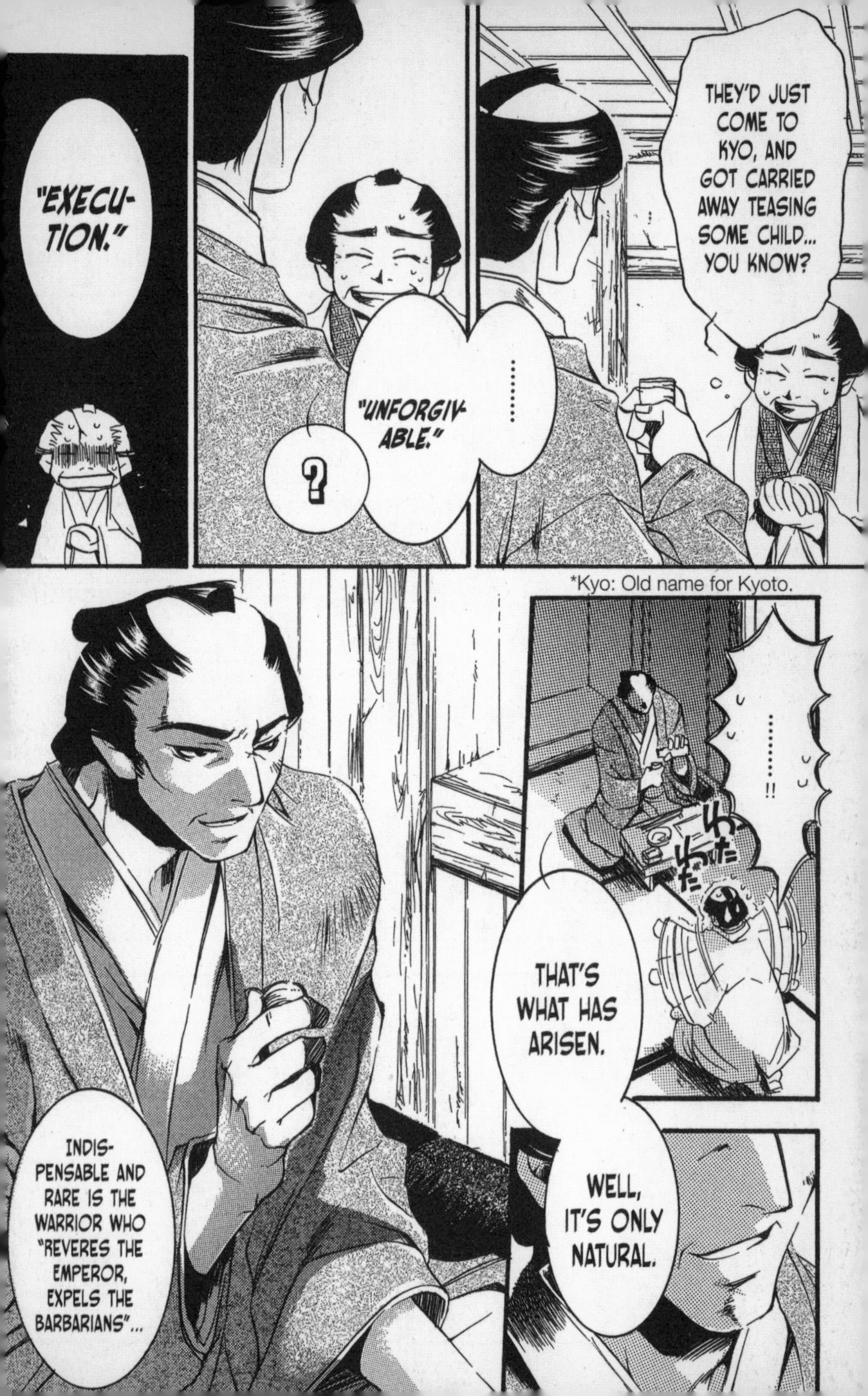
THEY'D JUST COME TO KYO, AND GOT CARRIED AWAY TEASING SOME CHILD... YOU KNOW?
......
"UNFORGIVABLE."
?
"EXECUTION."
......!!
THAT'S WHAT HAS ARISEN.
WELL, IT'S ONLY NATURAL.
INDISPENSABLE AND RARE IS THE WARRIOR WHO "REVERES THE EMPEROR, EXPELS THE BARBARIANS"...
*Kyo: Old name for Kyoto.

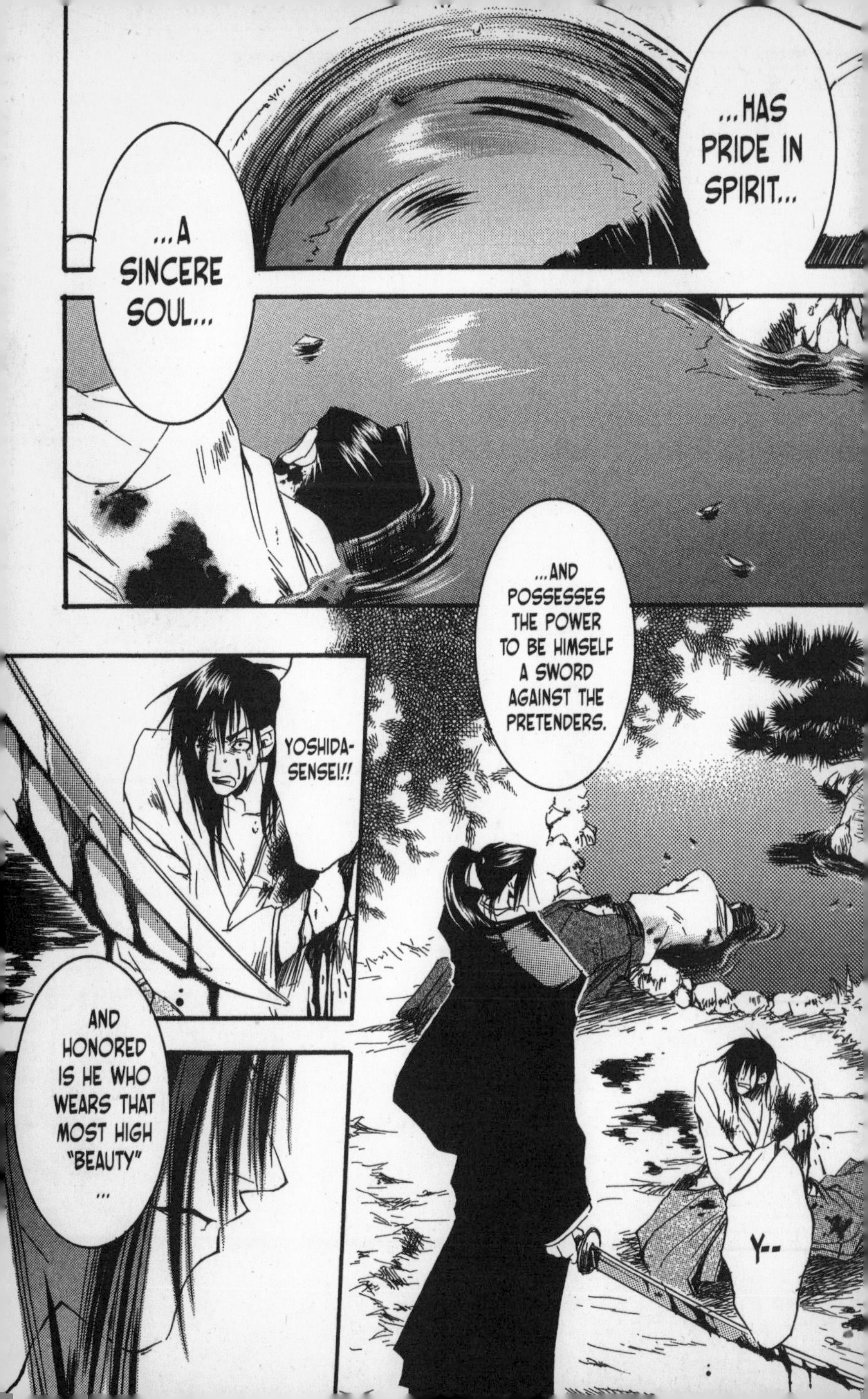
...HAS PRIDE IN SPIRIT...
...A SINCERE SOUL...
...AND POSSESSES THE POWER TO BE HIMSELF A SWORD AGAINST THE PRETENDERS.
Y--
YOSHIDA-SENSEI!!
AND HONORED IS HE WHO WEARS THAT MOST HIGH "BEAUTY" ...

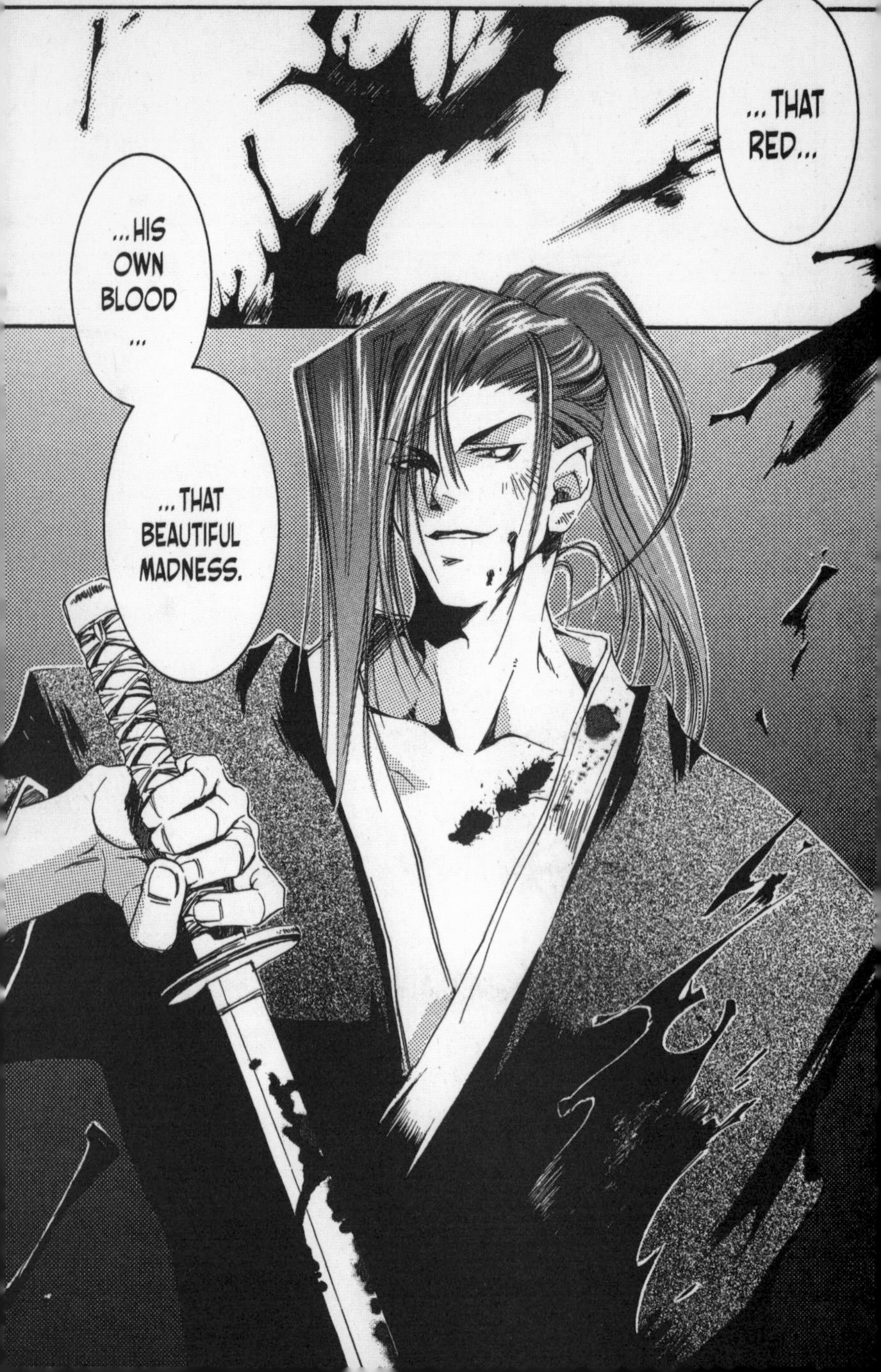
...THAT RED...
...HIS OWN BLOOD ...
...THAT BEAUTIFUL MADNESS.

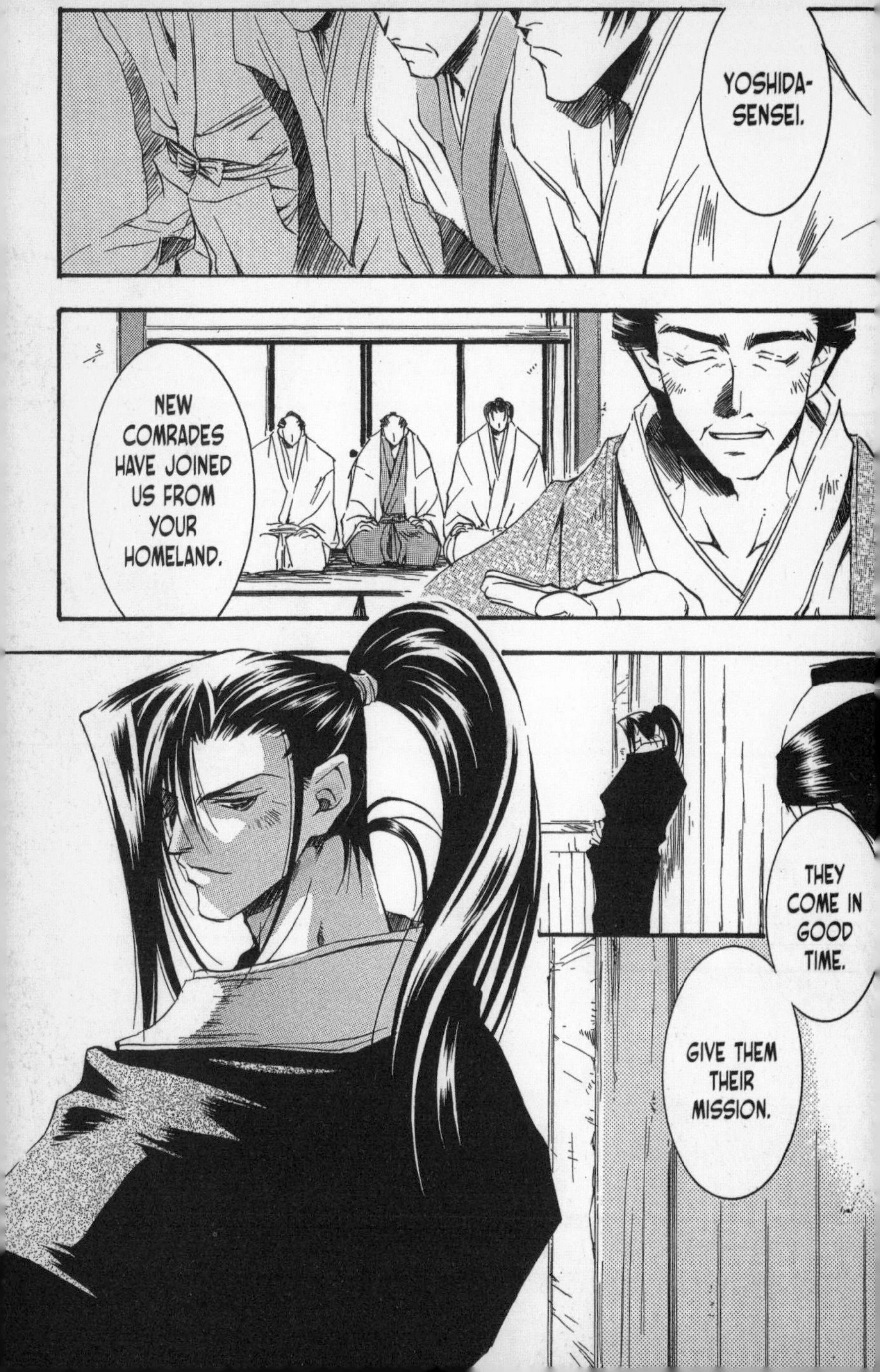
YOSHIDA-SENSEI.
NEW COMRADES HAVE JOINED US FROM YOUR HOMELAND.
THEY COME IN GOOD TIME.
GIVE THEM THEIR MISSION.

Act. 7
I'm a Loser

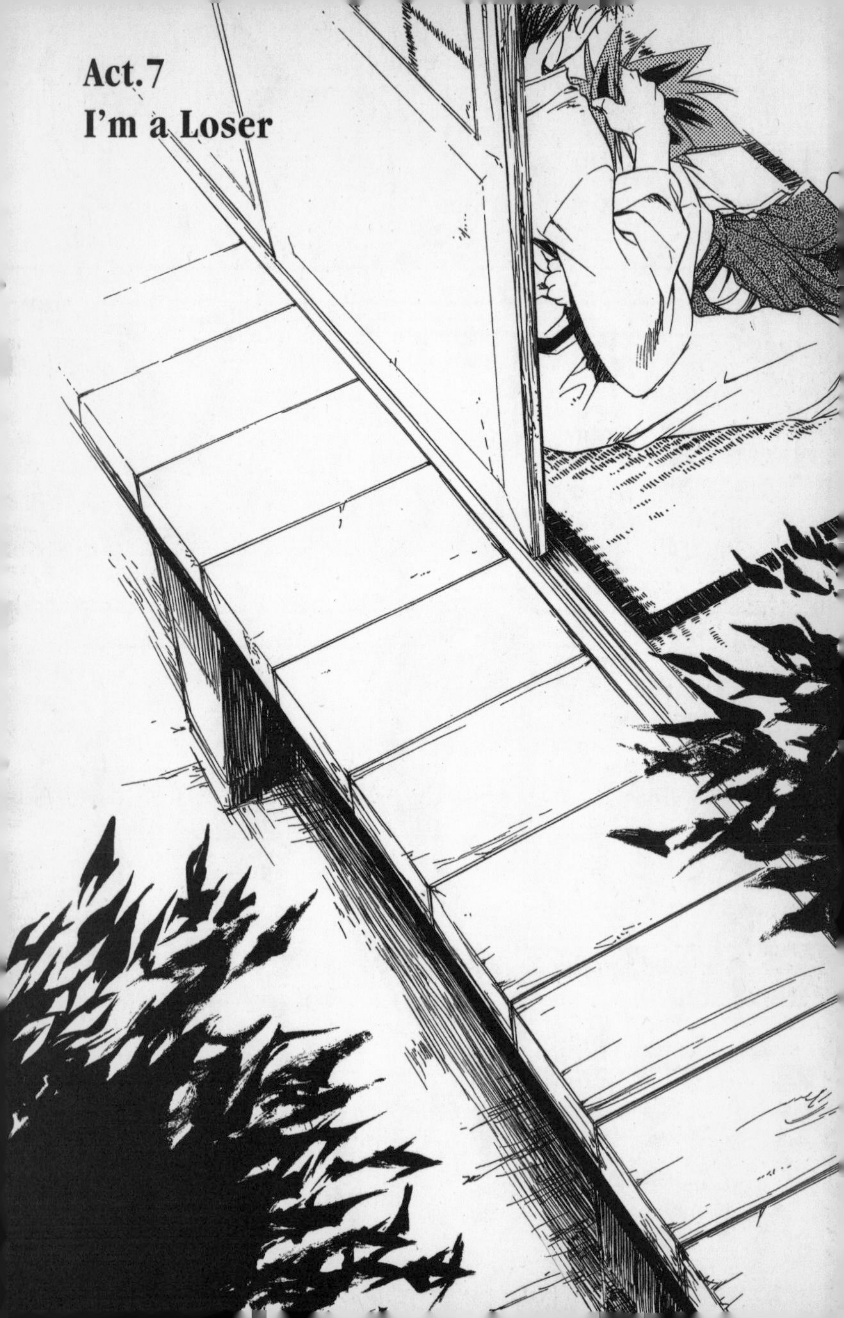

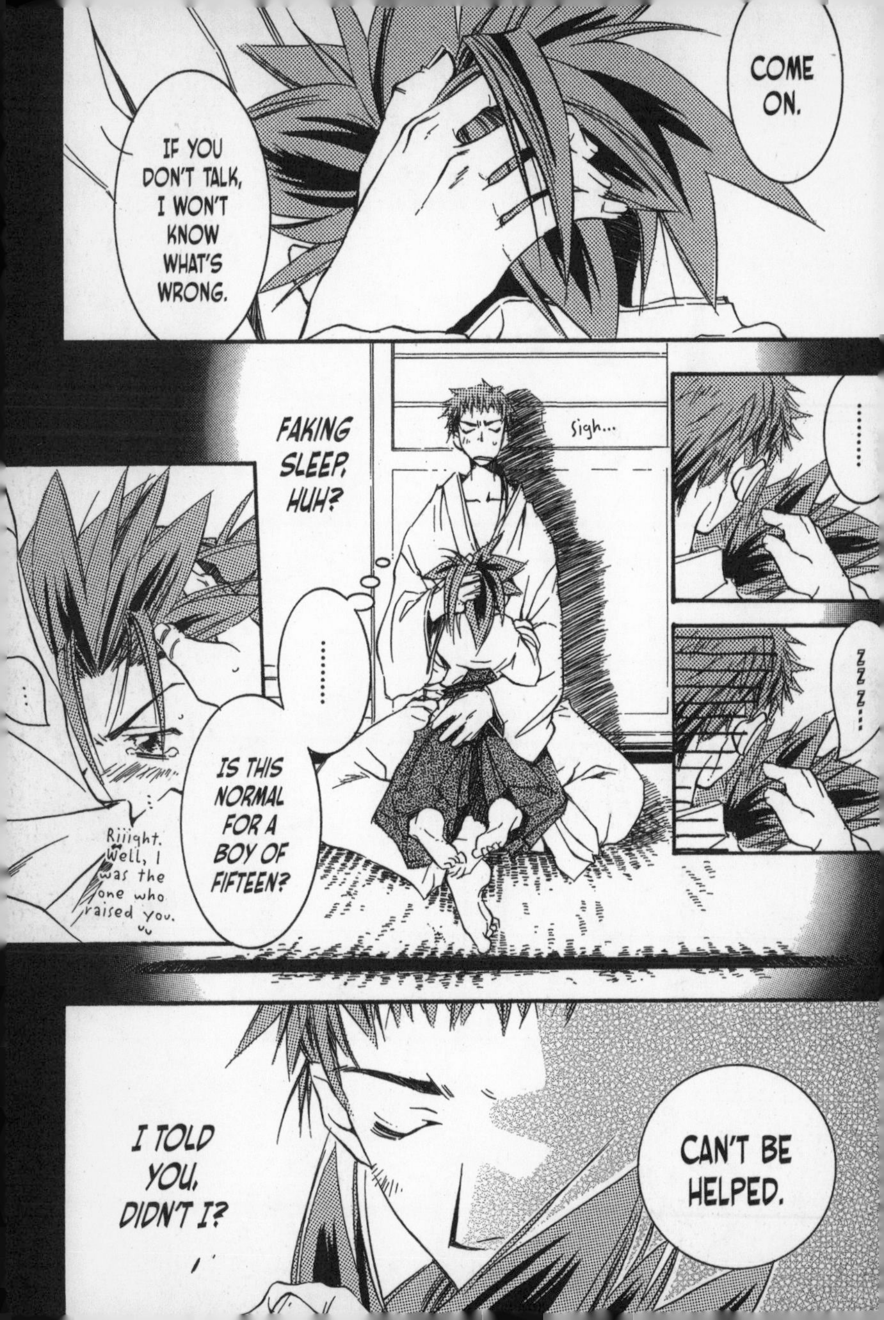
COME ON.
IF YOU DON'T TALK, I WON'T KNOW WHAT'S WRONG.
......
ZZZ...
Sigh...
FAKING SLEEP, HUH?
......
IS THIS NORMAL FOR A BOY OF FIFTEEN?
...
Riiight. Well, I was the one who raised you.
CAN'T BE HELPED.
I TOLD YOU. DIDN'T I?

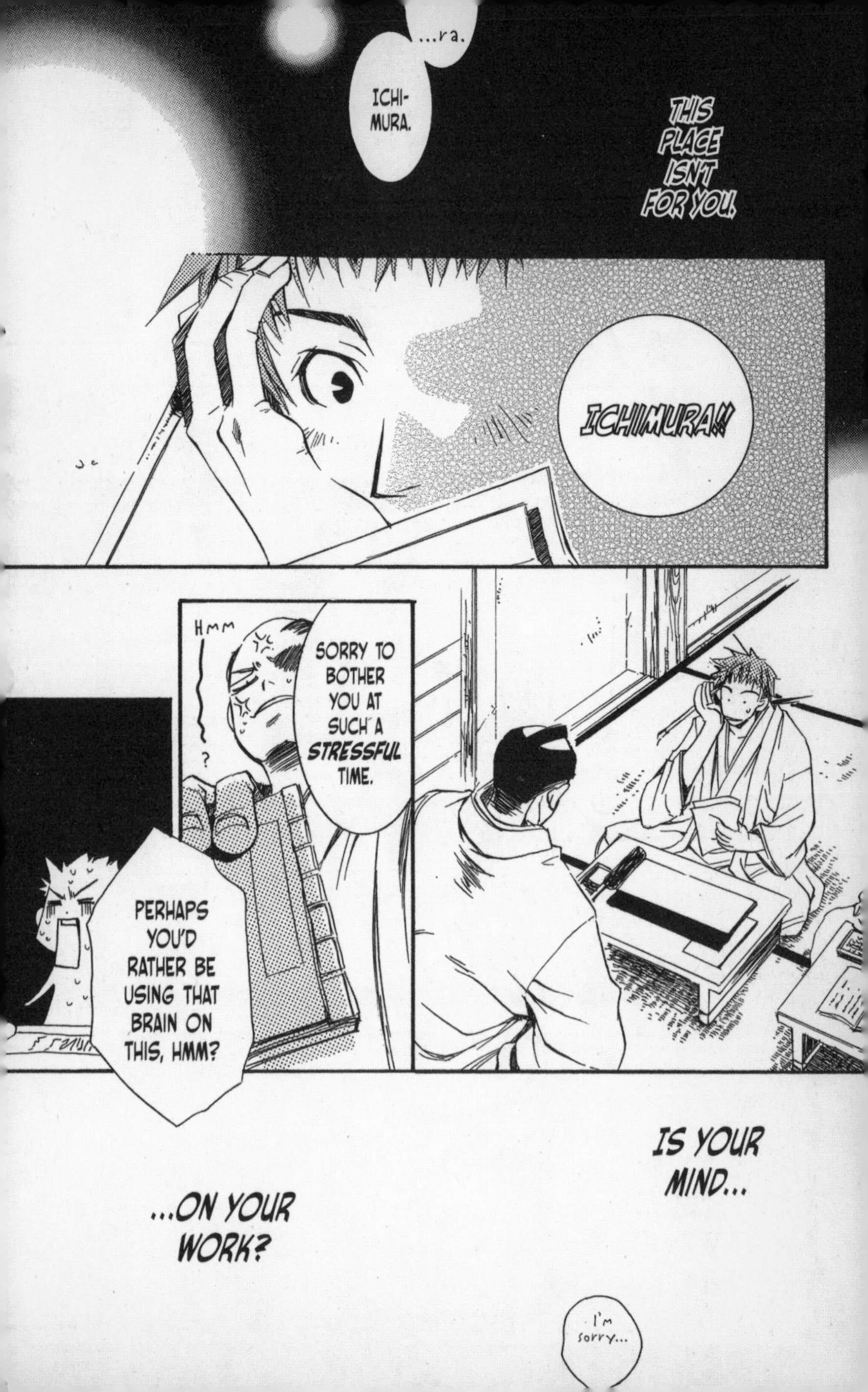
THIS PLACE ISN'T FOR YOU.
...ra.
ICHI-MURA.
ICHIMURA!!
SORRY TO BOTHER YOU AT SUCH A STRESSFUL TIME.
HMM ?
PERHAPS YOU'D RATHER BE USING THAT BRAIN ON THIS, HMM?
IS YOUR MIND...
...ON YOUR WORK?
I'm sorry...

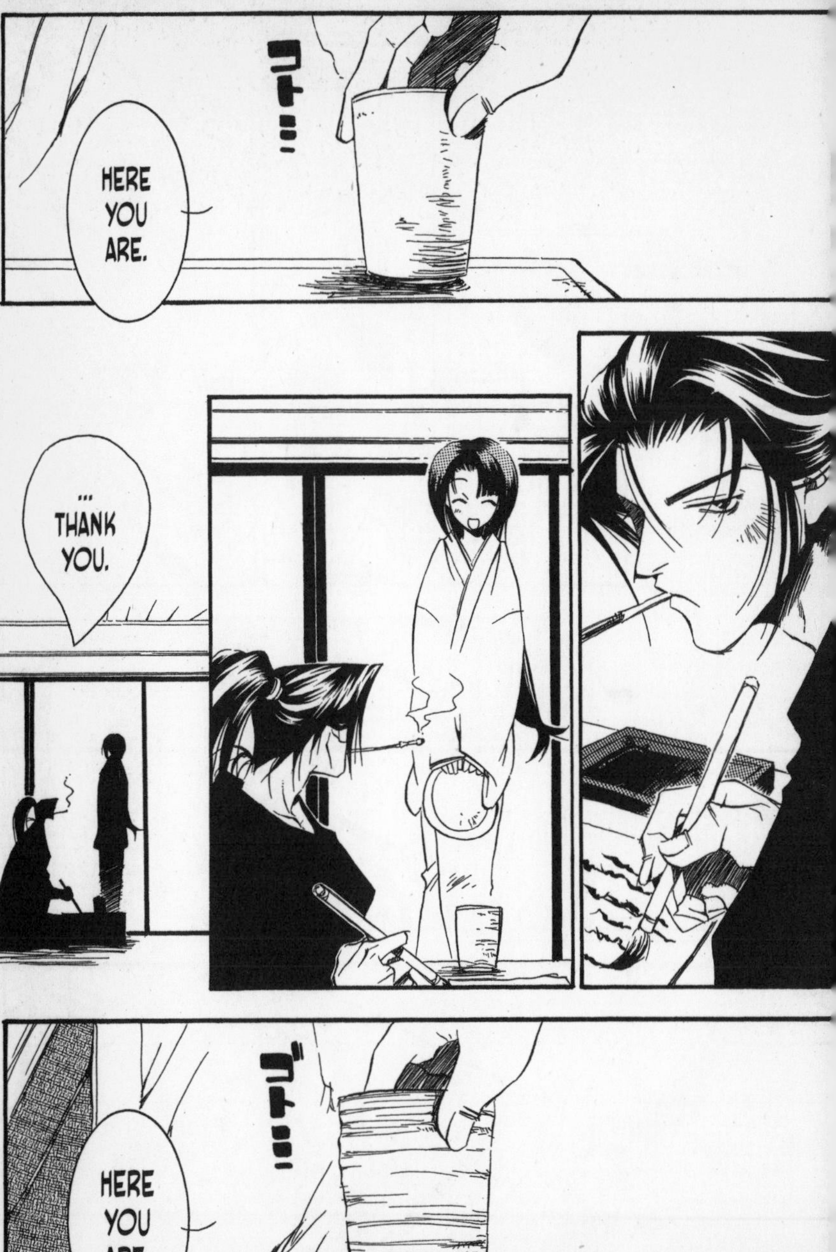
コトッ
HERE YOU ARE.
... THANK YOU.
ゴトッ
HERE YOU ARE.

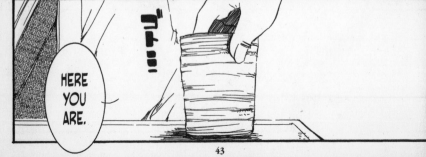

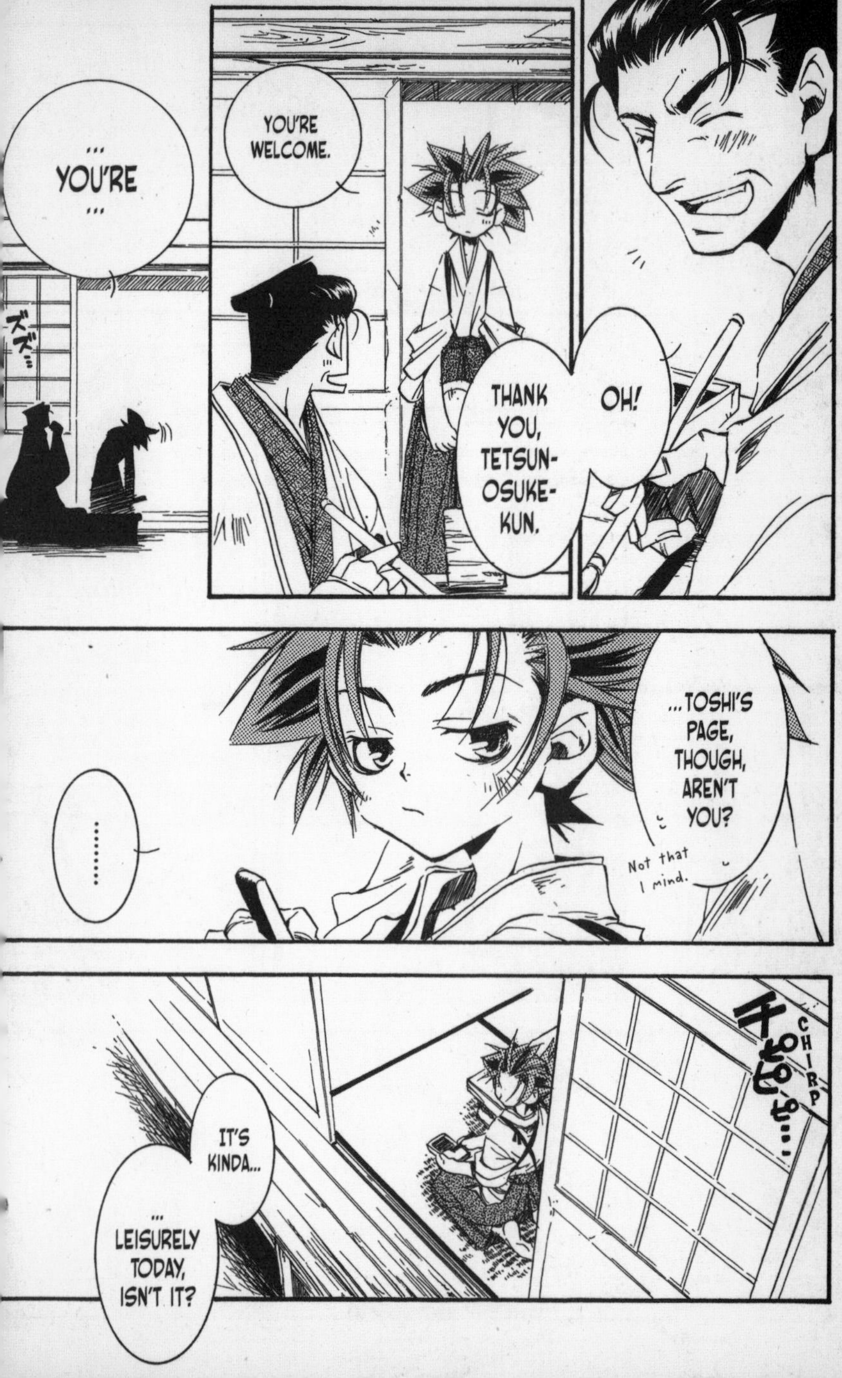
OH!
THANK YOU, TETSUN-OSUKE-KUN.
YOU'RE WELCOME.
... YOU'RE ...
ズズ…
...TOSHI'S PAGE, THOUGH, AREN'T YOU?
Not that I mind.
....
チピピ…
CHIRP
IT'S KINDA...
... LEISURELY TODAY, ISN'T IT?

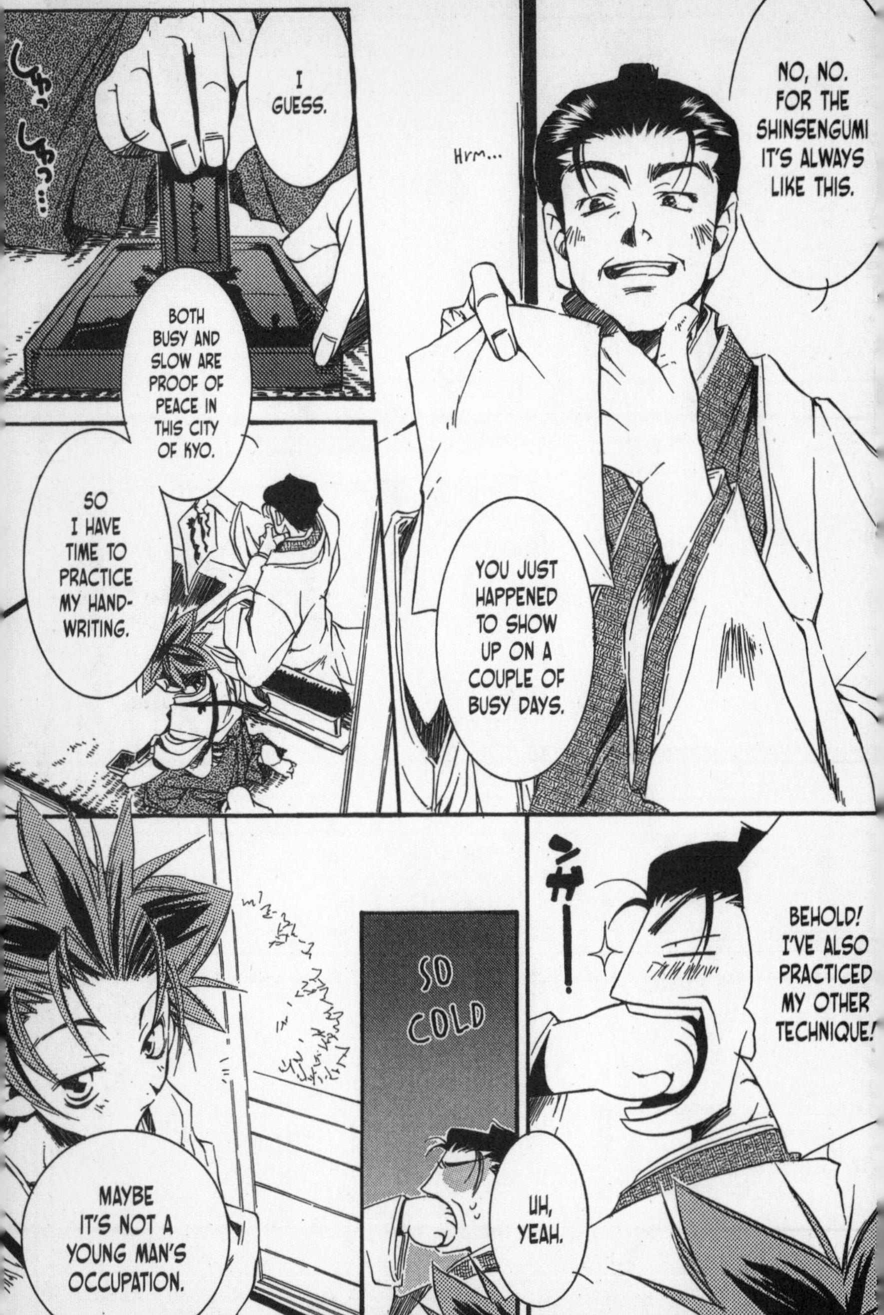
NO, NO. FOR THE SHINSENGUMI IT'S ALWAYS LIKE THIS.
Hrm...
YOU JUST HAPPENED TO SHOW UP ON A COUPLE OF BUSY DAYS.
I GUESS.
BOTH BUSY AND SLOW ARE PROOF OF PEACE IN THIS CITY OF KYO.
SO I HAVE TIME TO PRACTICE MY HAND-WRITING.
BEHOLD! I'VE ALSO PRACTICED MY OTHER TECHNIQUE!
SO COLD
UH, YEAH.
MAYBE IT'S NOT A YOUNG MAN'S OCCUPATION.

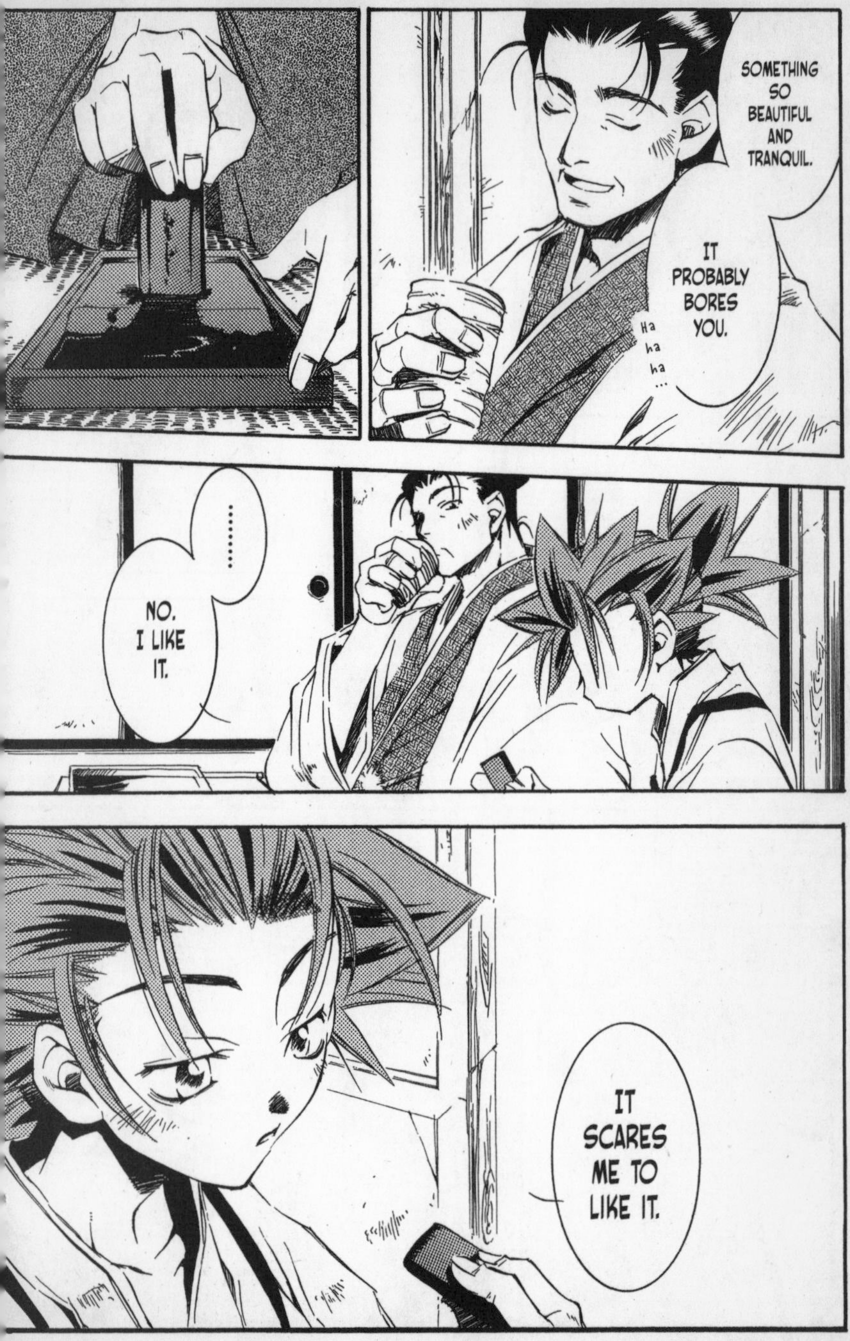
SOMETHING SO BEAUTIFUL AND TRANQUIL.
IT PROBABLY BORES YOU.
Ha ha ha ...
......
NO. I LIKE IT.
IT SCARES ME TO LIKE IT.

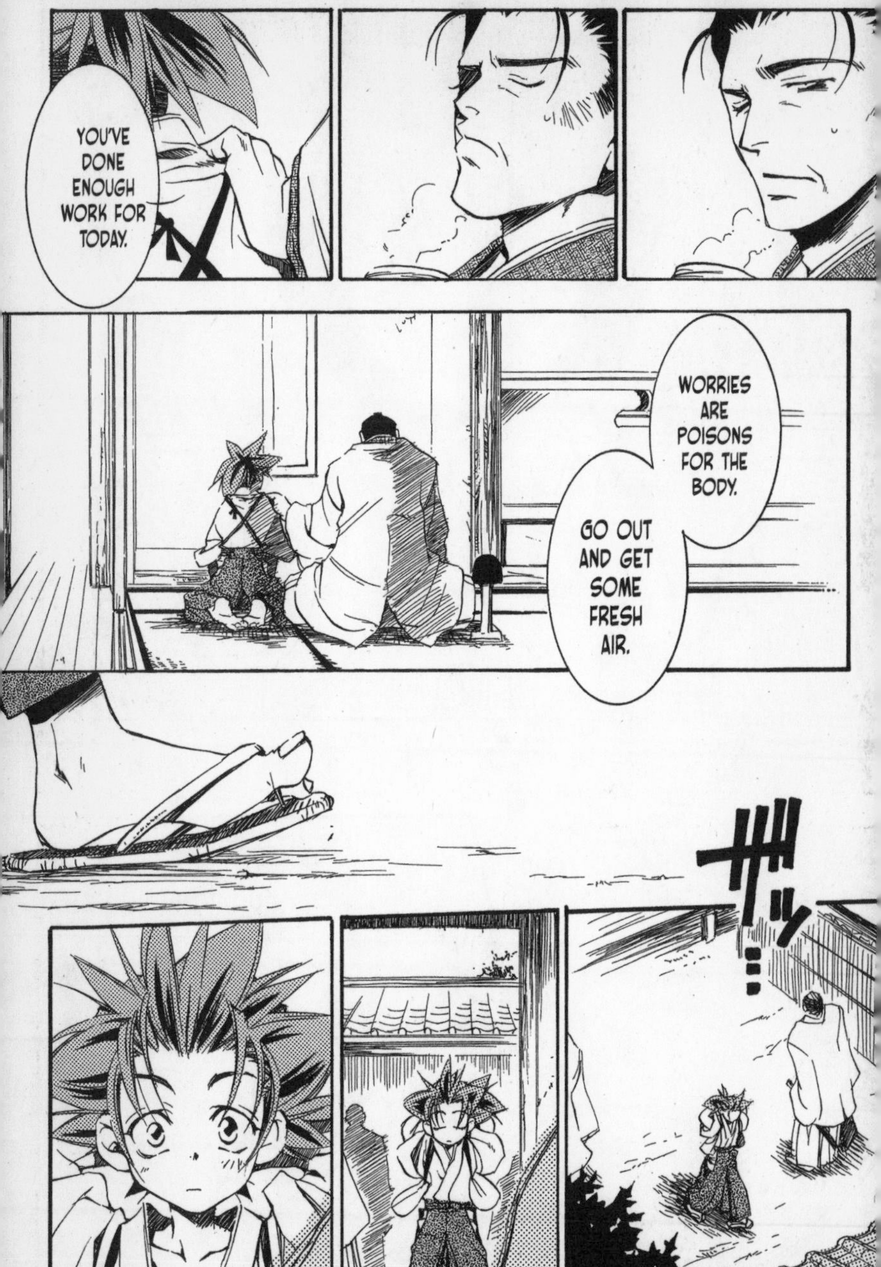
YOU'VE DONE ENOUGH WORK FOR TODAY.
WORRIES ARE POISONS FOR THE BODY.
GO OUT AND GET SOME FRESH AIR.
ザッ…

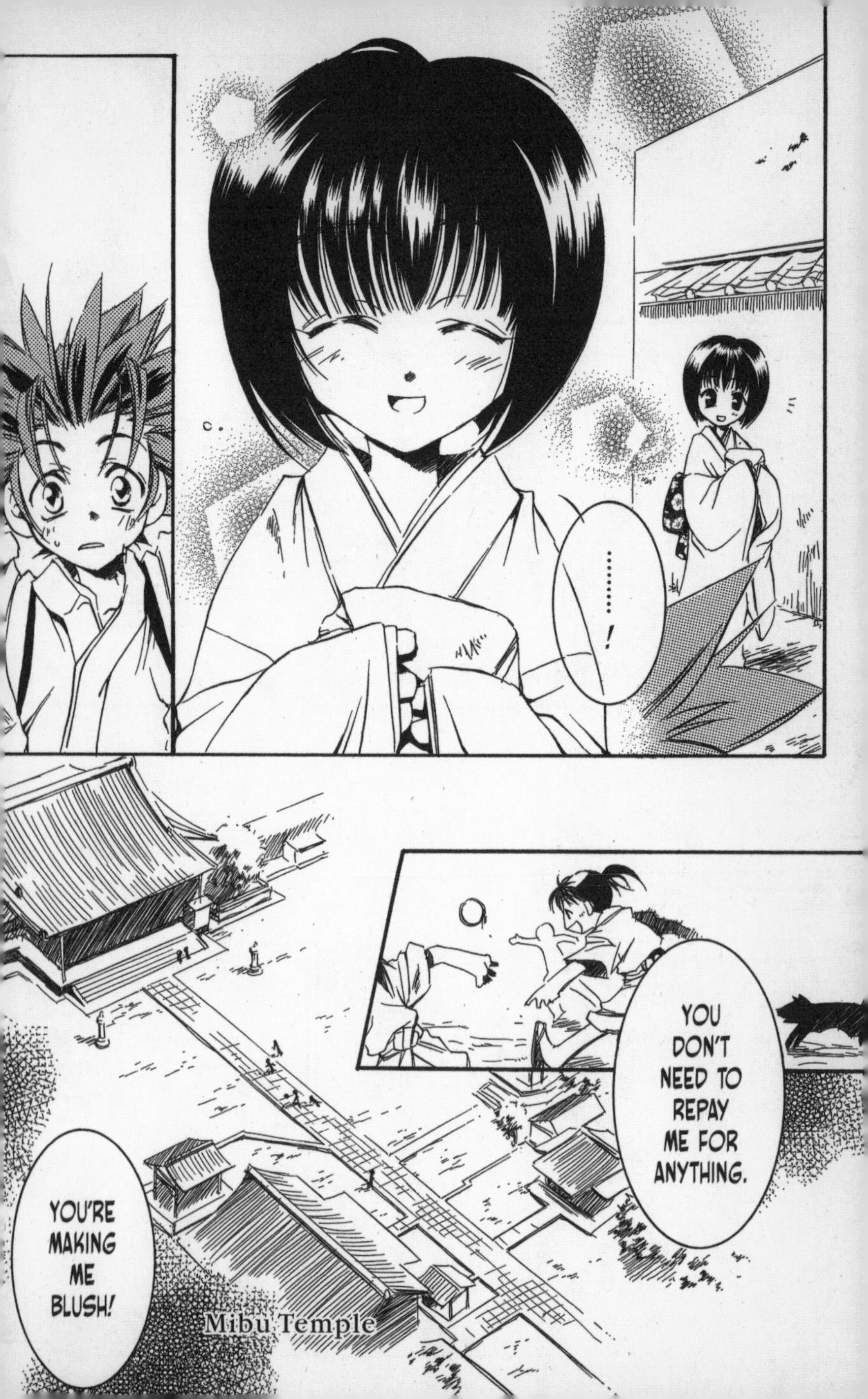
......!
YOU DON'T NEED TO REPAY ME FOR ANYTHING.
YOU'RE MAKING ME BLUSH!
Mibu Temple

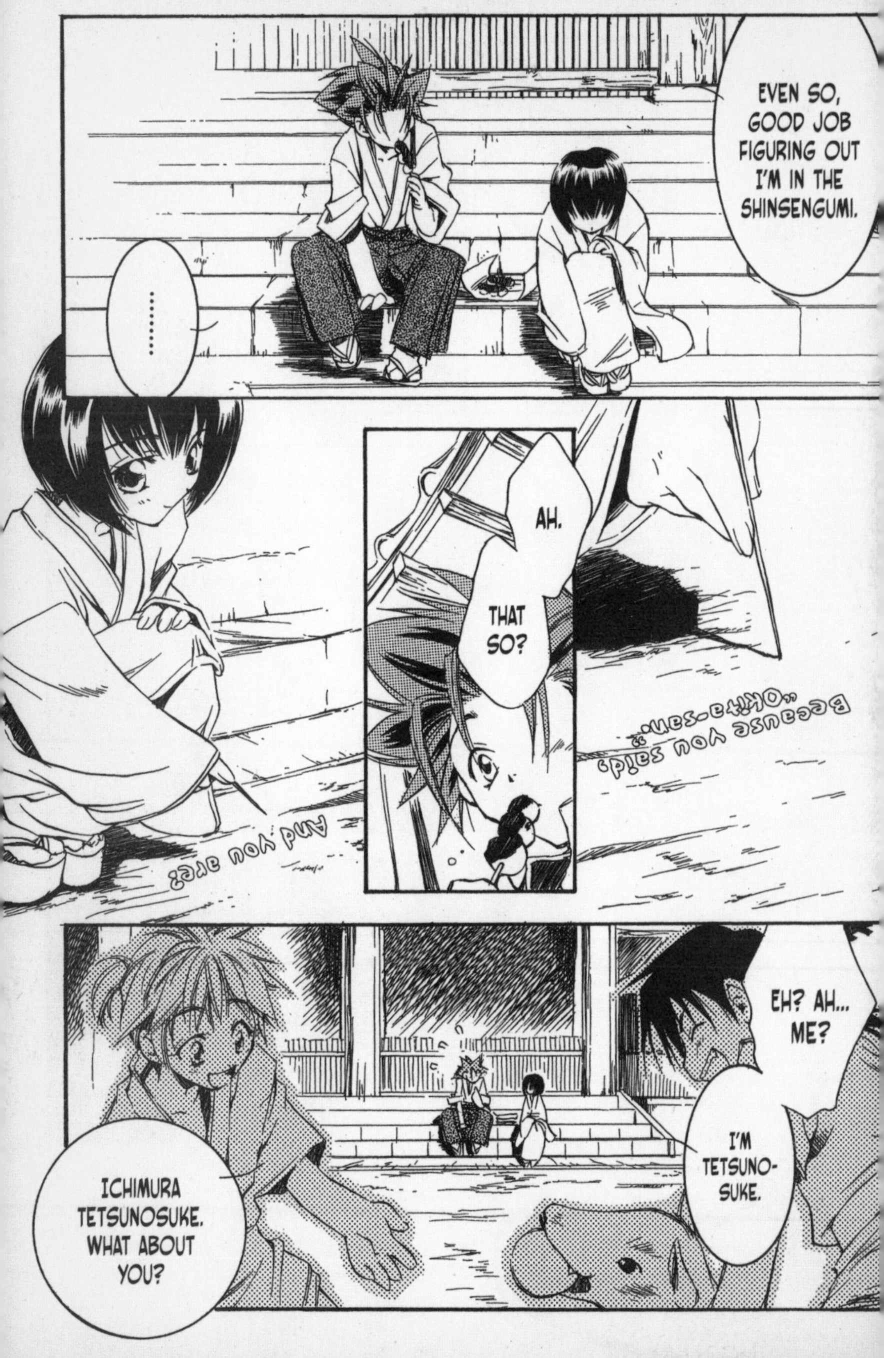

EVEN SO, GOOD JOB FIGURING OUT I'M IN THE SHINSENGUMI.
……
Because you said, "Okita-san."
AH.
THAT SO?
And you are?
EH? AH... ME?
I'M TETSUNO-SUKE.
ICHIMURA TETSUNOSUKE. WHAT ABOUT YOU?

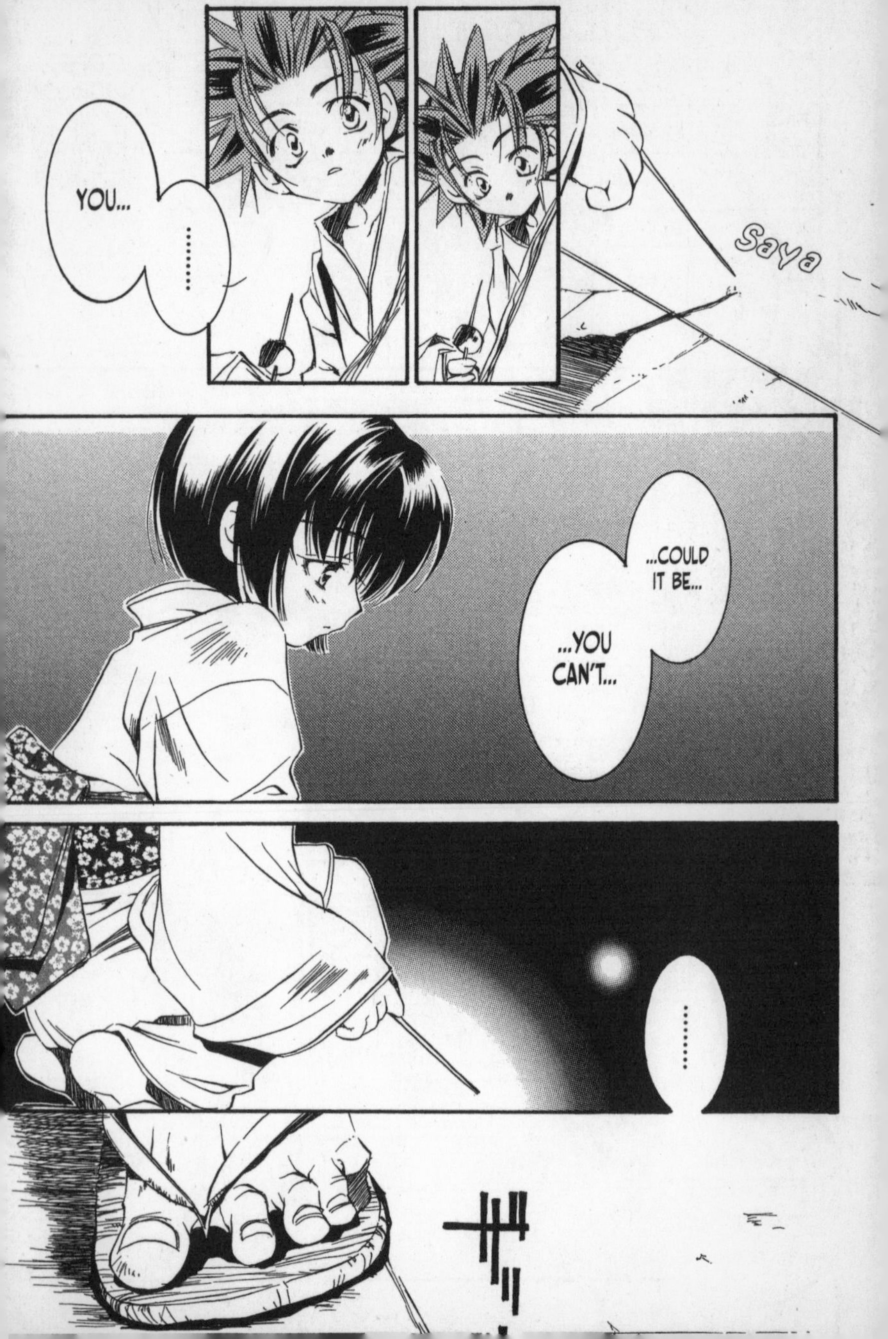
Saya
YOU...
......
...COULD IT BE...
...YOU CAN'T...
......

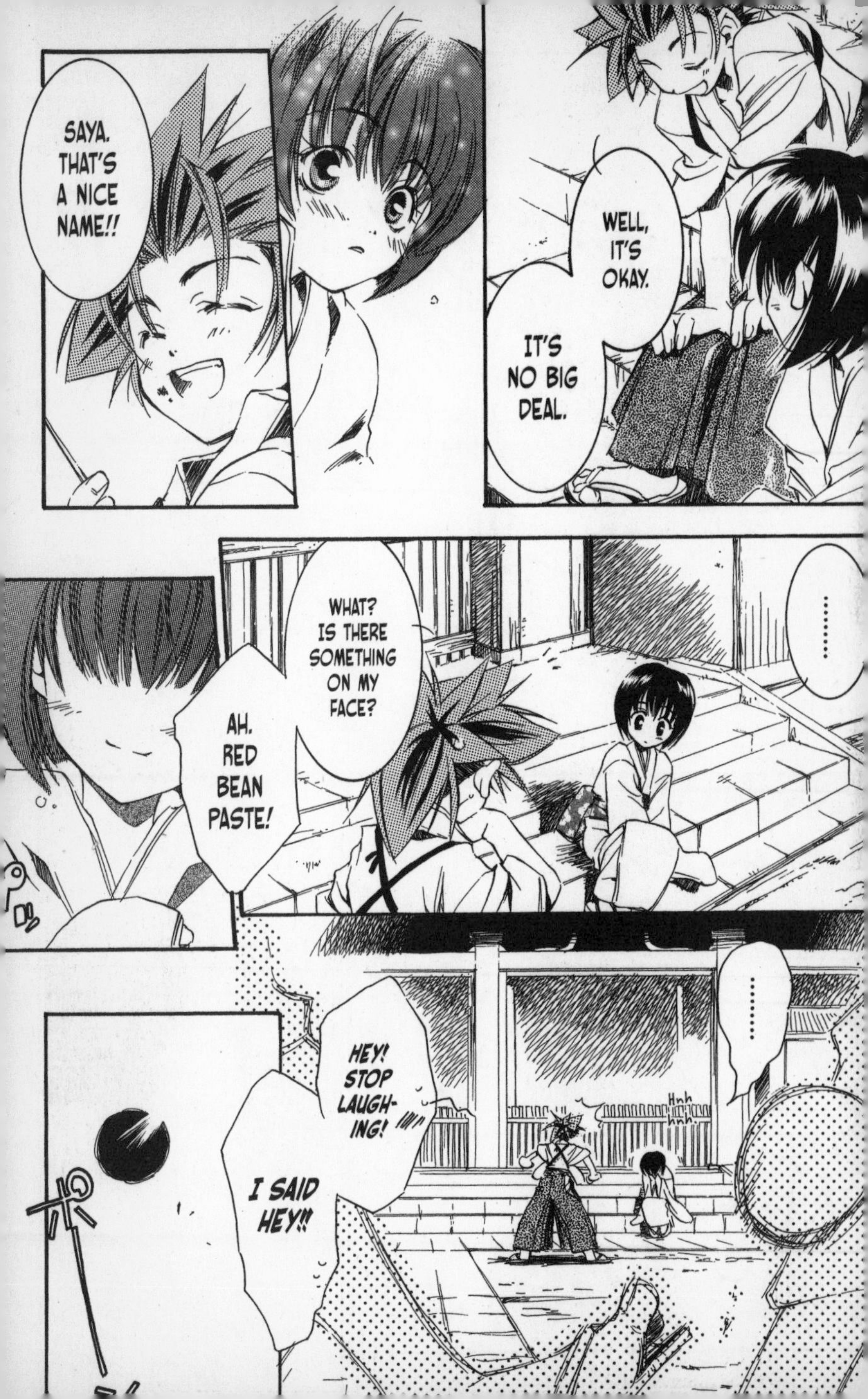
WELL, IT'S OKAY.
IT'S NO BIG DEAL.
SAYA. THAT'S A NICE NAME!!
......
WHAT? IS THERE SOMETHING ON MY FACE?
AH. RED BEAN PASTE!
......
Hnh hnh.
HEY! STOP LAUGHING!
I SAID HEY!!

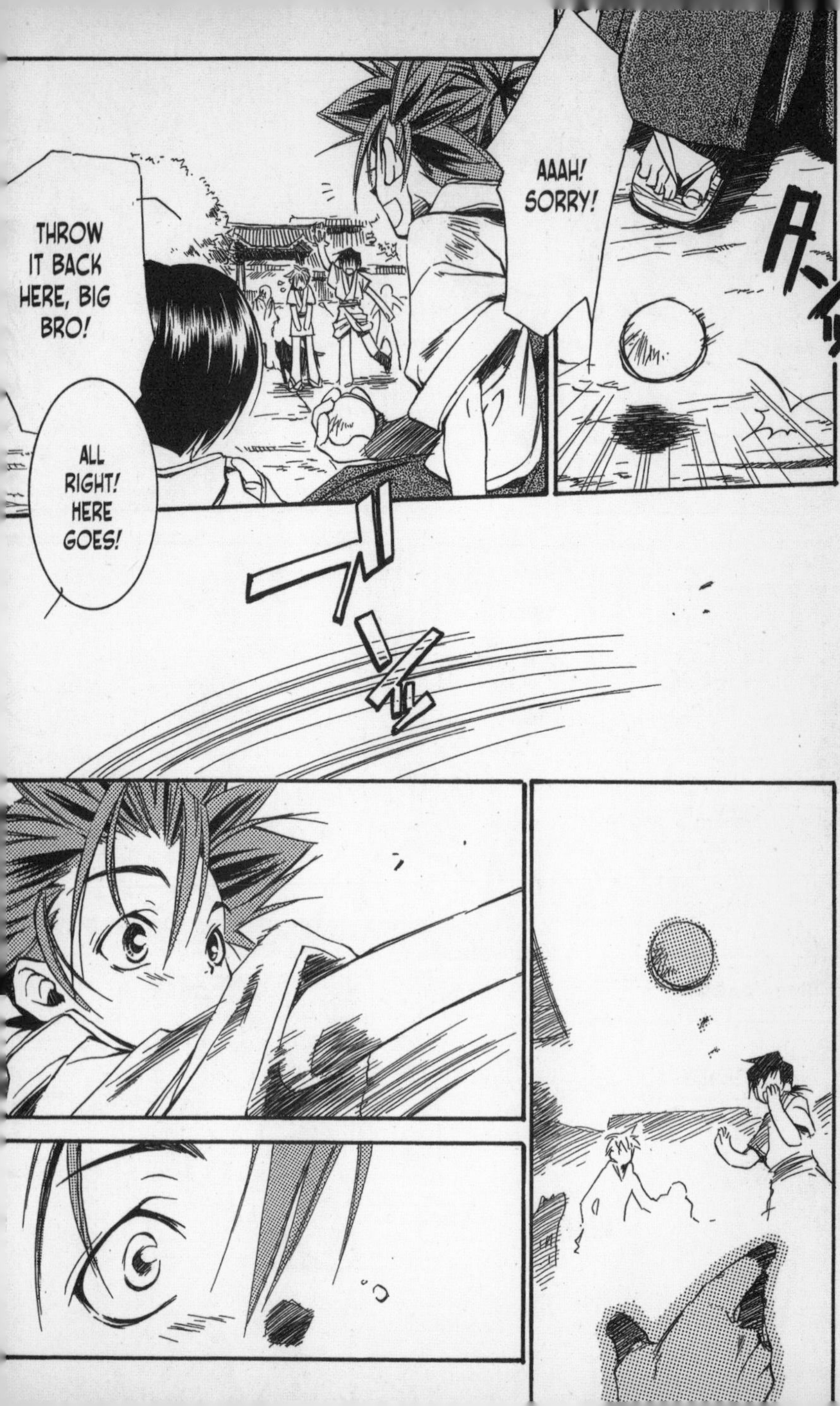
AAAH! SORRY!
THROW IT BACK HERE, BIG BRO!
ALL RIGHT! HERE GOES!

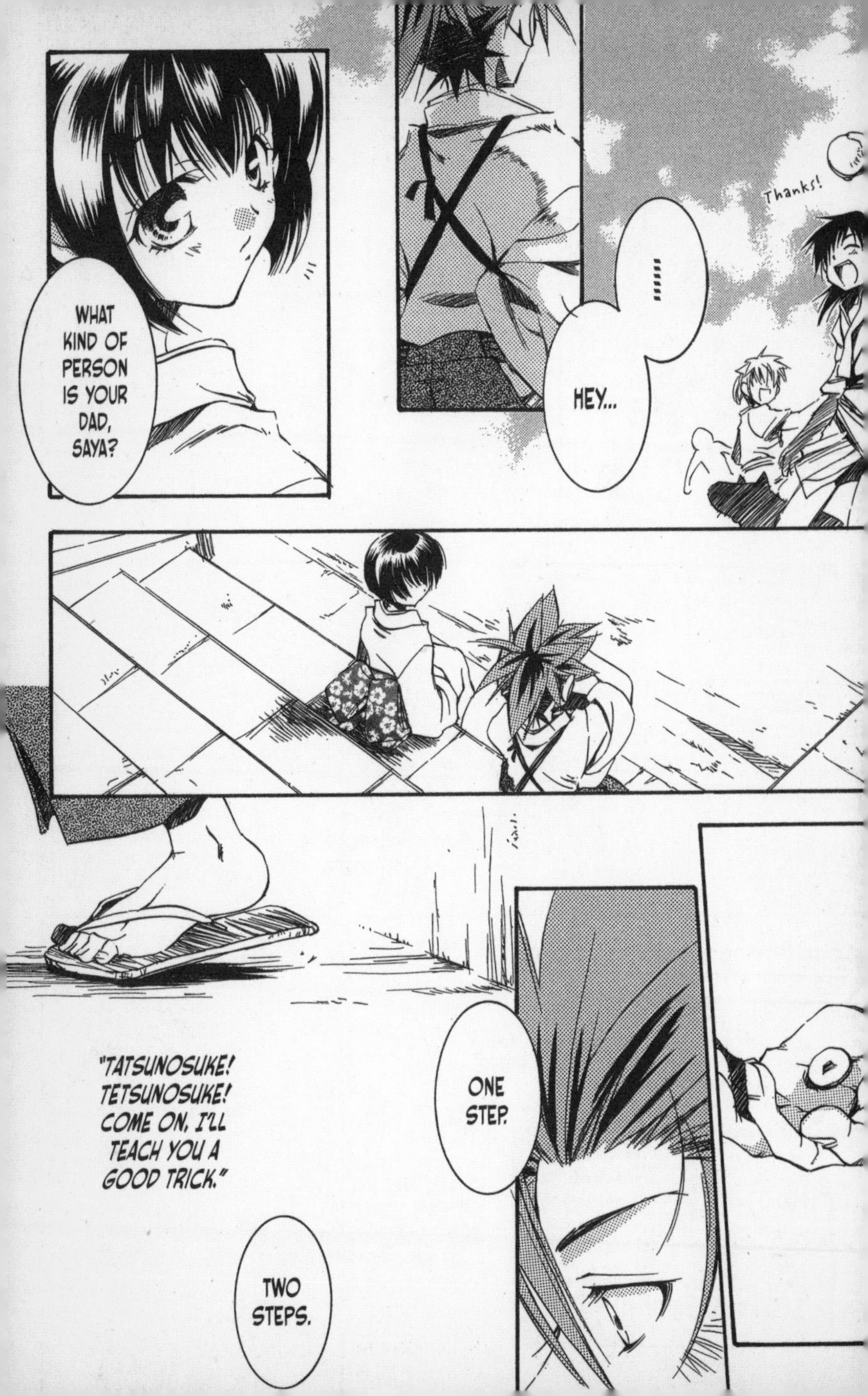
Thanks!
......
HEY...
WHAT KIND OF PERSON IS YOUR DAD, SAYA?
ONE STEP.
"TATSUNOSUKE! TETSUNOSUKE! COME ON, I'LL TEACH YOU A GOOD TRICK."
TWO STEPS.

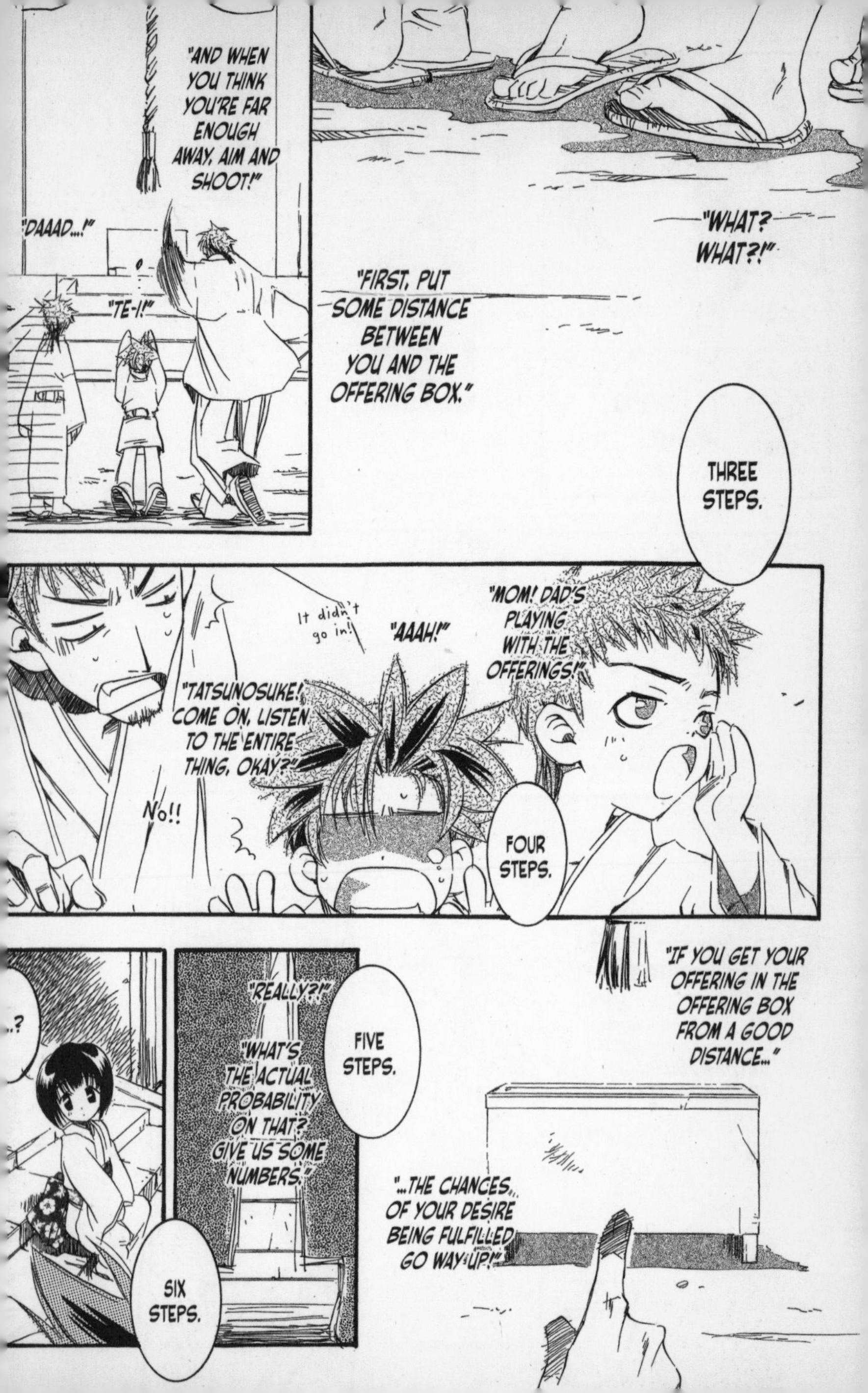
"WHAT? WHAT?!"
"FIRST, PUT SOME DISTANCE BETWEEN YOU AND THE OFFERING BOX."
"AND WHEN YOU THINK YOU'RE FAR ENOUGH AWAY, AIM AND SHOOT!"
"DAAAD...!"
"TE-I!"
THREE STEPS.
"MOM! DAD'S PLAYING WITH THE OFFERINGS!"
FOUR STEPS.
"AAAH!"
It didn't go in!
"TATSUNOSUKE! COME ON, LISTEN TO THE ENTIRE THING, OKAY?"
No!!
"IF YOU GET YOUR OFFERING IN THE OFFERING BOX FROM A GOOD DISTANCE..."
"...THE CHANCES OF YOUR DESIRE BEING FULFILLED GO WAY UP!"
FIVE STEPS.
"REALLY?!"
"WHAT'S THE ACTUAL PROBABILITY ON THAT? GIVE US SOME NUMBERS."
SIX STEPS.
..?

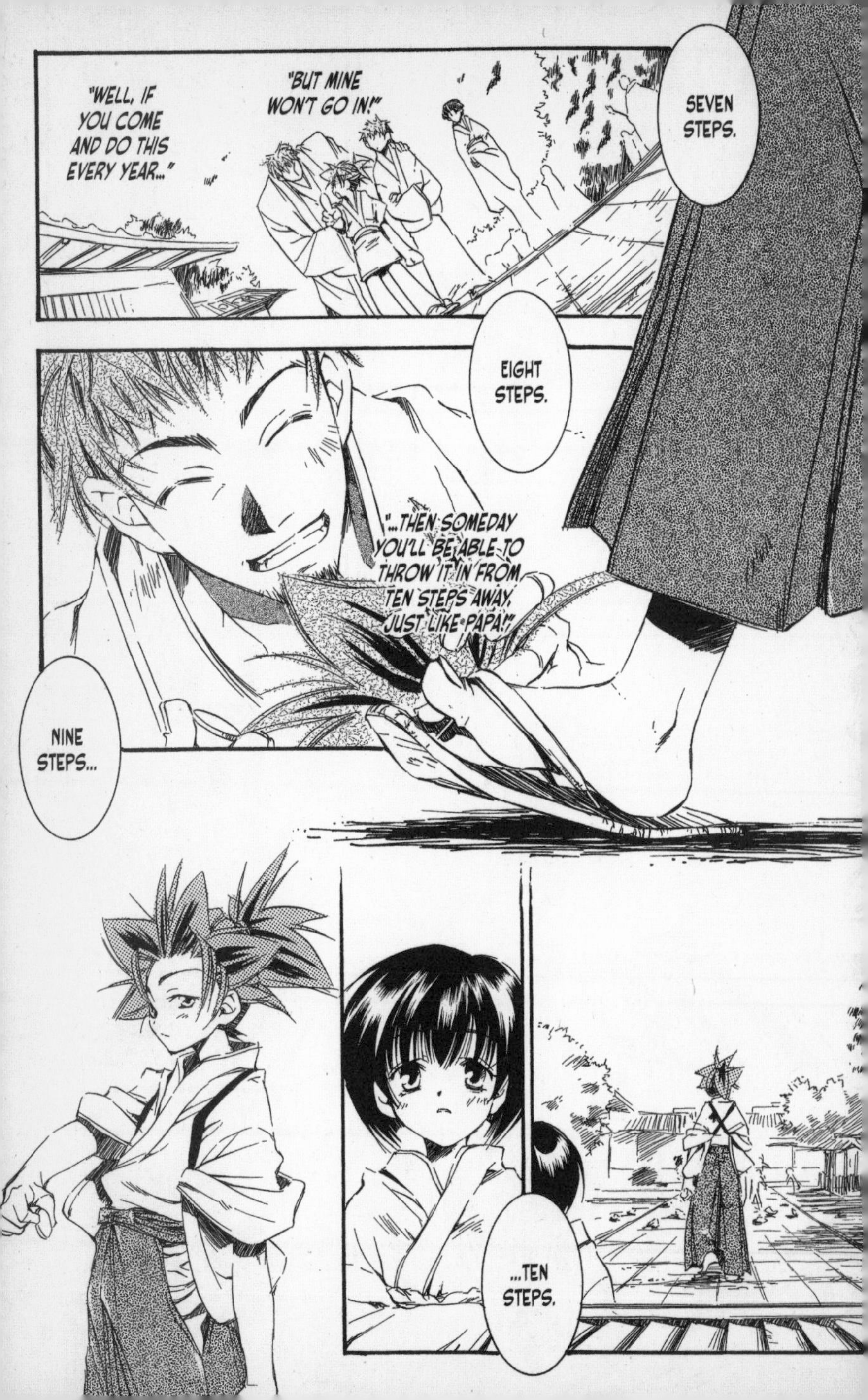
SEVEN STEPS.
"BUT MINE WON'T GO IN!"
"WELL, IF YOU COME AND DO THIS EVERY YEAR..."
EIGHT STEPS.
"...THEN SOMEDAY YOU'LL BE ABLE TO THROW IT IN FROM TEN STEPS AWAY. JUST LIKE PAPA!"
NINE STEPS...
...TEN STEPS.

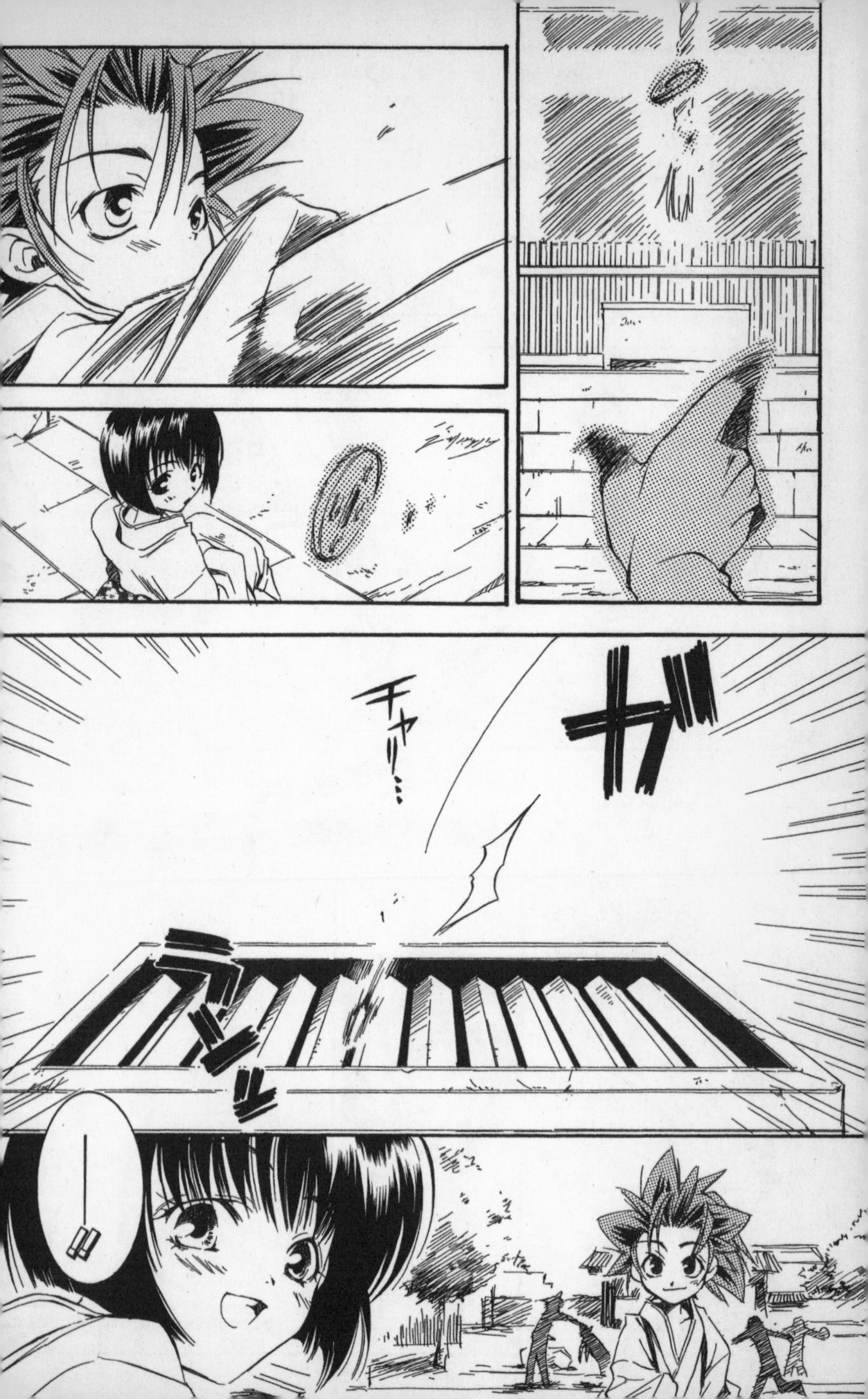
ガ
チャリ…
ラン
…!!

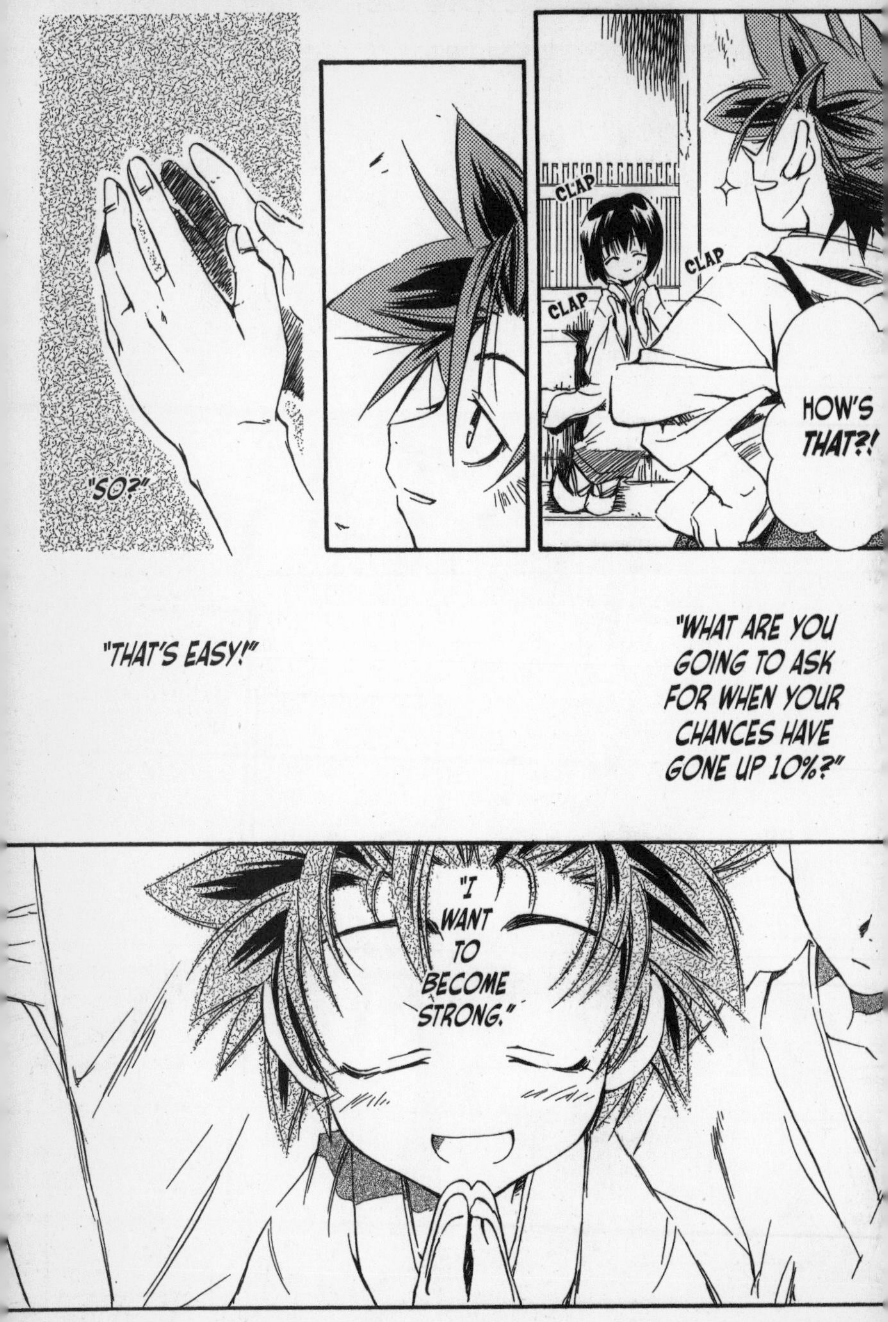
CLAP
CLAP
CLAP
HOW'S THAT?!
"SO?"
"WHAT ARE YOU GOING TO ASK FOR WHEN YOUR CHANCES HAVE GONE UP 10%?"
"THAT'S EASY!"
"I WANT TO BECOME STRONG."

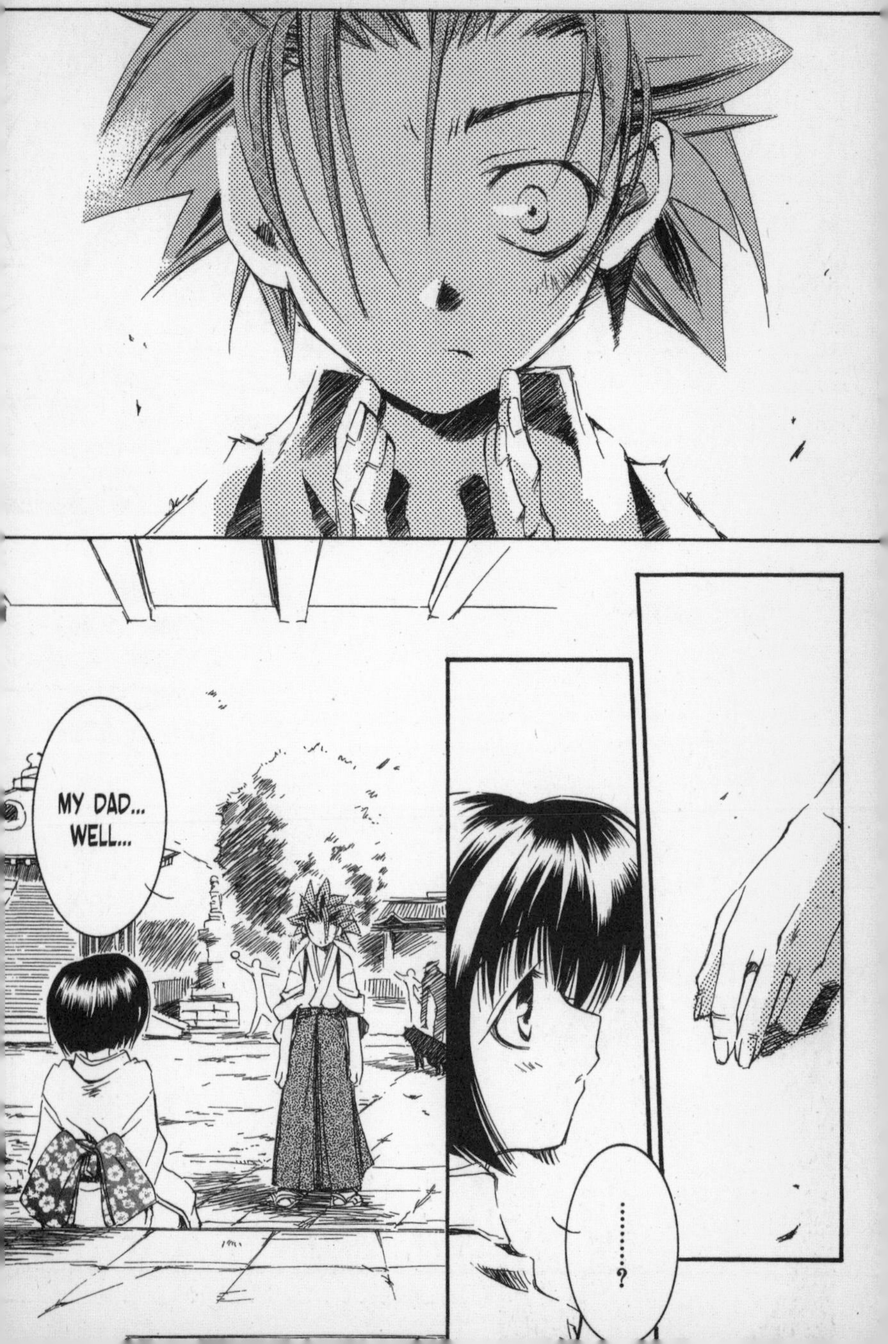
......?
MY DAD... WELL...

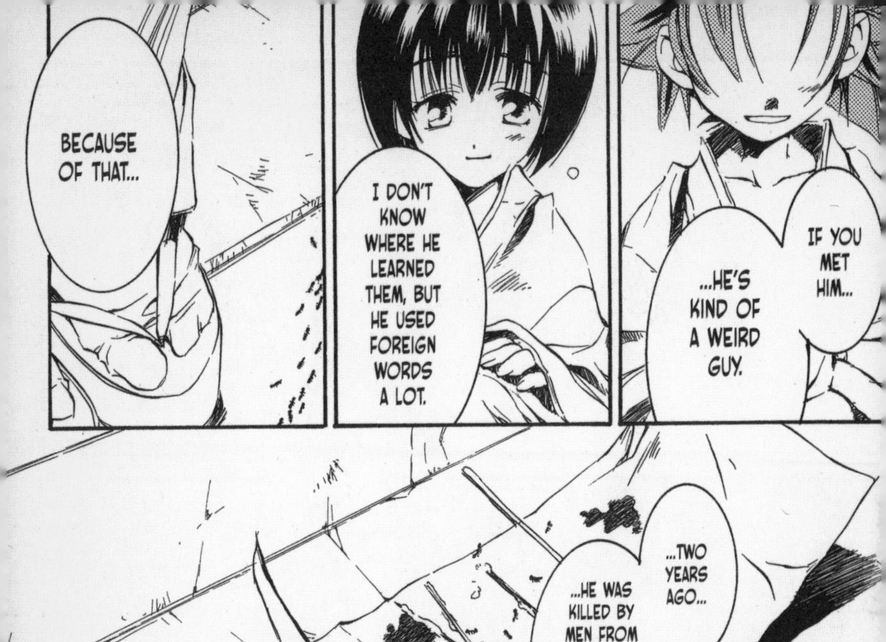
IF YOU MET HIM...
...HE'S KIND OF A WEIRD GUY.
I DON'T KNOW WHERE HE LEARNED THEM, BUT HE USED FOREIGN WORDS A LOT.
BECAUSE OF THAT...
...TWO YEARS AGO...
...HE WAS KILLED BY MEN FROM CHOUSHUU. "EXPEL THE BARBARIANS," THEY SAID.
MOM GOT CAUGHT UP IN IT, TOO.
NOW IT'S JUST ME AND TATSU.

"Expel the barbarians": Those who are "sonnou joui" seek to repel all foreigners and foreign influence from Japan.

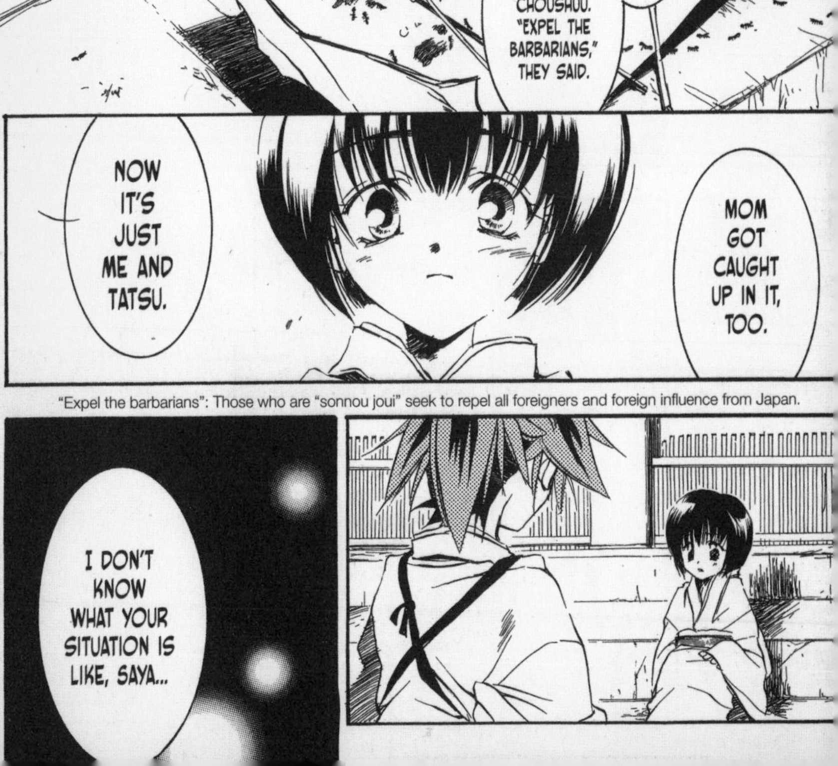
I DON'T KNOW WHAT YOUR SITUATION IS LIKE, SAYA...

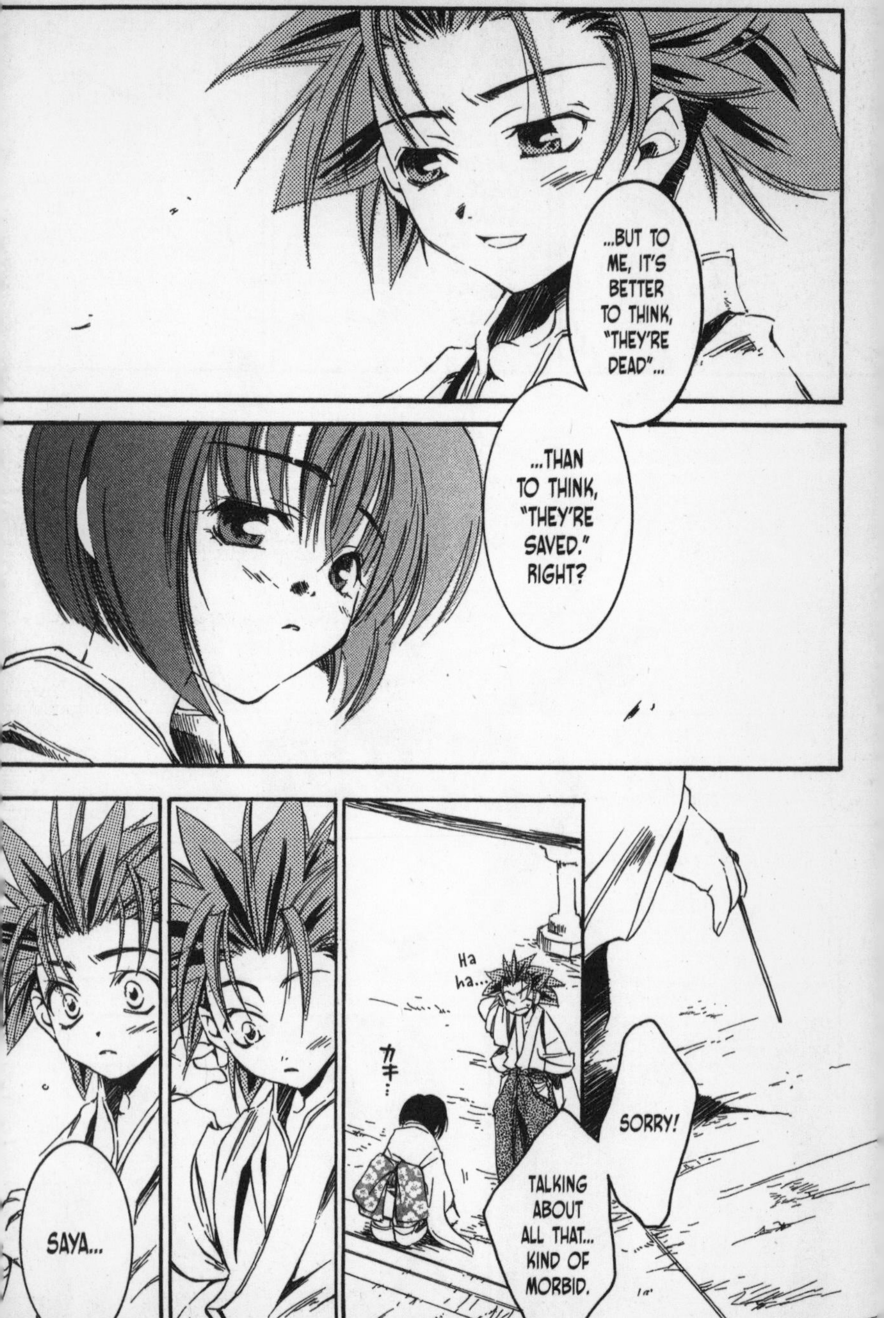
...BUT TO ME, IT'S BETTER TO THINK, "THEY'RE DEAD"...
...THAN TO THINK, "THEY'RE SAVED." RIGHT?
Ha ha...
カキ..
SORRY!
TALKING ABOUT ALL THAT... KIND OF MORBID.
SAYA...

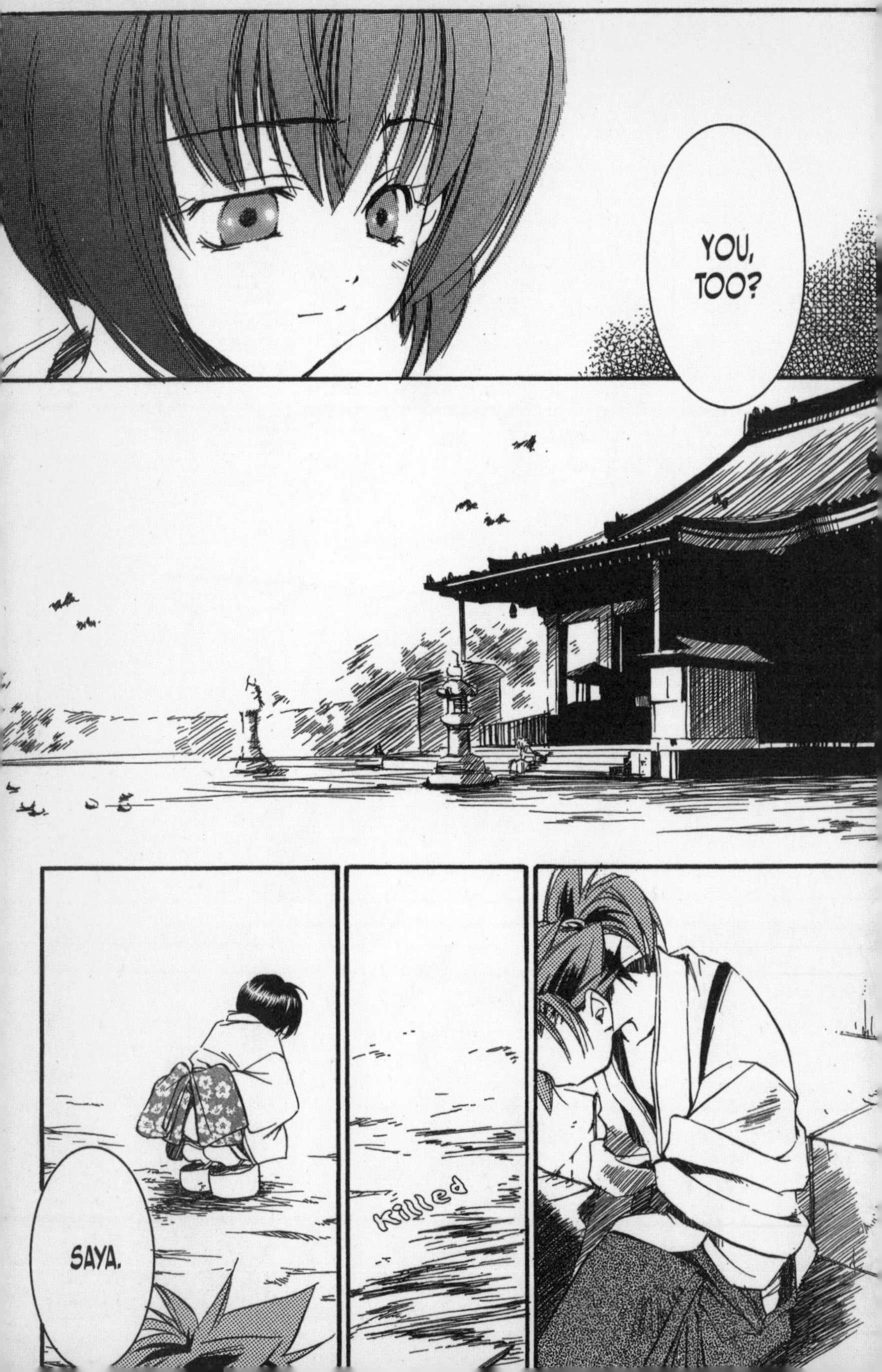
YOU, TOO?
Killed
SAYA.

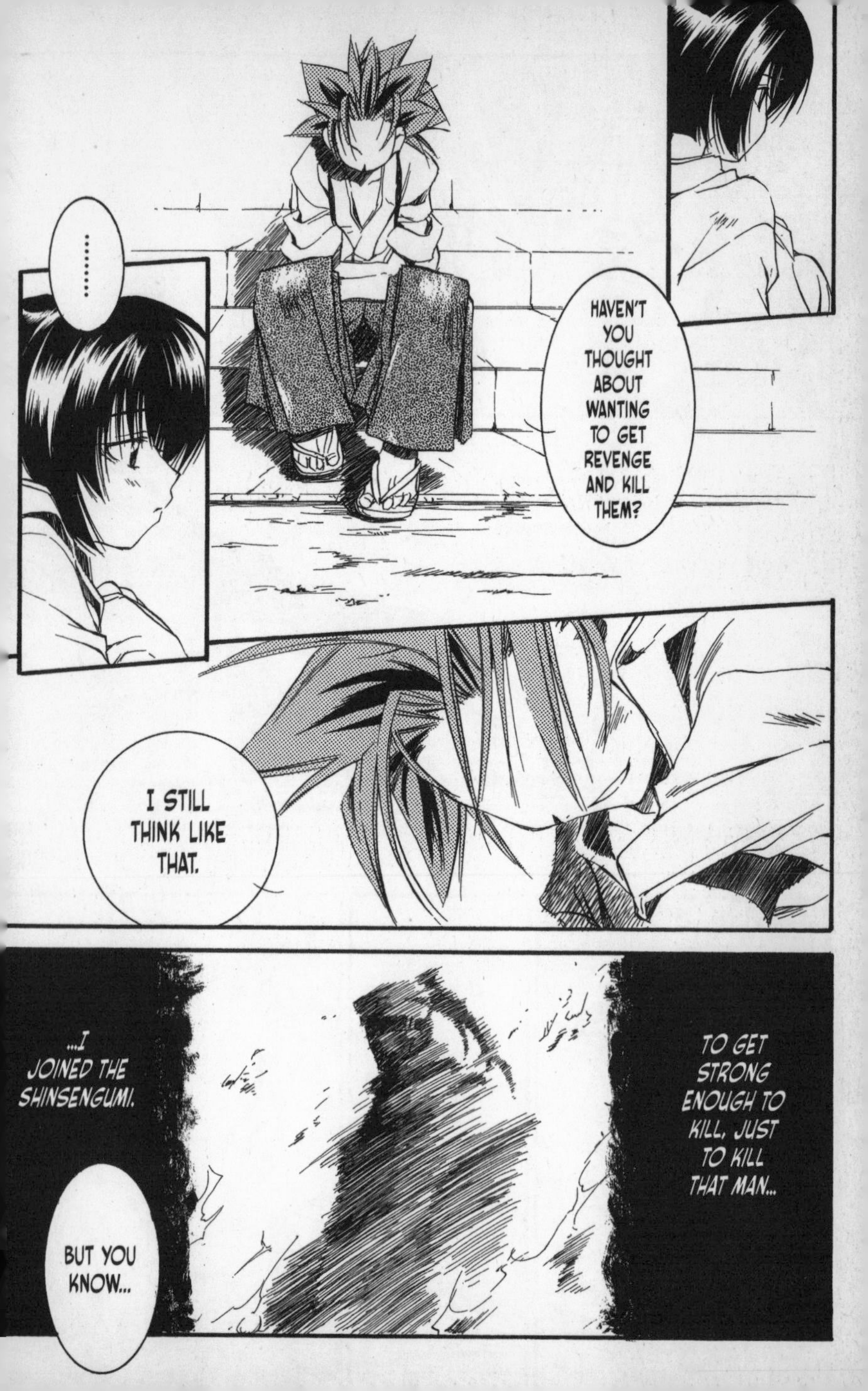
HAVEN'T YOU THOUGHT ABOUT WANTING TO GET REVENGE AND KILL THEM?
......
I STILL THINK LIKE THAT.
TO GET STRONG ENOUGH TO KILL, JUST TO KILL THAT MAN...
...I JOINED THE SHINSENGUMI.
BUT YOU KNOW...

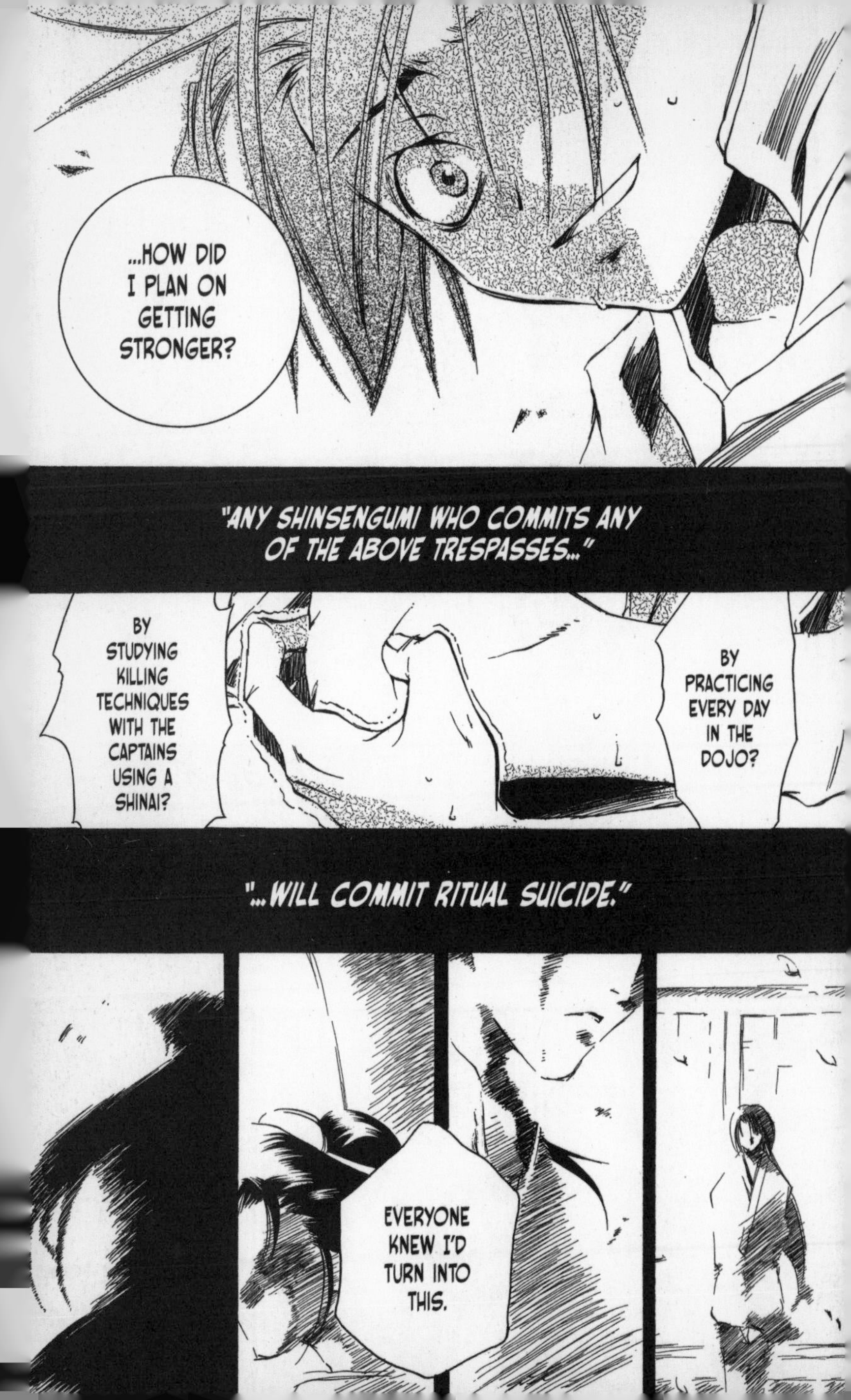
...HOW DID I PLAN ON GETTING STRONGER?
"ANY SHINSENGUMI WHO COMMITS ANY OF THE ABOVE TRESPASSES..."
BY PRACTICING EVERY DAY IN THE DOJO?
BY STUDYING KILLING TECHNIQUES WITH THE CAPTAINS USING A SHINAI?
"...WILL COMMIT RITUAL SUICIDE."
EVERYONE KNEW I'D TURN INTO THIS.

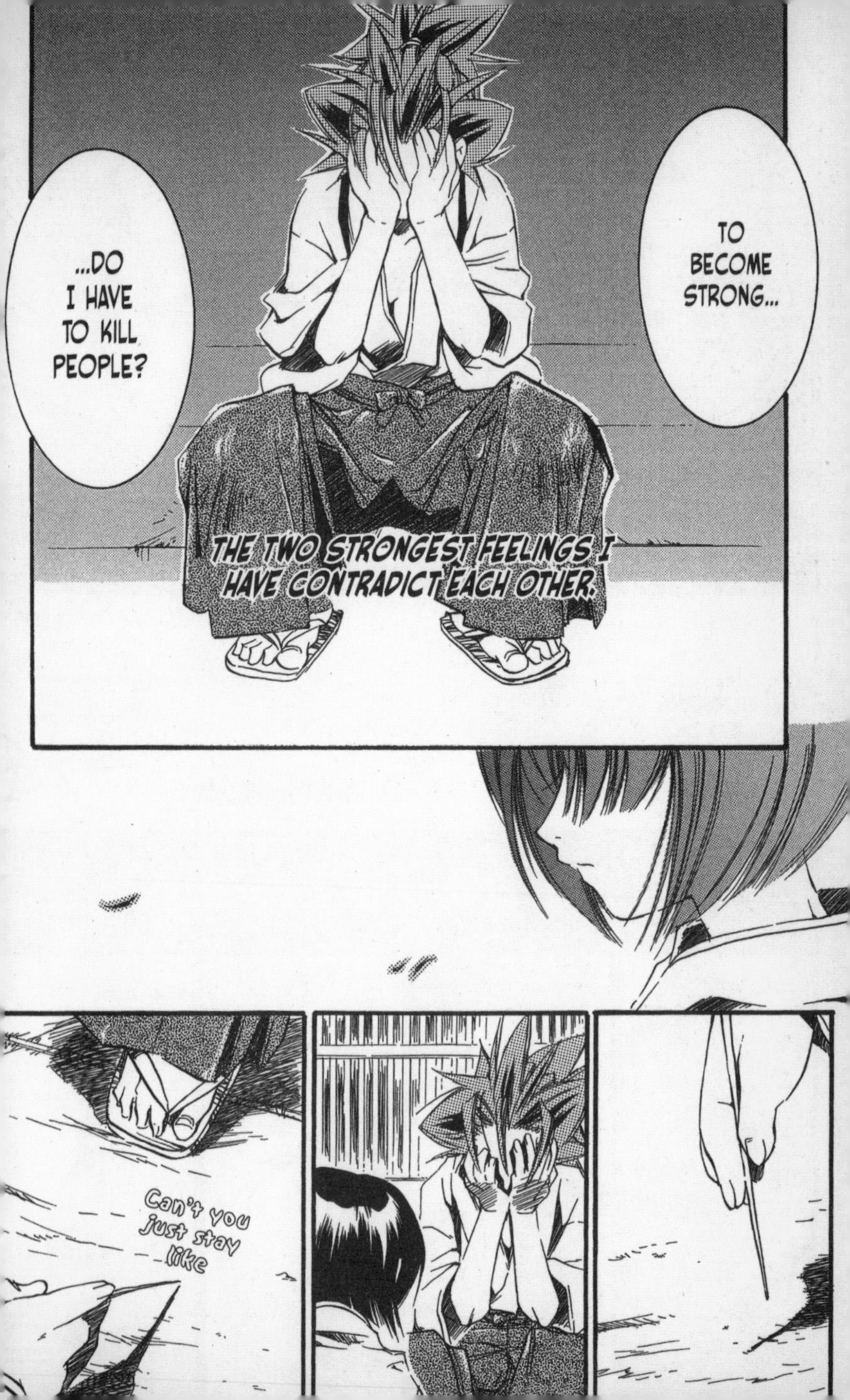
TO BECOME STRONG...
...DO I HAVE TO KILL PEOPLE?
THE TWO STRONGEST FEELINGS I HAVE CONTRADICT EACH OTHER.
Can't you just stay like

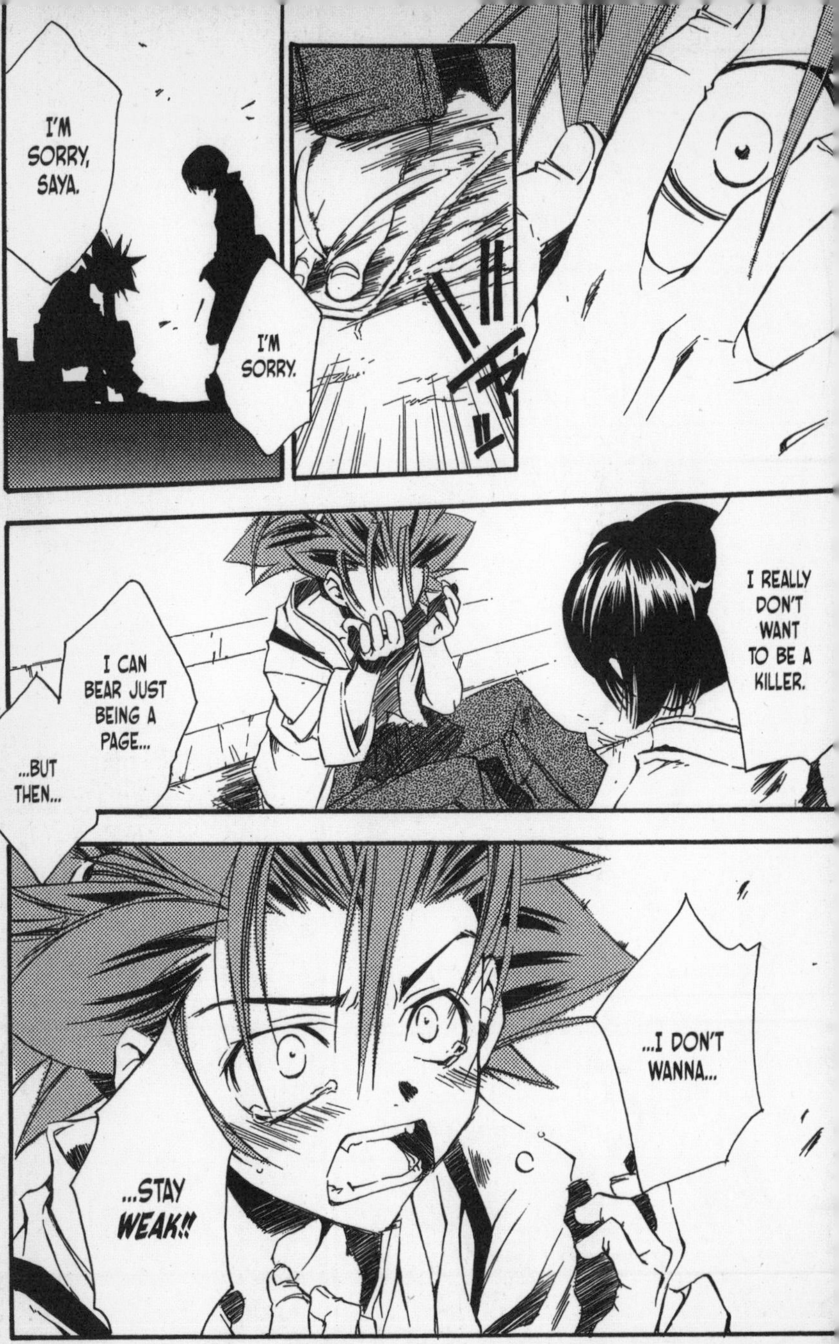
I'M SORRY.
I'M SORRY, SAYA.
I REALLY DON'T WANT TO BE A KILLER.
I CAN BEAR JUST BEING A PAGE...
...BUT THEN...
...I DON'T WANNA...
...STAY WEAK!!

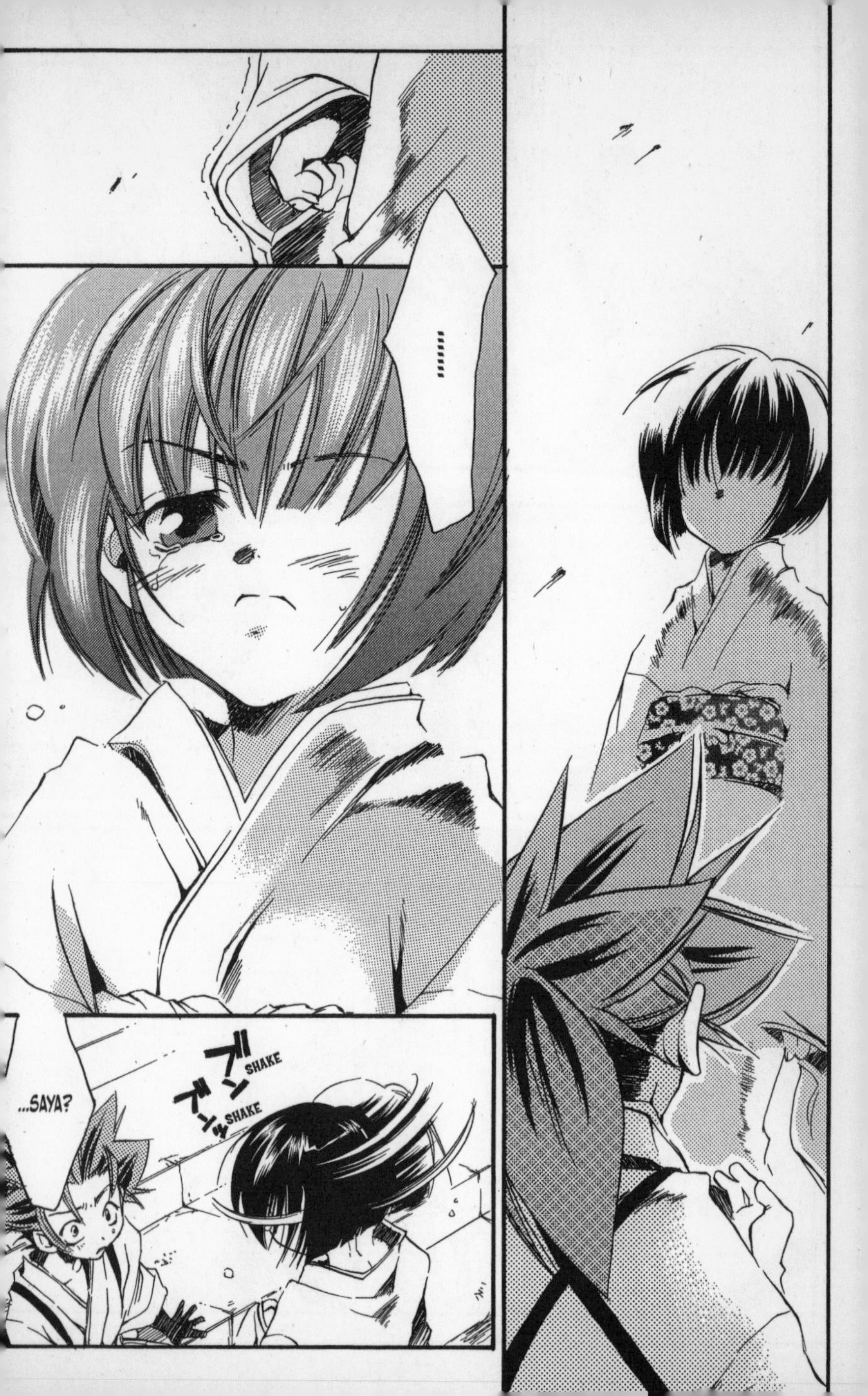
......
...SAYA?
ブン SHAKE
ブンッ SHAKE

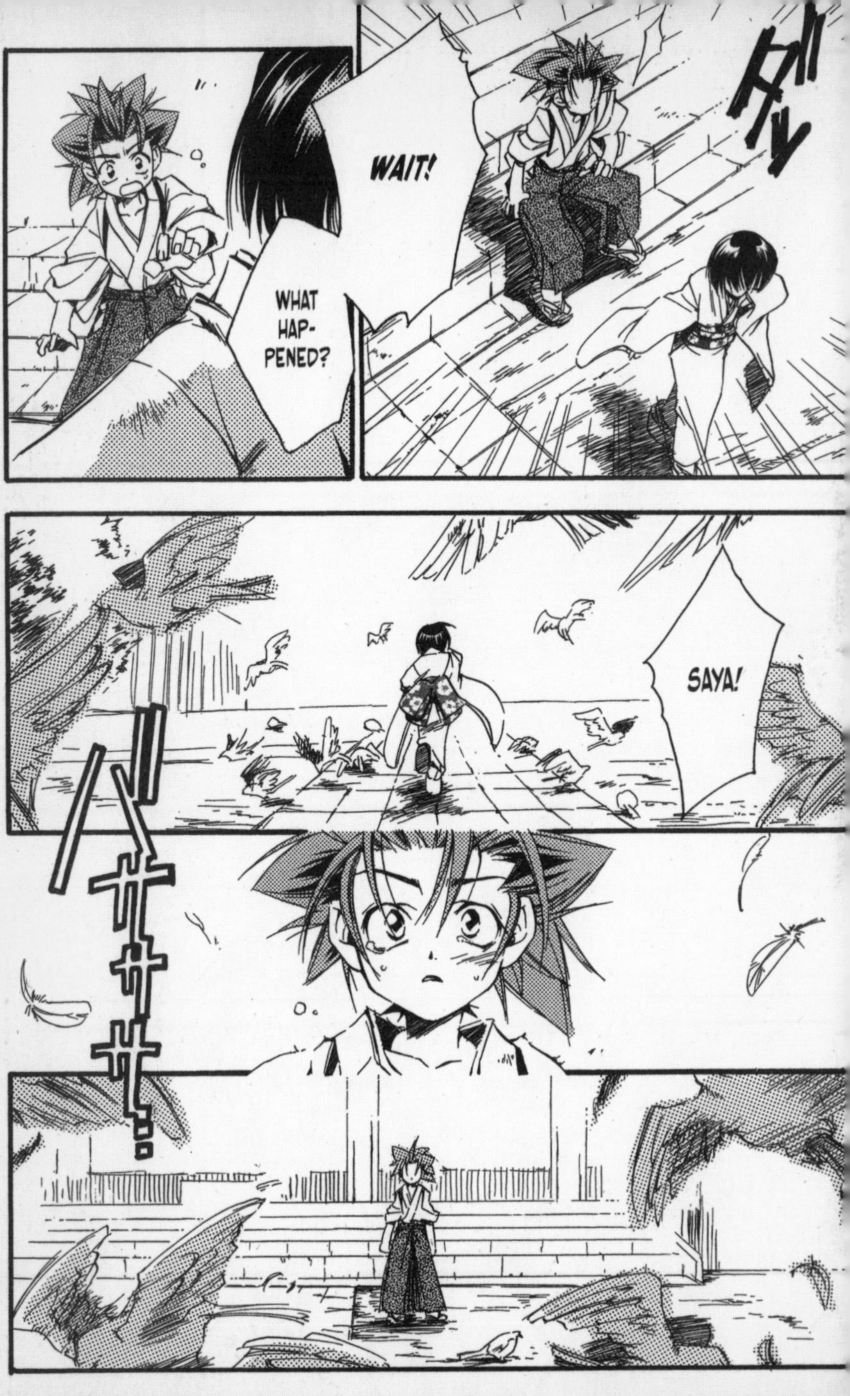
WAIT!
WHAT HAP-PENED?
SAYA!

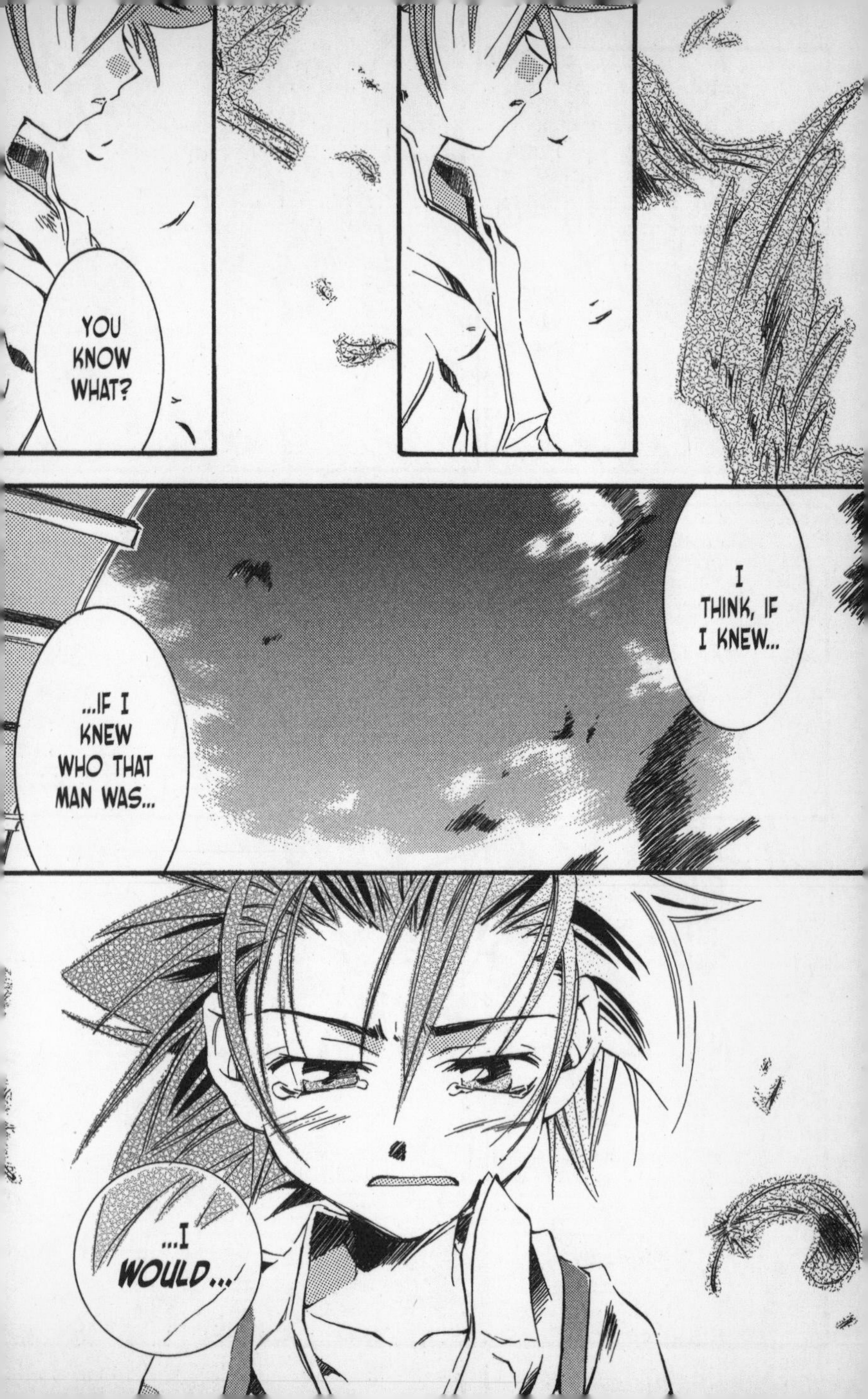
YOU KNOW WHAT?
I THINK, IF I KNEW...
...IF I KNEW WHO THAT MAN WAS...
...I WOULD...

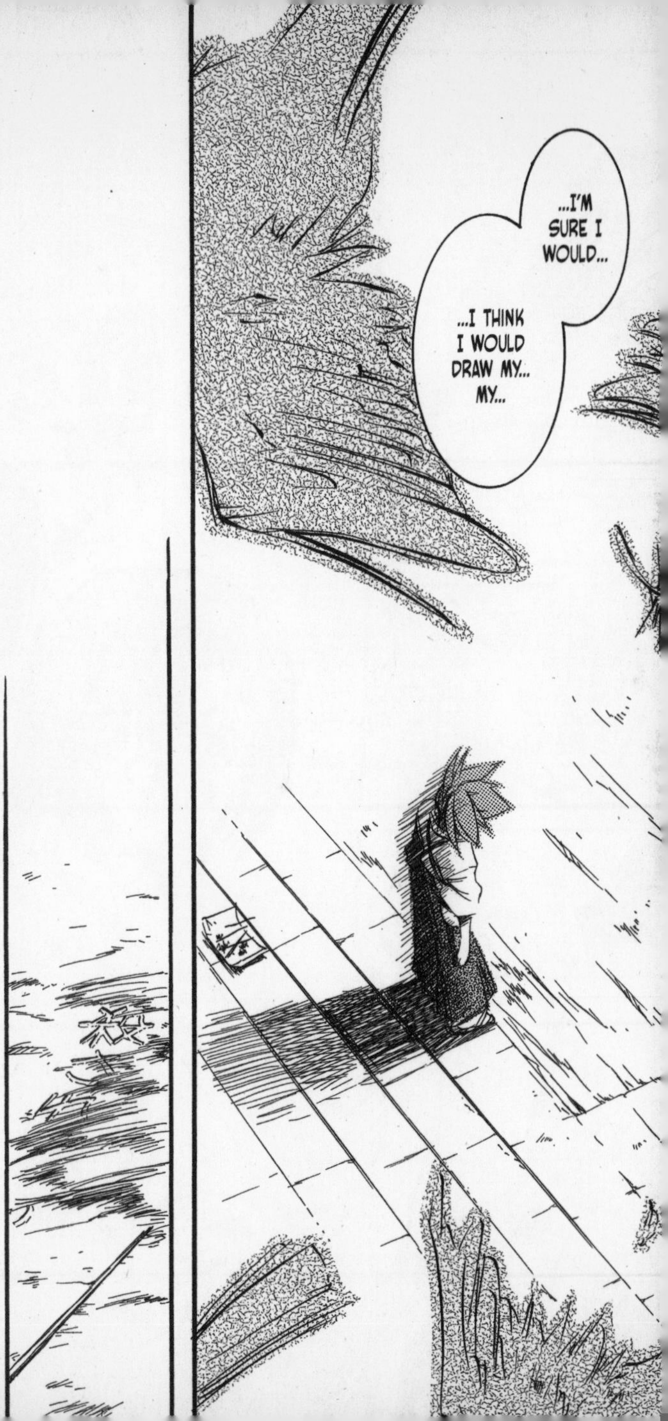
...I'M SURE I WOULD...
...I THINK I WOULD DRAW MY... MY...

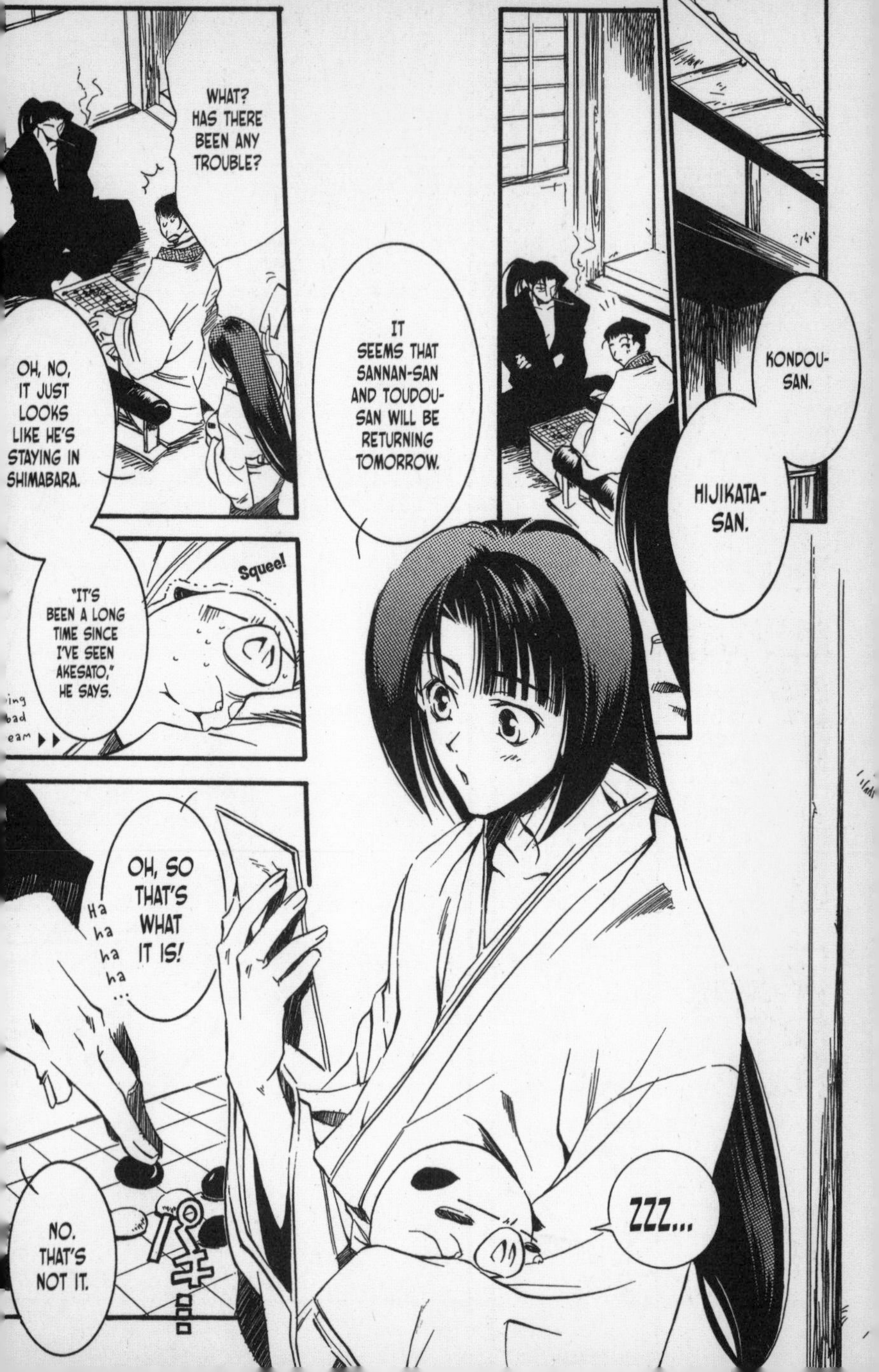
KONDOU-SAN.
HIJIKATA-SAN.
IT SEEMS THAT SANNAN-SAN AND TOUDOU-SAN WILL BE RETURNING TOMORROW.
WHAT? HAS THERE BEEN ANY TROUBLE?
OH, NO, IT JUST LOOKS LIKE HE'S STAYING IN SHIMABARA.
Squee!
"IT'S BEEN A LONG TIME SINCE I'VE SEEN AKESATO," HE SAYS.
OH, SO THAT'S WHAT IT IS!
Ha ha ha ha...
NO. THAT'S NOT IT.
ZZZ...

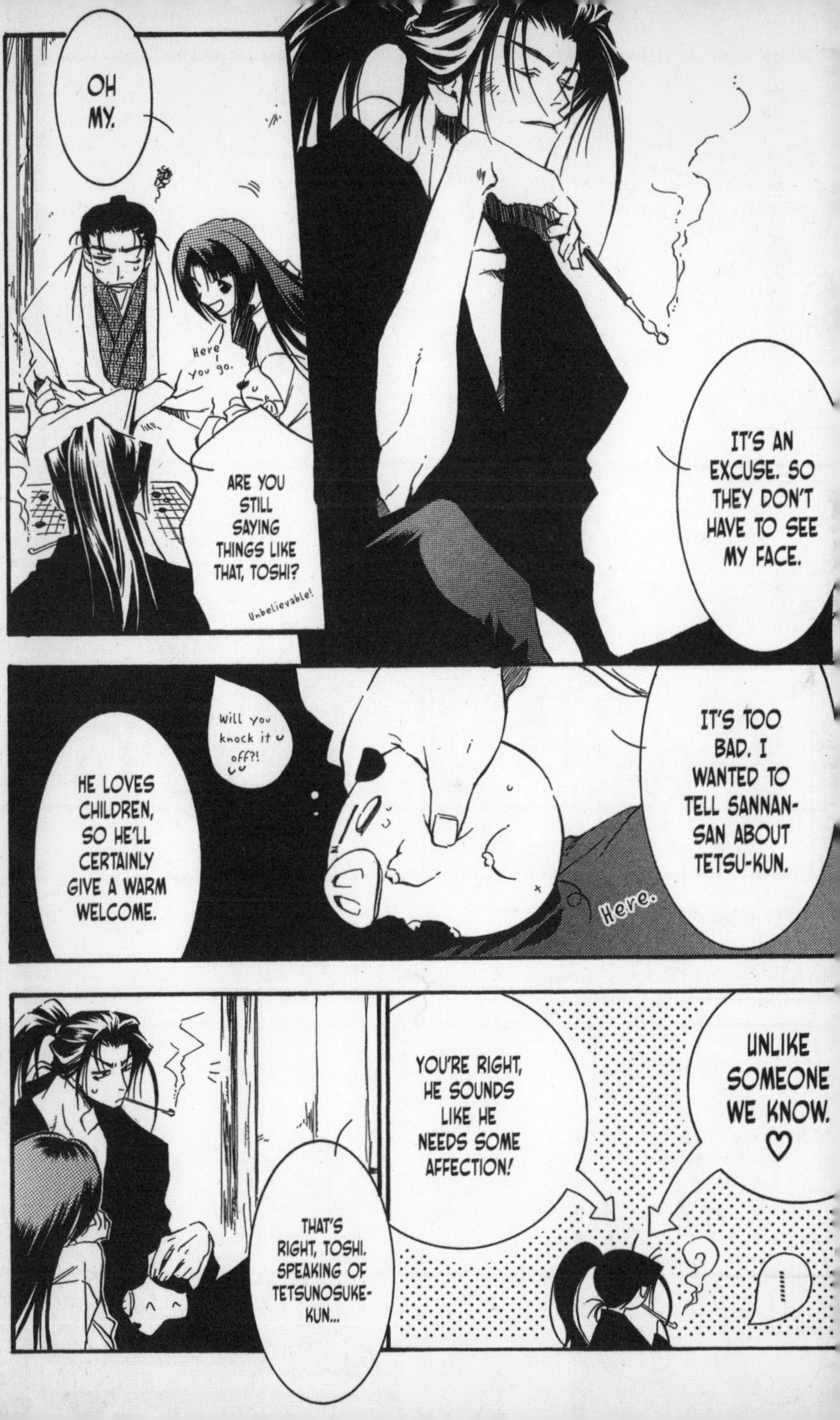
IT'S AN EXCUSE. SO THEY DON'T HAVE TO SEE MY FACE.
OH MY.
Here you go.
ARE YOU STILL SAYING THINGS LIKE THAT, TOSHI?
Unbelievable!
IT'S TOO BAD. I WANTED TO TELL SANNAN-SAN ABOUT TETSU-KUN.
Here.
Will you knock it off?!
HE LOVES CHILDREN, SO HE'LL CERTAINLY GIVE A WARM WELCOME.
UNLIKE SOMEONE WE KNOW. ♡
YOU'RE RIGHT, HE SOUNDS LIKE HE NEEDS SOME AFFECTION!
......
THAT'S RIGHT, TOSHI. SPEAKING OF TETSUNOSUKE-KUN...

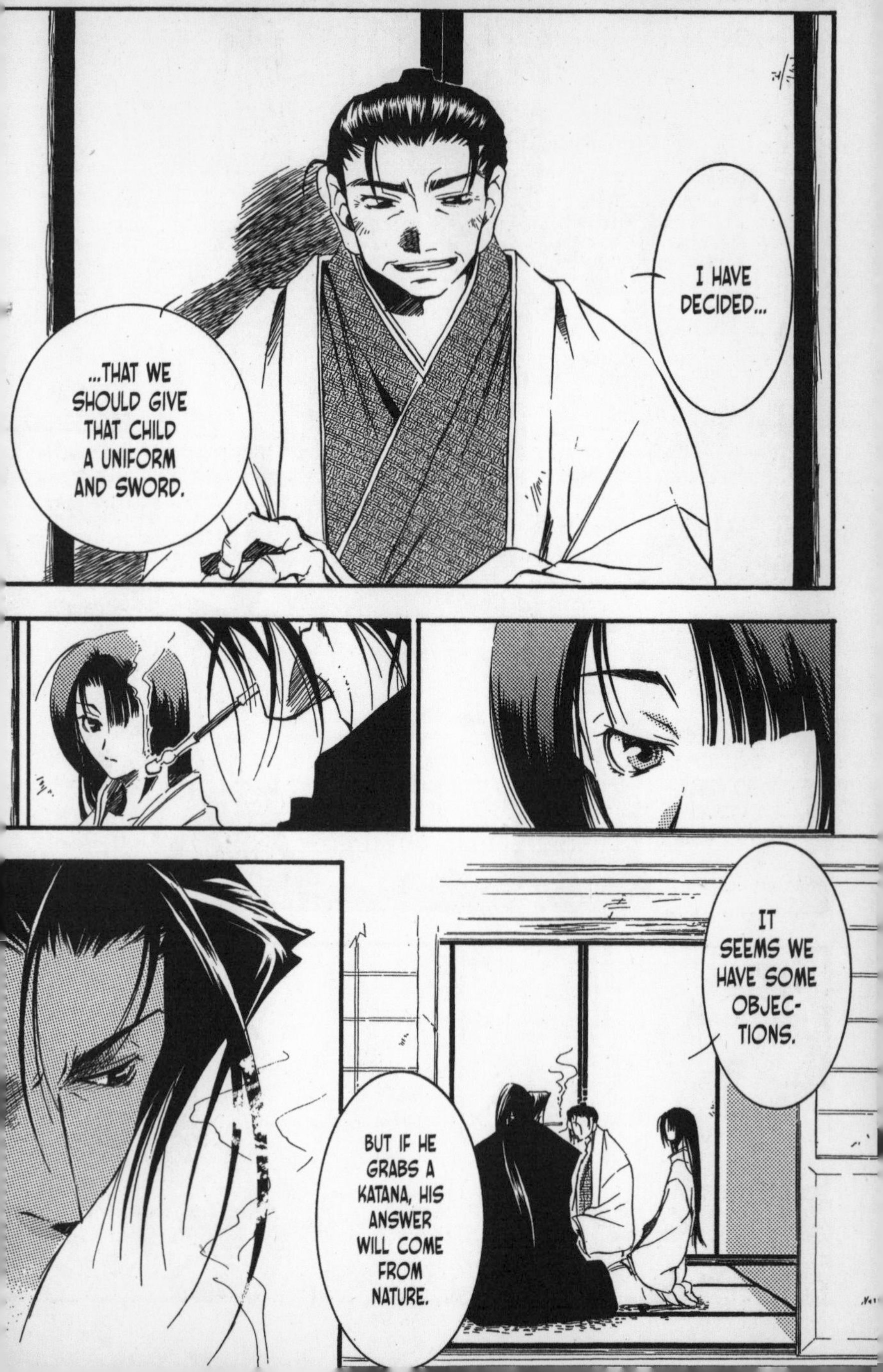
I HAVE DECIDED...
...THAT WE SHOULD GIVE THAT CHILD A UNIFORM AND SWORD.
IT SEEMS WE HAVE SOME OBJEC- TIONS.
BUT IF HE GRABS A KATANA, HIS ANSWER WILL COME FROM NATURE.

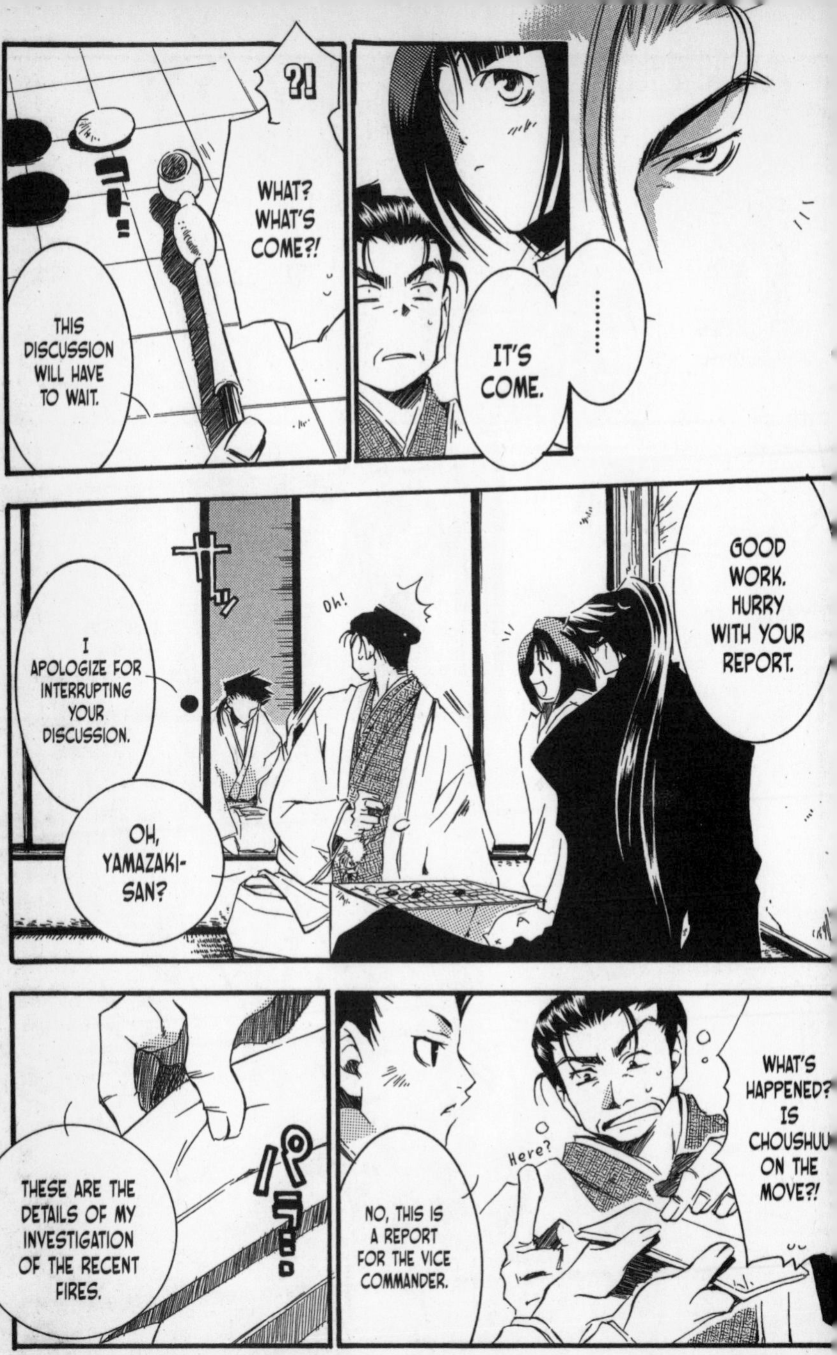
......
IT'S COME.
?!
WHAT? WHAT'S COME?!
THIS DISCUSSION WILL HAVE TO WAIT.
GOOD WORK. HURRY WITH YOUR REPORT.
Oh!
I APOLOGIZE FOR INTERRUPTING YOUR DISCUSSION.
OH, YAMAZAKI-SAN?
WHAT'S HAPPENED? IS CHOUSHUU ON THE MOVE?!
Here?
NO, THIS IS A REPORT FOR THE VICE COMMANDER.
THESE ARE THE DETAILS OF MY INVESTIGATION OF THE RECENT FIRES.

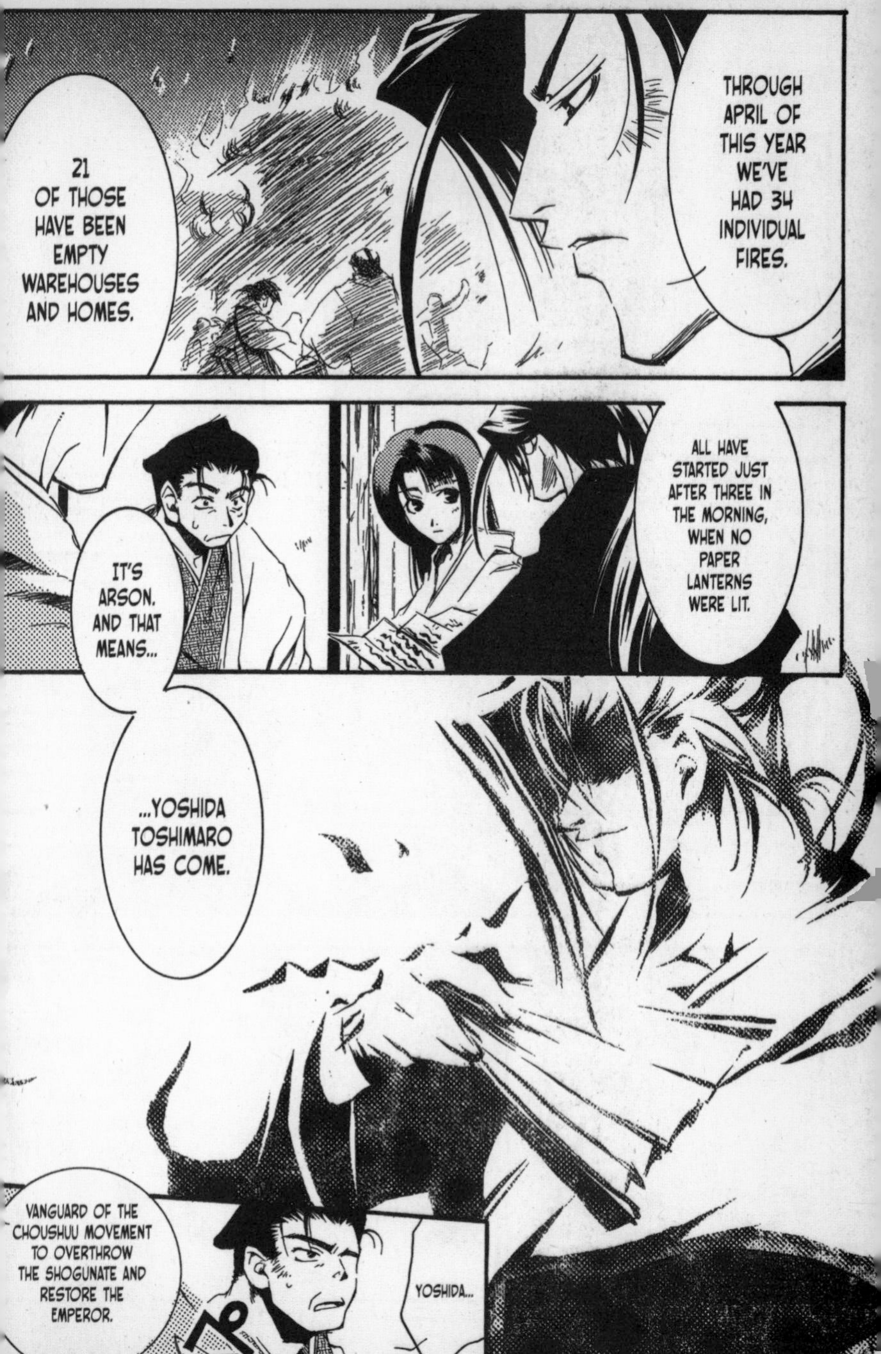
THROUGH APRIL OF THIS YEAR WE'VE HAD 34 INDIVIDUAL FIRES.
21 OF THOSE HAVE BEEN EMPTY WAREHOUSES AND HOMES.
ALL HAVE STARTED JUST AFTER THREE IN THE MORNING, WHEN NO PAPER LANTERNS WERE LIT.
IT'S ARSON. AND THAT MEANS...
...YOSHIDA TOSHIMARO HAS COME.
YOSHIDA...
VANGUARD OF THE CHOUSHUU MOVEMENT TO OVERTHROW THE SHOGUNATE AND RESTORE THE EMPEROR.

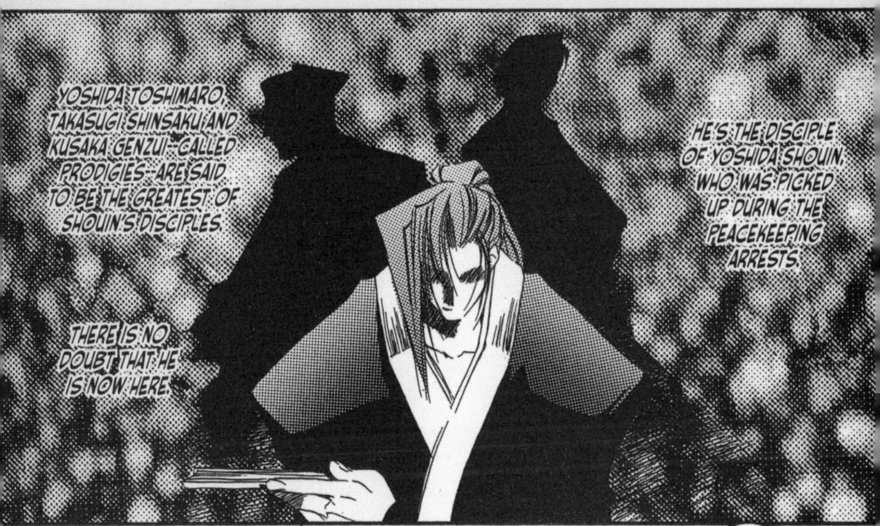
HE'S THE DISCIPLE OF YOSHIDA SHOUIN, WHO WAS PICKED UP DURING THE PEACEKEEPING ARRESTS.
YOSHIDA TOSHIMARO, TAKASUGI SHINSAKU AND KUSAKA GENZUI--CALLED PRODIGIES--ARE SAID TO BE THE GREATEST OF SHOUIN'S DISCIPLES.
THERE IS NO DOUBT THAT HE IS NOW HERE.

Peacekeeping arrests: The 1858 suppression of the anti-shogunate "sonnou joui" movement.

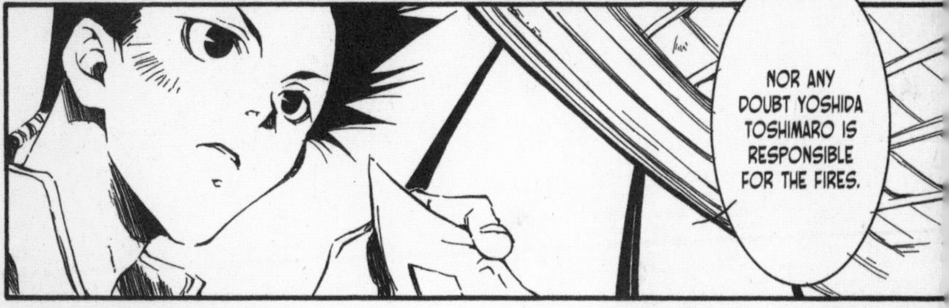
NOR ANY DOUBT YOSHIDA TOSHIMARO IS RESPONSIBLE FOR THE FIRES.

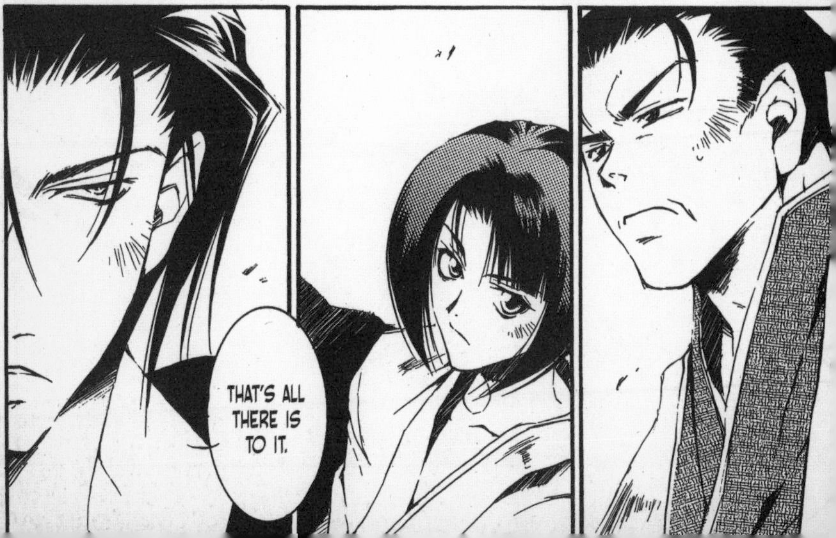
THAT'S ALL THERE IS TO IT.

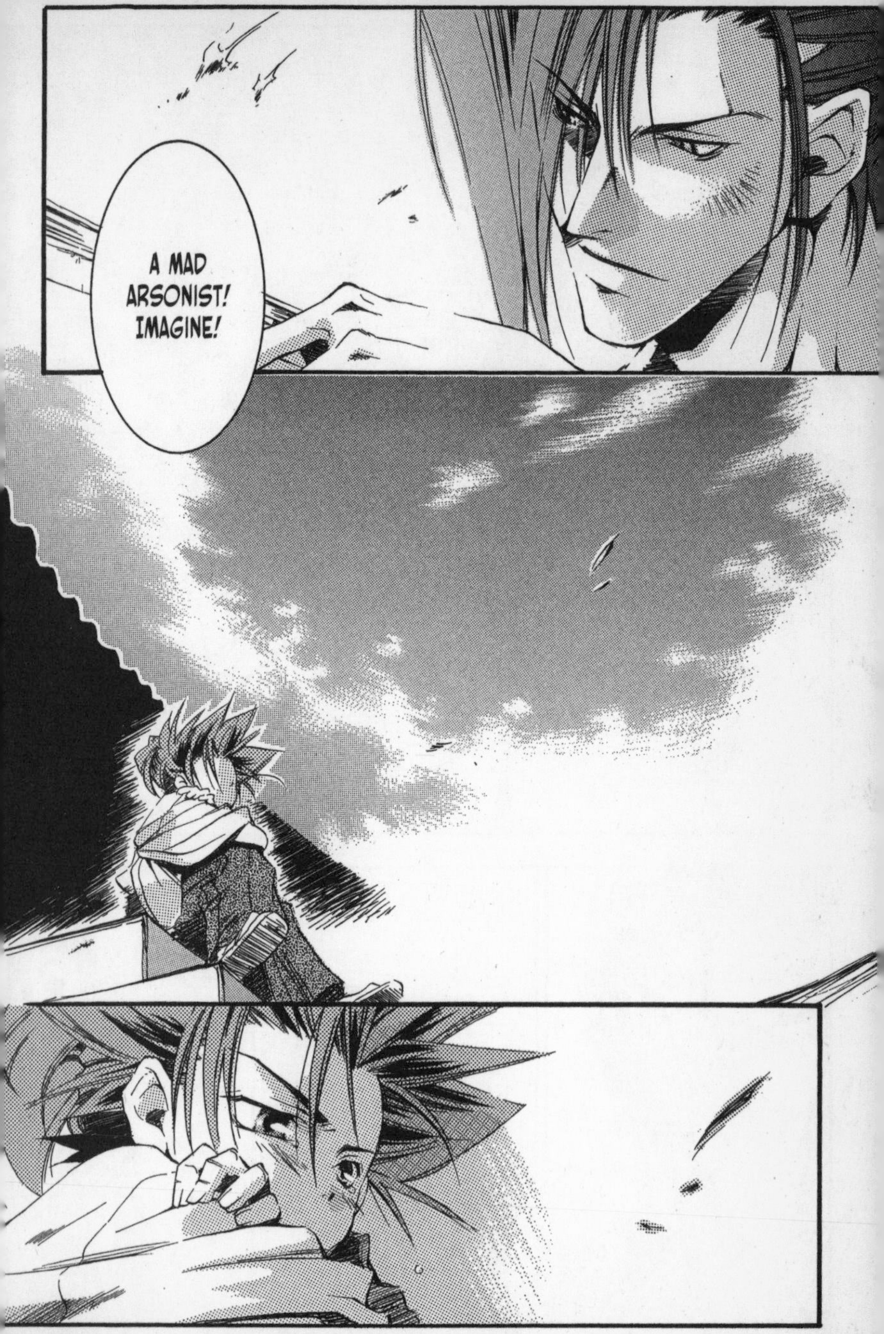
A MAD ARSONIST! IMAGINE!

Act.8
Get Back

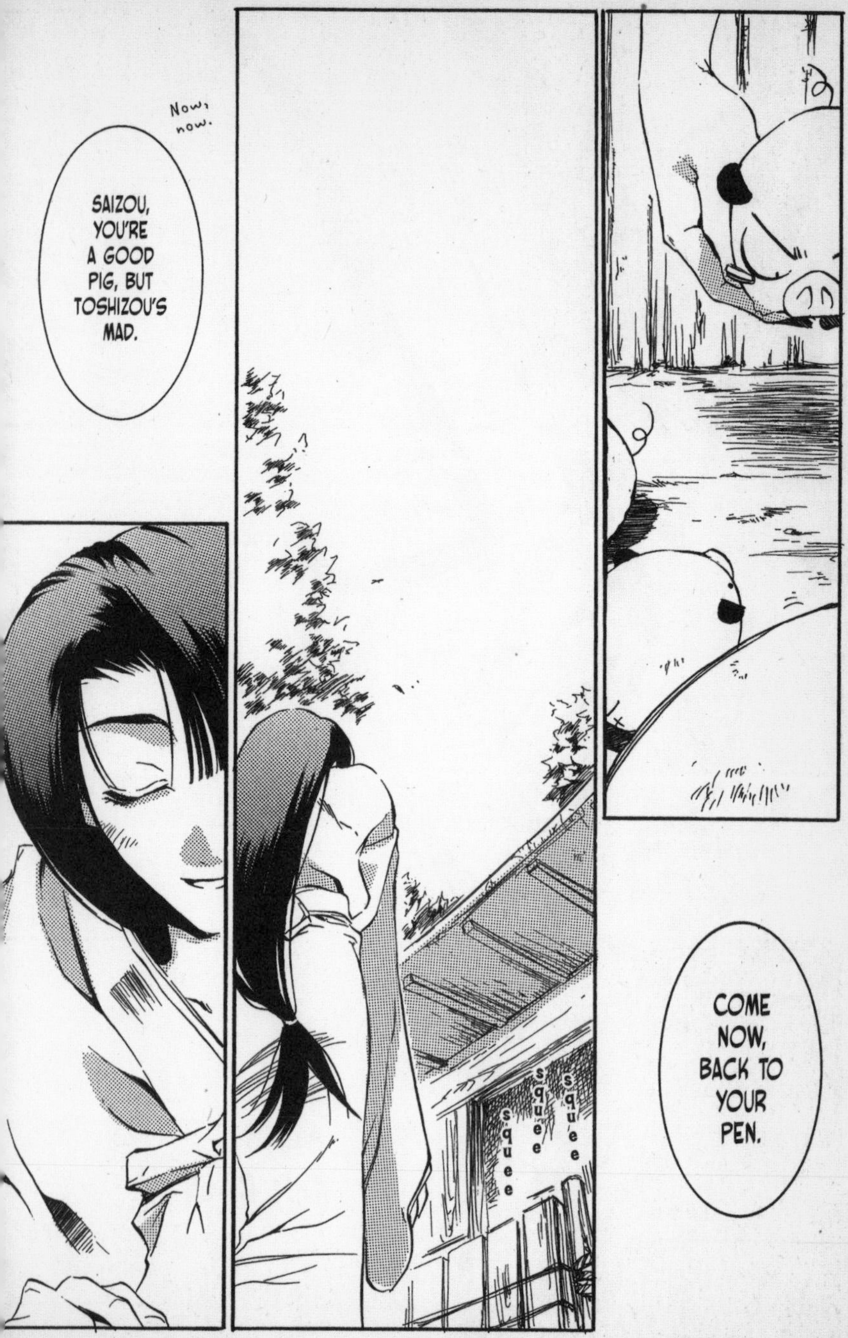
COME NOW, BACK TO YOUR PEN.
squee
squee
squee
Now, now.
SAIZOU, YOU'RE A GOOD PIG, BUT TOSHIZOU'S MAD.

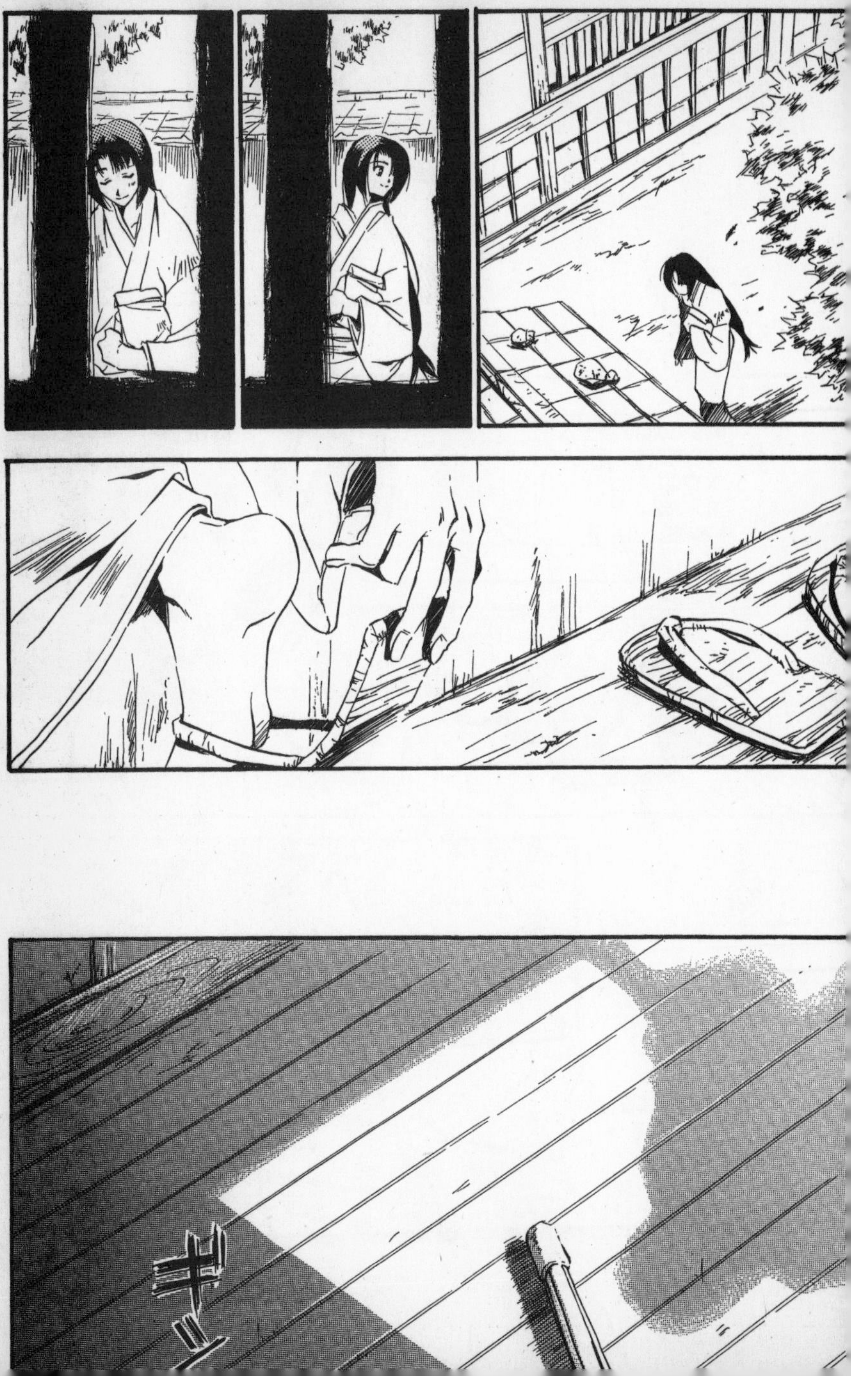
ギ

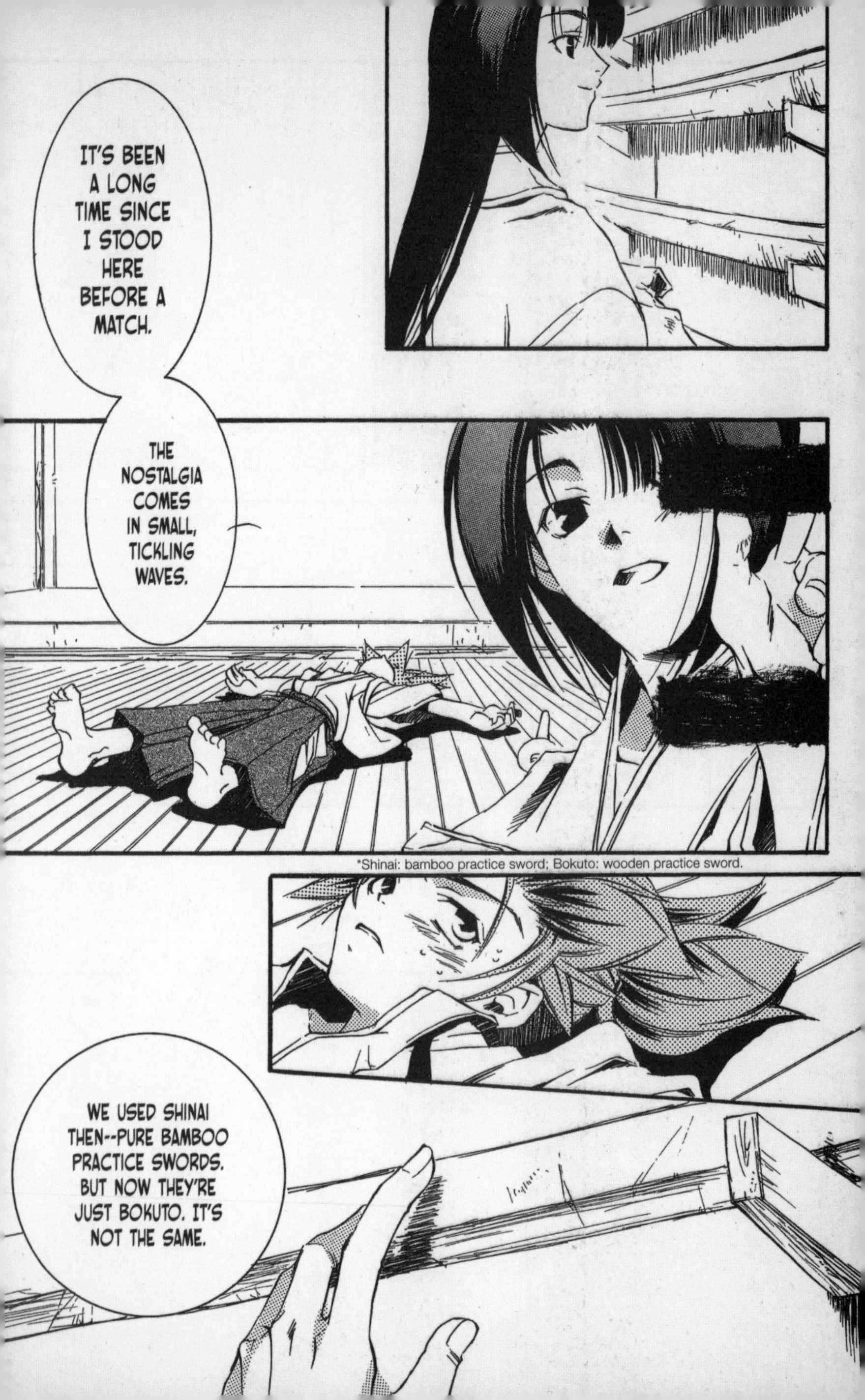
IT'S BEEN A LONG TIME SINCE I STOOD HERE BEFORE A MATCH.
THE NOSTALGIA COMES IN SMALL, TICKLING WAVES.
WE USED SHINAI THEN--PURE BAMBOO PRACTICE SWORDS. BUT NOW THEY'RE JUST BOKUTO. IT'S NOT THE SAME.

*Shinai: bamboo practice sword; Bokuto: wooden practice sword.

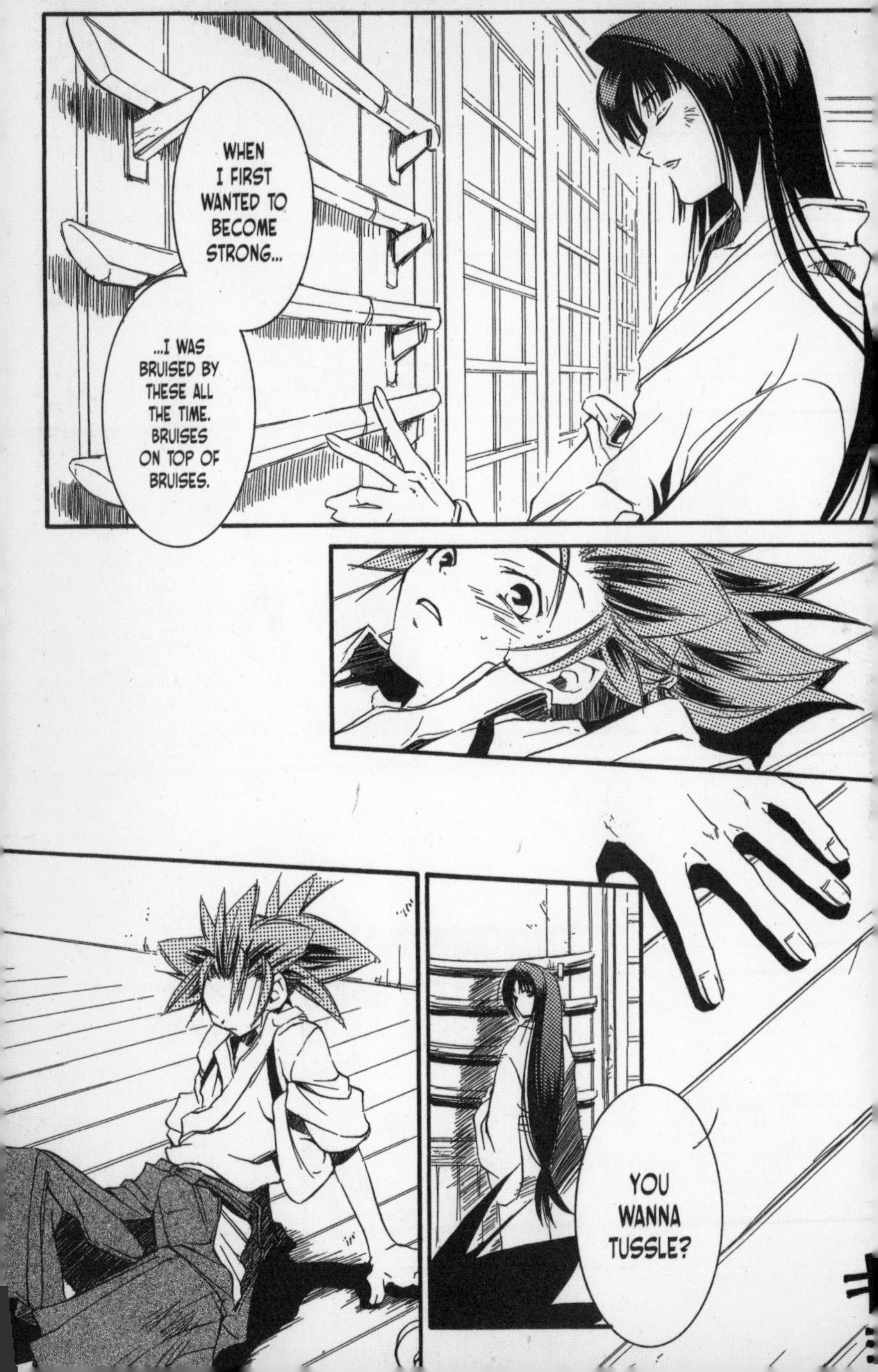
WHEN I FIRST WANTED TO BECOME STRONG...
...I WAS BRUISED BY THESE ALL THE TIME. BRUISES ON TOP OF BRUISES.
YOU WANNA TUSSLE?

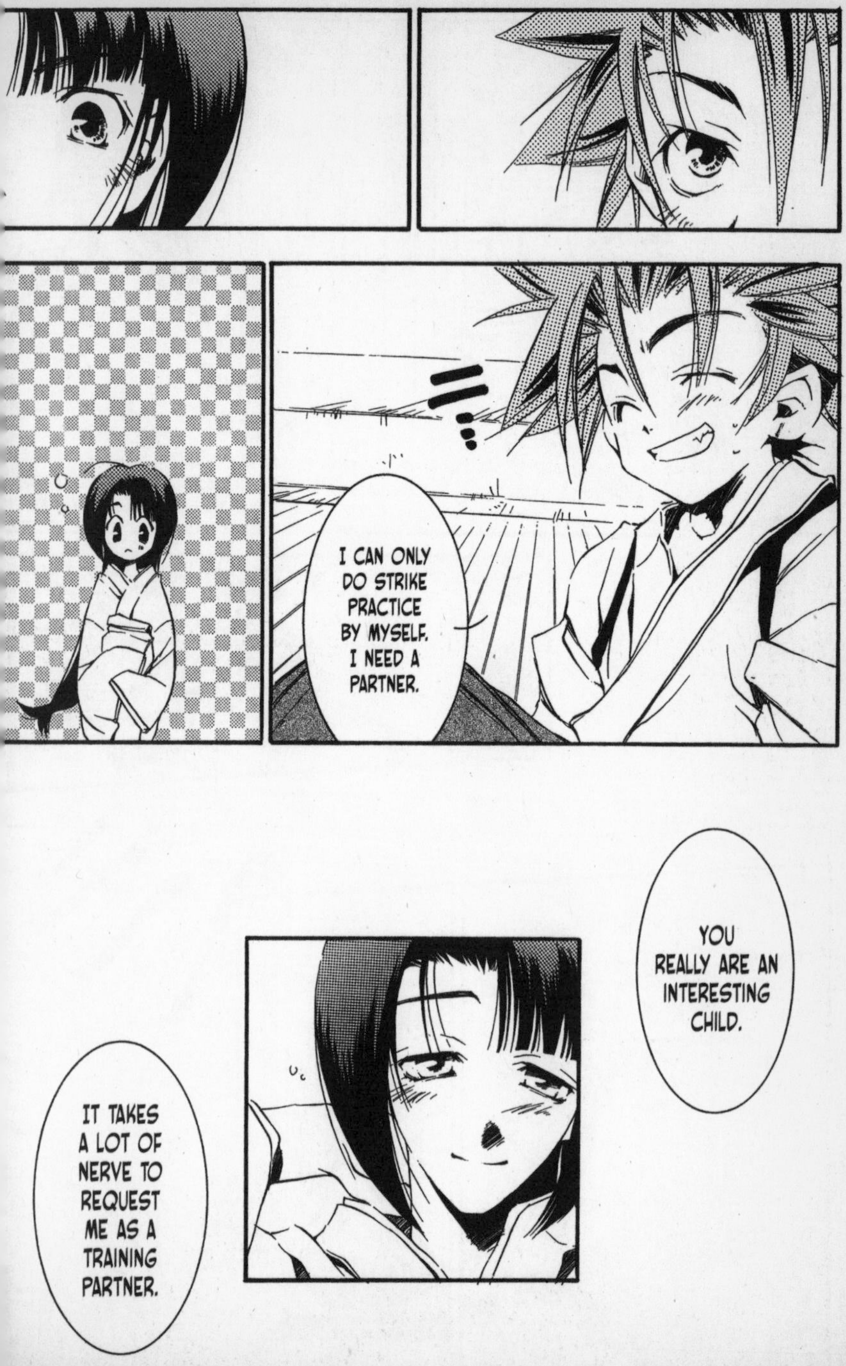
I CAN ONLY DO STRIKE PRACTICE BY MYSELF. I NEED A PARTNER.
YOU REALLY ARE AN INTERESTING CHILD.
IT TAKES A LOT OF NERVE TO REQUEST ME AS A TRAINING PARTNER.

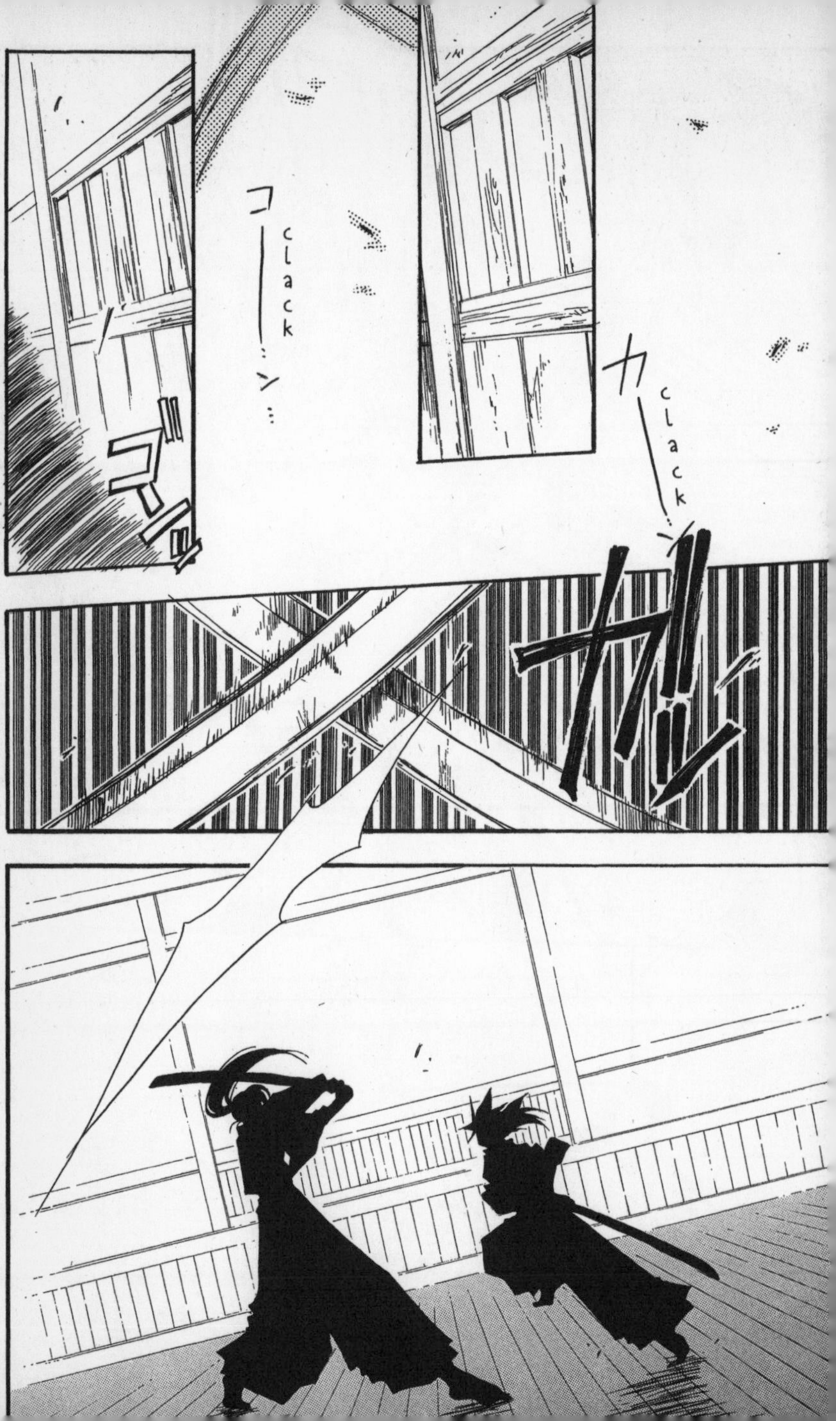カー
clack
コ—…ン…
clack
ゴゴ
ガッ

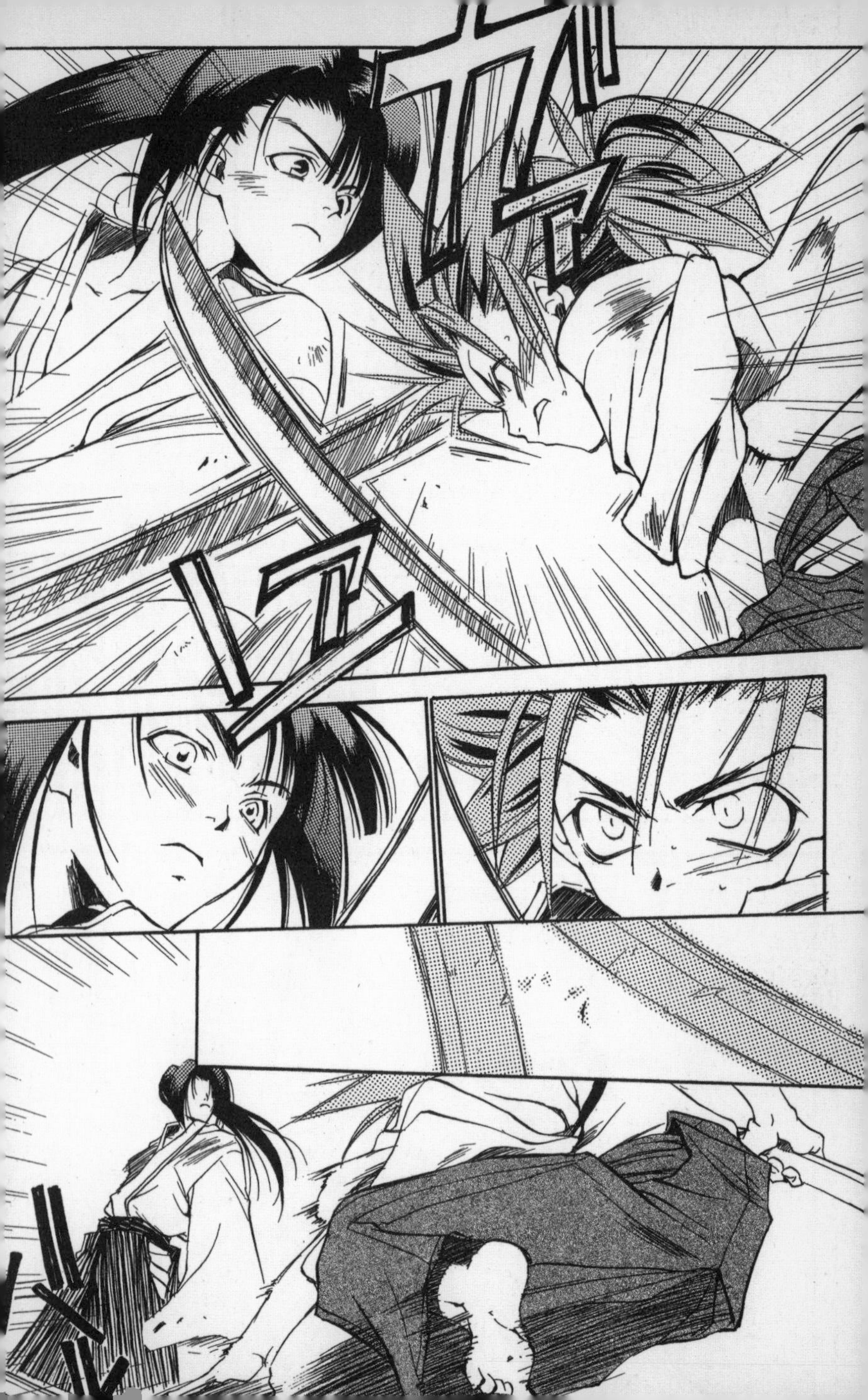

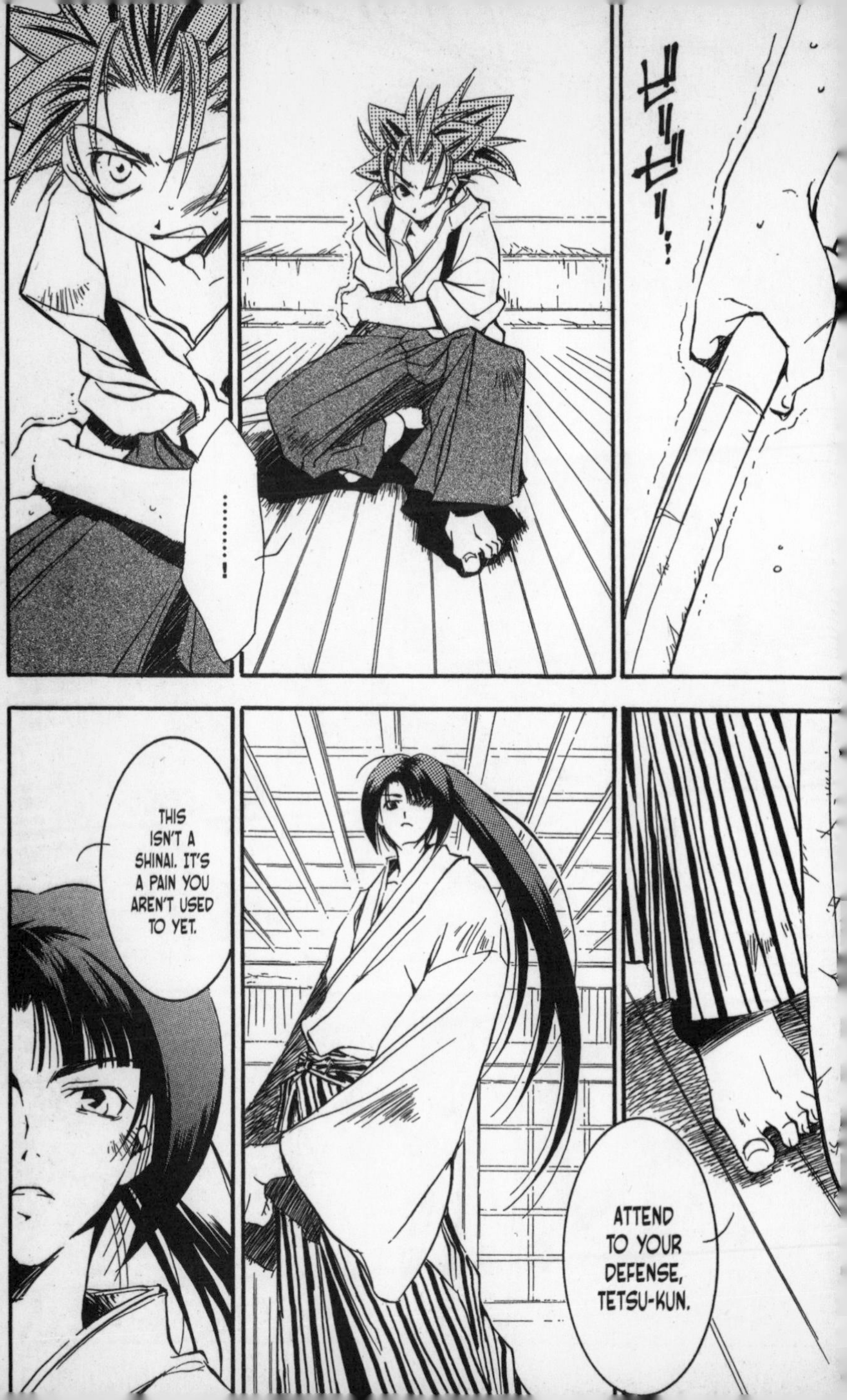
ピリピリッ!!
……!
ATTEND TO YOUR DEFENSE, TETSU-KUN.
THIS ISN'T A SHINAI. IT'S A PAIN YOU AREN'T USED TO YET.

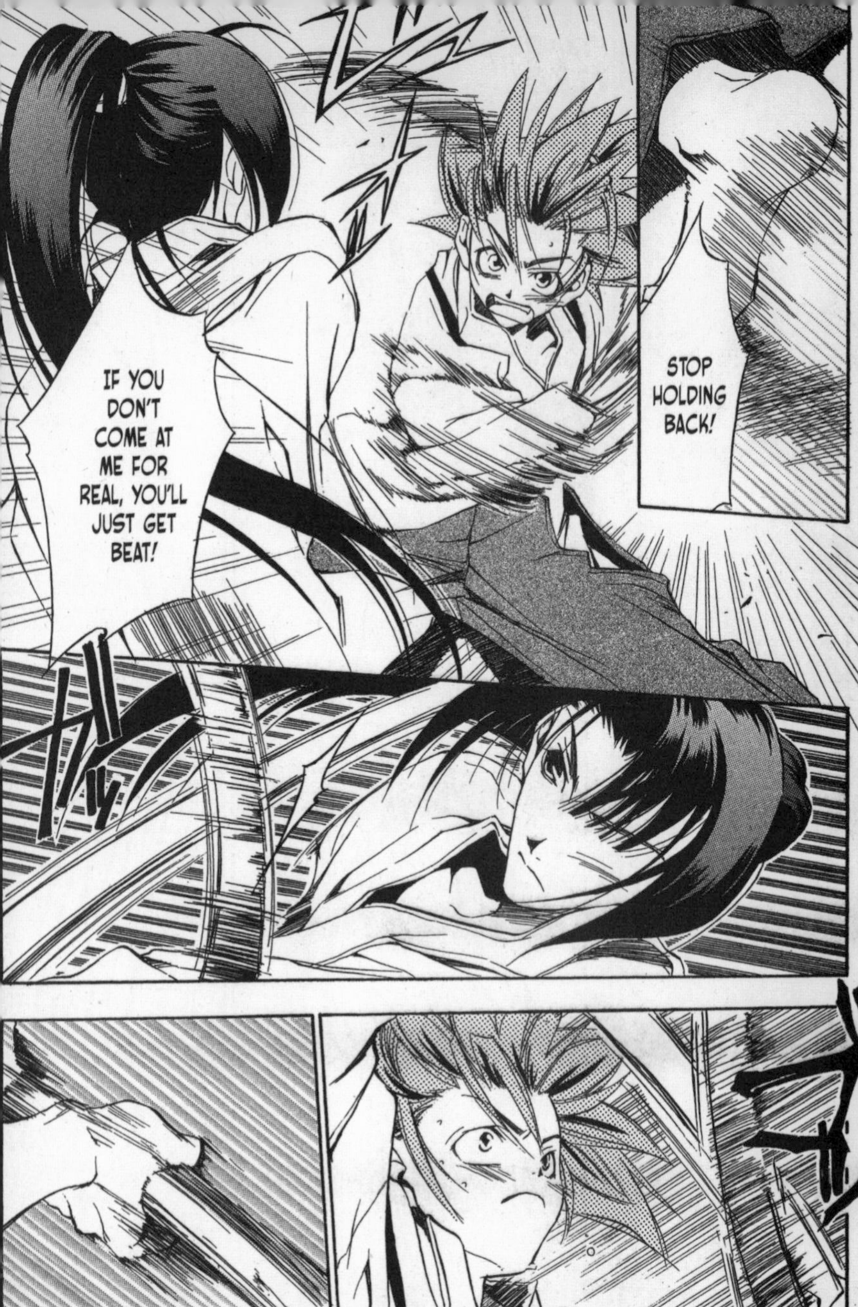
STOP HOLDING BACK!
IF YOU DON'T COME AT ME FOR REAL, YOU'LL JUST GET BEAT!

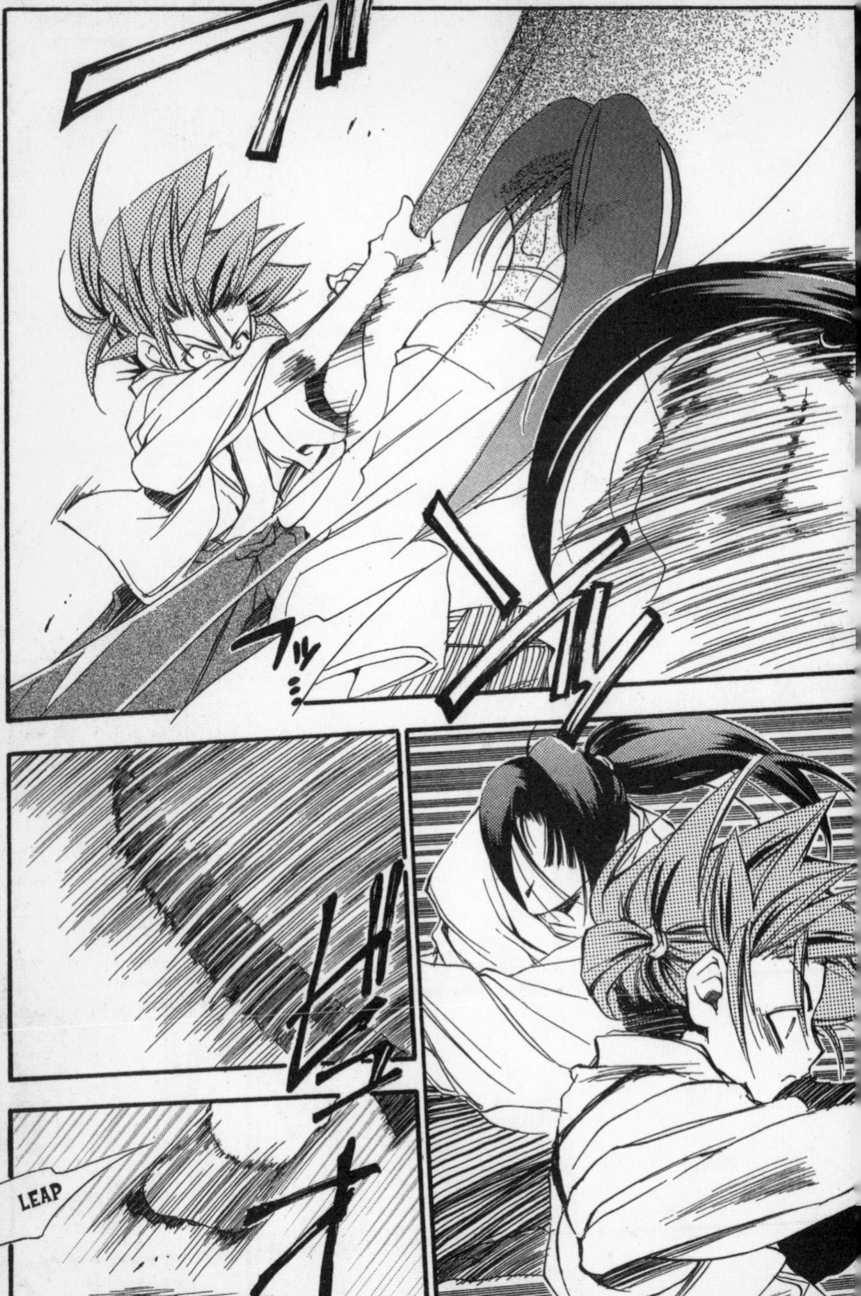

LEAP

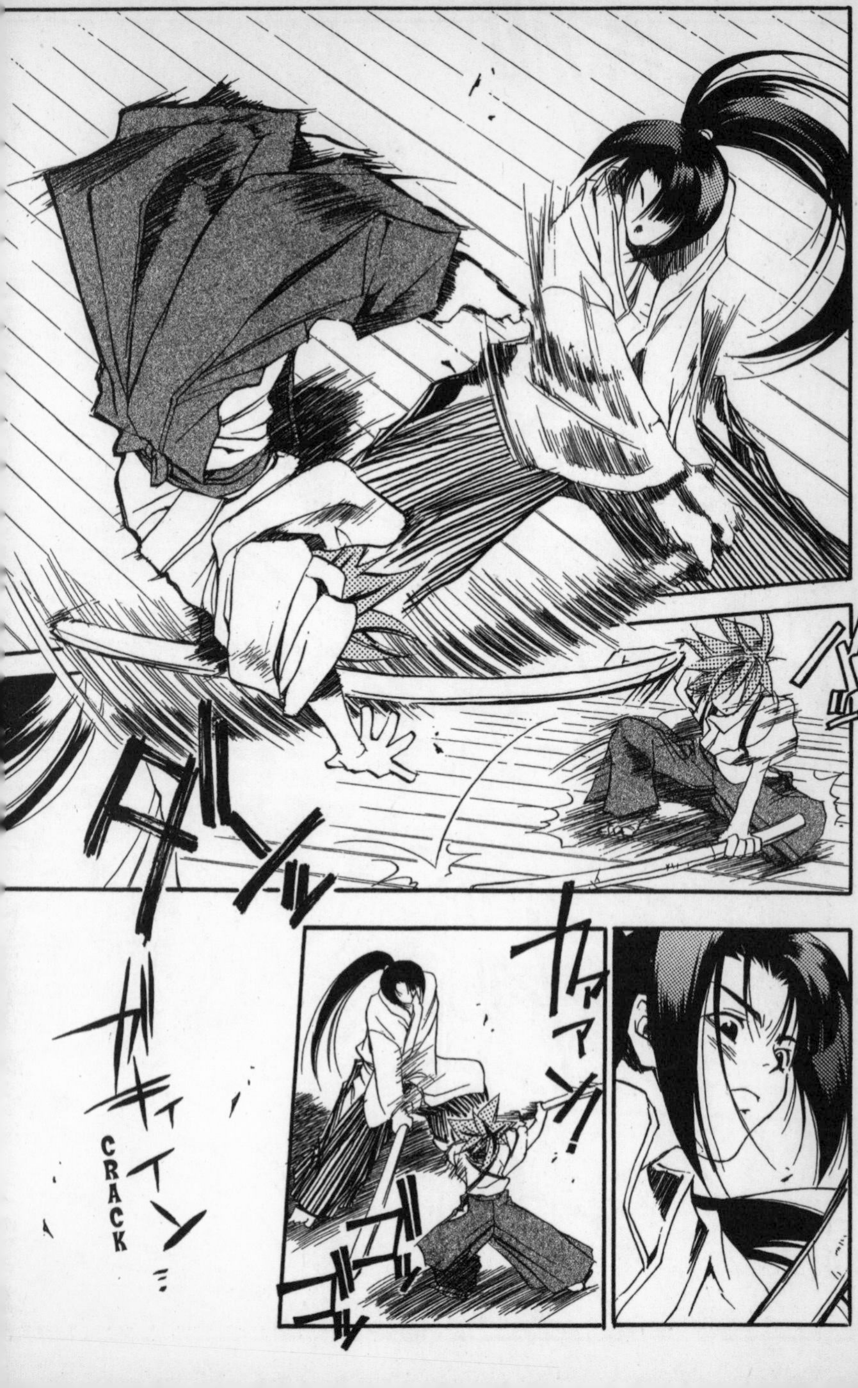
CRACK

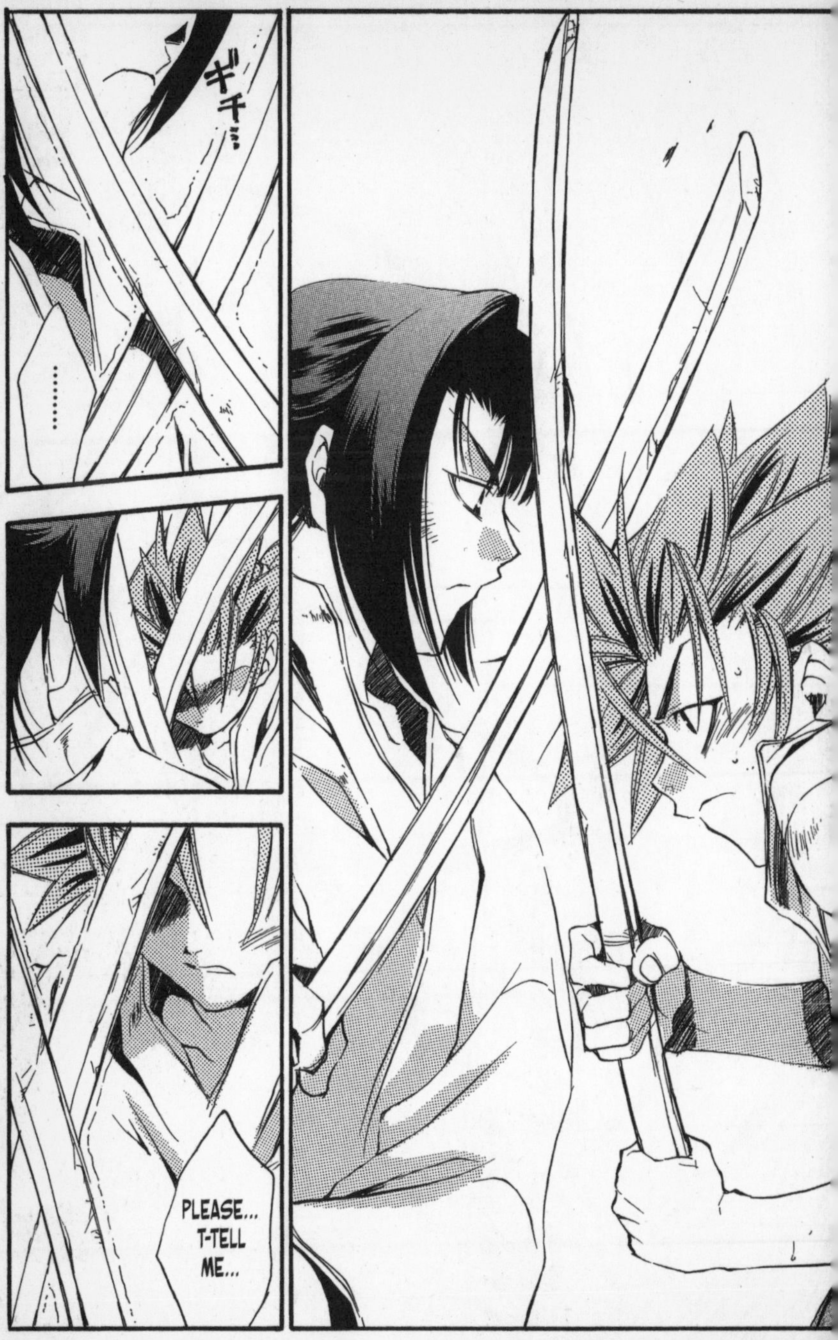
ギチ
....
PLEASE... T-TELL ME...

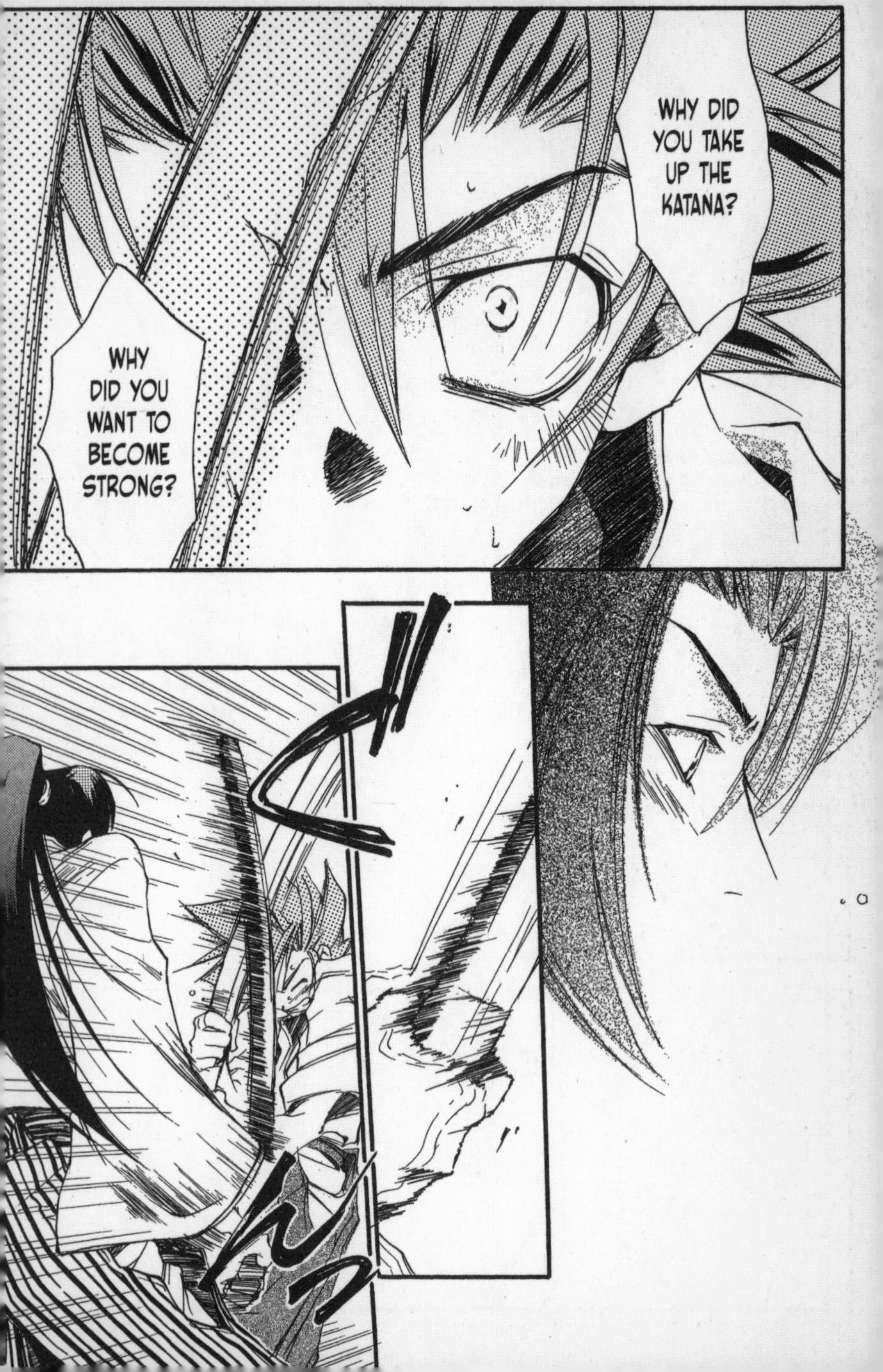
WHY DID YOU TAKE UP THE KATANA?
WHY DID YOU WANT TO BECOME STRONG?

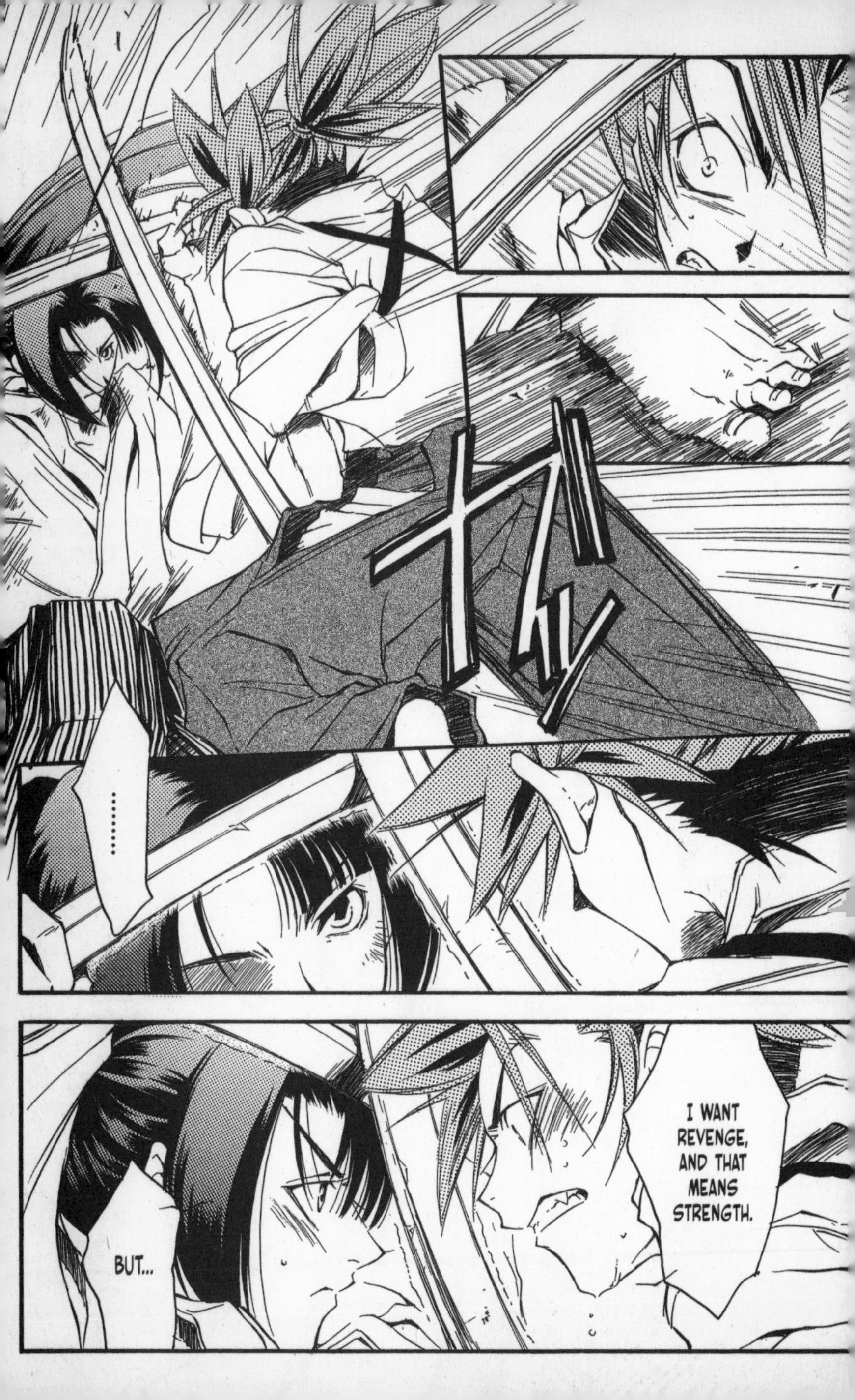
......
I WANT REVENGE, AND THAT MEANS STRENGTH.
BUT...

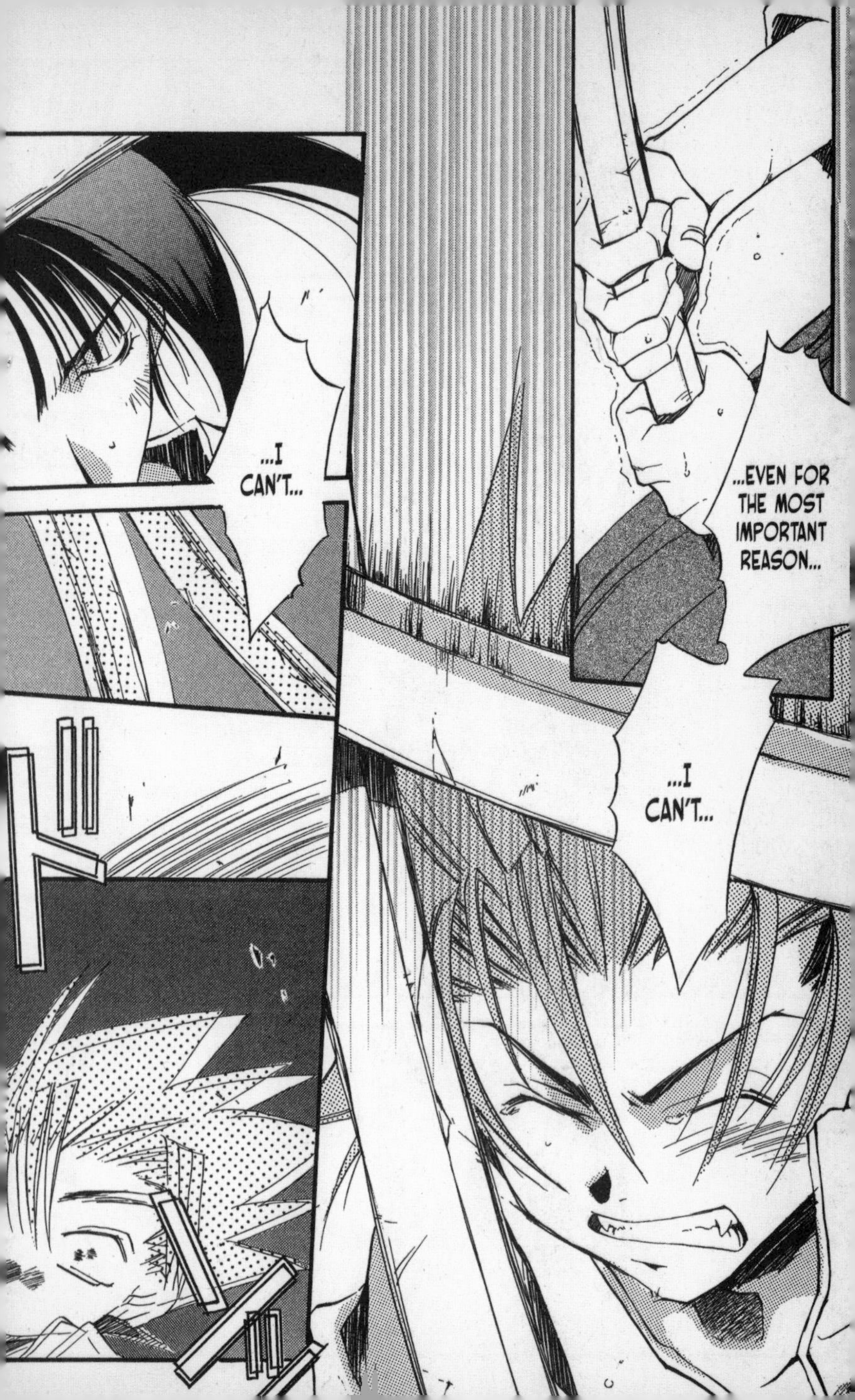
...EVEN FOR THE MOST IMPORTANT REASON...
...I CAN'T...
...I CAN'T...

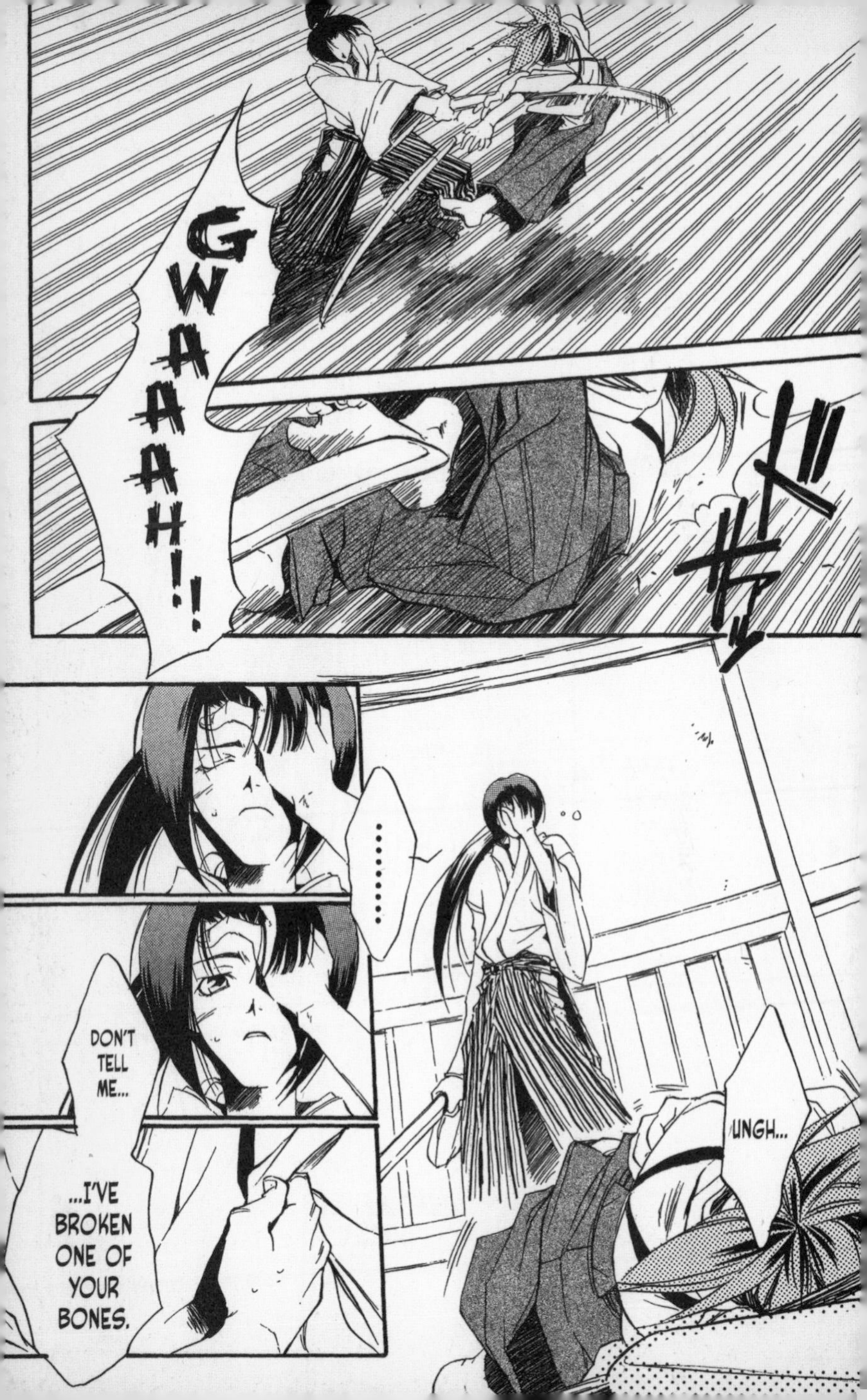
GWAAAH!!
......
UNGH...
DON'T TELL ME...
...I'VE BROKEN ONE OF YOUR BONES.

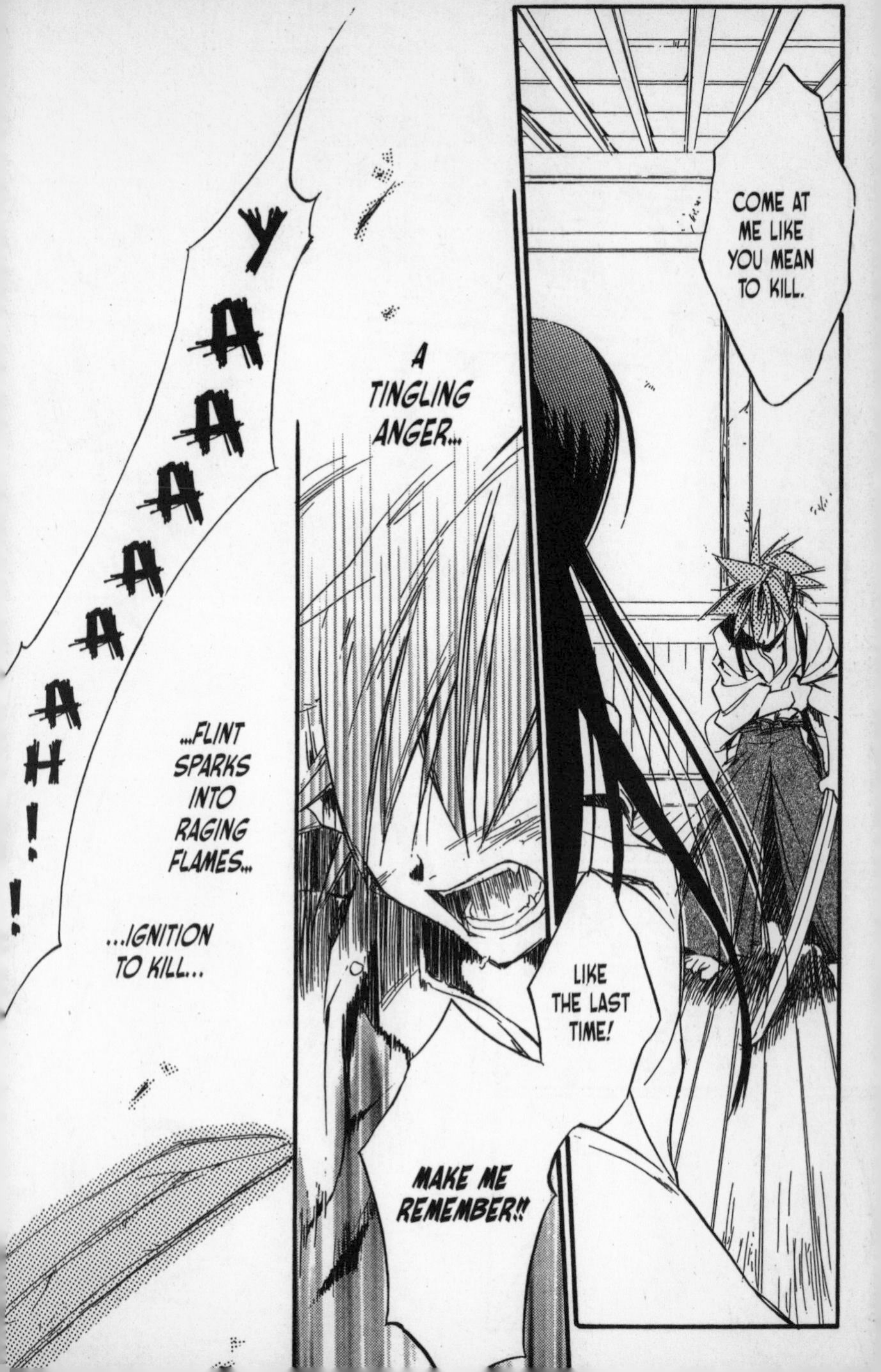
COME AT ME LIKE YOU MEAN TO KILL.
A TINGLING ANGER...
LIKE THE LAST TIME!
MAKE ME REMEMBER!!
YAAAAAAH!!
...FLINT SPARKS INTO RAGING FLAMES...
...IGNITION TO KILL...

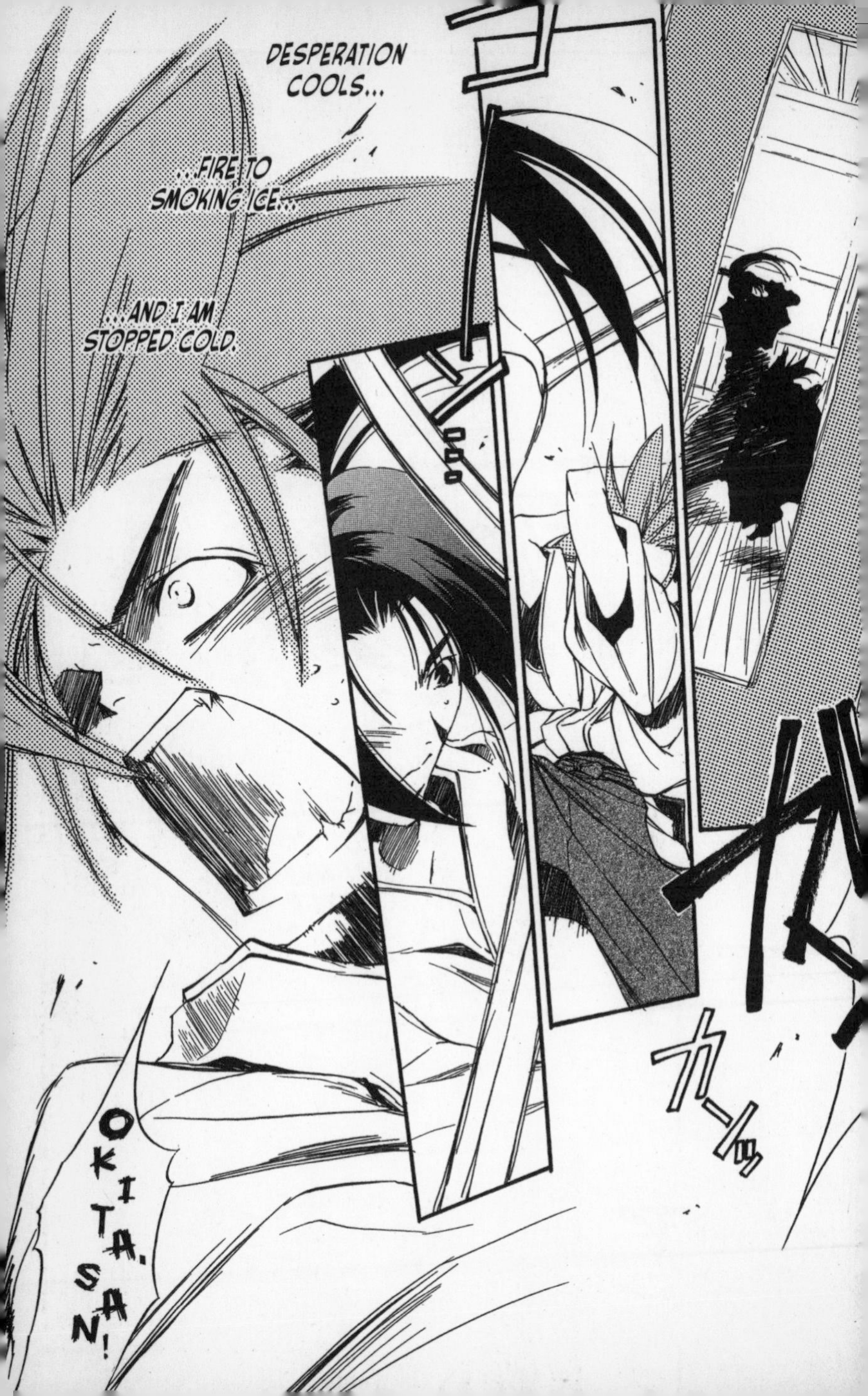
DESPERATION COOLS...
...FIRE TO SMOKING ICE...
...AND I AM STOPPED COLD.
OKITA-SAN!

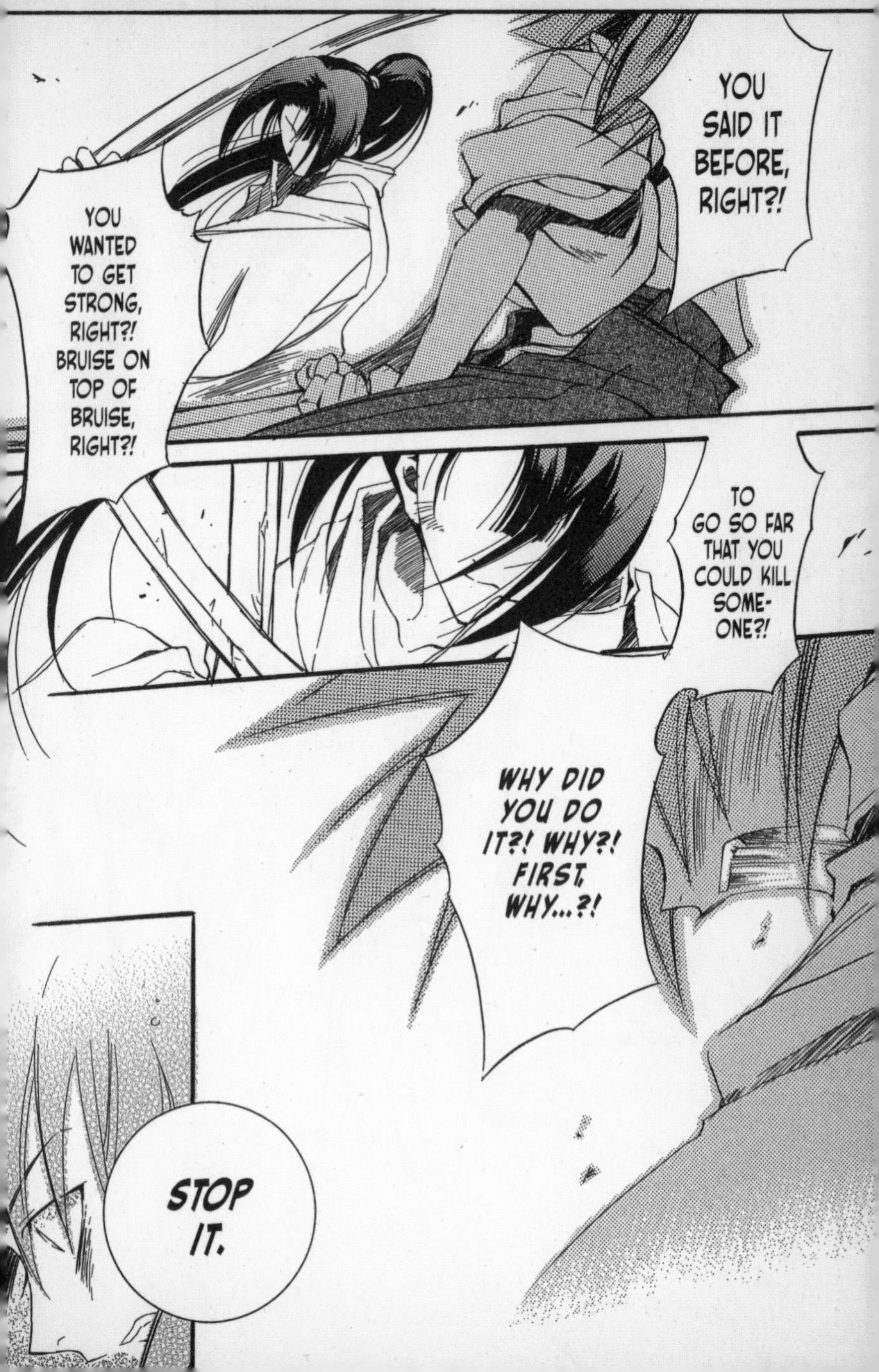
YOU SAID IT BEFORE, RIGHT?!
YOU WANTED TO GET STRONG, RIGHT?! BRUISE ON TOP OF BRUISE, RIGHT?!
TO GO SO FAR THAT YOU COULD KILL SOME-ONE?!
WHY DID YOU DO IT?! WHY?! FIRST, WHY...?!
STOP IT.

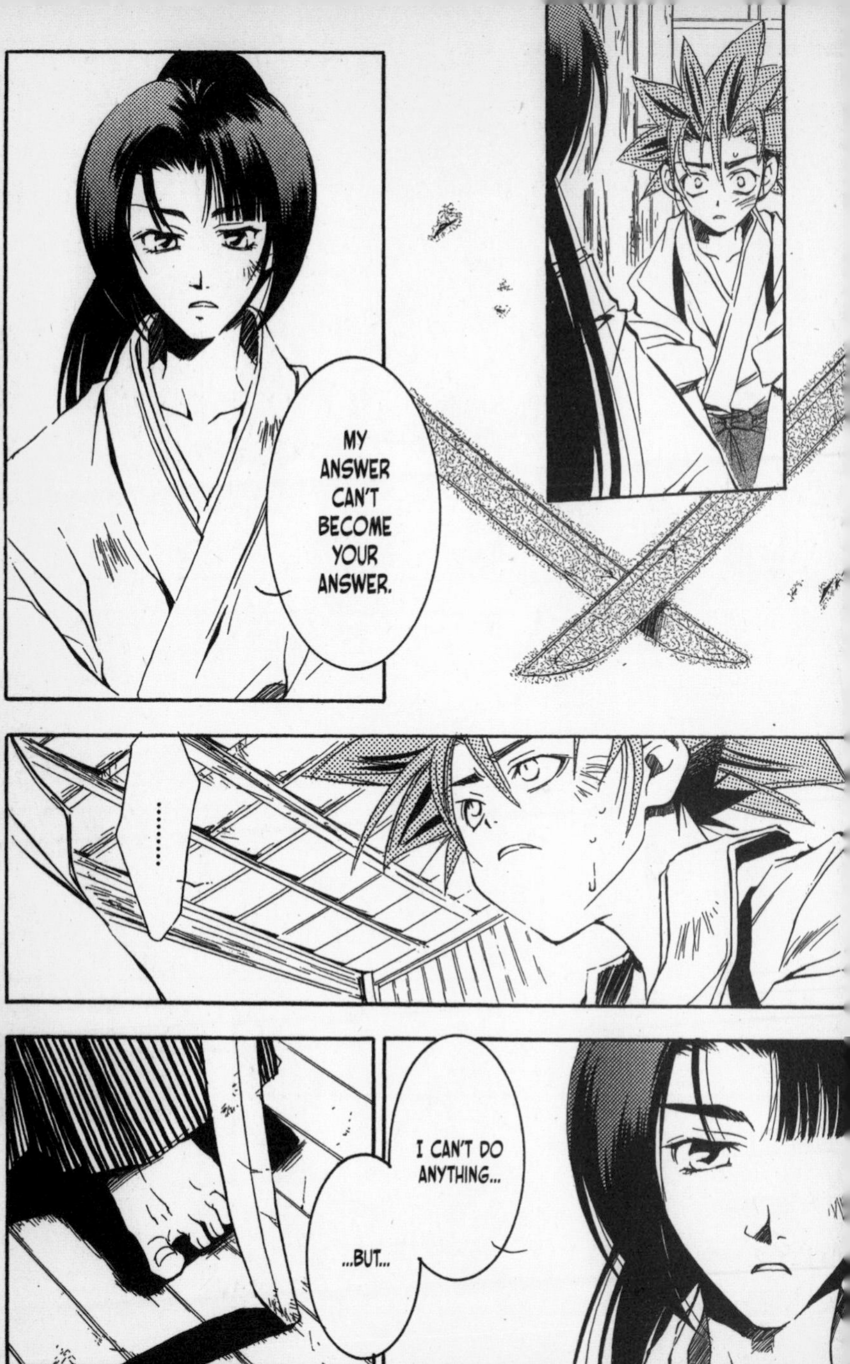
MY ANSWER CAN'T BECOME YOUR ANSWER.
......
I CAN'T DO ANYTHING...
...BUT...

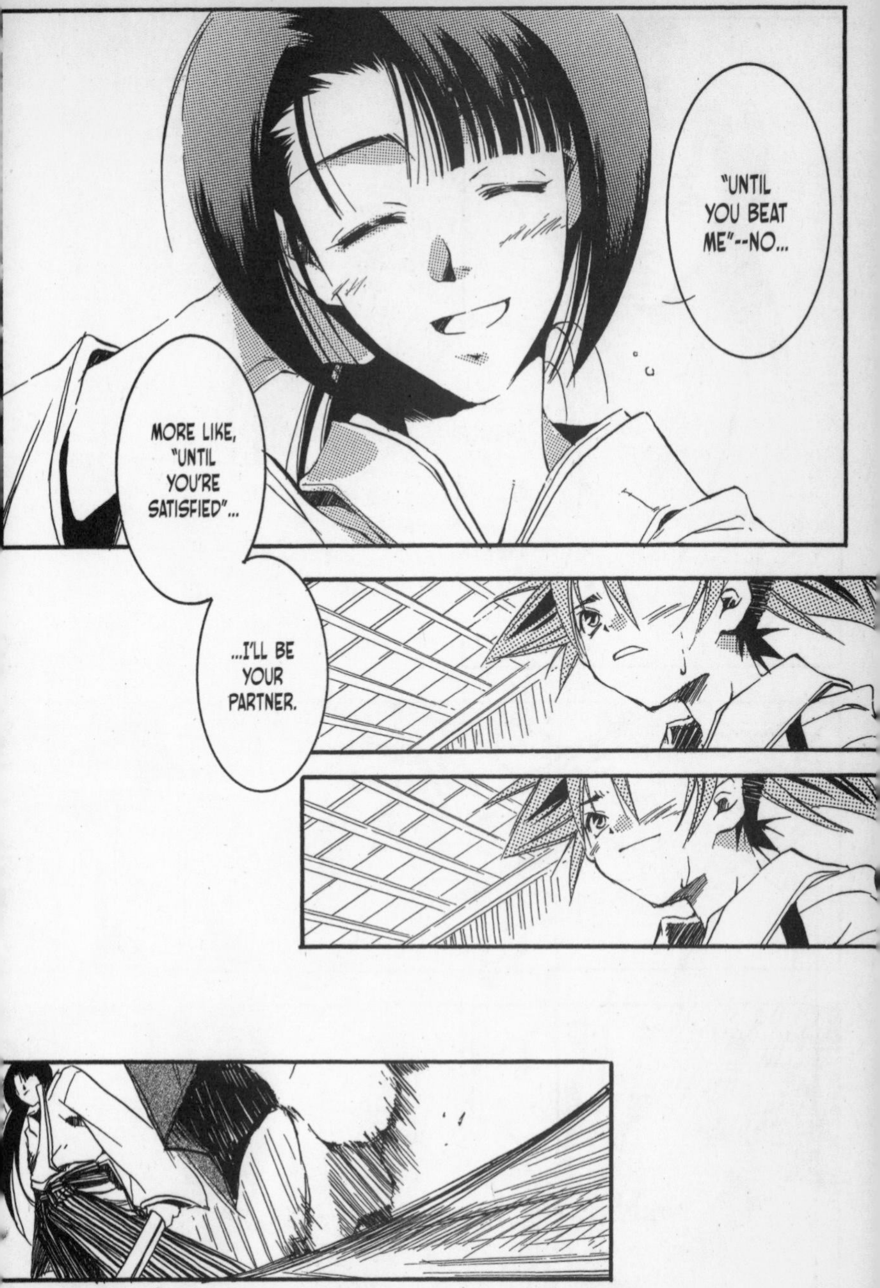
"UNTIL YOU BEAT ME"--NO...
MORE LIKE, "UNTIL YOU'RE SATISFIED"...
...I'LL BE YOUR PARTNER.

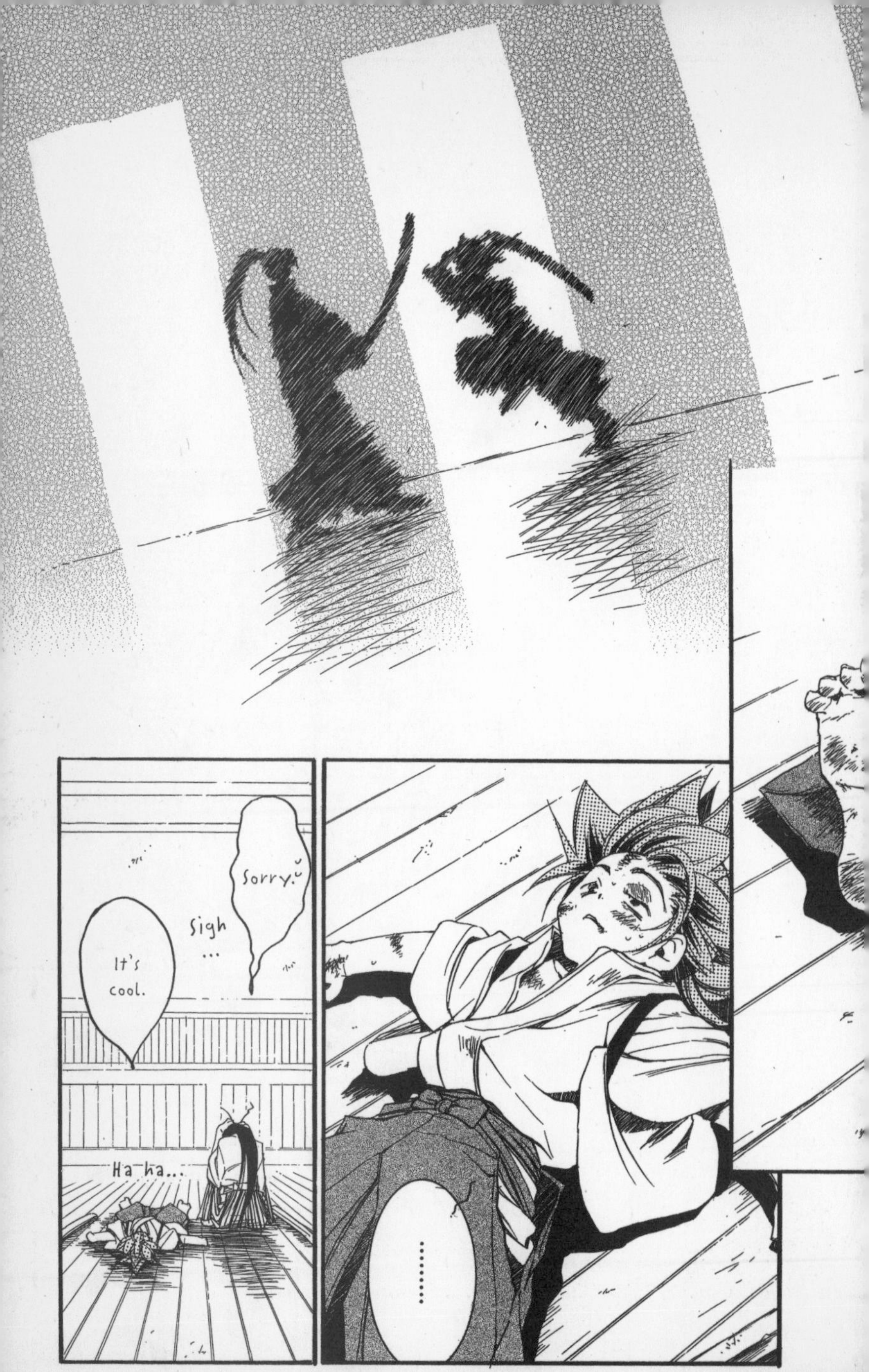

......
Sorry.
Sigh...
It's cool.
Ha ha...

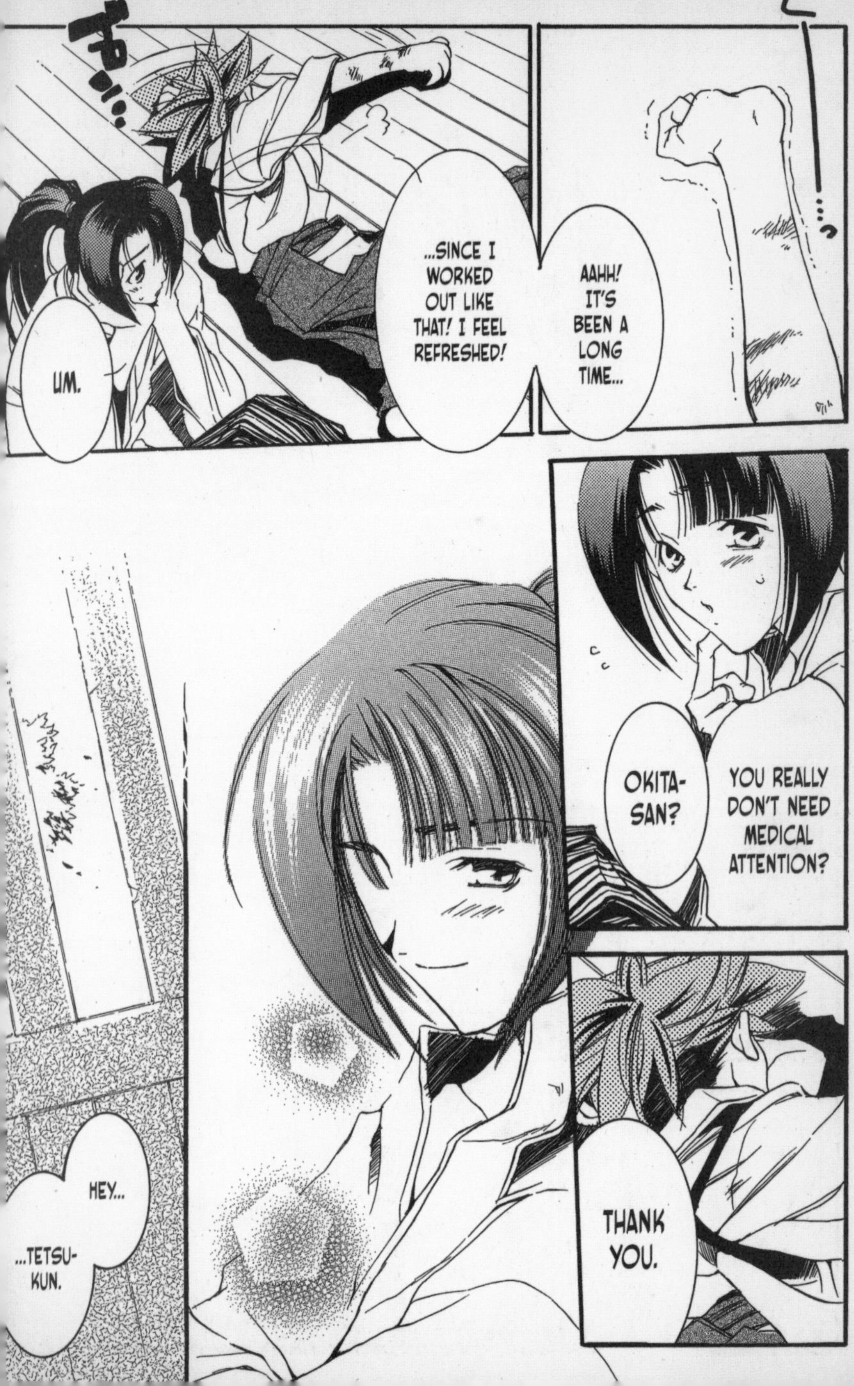
AAHH! IT'S BEEN A LONG TIME...
...SINCE I WORKED OUT LIKE THAT! I FEEL REFRESHED!
UM.
YOU REALLY DON'T NEED MEDICAL ATTENTION?
OKITA-SAN?
THANK YOU.
HEY... ...TETSU-KUN.

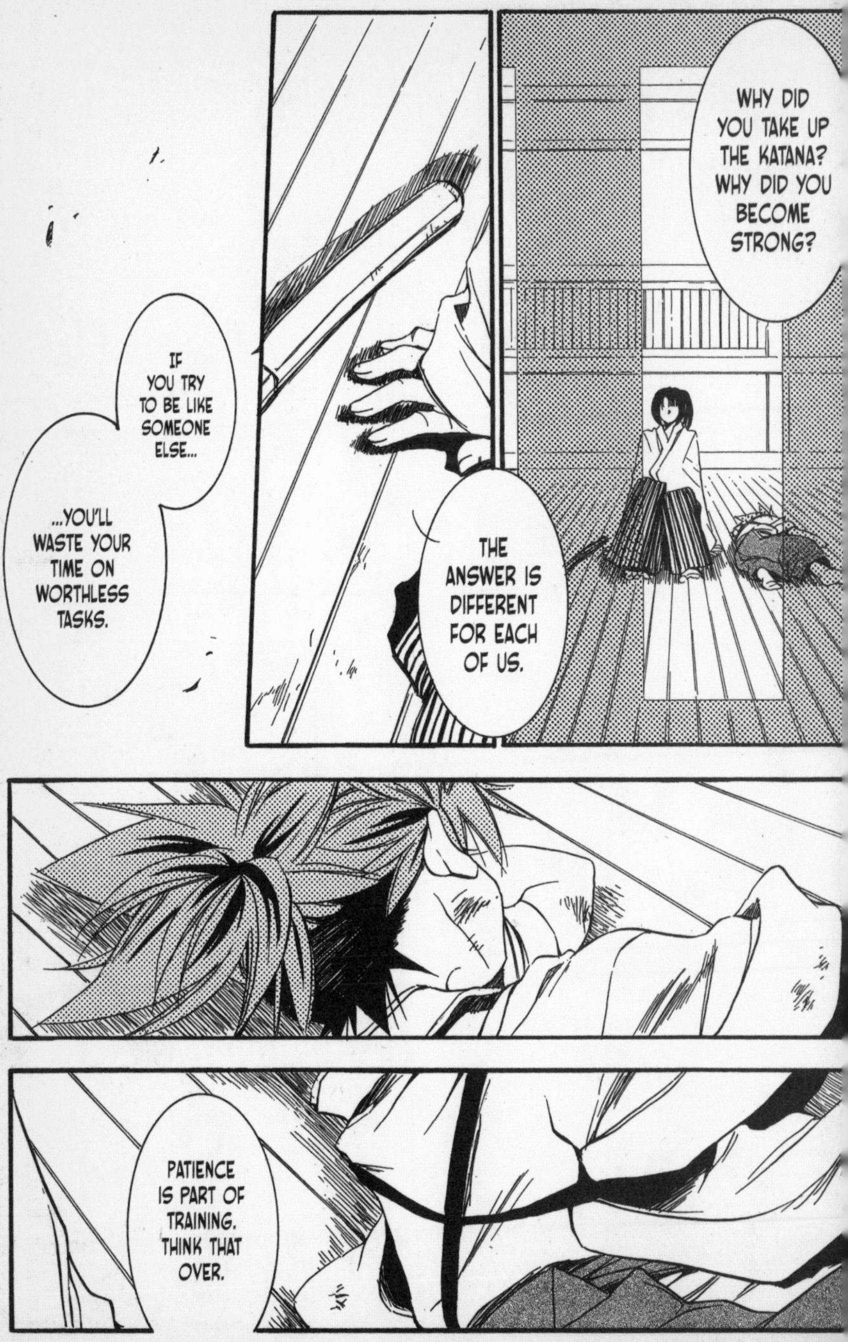
WHY DID YOU TAKE UP THE KATANA? WHY DID YOU BECOME STRONG?
THE ANSWER IS DIFFERENT FOR EACH OF US.
IF YOU TRY TO BE LIKE SOMEONE ELSE...
...YOU'LL WASTE YOUR TIME ON WORTHLESS TASKS.
PATIENCE IS PART OF TRAINING. THINK THAT OVER.

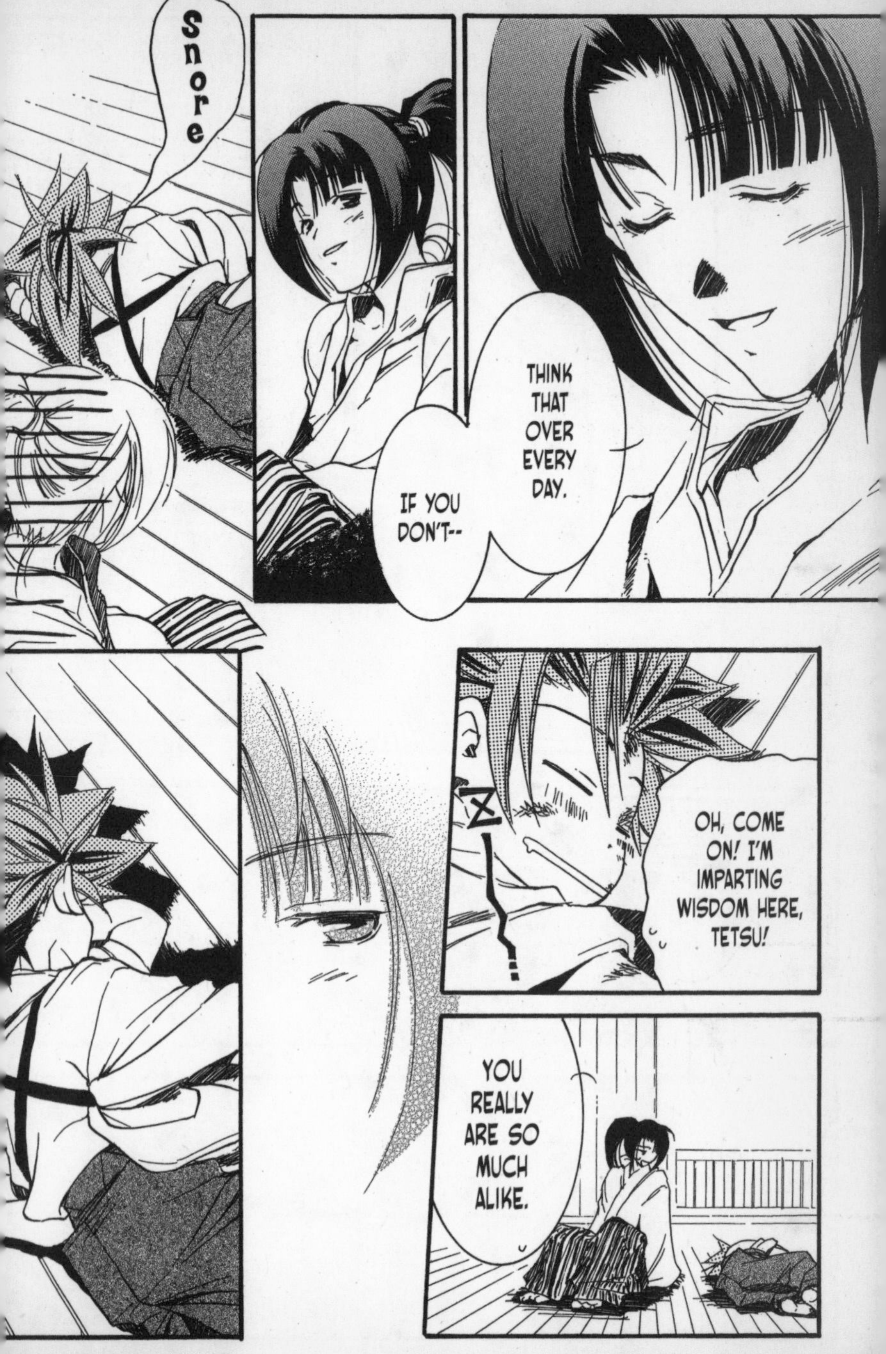
THINK THAT OVER EVERY DAY.
IF YOU DON'T--
Snore
OH, COME ON! I'M IMPARTING WISDOM HERE, TETSU!
Z
YOU REALLY ARE SO MUCH ALIKE.

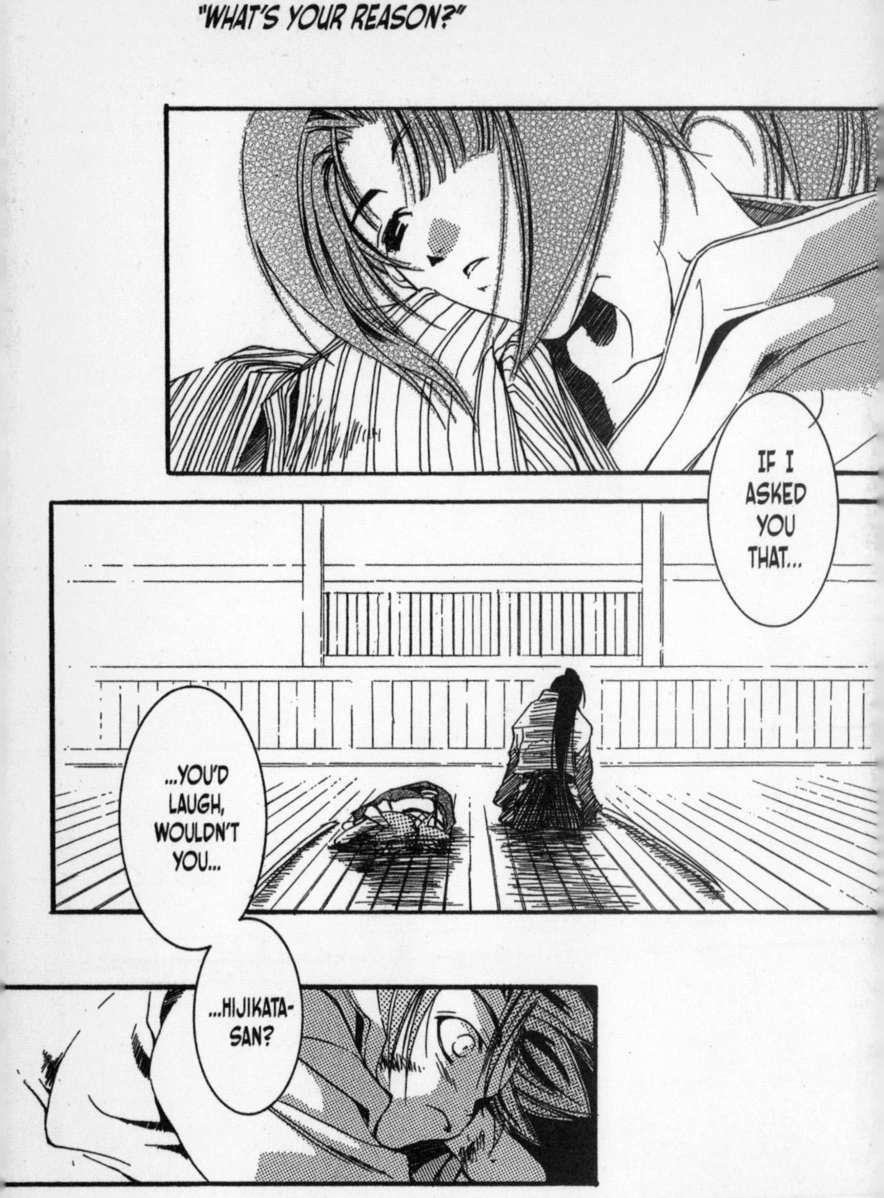
"WHAT'S YOUR REASON?"
IF I ASKED YOU THAT...
...YOU'D LAUGH, WOULDN'T YOU...
...HIJIKATA-SAN?

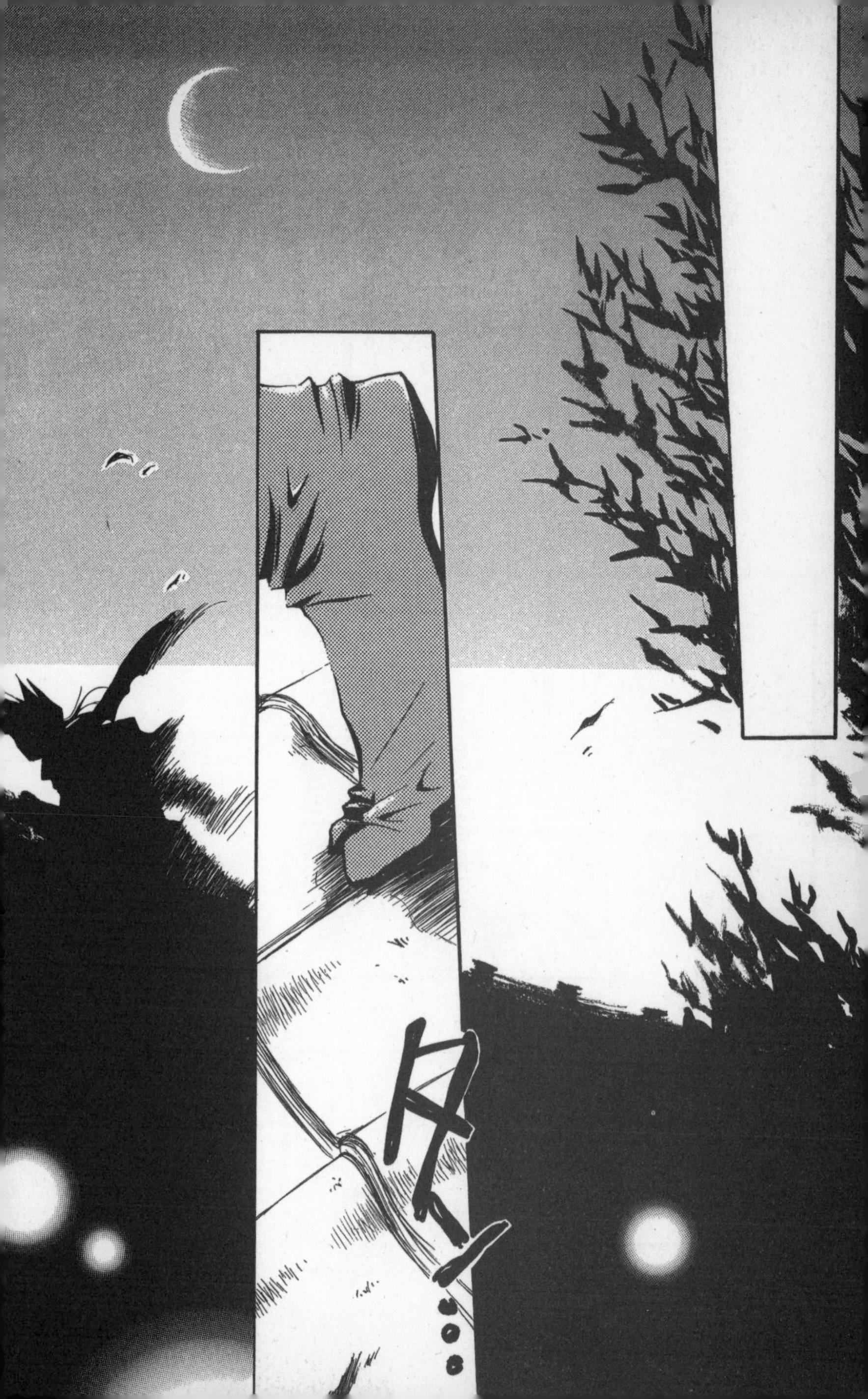

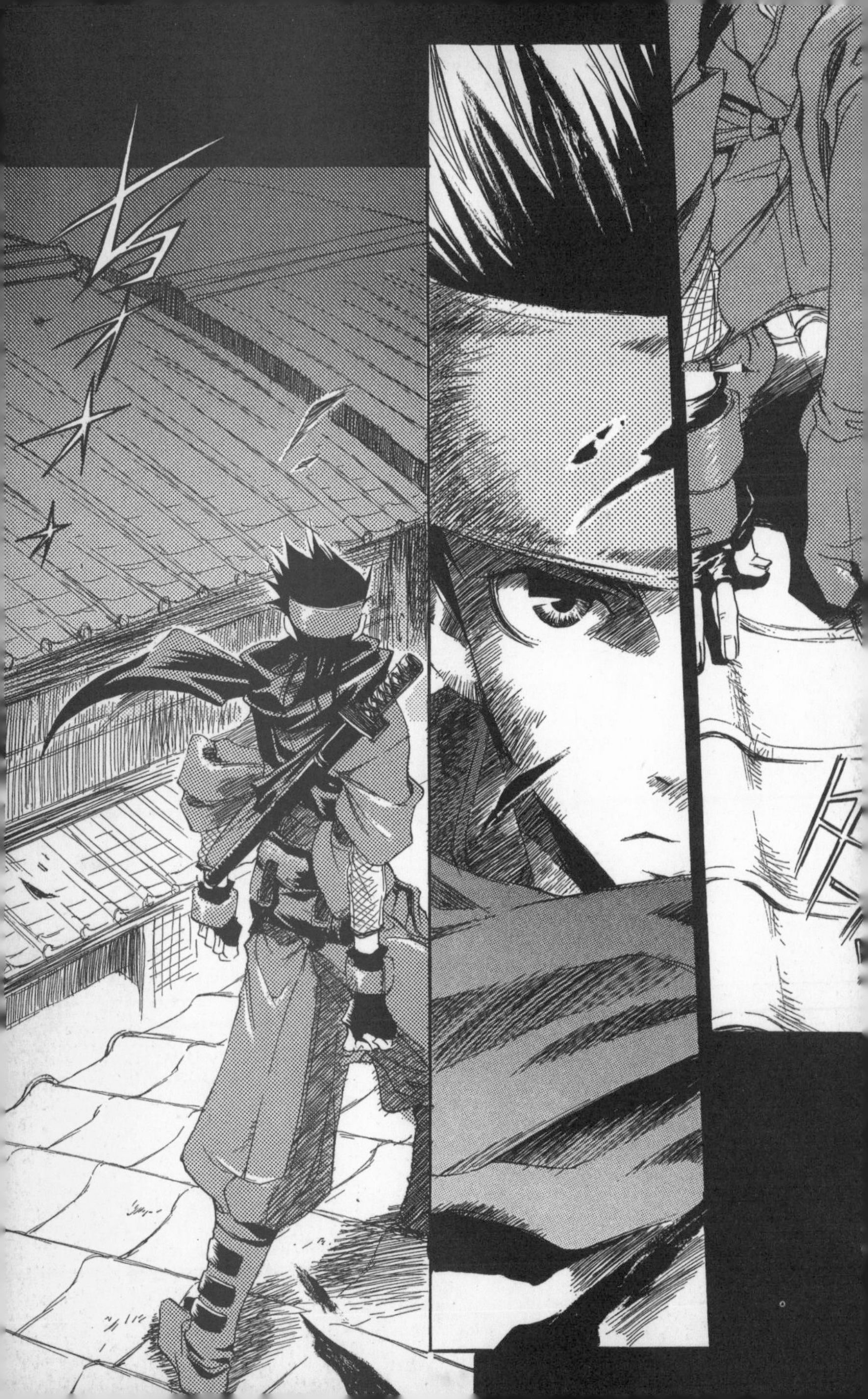

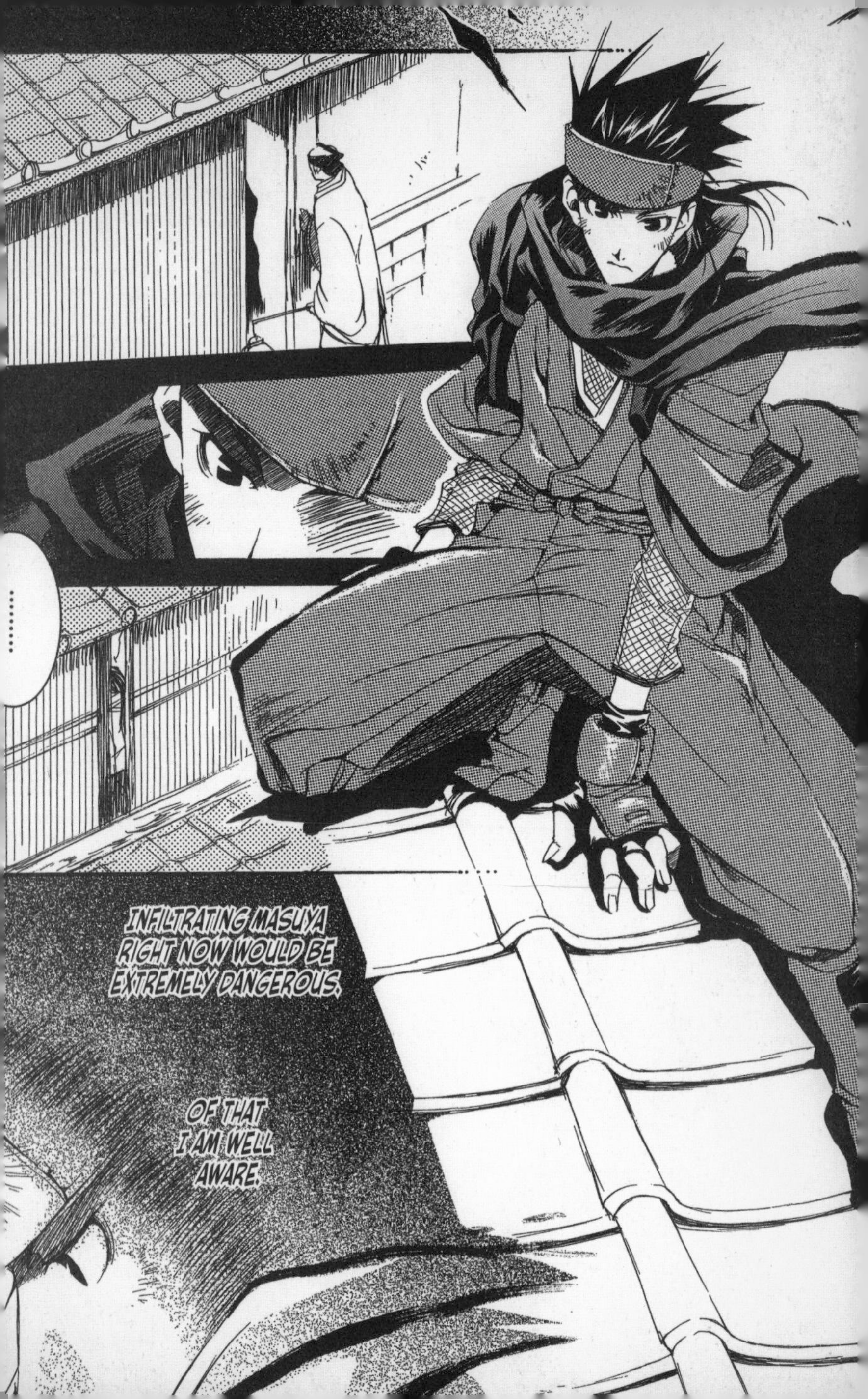
......
INFILTRATING MASUYA RIGHT NOW WOULD BE EXTREMELY DANGEROUS.
OF THAT I AM WELL AWARE.

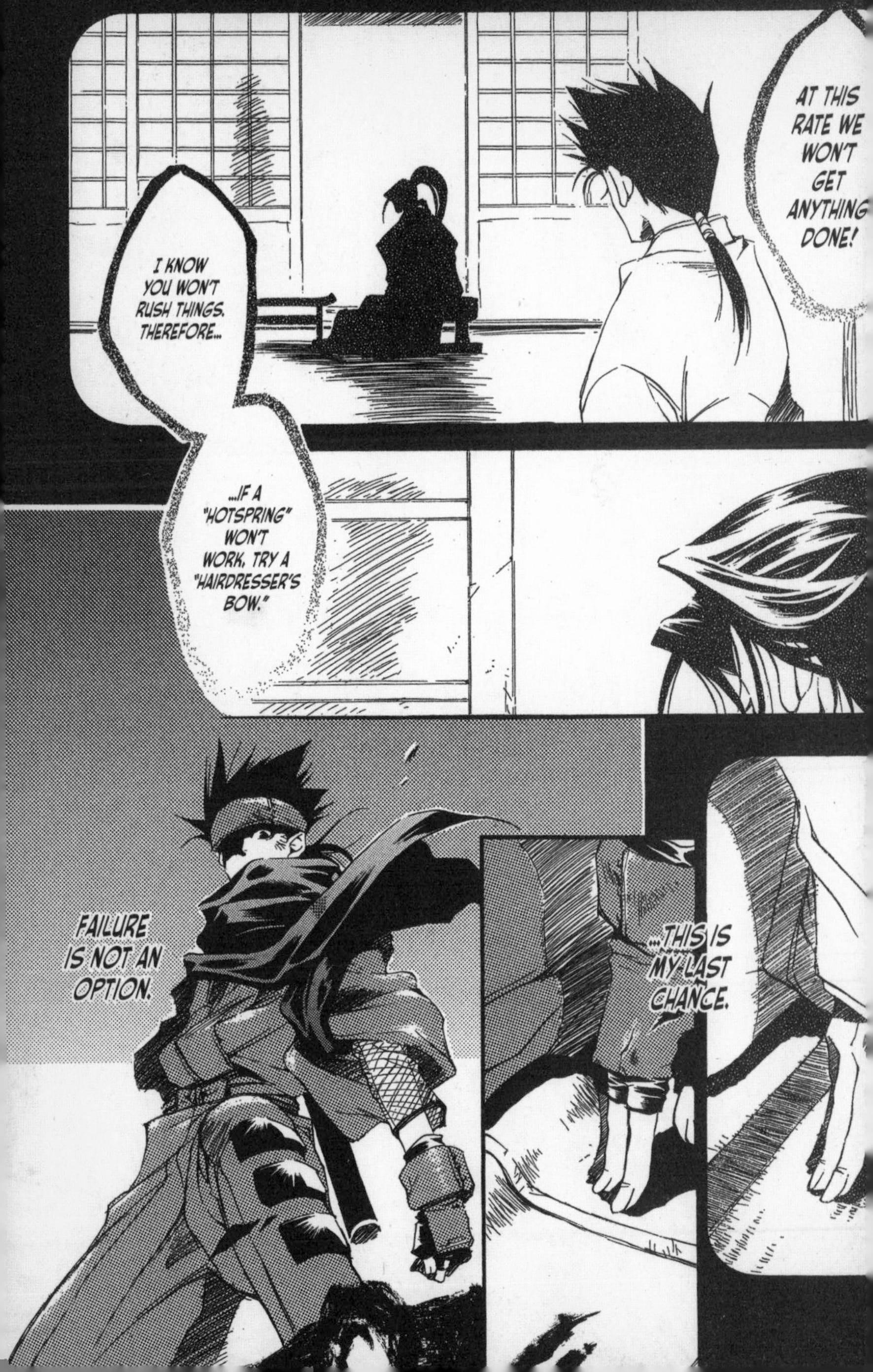
AT THIS RATE WE WON'T GET ANYTHING DONE!
I KNOW YOU WON'T RUSH THINGS. THEREFORE...
...IF A "HOTSPRING" WON'T WORK, TRY A "HAIRDRESSER'S BOW."
...THIS IS MY LAST CHANCE.
FAILURE IS NOT AN OPTION.

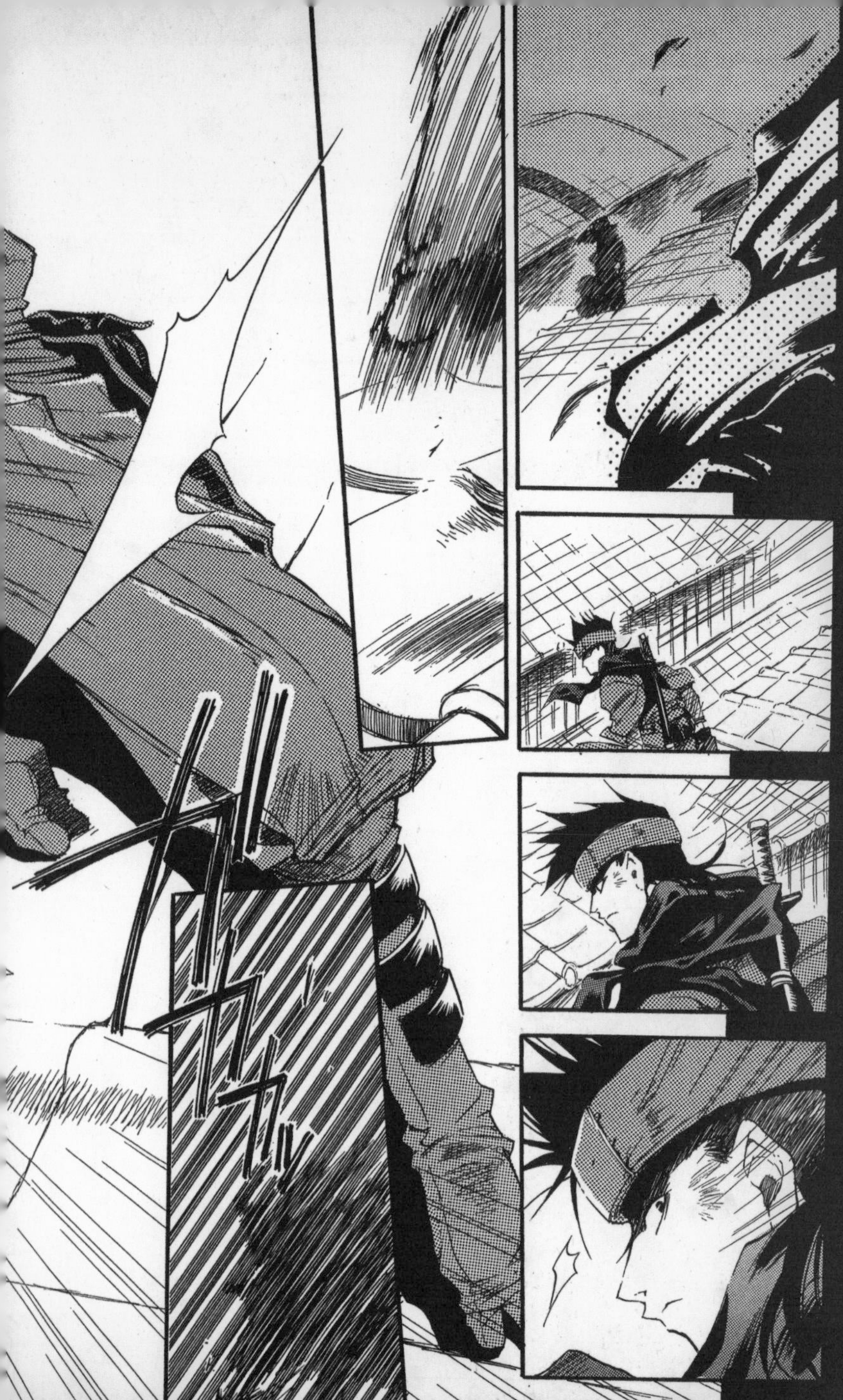

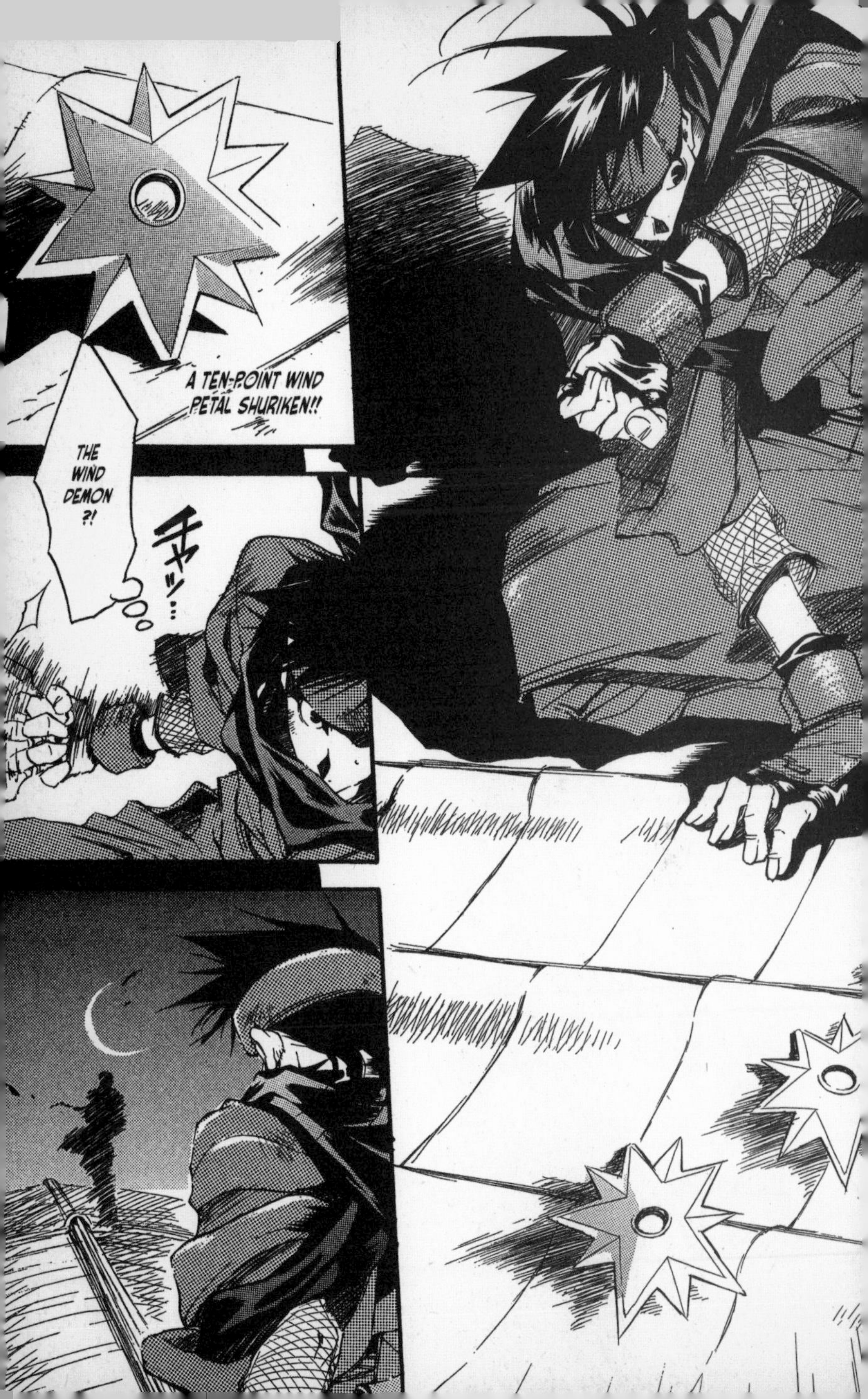
A TEN-POINT WIND PETAL SHURIKEN!!
THE WIND DEMON ?!
チャッ…

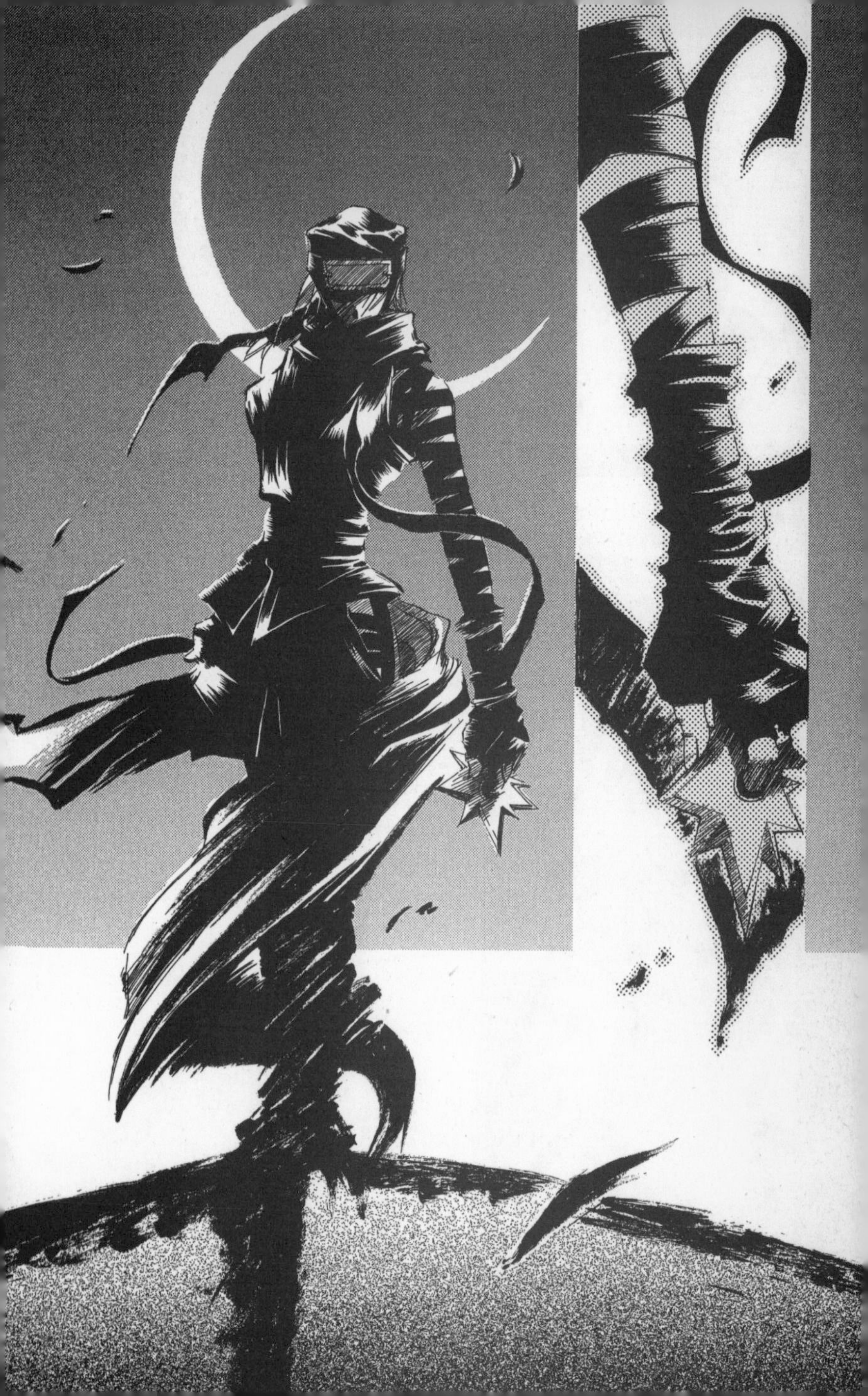

Act.9
All I've Got to Do

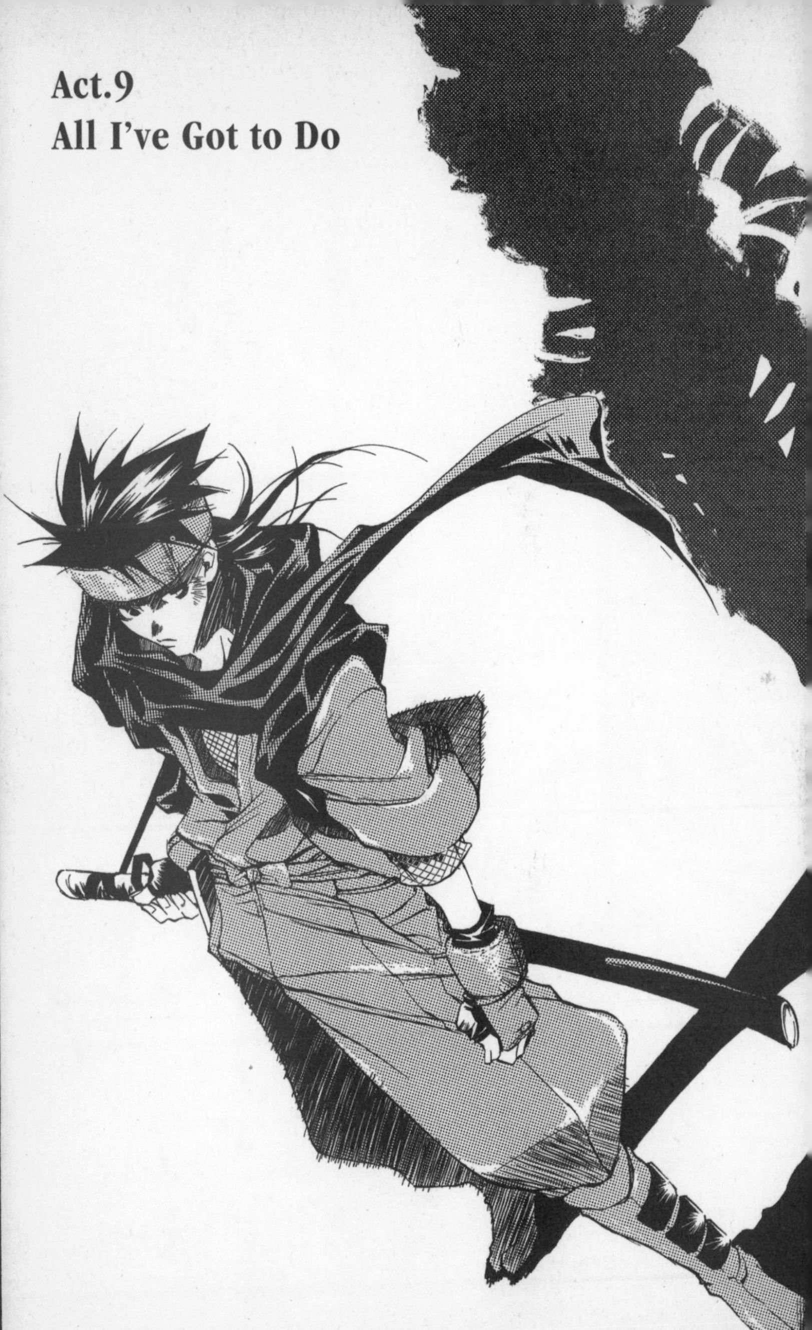

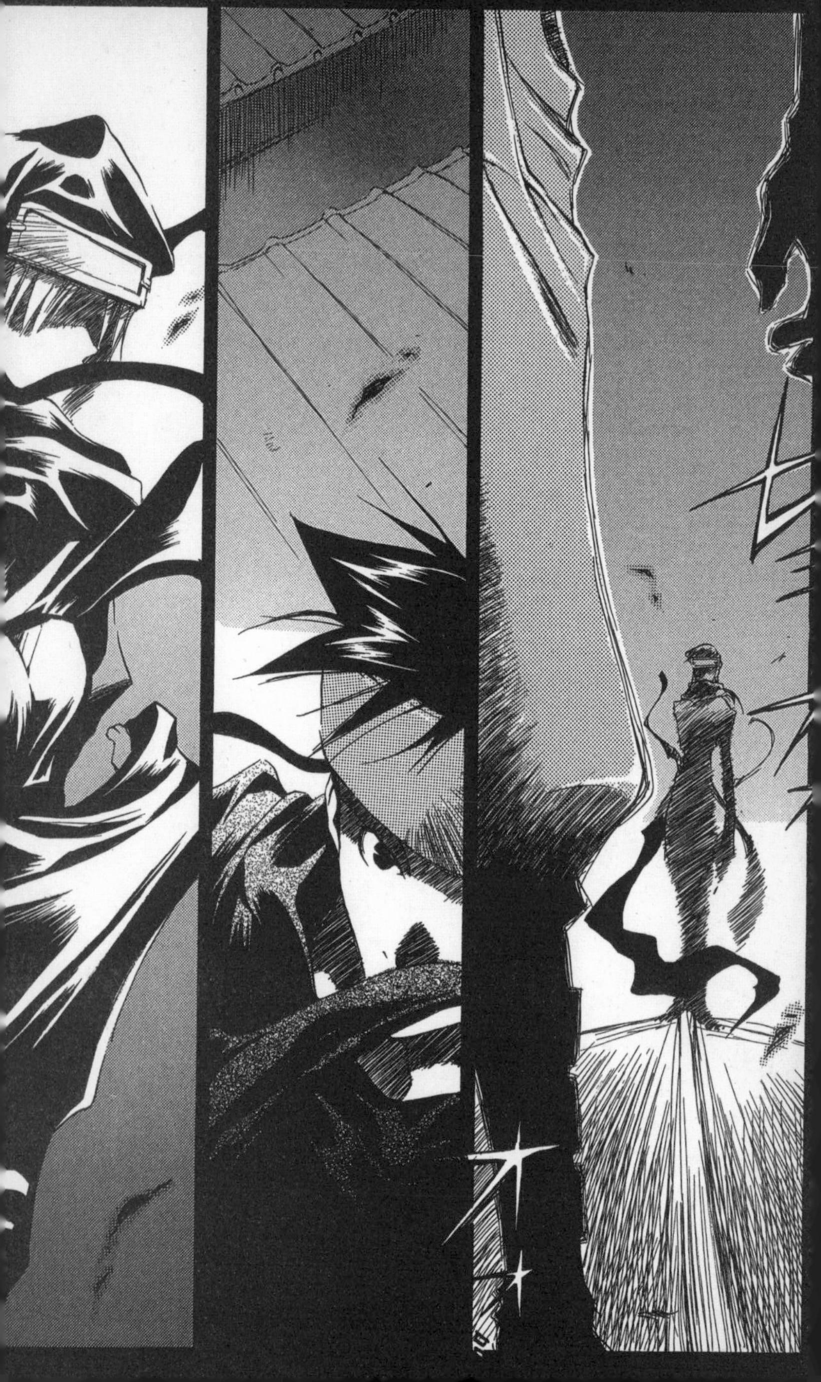

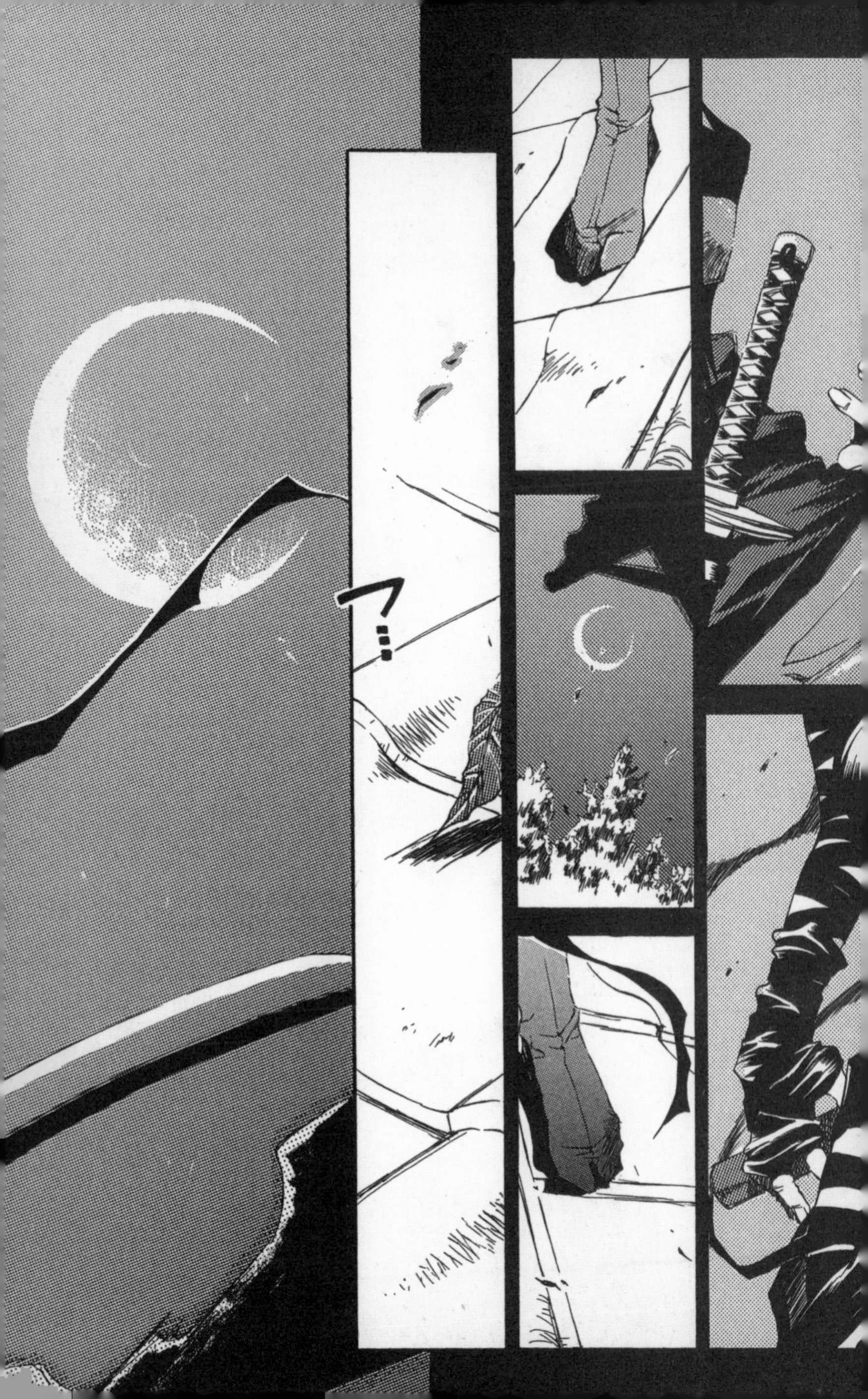
フ…

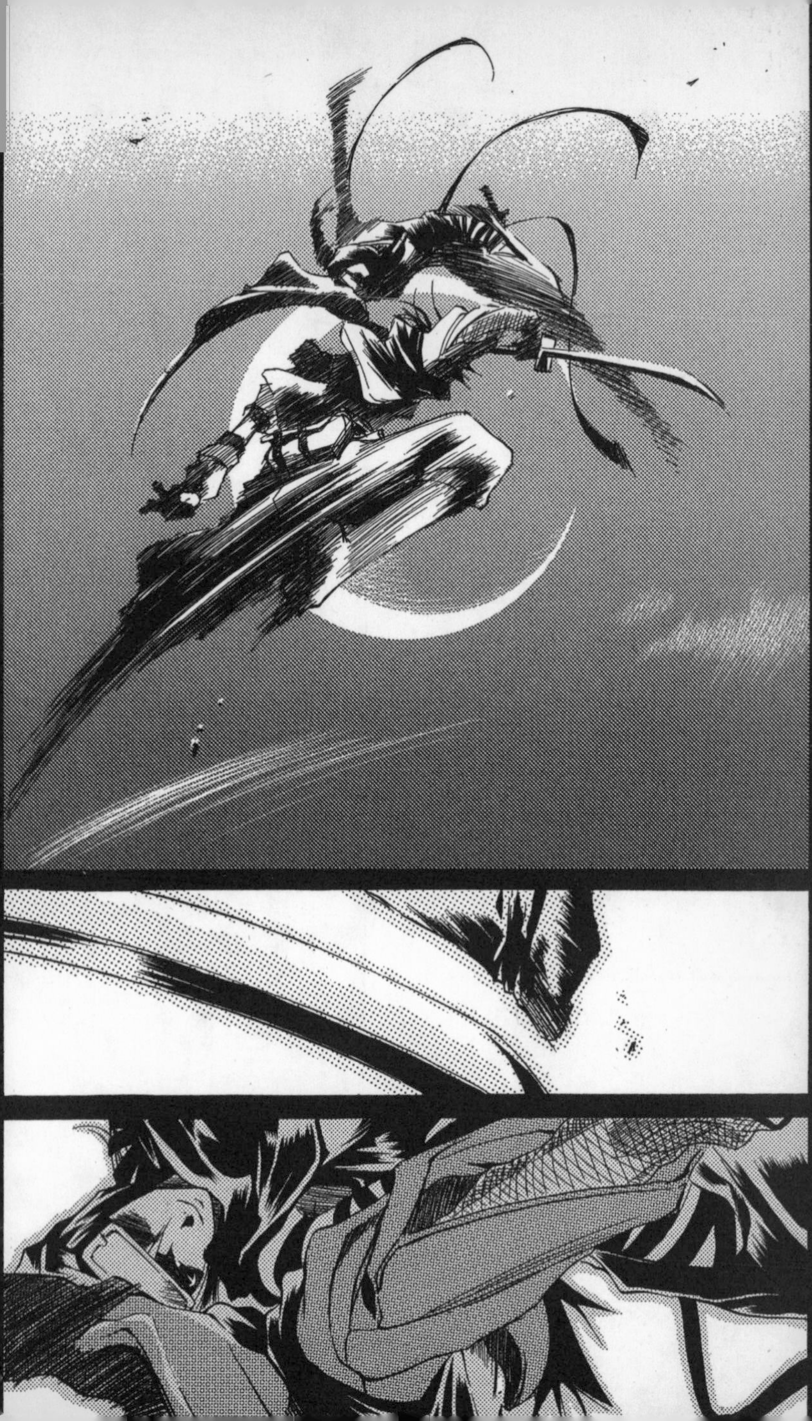

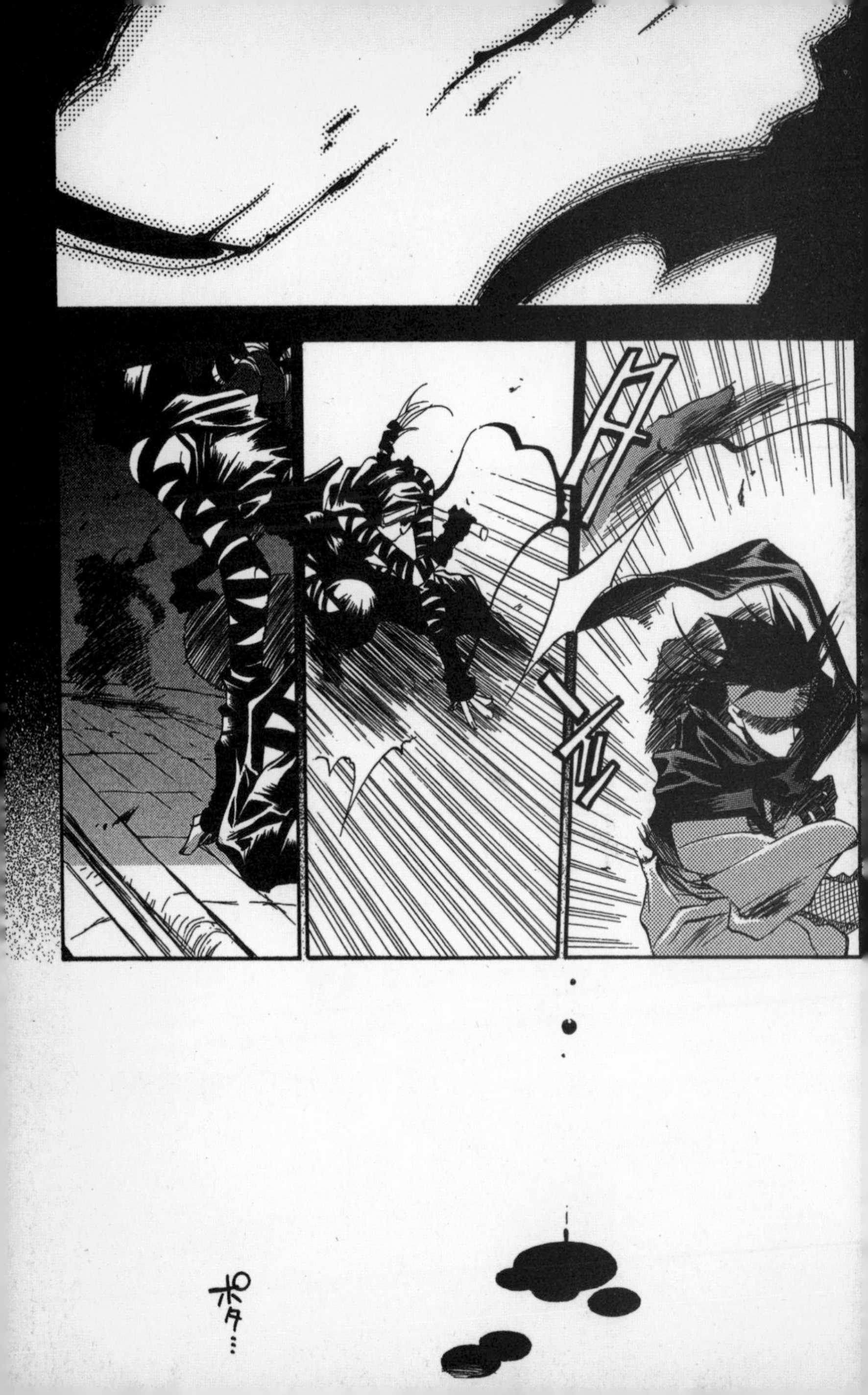
ポタ…

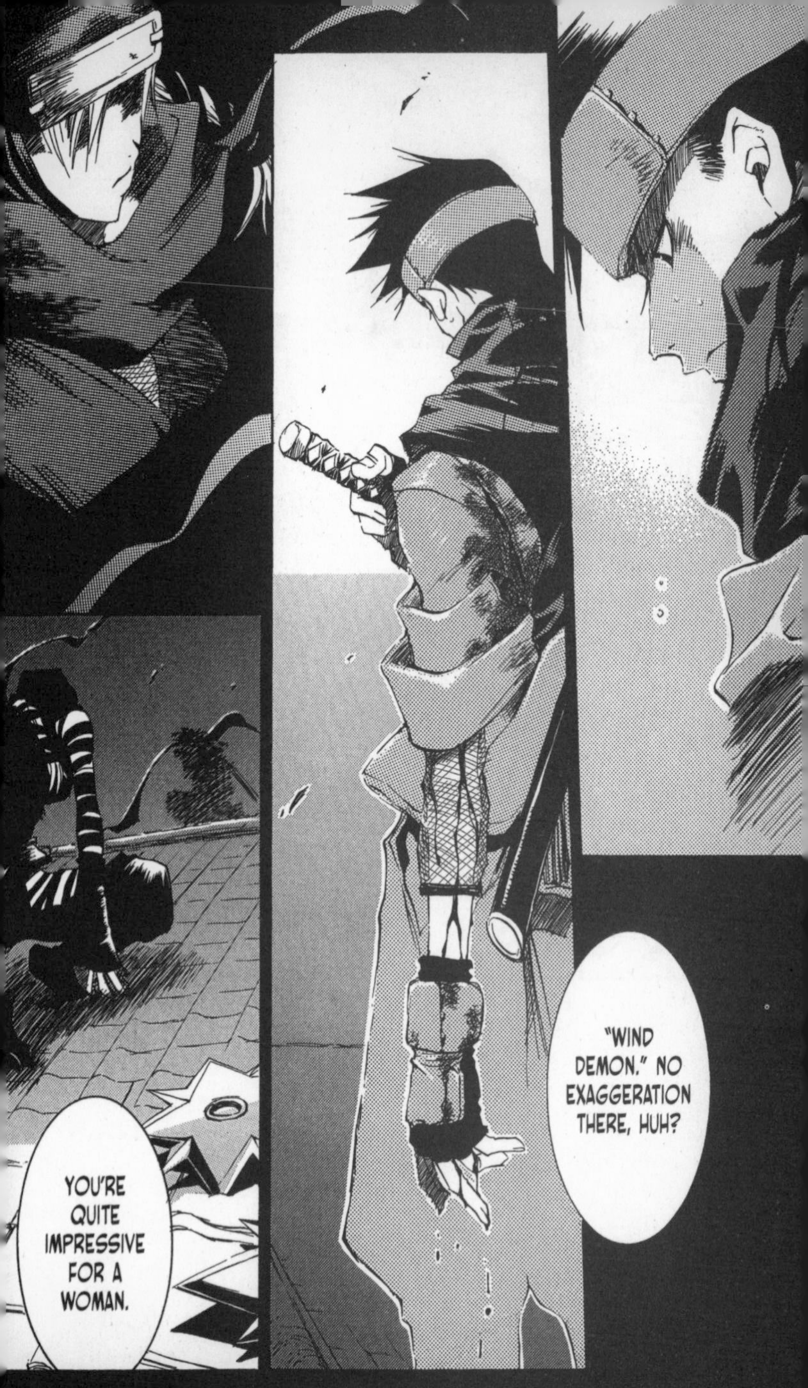
"WIND DEMON." NO EXAGGERATION THERE, HUH?
YOU'RE QUITE IMPRESSIVE FOR A WOMAN.

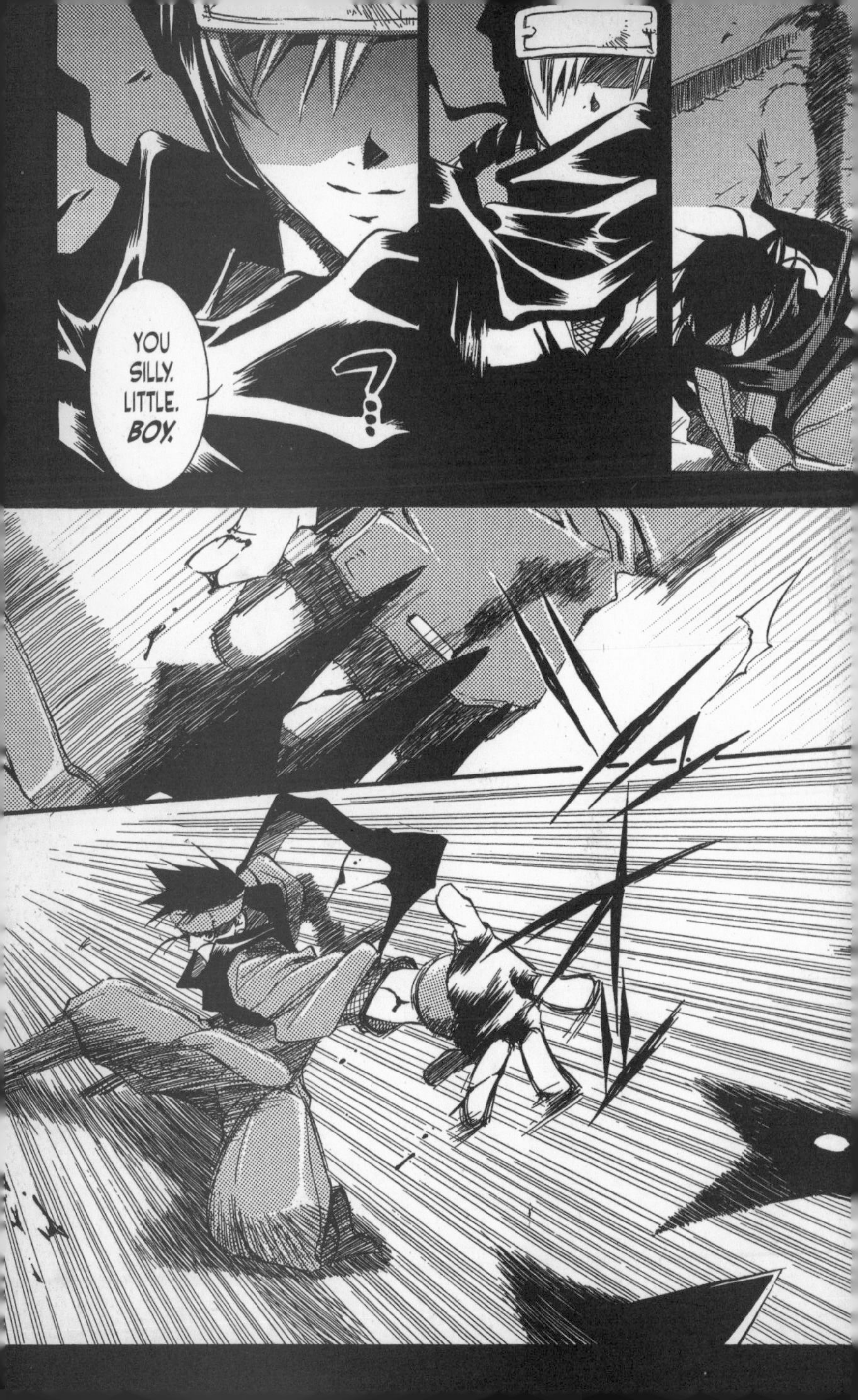
YOU SILLY. LITTLE. *BOY.*
?

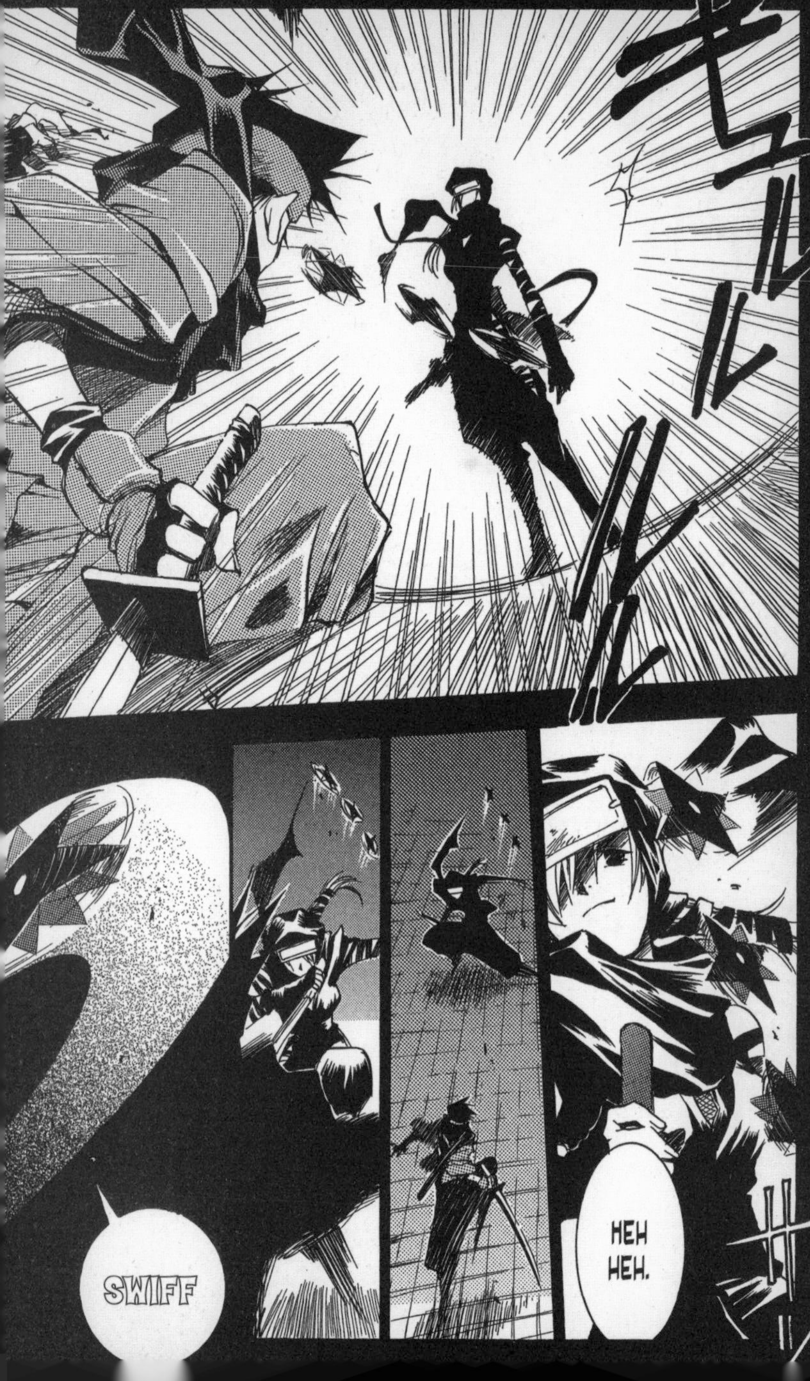
ギュルルルル
HEH
HEH.
SWIFF

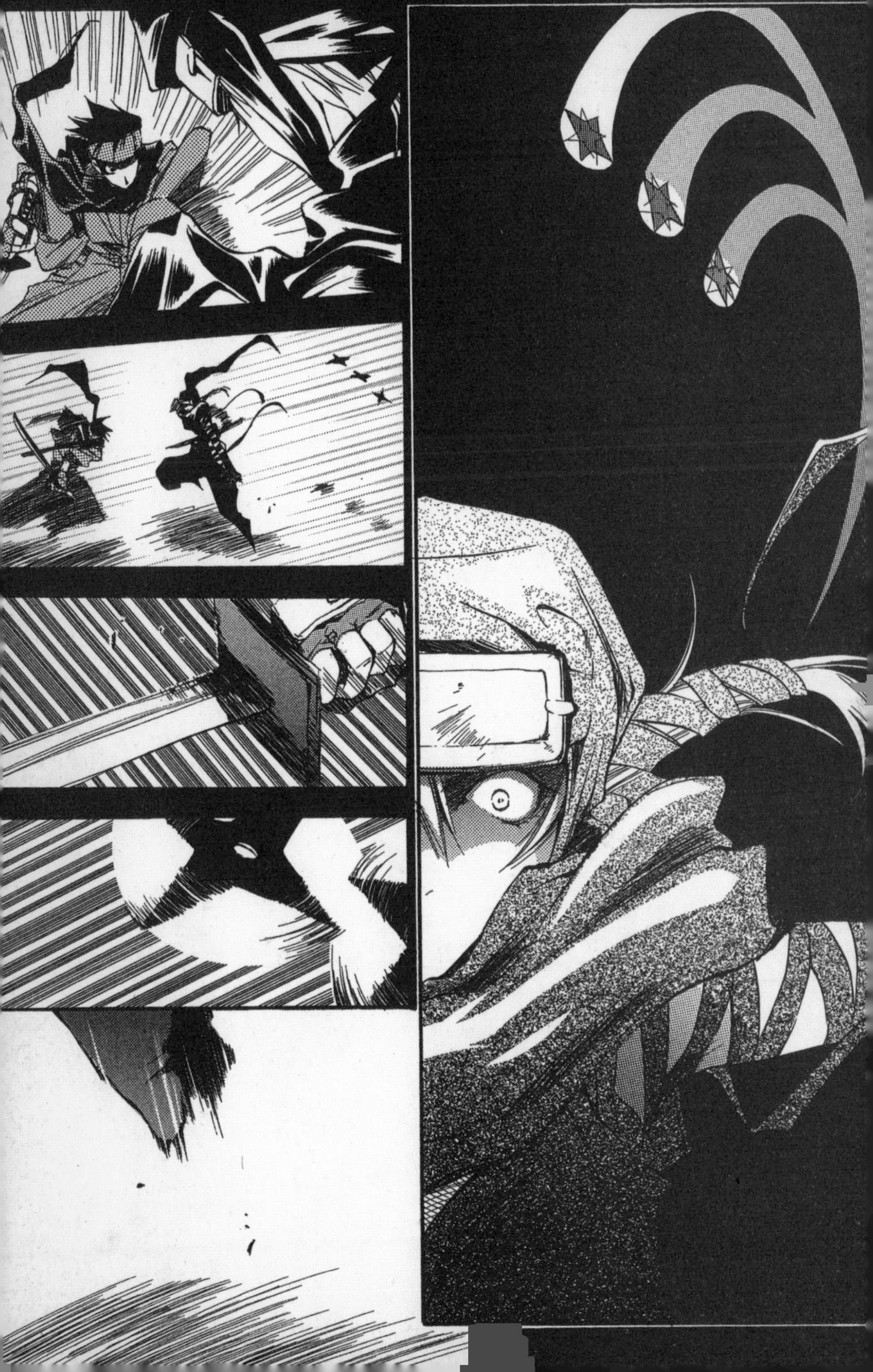

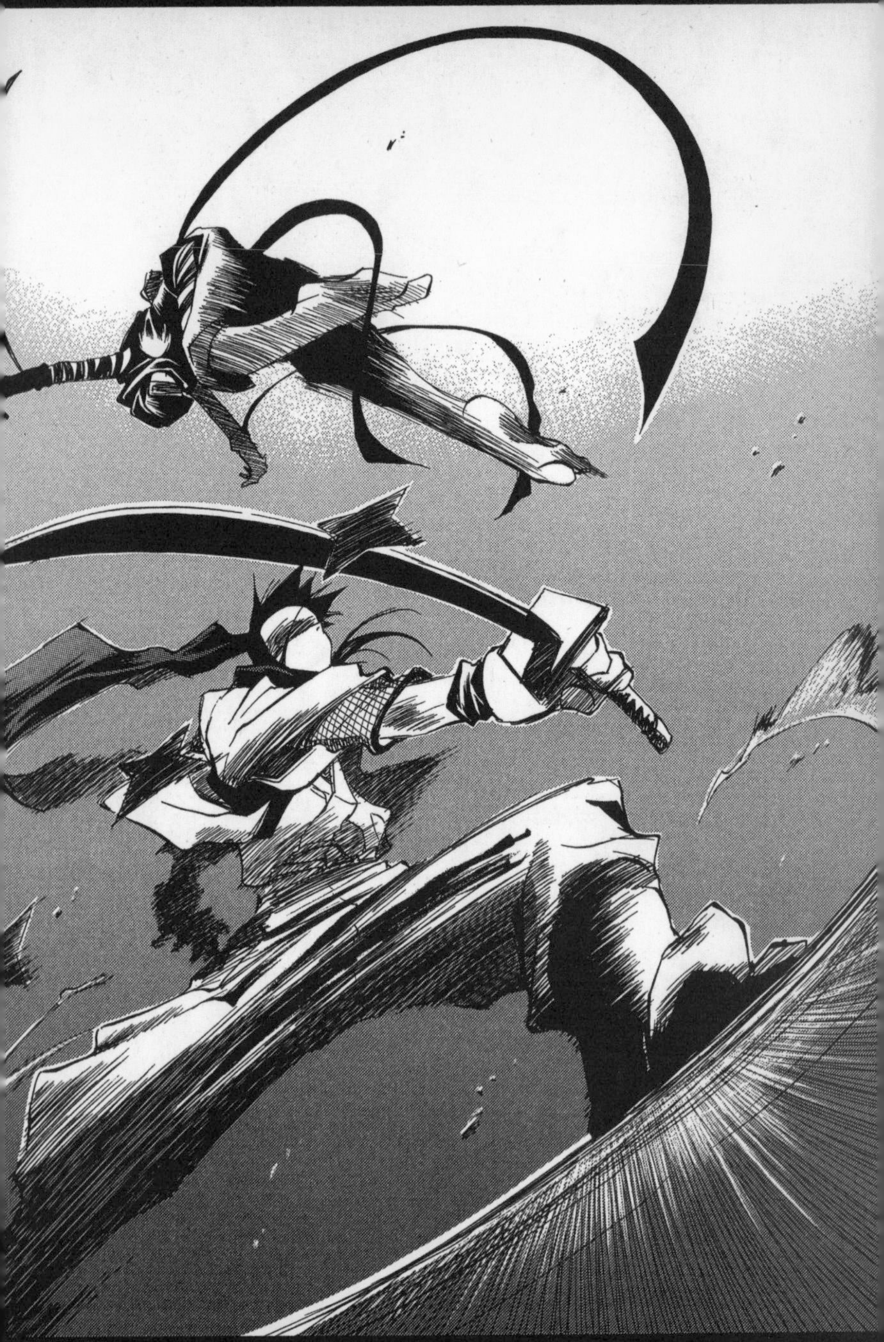

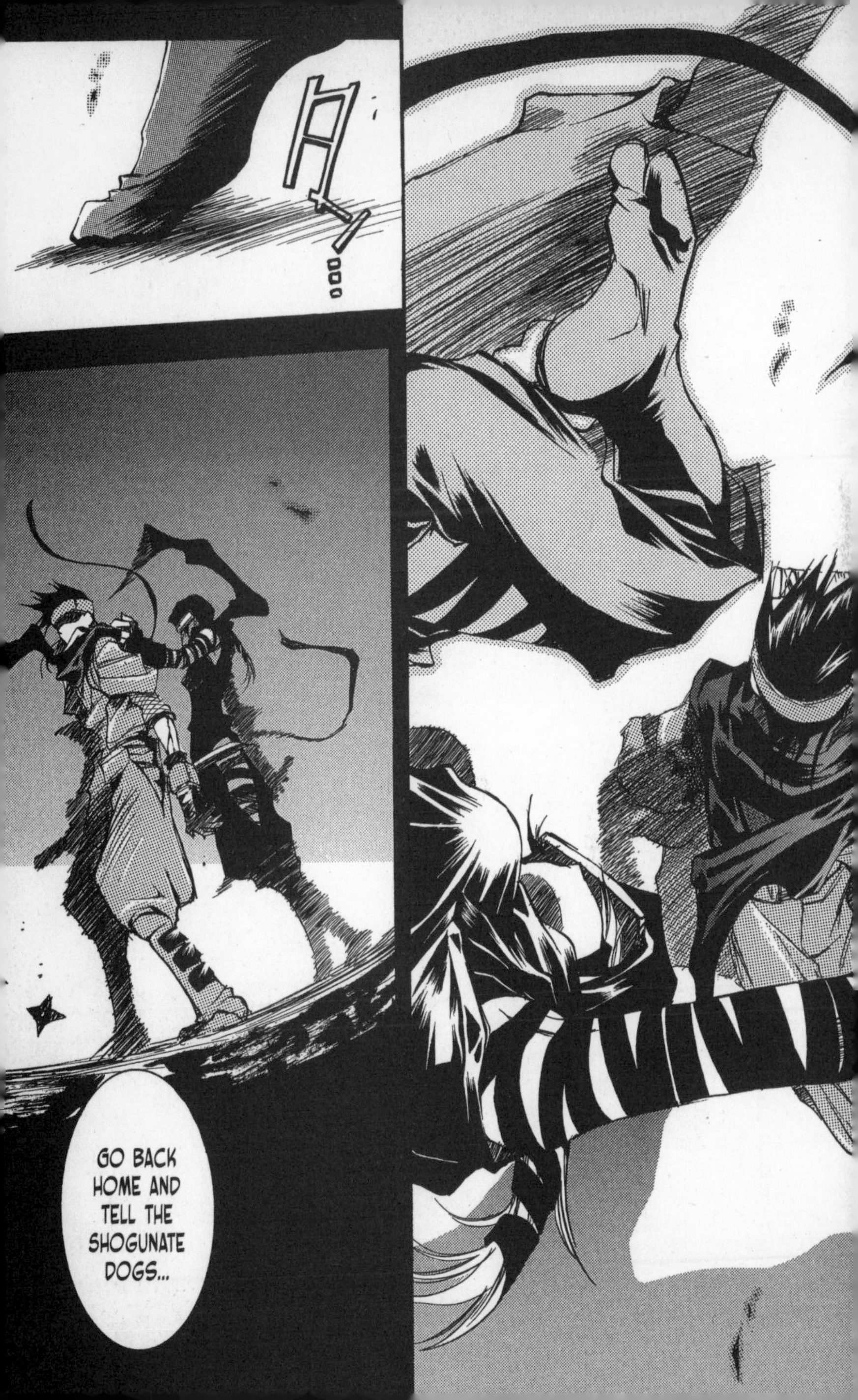
GO BACK HOME AND TELL THE SHOGUNATE DOGS...

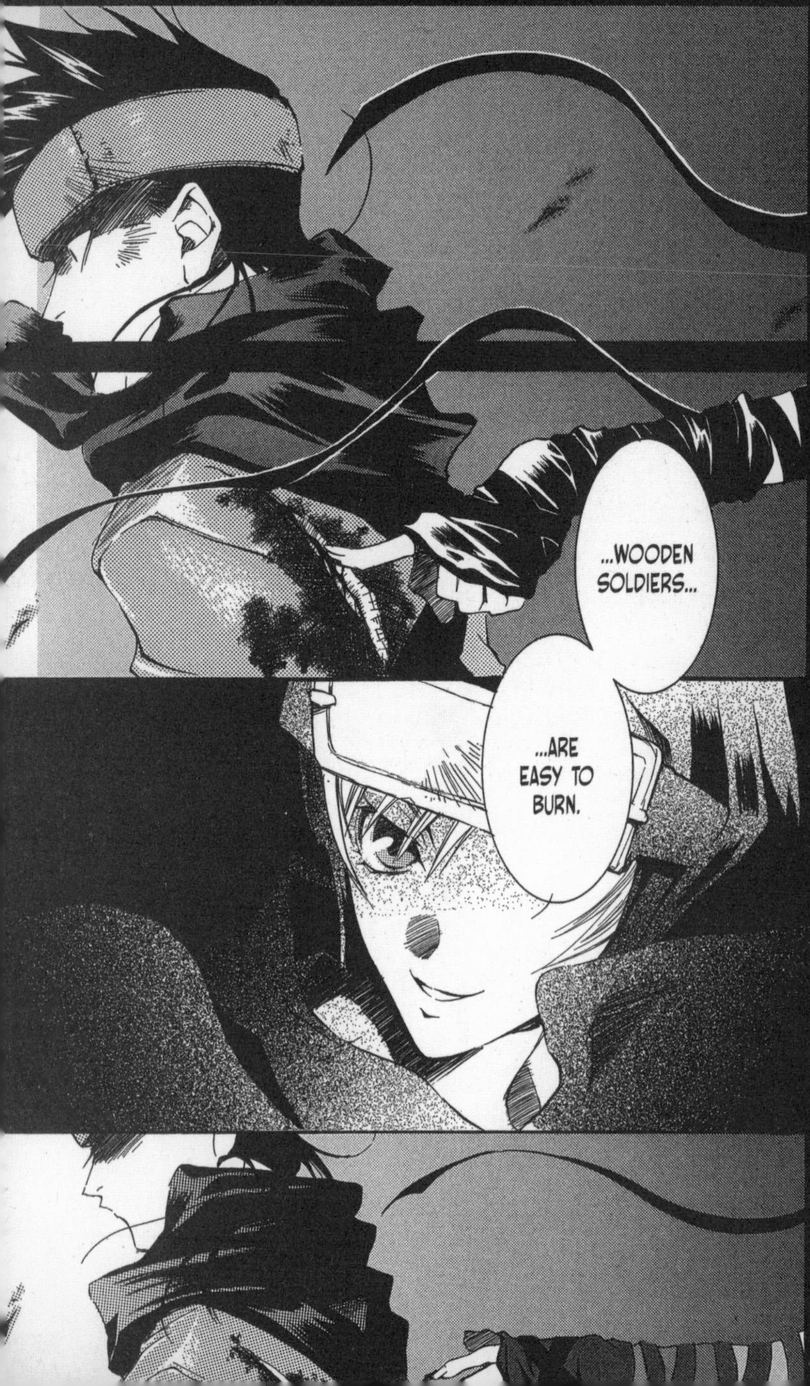
...WOODEN SOLDIERS...
...ARE EASY TO BURN.

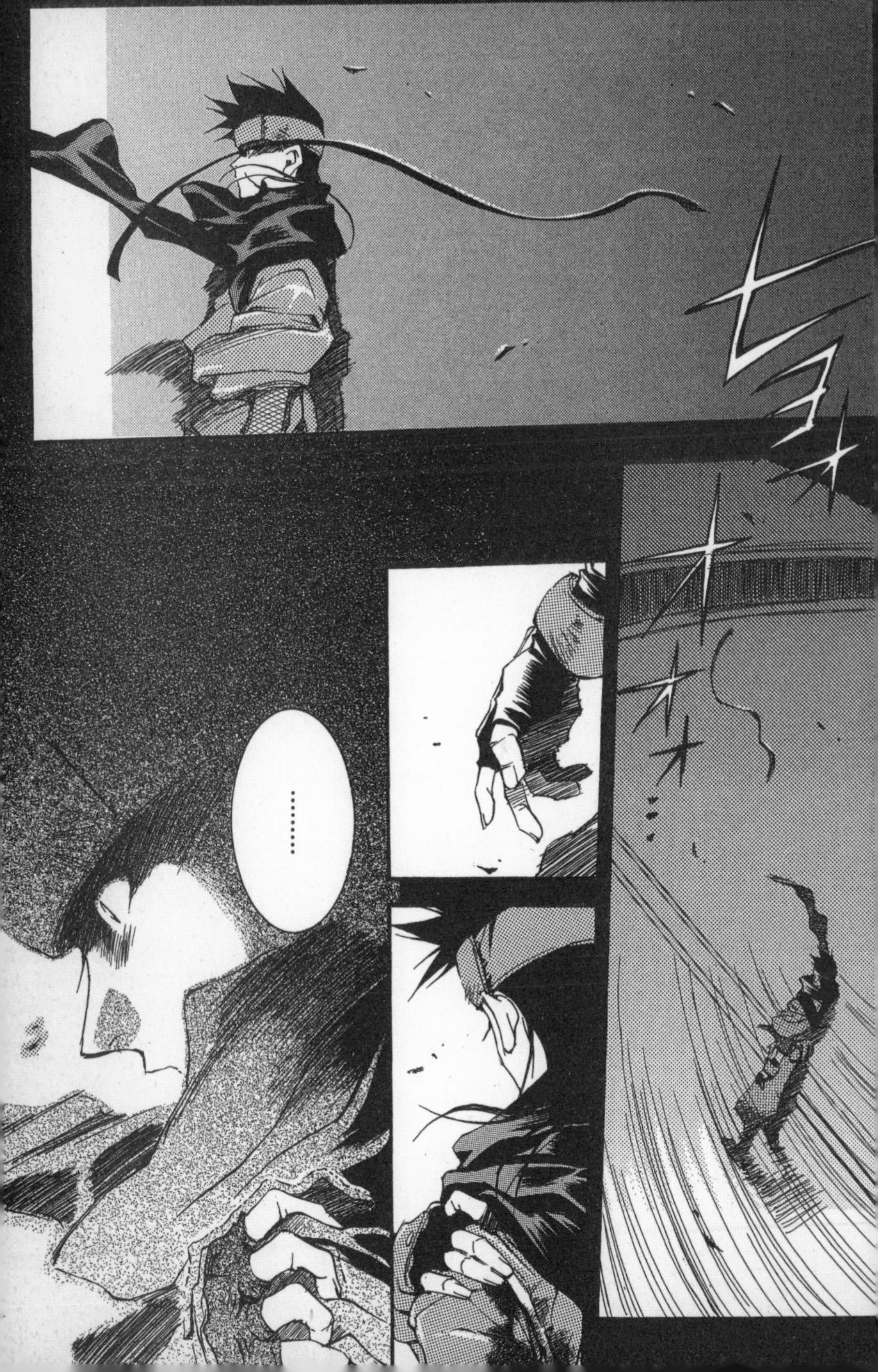

……

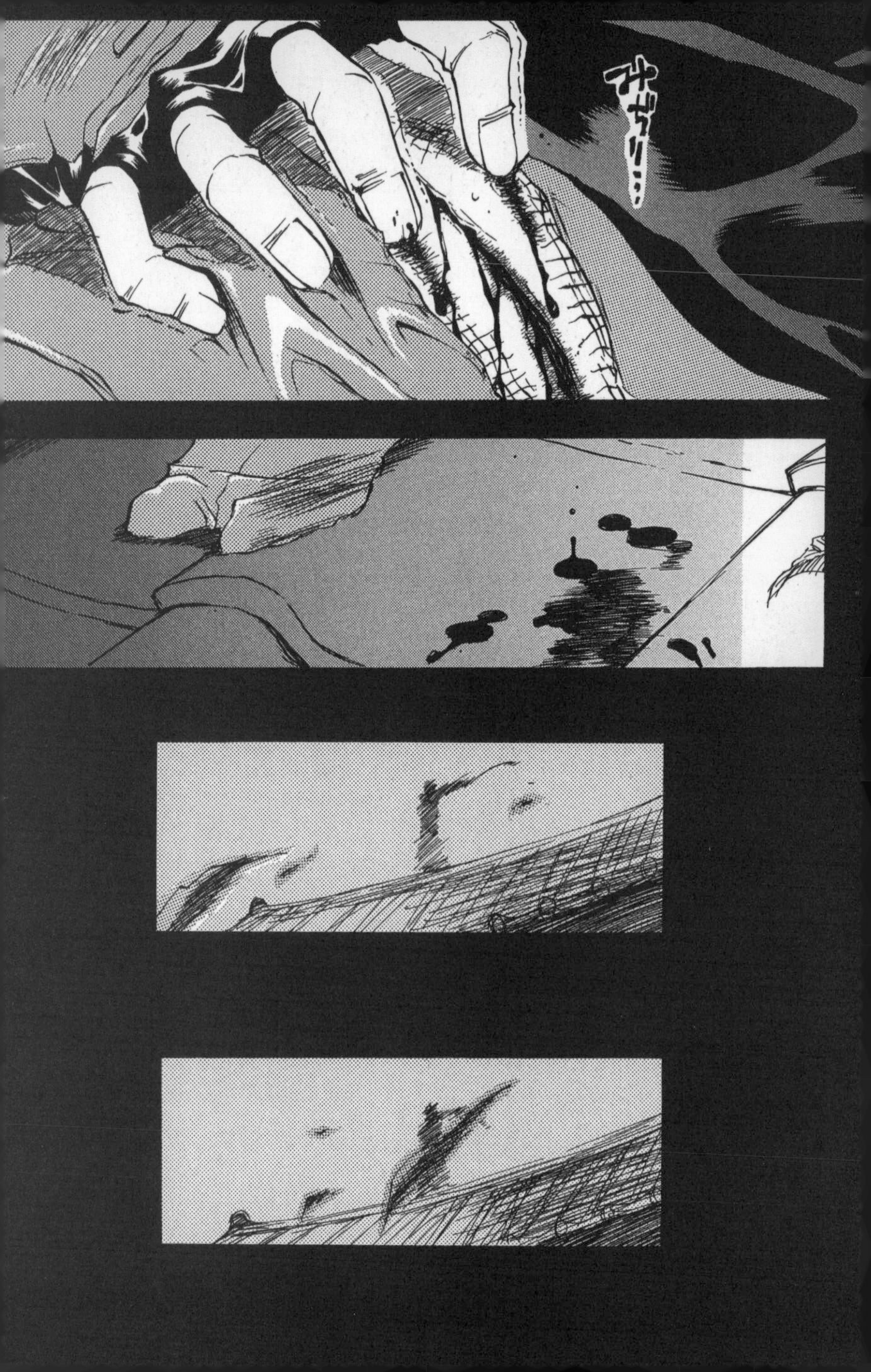
みぢりーっ

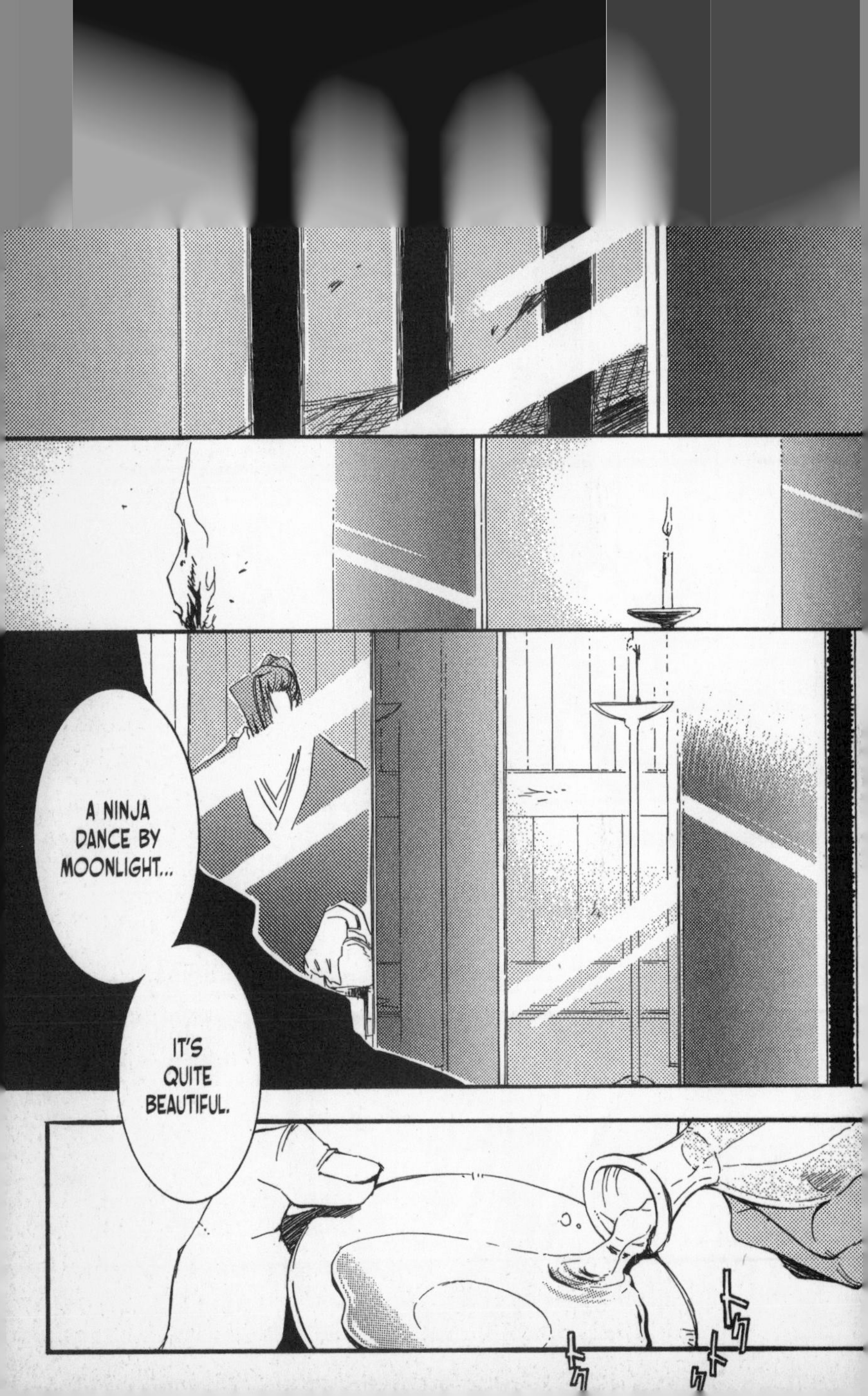
A NINJA DANCE BY MOONLIGHT...
IT'S QUITE BEAUTIFUL.

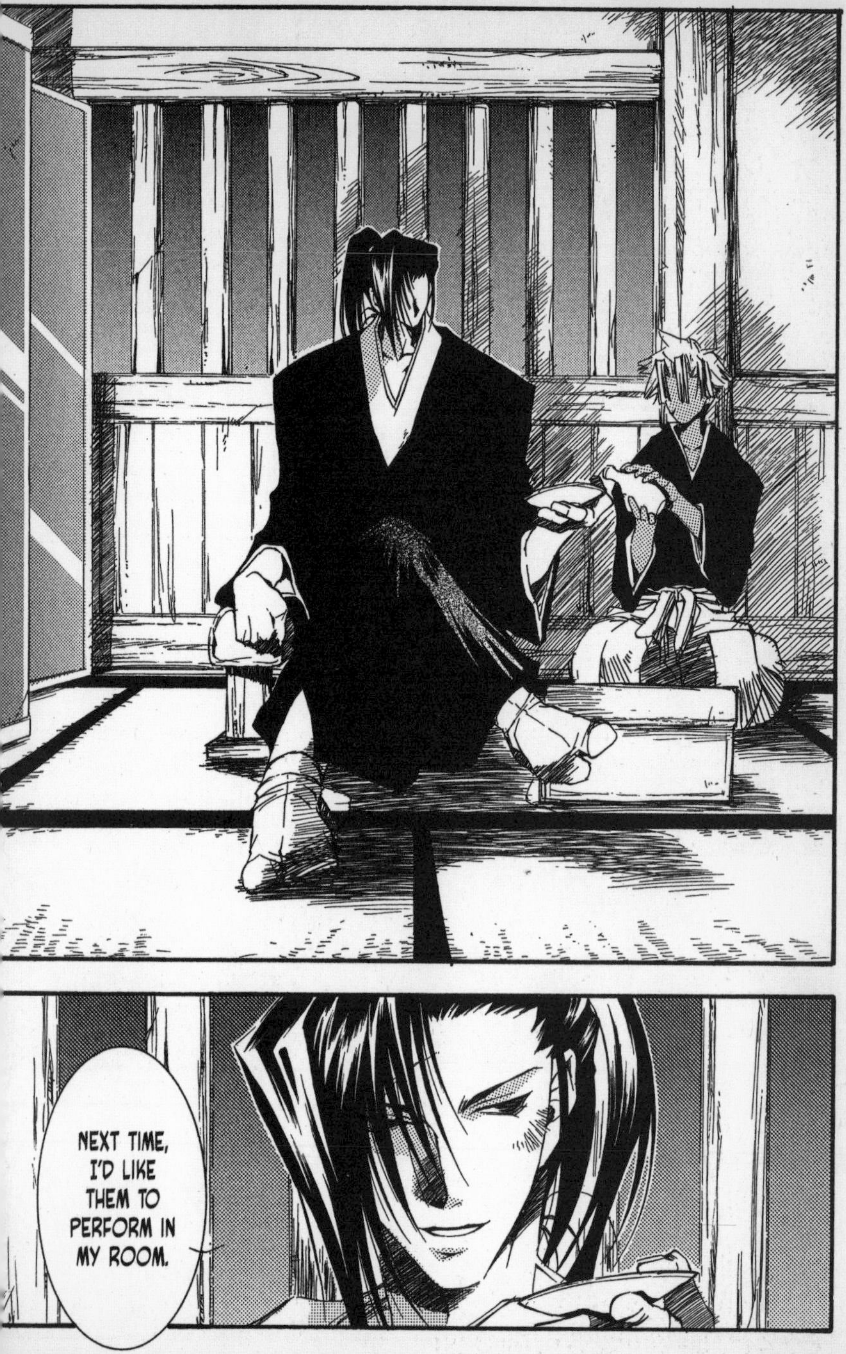
NEXT TIME, I'D LIKE THEM TO PERFORM IN MY ROOM.

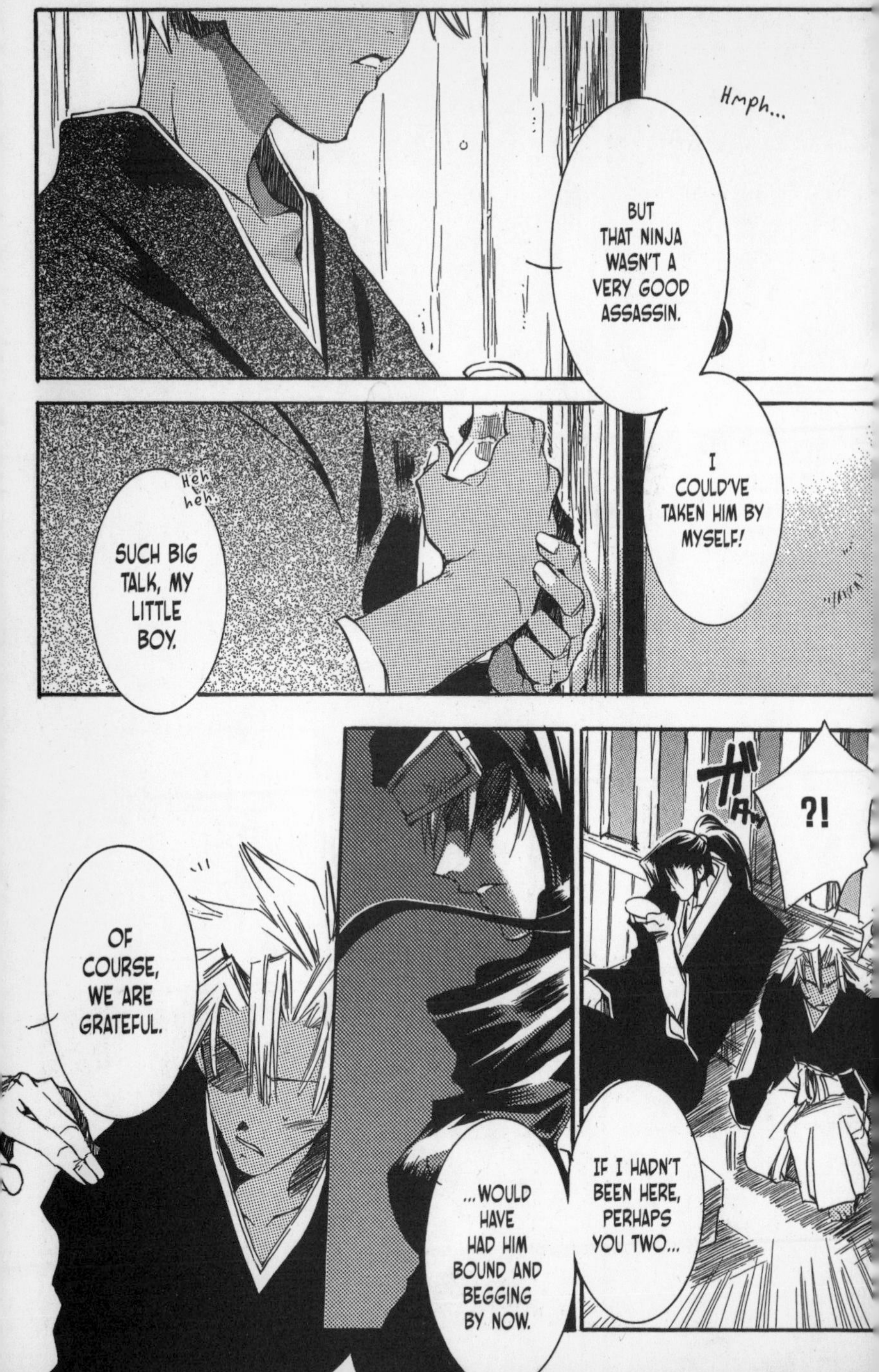
Hmph...
BUT THAT NINJA WASN'T A VERY GOOD ASSASSIN.
I COULD'VE TAKEN HIM BY MYSELF!
Heh heh.
SUCH BIG TALK, MY LITTLE BOY.
?!
IF I HADN'T BEEN HERE, PERHAPS YOU TWO...
...WOULD HAVE HAD HIM BOUND AND BEGGING BY NOW.
OF COURSE, WE ARE GRATEFUL.

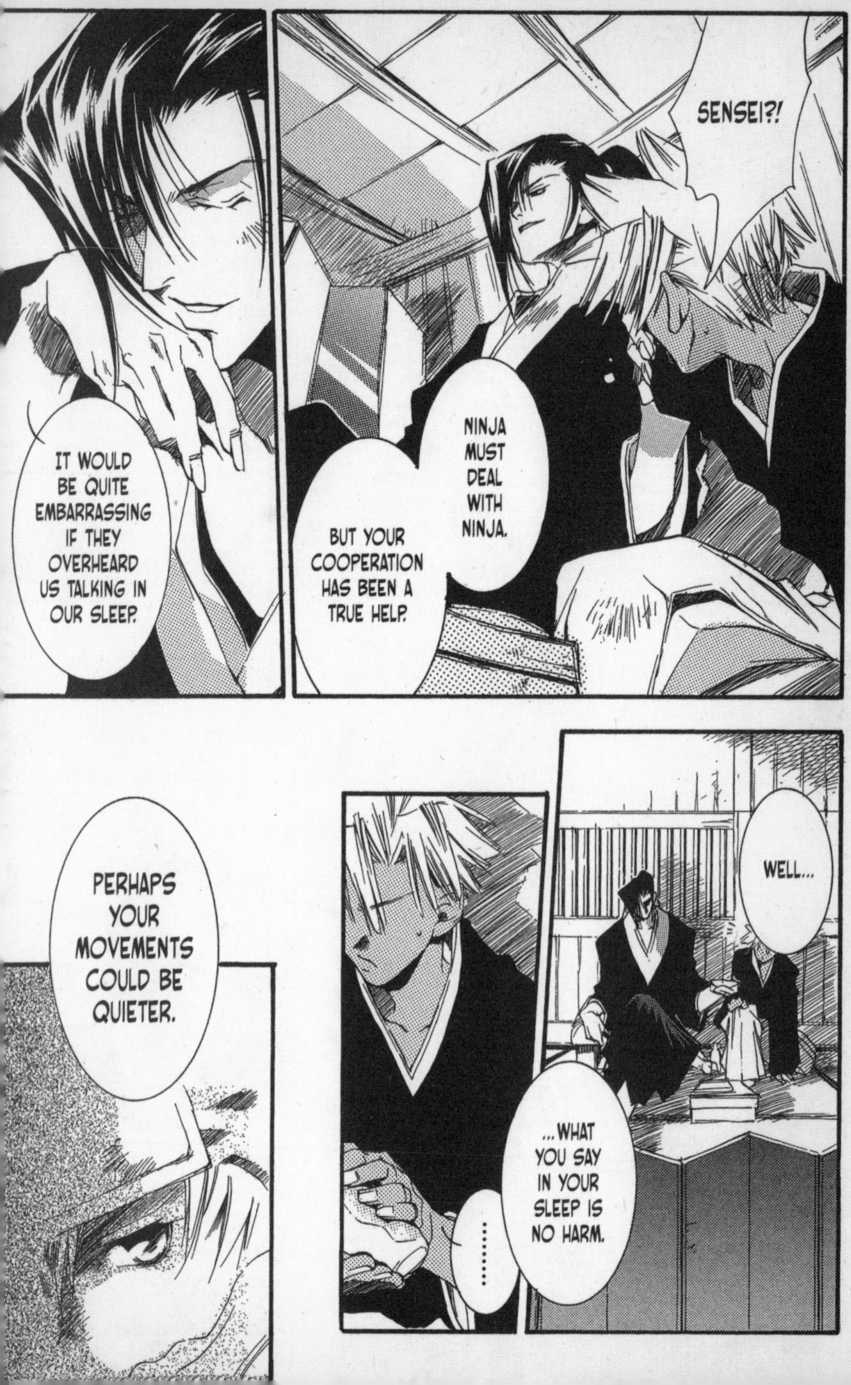
SENSEI?!
NINJA MUST DEAL WITH NINJA.
BUT YOUR COOPERATION HAS BEEN A TRUE HELP.
IT WOULD BE QUITE EMBARRASSING IF THEY OVERHEARD US TALKING IN OUR SLEEP.
WELL...
...WHAT YOU SAY IN YOUR SLEEP IS NO HARM.
....
PERHAPS YOUR MOVEMENTS COULD BE QUIETER.

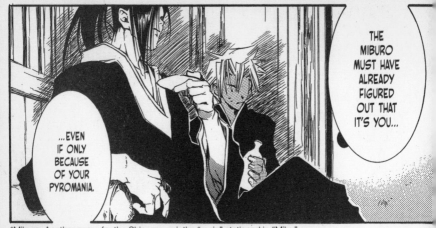

THE MIBURO MUST HAVE ALREADY FIGURED OUT THAT IT'S YOU...
...EVEN IF ONLY BECAUSE OF YOUR PYROMANIA.
I CAN'T HELP YOU IF YOU REVEAL YOURSELF.
AH. YOU'VE FINALLY SAID IT.
THAT *ITSELF* IS WHY...
...IT'S NOW EASIER FOR US TO MAKE OUR MOVE.
THEY KNOW WE ARE HERE, AND YET INSTEAD OF SETTING THEIR SOLDIERS UPON US THEY SEND *NINJA.*

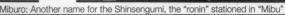

*Miburo: Another name for the Shinsengumi, the "ronin" stationed in "Mibu"

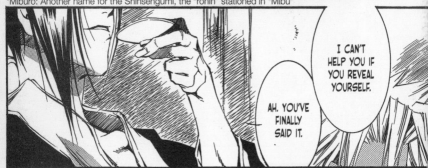

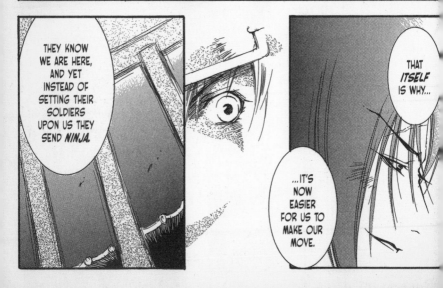

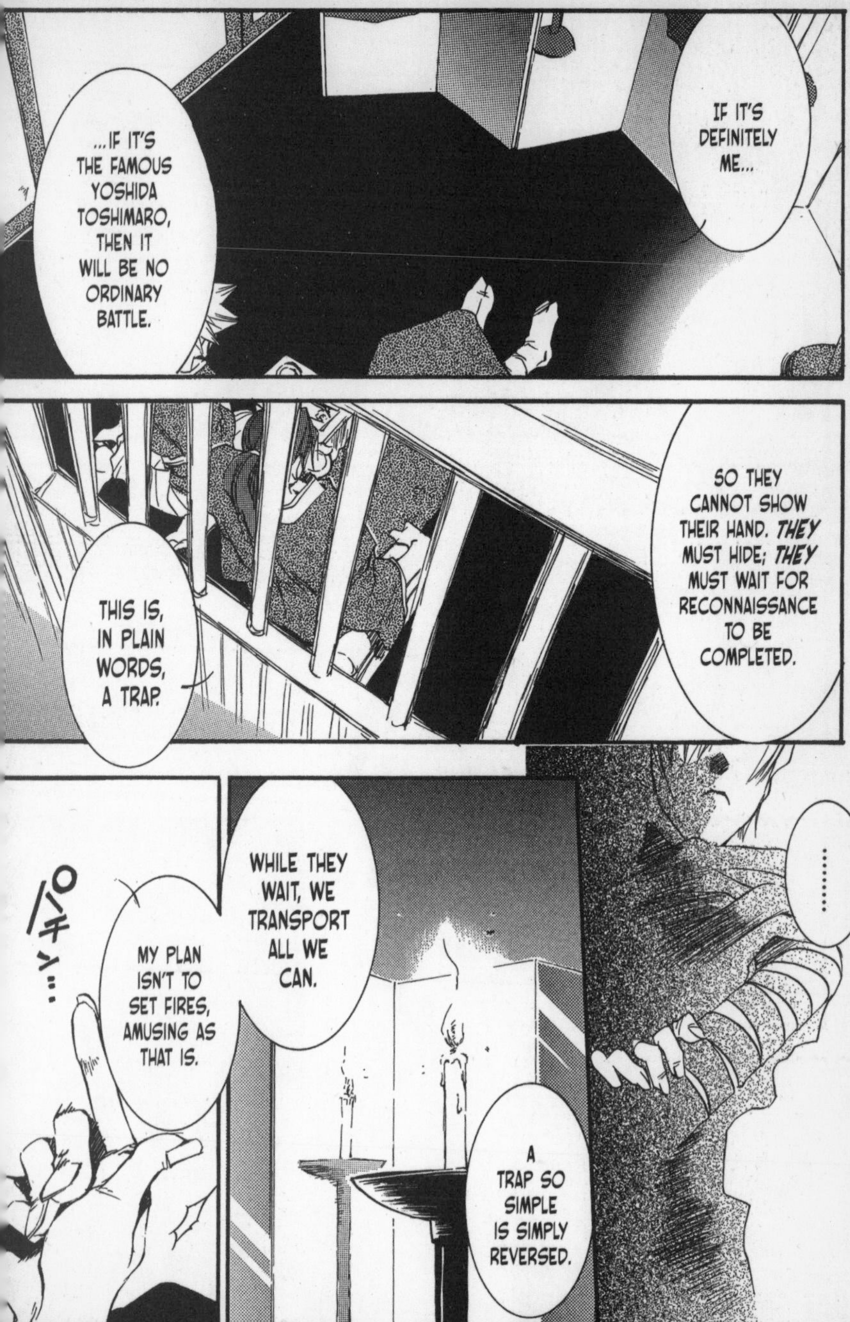
IF IT'S DEFINITELY ME...
...IF IT'S THE FAMOUS YOSHIDA TOSHIMARO, THEN IT WILL BE NO ORDINARY BATTLE.
SO THEY CANNOT SHOW THEIR HAND. *THEY* MUST HIDE; *THEY* MUST WAIT FOR RECONNAISSANCE TO BE COMPLETED.
THIS IS, IN PLAIN WORDS, A TRAP.
......
A TRAP SO SIMPLE IS SIMPLY REVERSED.
WHILE THEY WAIT, WE TRANSPORT ALL WE CAN.
MY PLAN ISN'T TO SET FIRES, AMUSING AS THAT IS.
パキン…

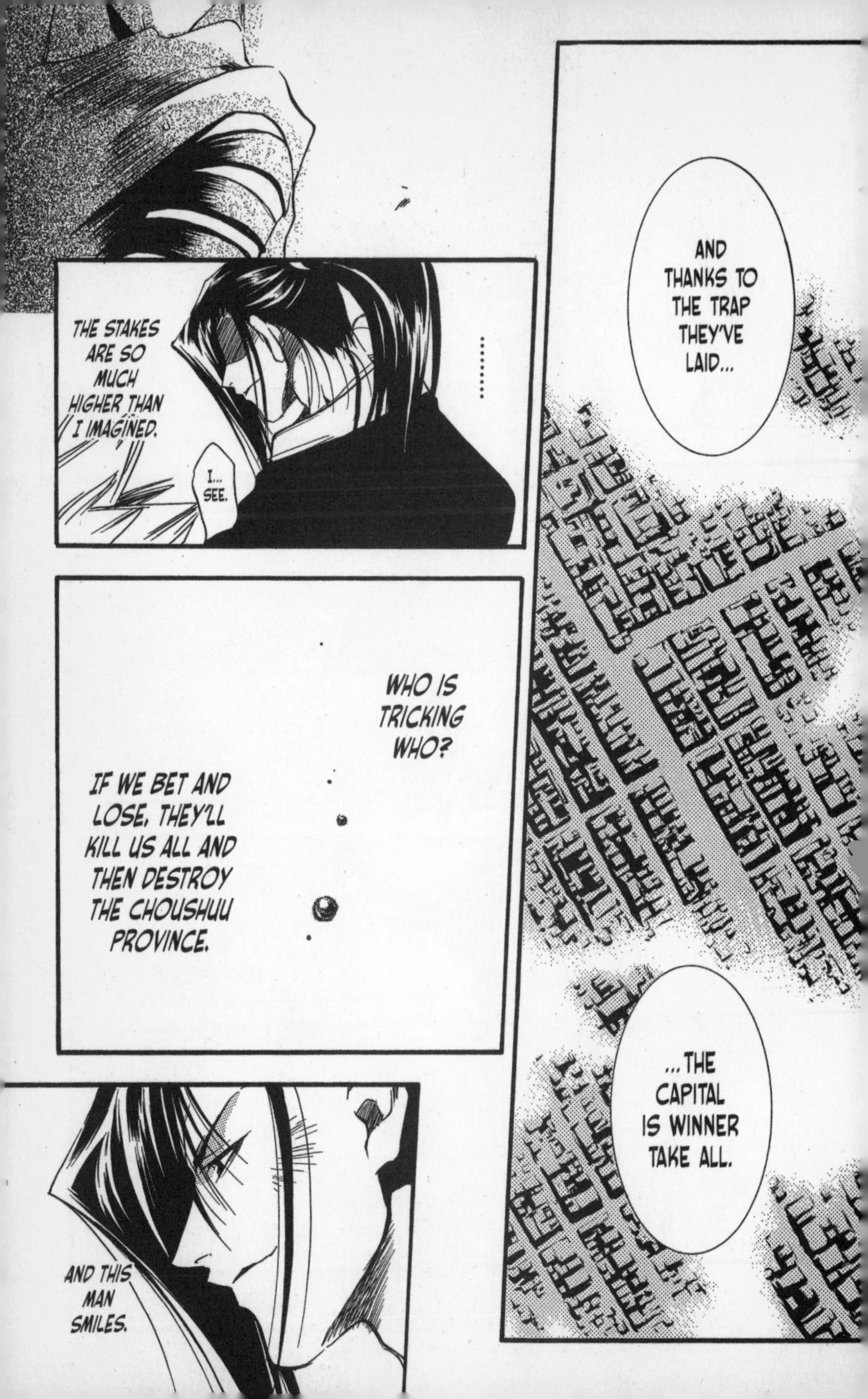
AND THANKS TO THE TRAP THEY'VE LAID...
...THE CAPITAL IS WINNER TAKE ALL.
THE STAKES ARE SO MUCH HIGHER THAN I IMAGINED.
I... SEE.
....
WHO IS TRICKING WHO?
IF WE BET AND LOSE, THEY'LL KILL US ALL AND THEN DESTROY THE CHOUSHUU PROVINCE.
AND THIS MAN SMILES.

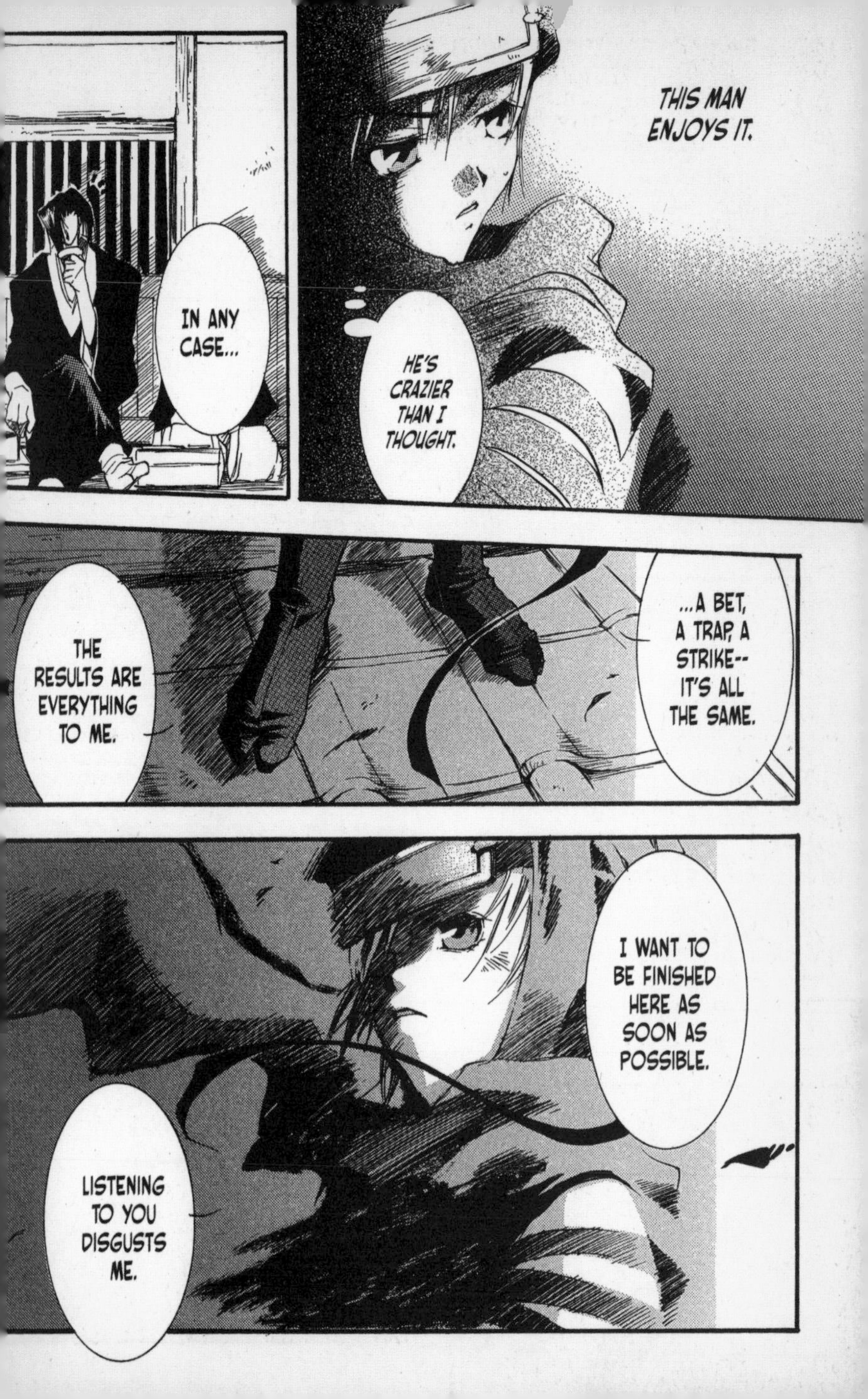
THIS MAN ENJOYS IT.
HE'S CRAZIER THAN I THOUGHT.
IN ANY CASE...
...A BET, A TRAP, A STRIKE-- IT'S ALL THE SAME.
THE RESULTS ARE EVERYTHING TO ME.
I WANT TO BE FINISHED HERE AS SOON AS POSSIBLE.
LISTENING TO YOU DISGUSTS ME.

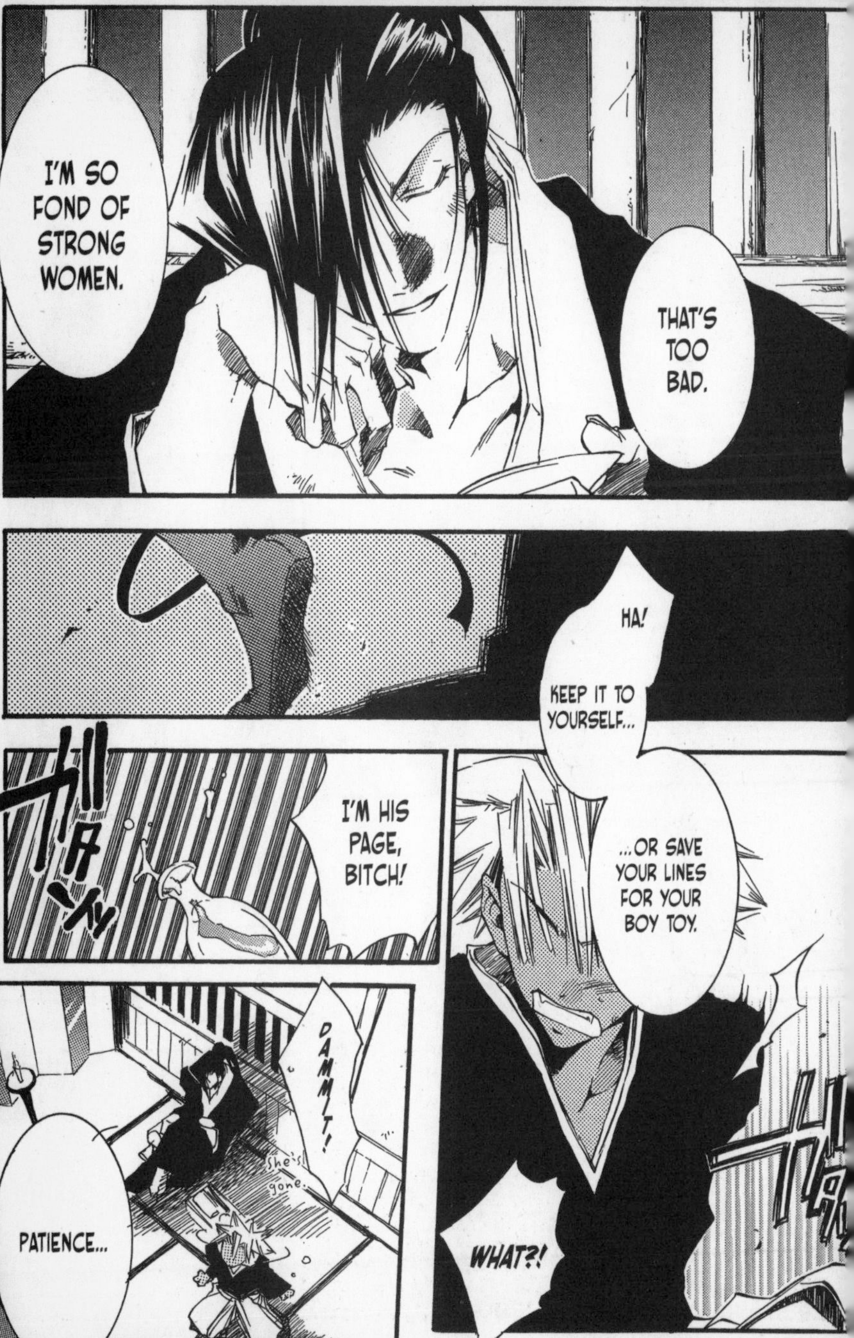
I'M SO FOND OF STRONG WOMEN.
THAT'S TOO BAD.
HA!
KEEP IT TO YOURSELF...
...OR SAVE YOUR LINES FOR YOUR BOY TOY.
WHAT?!
I'M HIS PAGE, BITCH!
DAMMIT!
She's gone.
PATIENCE...

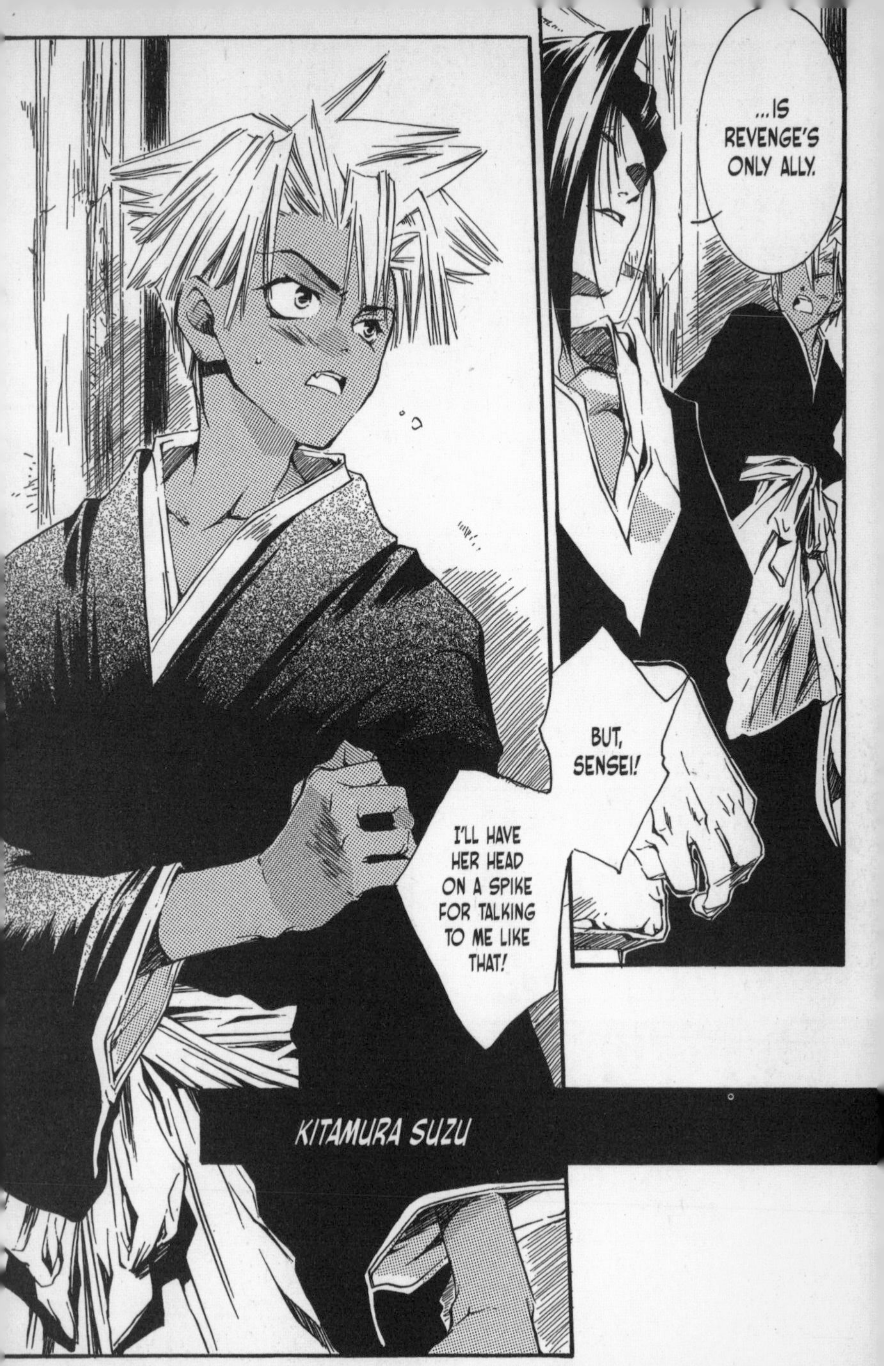
...IS REVENGE'S ONLY ALLY.
BUT, SENSEI!
I'LL HAVE HER HEAD ON A SPIKE FOR TALKING TO ME LIKE THAT!
KITAMURA SUZU

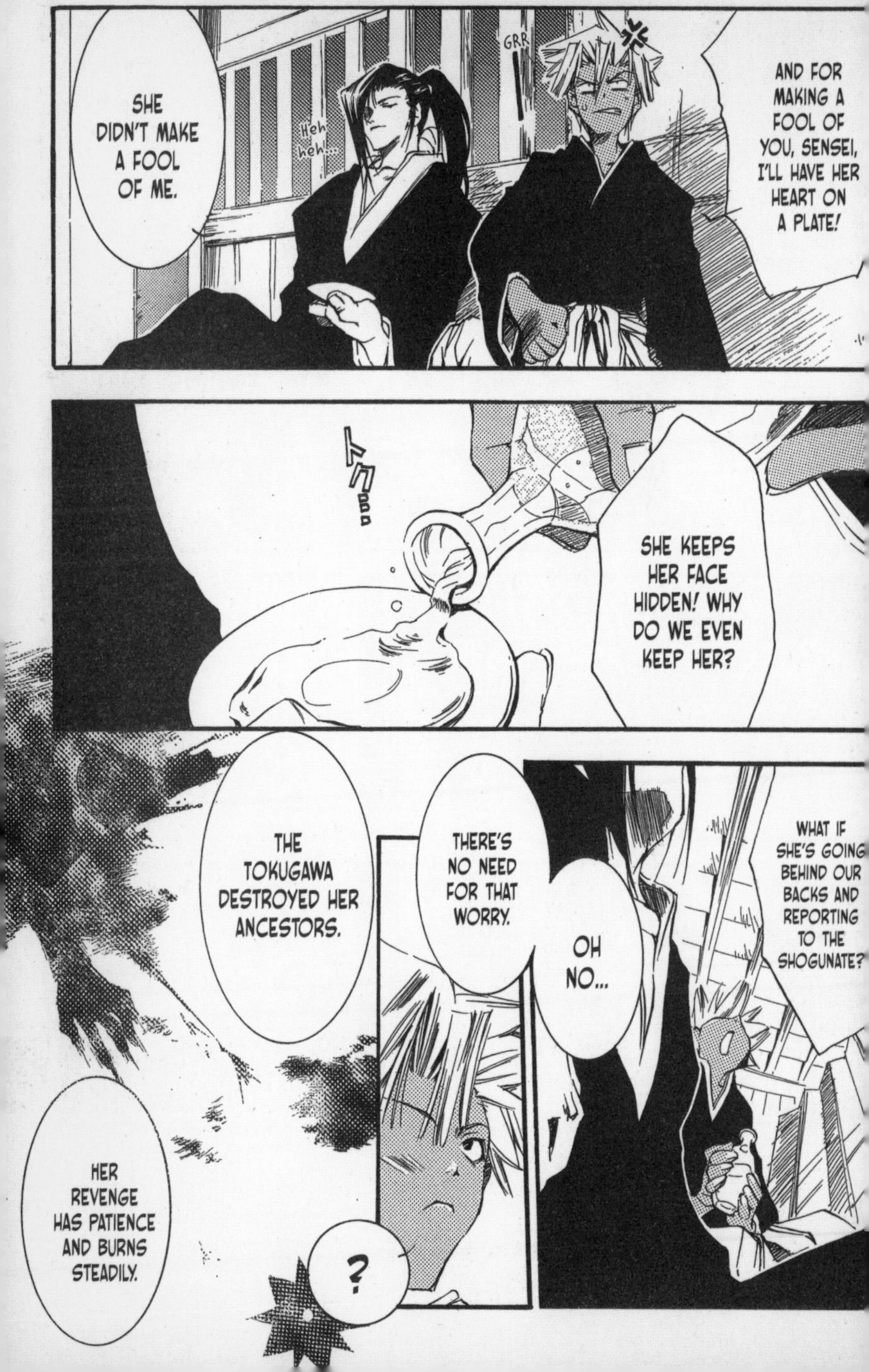
AND FOR MAKING A FOOL OF YOU, SENSEI, I'LL HAVE HER HEART ON A PLATE!
GRR
Heh heh!...
SHE DIDN'T MAKE A FOOL OF ME.
SHE KEEPS HER FACE HIDDEN! WHY DO WE EVEN KEEP HER?
トク
WHAT IF SHE'S GOING BEHIND OUR BACKS AND REPORTING TO THE SHOGUNATE?
OH NO...
THERE'S NO NEED FOR THAT WORRY.
THE TOKUGAWA DESTROYED HER ANCESTORS.
?
HER REVENGE HAS PATIENCE AND BURNS STEADILY.

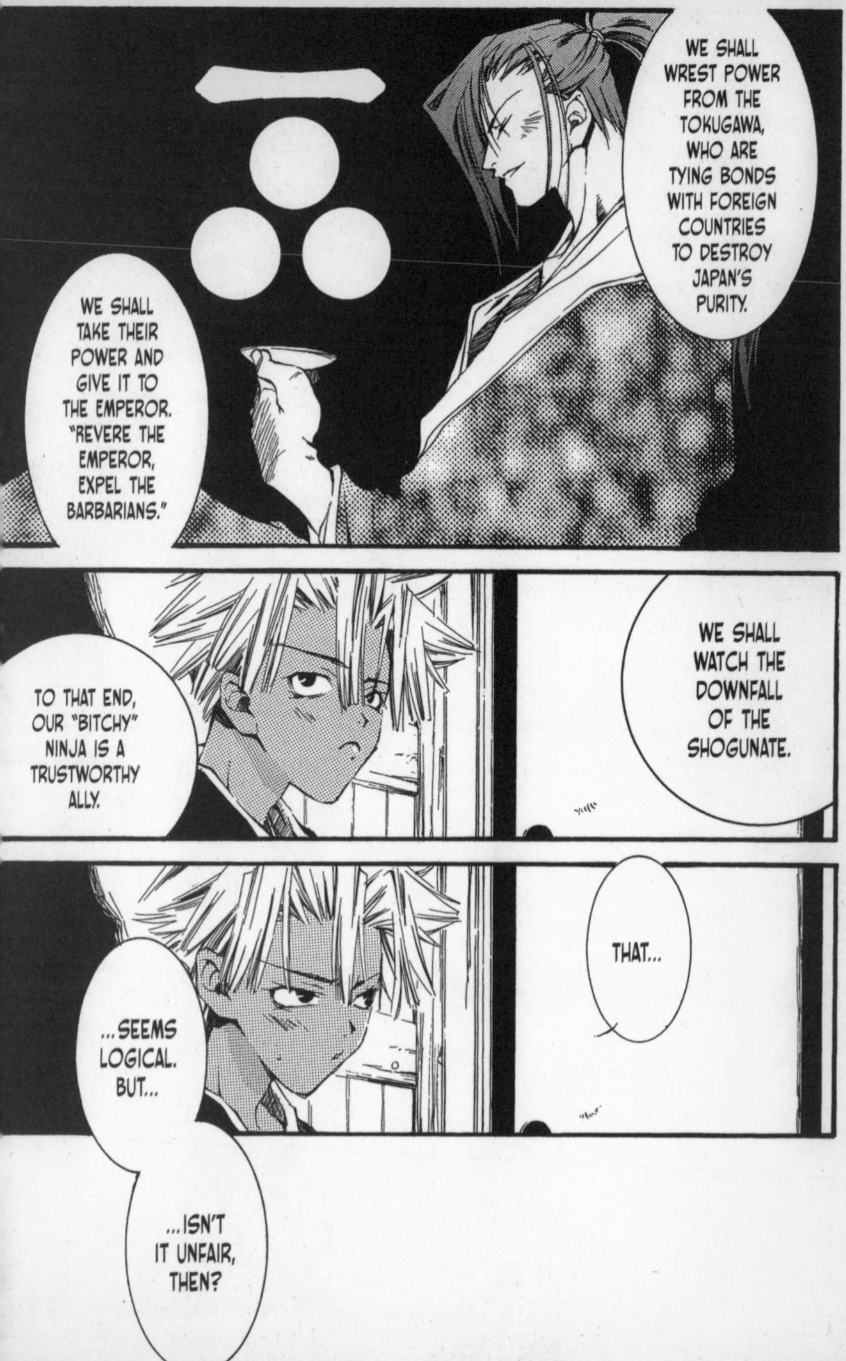
WE SHALL WREST POWER FROM THE TOKUGAWA, WHO ARE TYING BONDS WITH FOREIGN COUNTRIES TO DESTROY JAPAN'S PURITY.
WE SHALL TAKE THEIR POWER AND GIVE IT TO THE EMPEROR. "REVERE THE EMPEROR, EXPEL THE BARBARIANS."
WE SHALL WATCH THE DOWNFALL OF THE SHOGUNATE.
TO THAT END, OUR "BITCHY" NINJA IS A TRUSTWORTHY ALLY.
THAT...
...SEEMS LOGICAL. BUT...
...ISN'T IT UNFAIR, THEN?

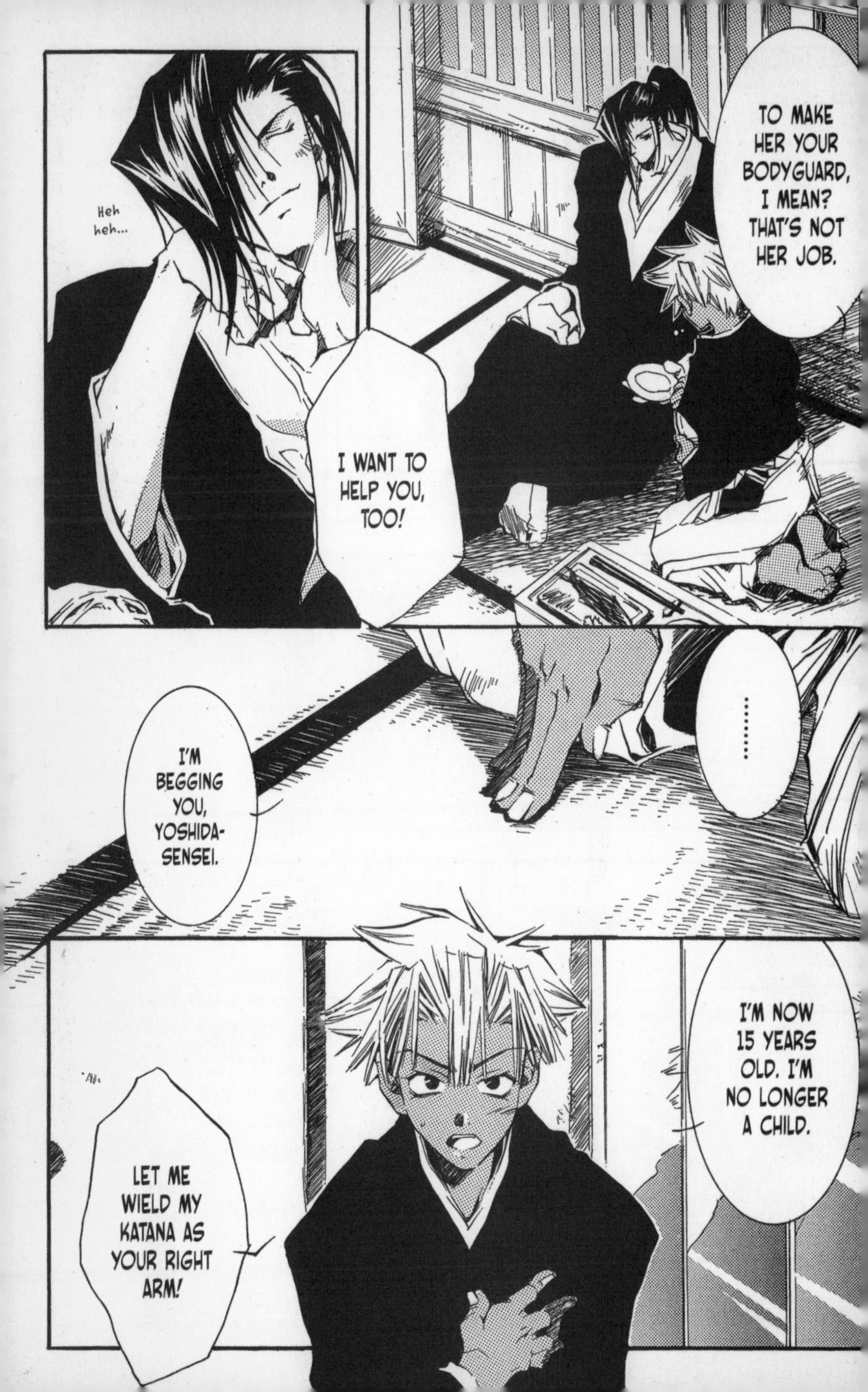
TO MAKE HER YOUR BODYGUARD, I MEAN? THAT'S NOT HER JOB.
I WANT TO HELP YOU, TOO!
Heh heh...
......
I'M BEGGING YOU, YOSHIDA-SENSEI.
I'M NOW 15 YEARS OLD. I'M NO LONGER A CHILD.
LET ME WIELD MY KATANA AS YOUR RIGHT ARM!

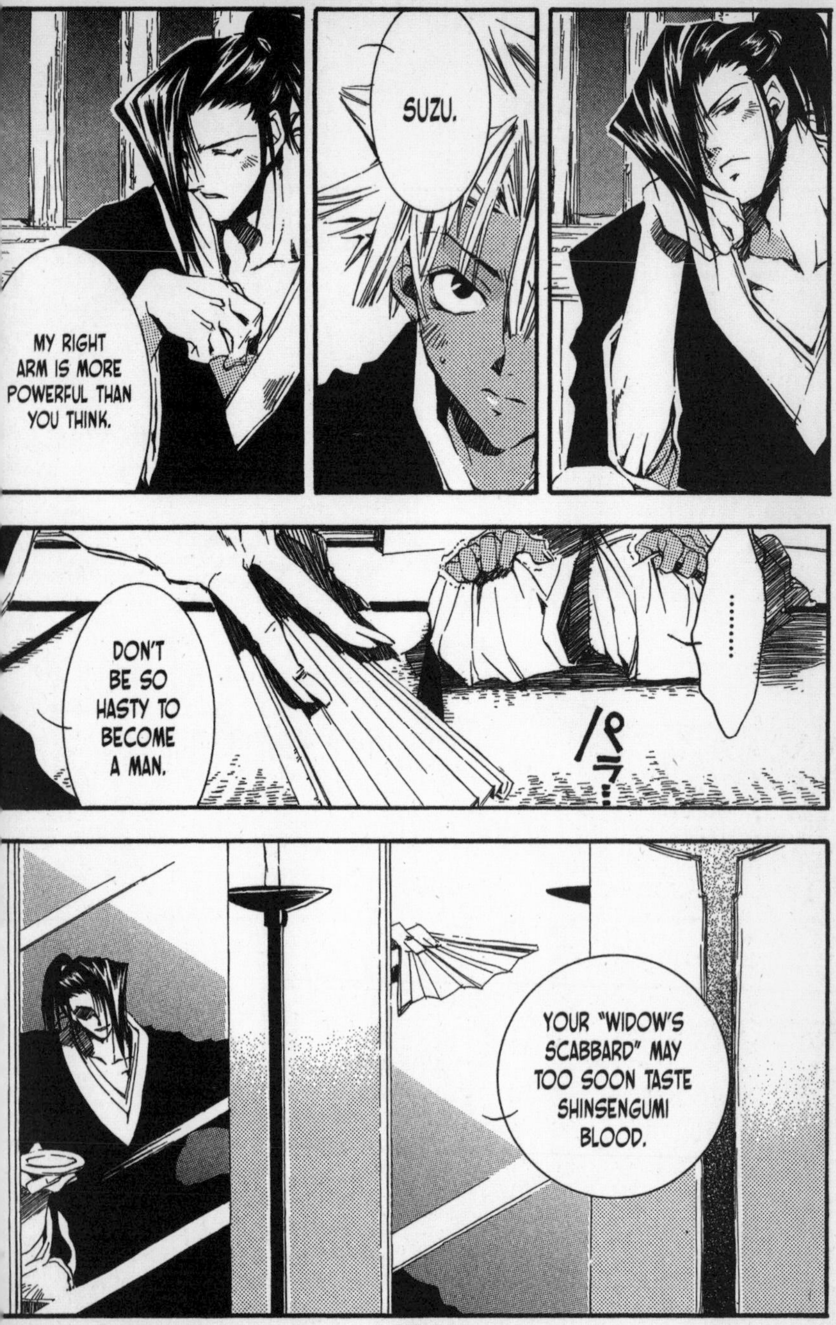
SUZU.
MY RIGHT ARM IS MORE POWERFUL THAN YOU THINK.
……
パラ…
DON'T BE SO HASTY TO BECOME A MAN.
YOUR "WIDOW'S SCABBARD" MAY TOO SOON TASTE SHINSENGUMI BLOOD.

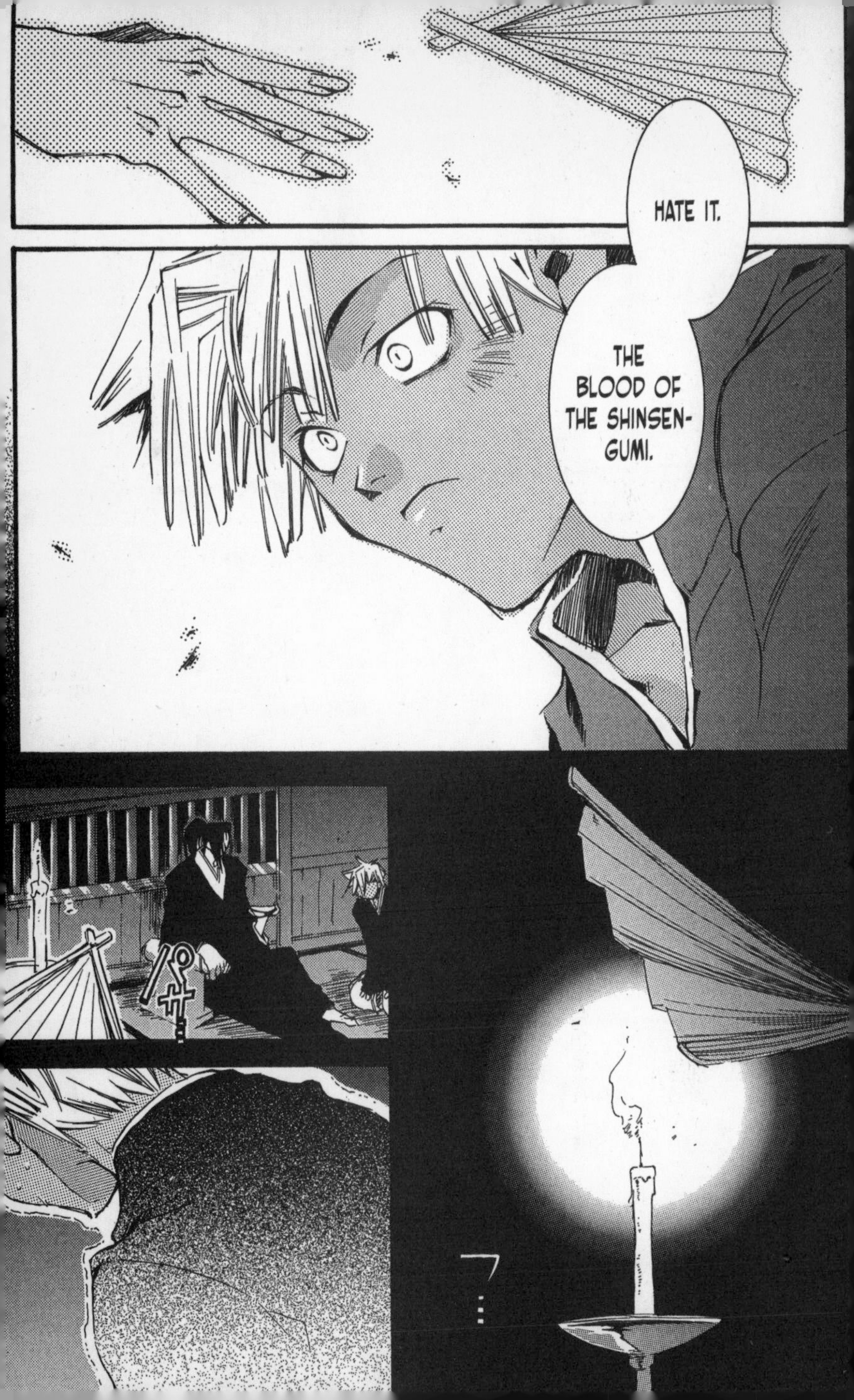
HATE IT.
THE BLOOD OF THE SHINSEN-GUMI.

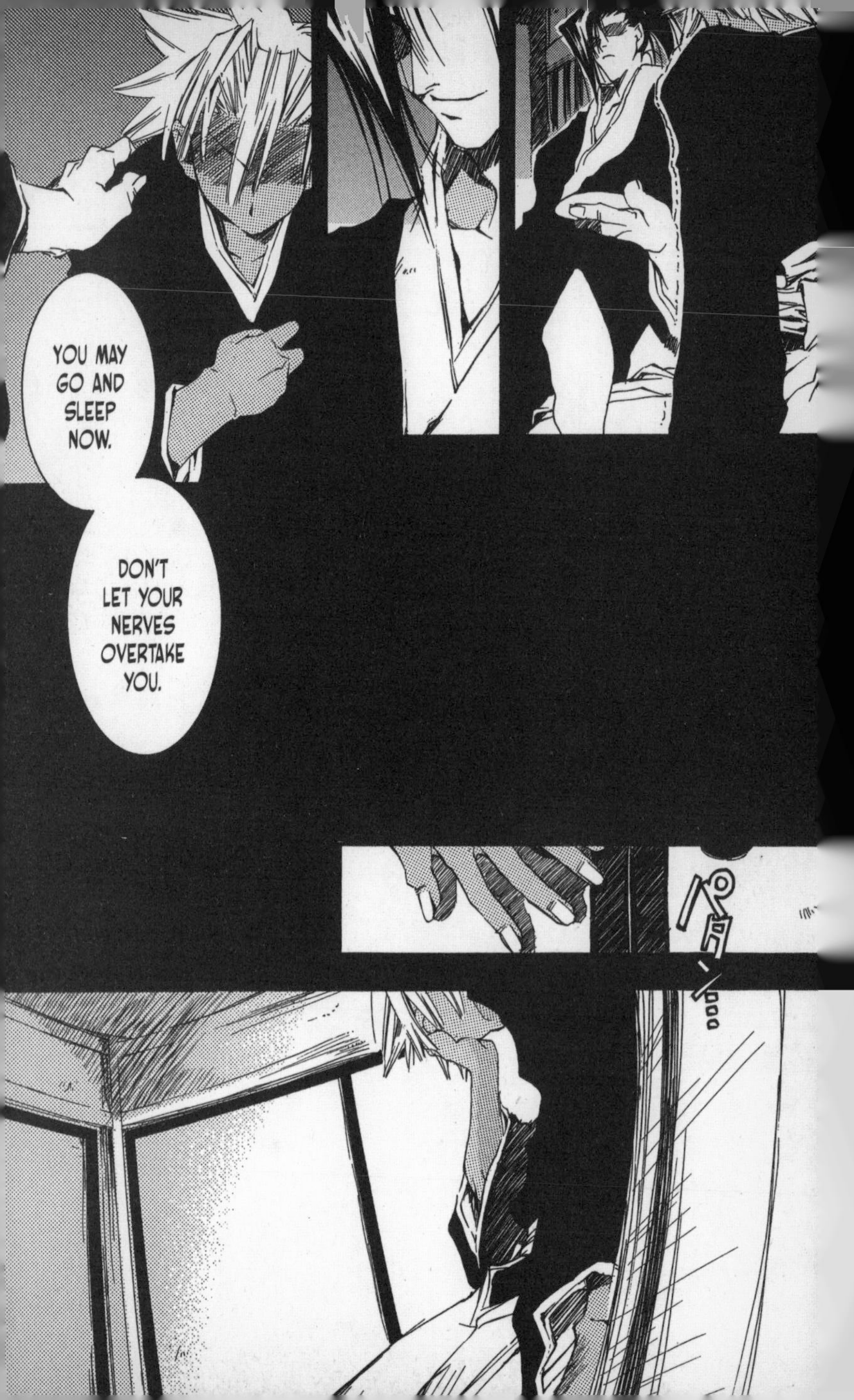
YOU MAY GO AND SLEEP NOW.
DON'T LET YOUR NERVES OVERTAKE YOU.

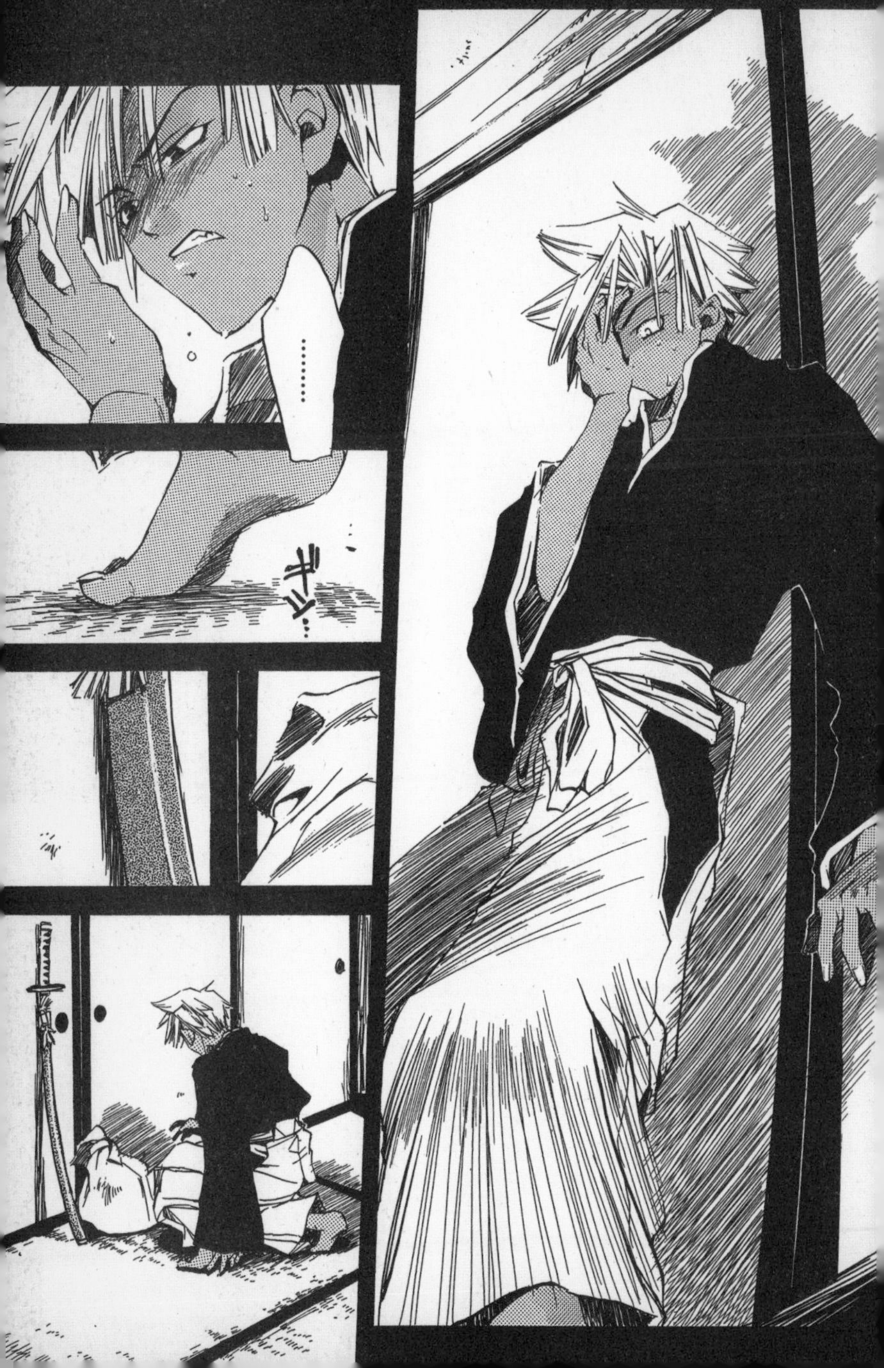
....
ギシ...

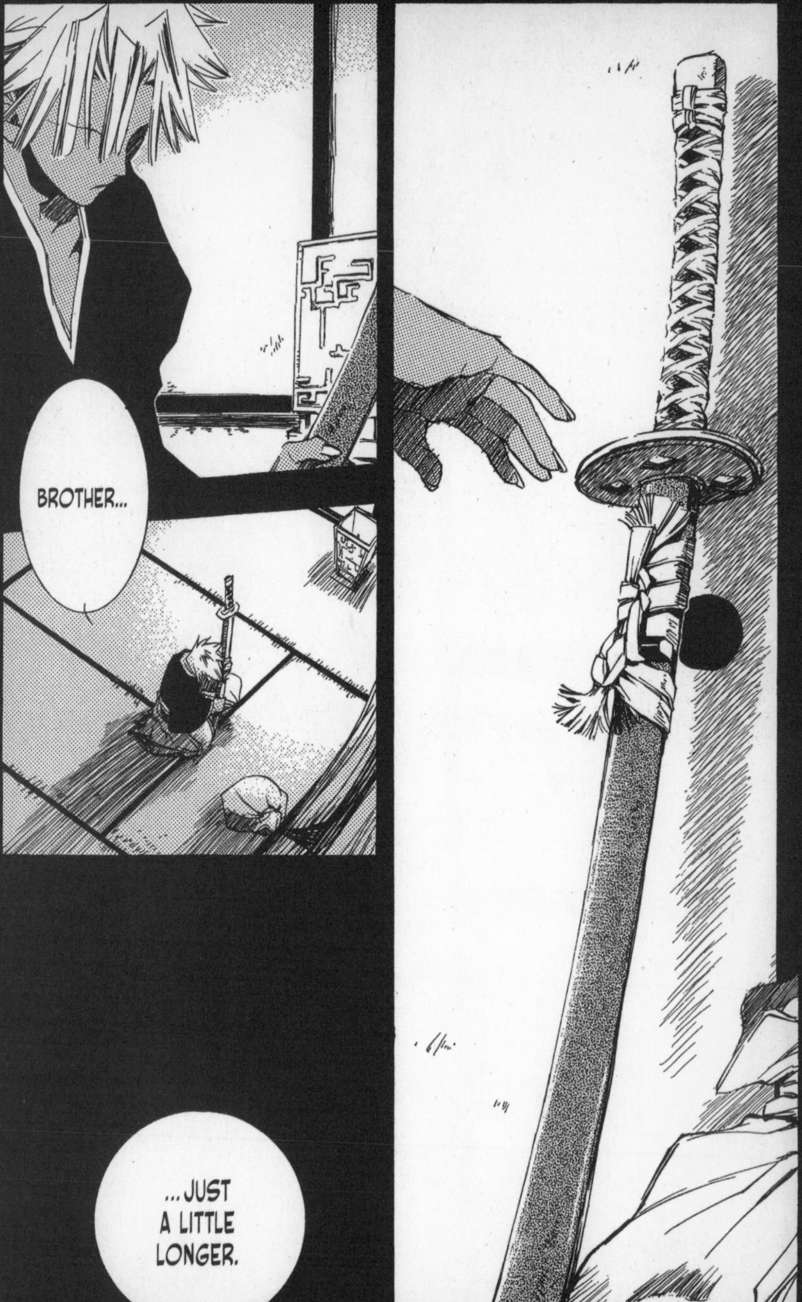
BROTHER...
...JUST A LITTLE LONGER.

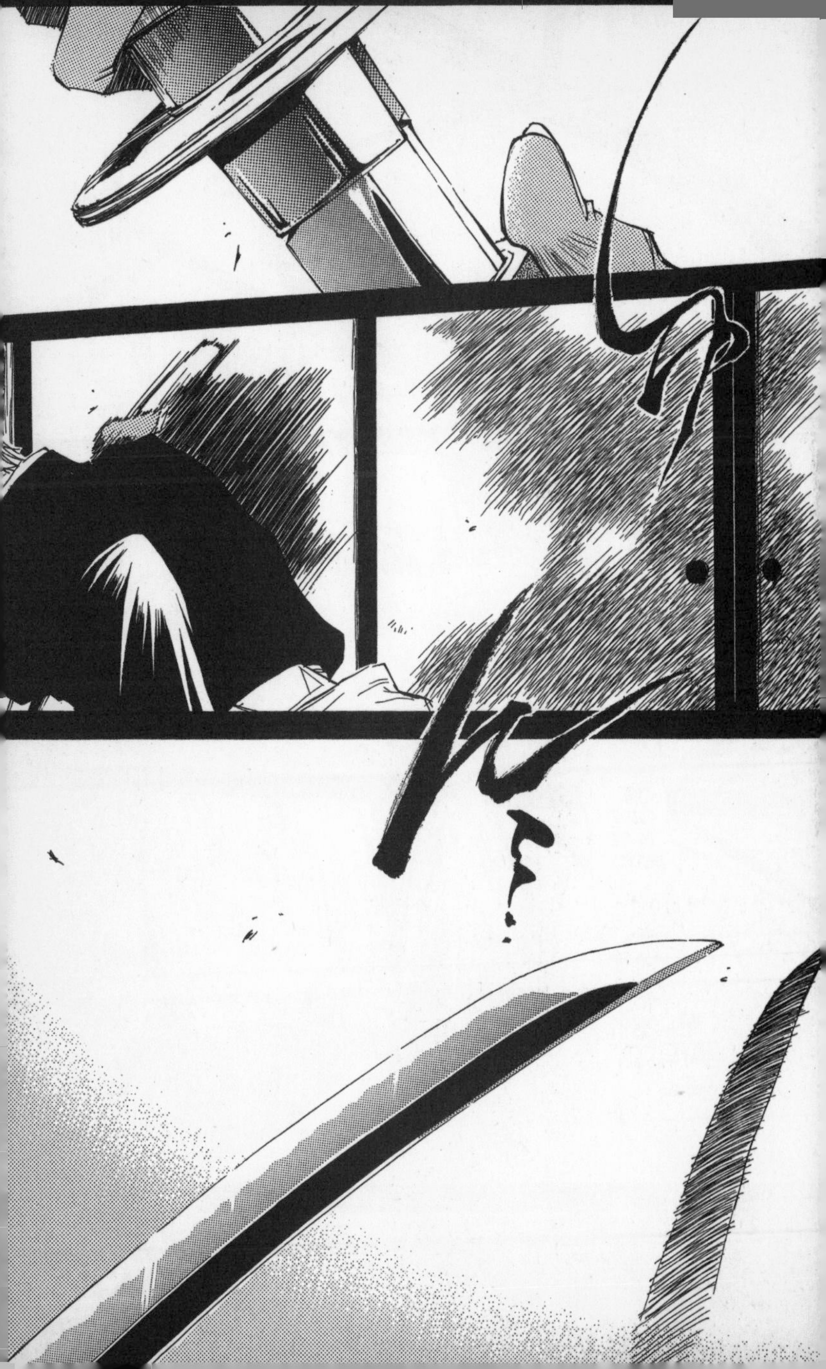

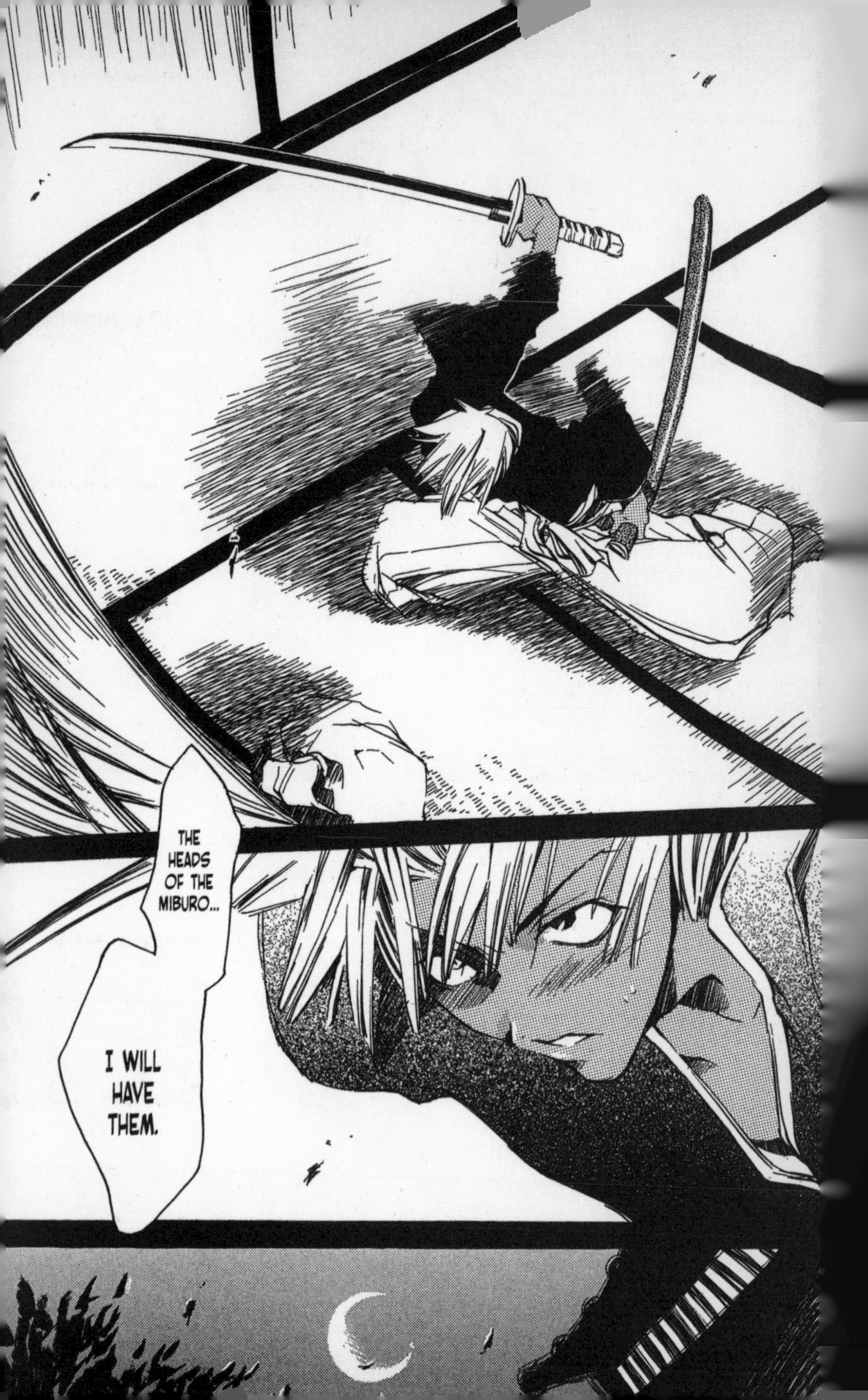
THE HEADS OF THE MIBURO...
I WILL HAVE THEM.

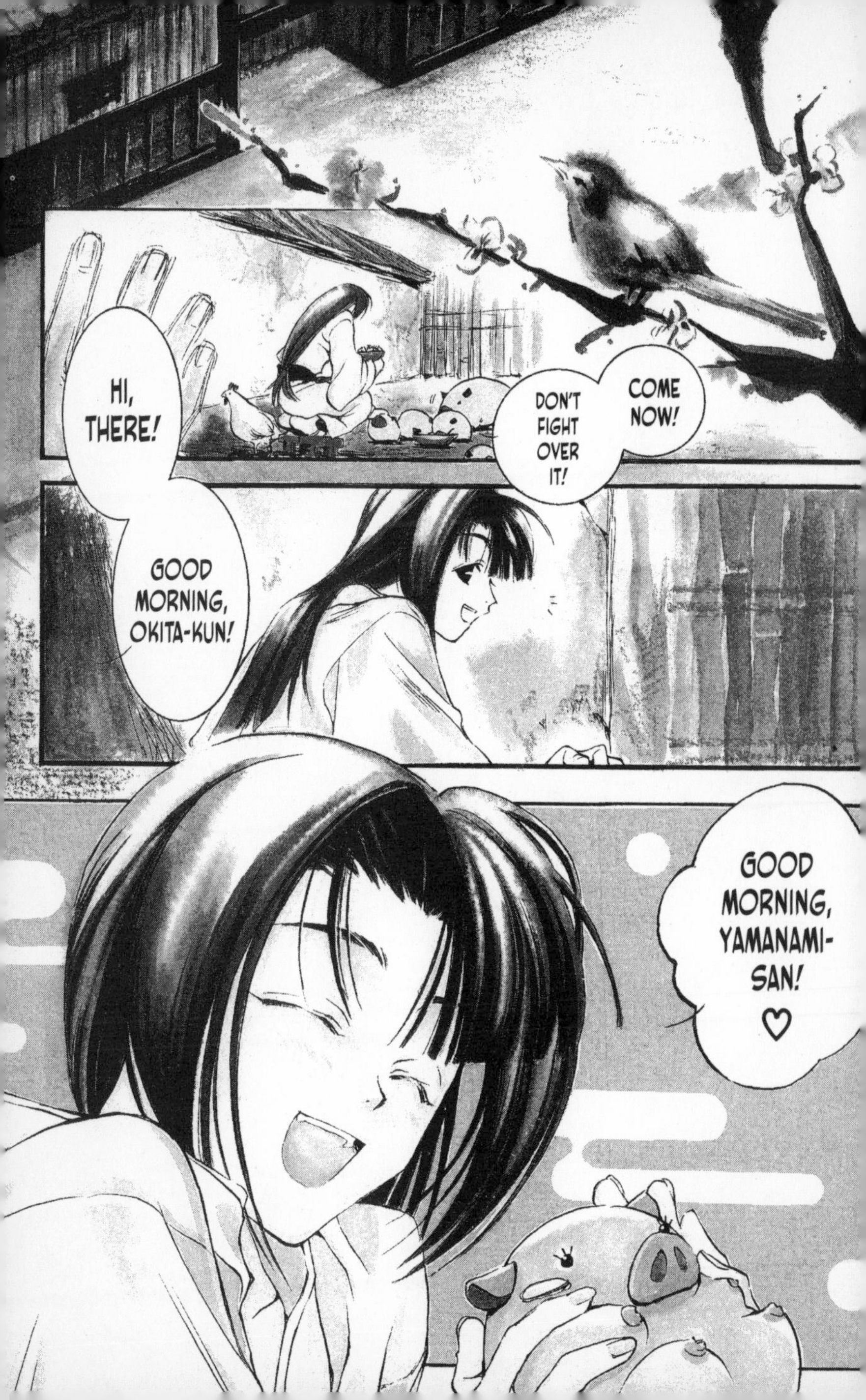
COME NOW!
DON'T FIGHT OVER IT!
HI, THERE!
GOOD MORNING, OKITA-KUN!
GOOD MORNING, YAMANAMI-SAN! ♡

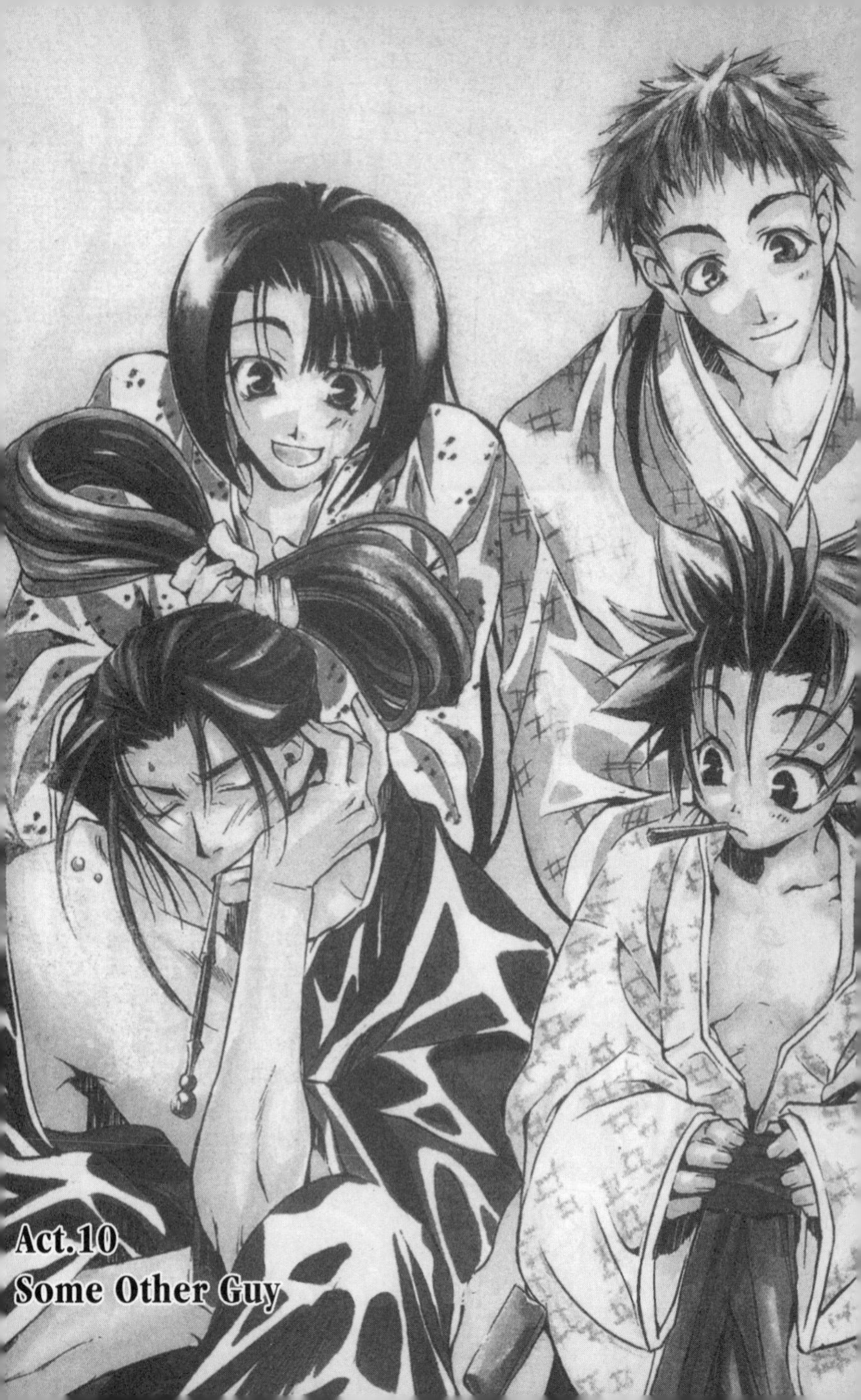

Act.10
Some Other Guy

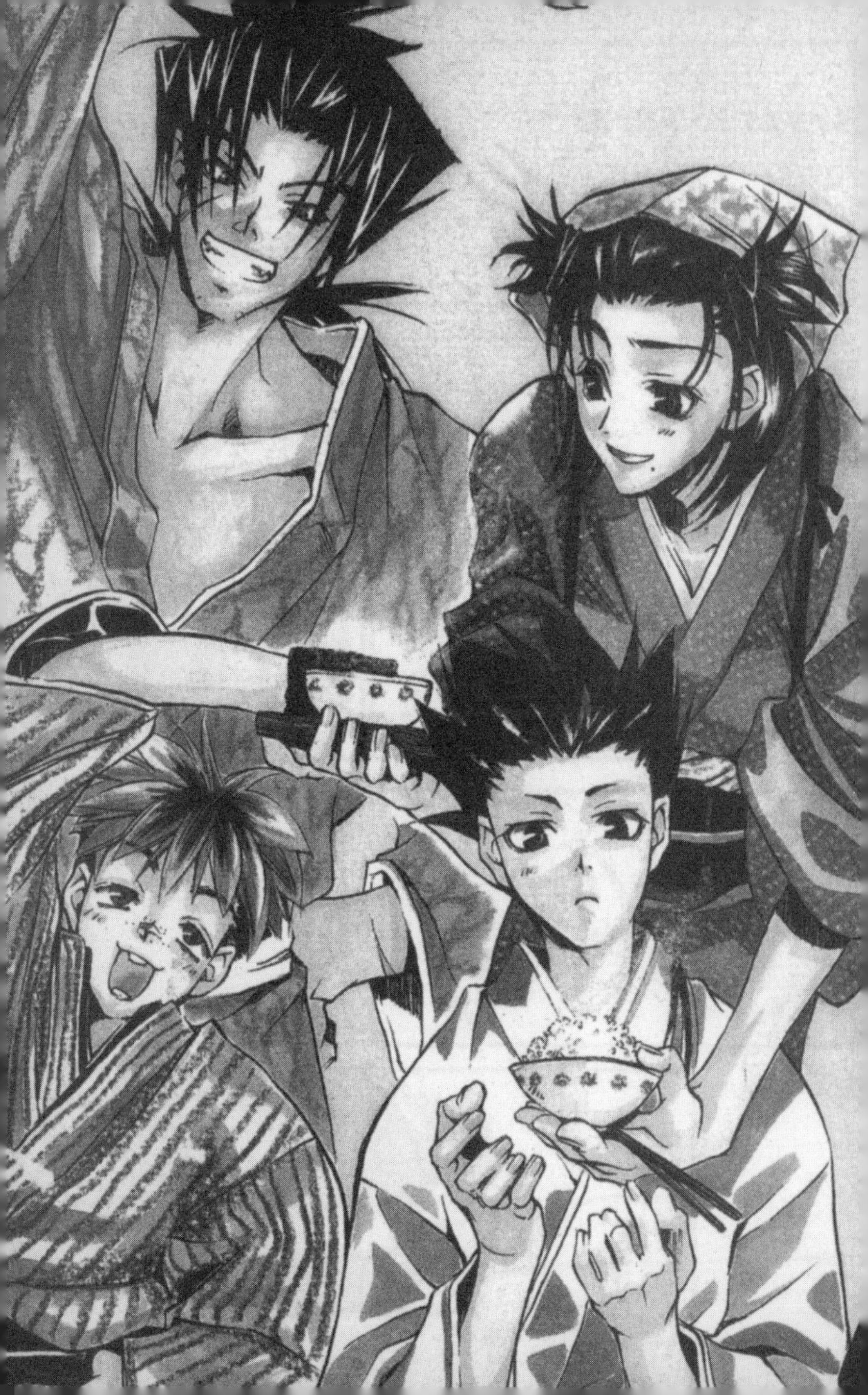

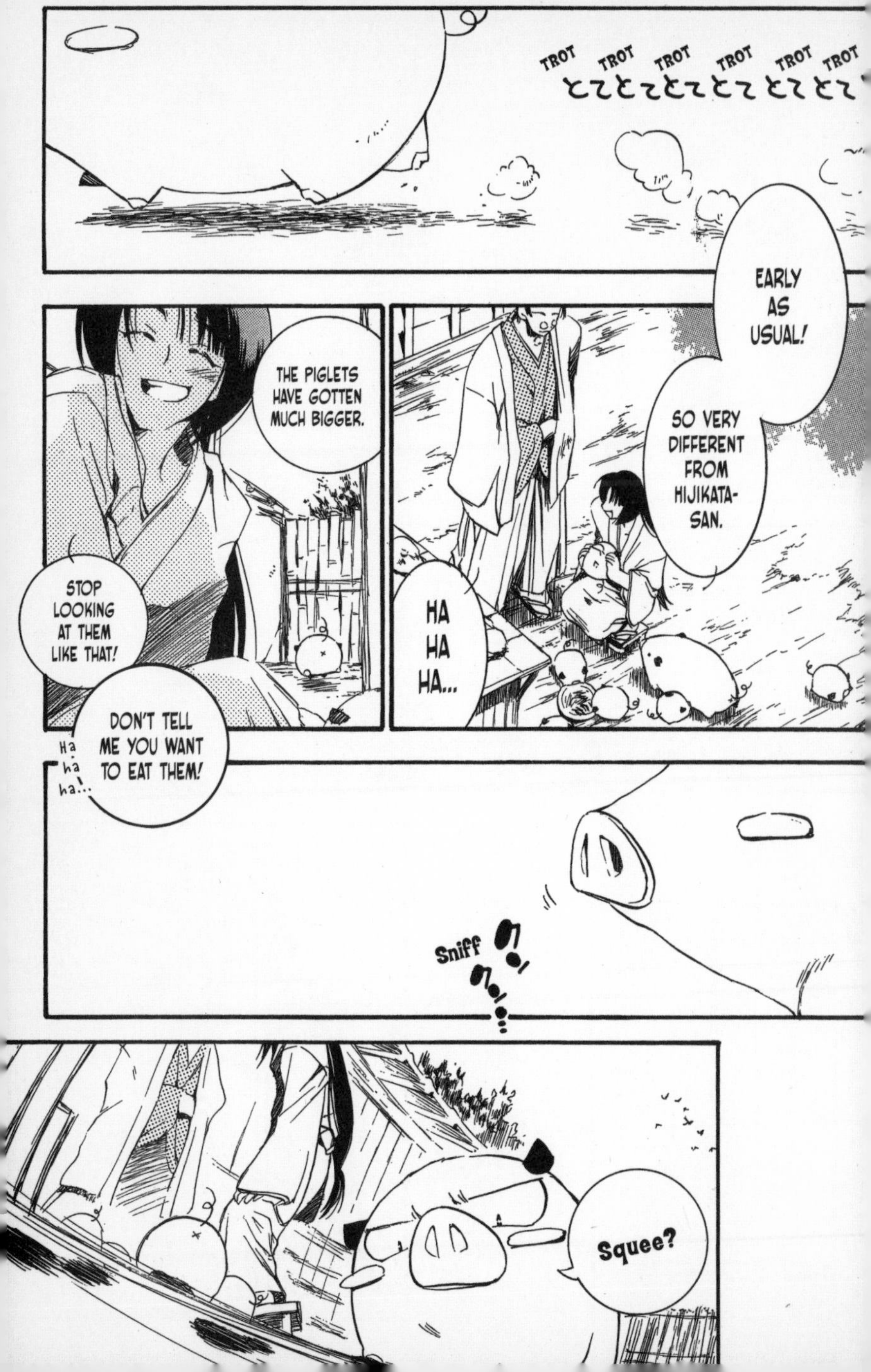
TROT TROT TROT TROT TROT TROT
とてとてとてとてとてとて
EARLY AS USUAL!
SO VERY DIFFERENT FROM HIJIKATA-SAN.
HA HA HA...
THE PIGLETS HAVE GOTTEN MUCH BIGGER.
STOP LOOKING AT THEM LIKE THAT!
DON'T TELL ME YOU WANT TO EAT THEM!
Ha ha ha...
Sniff
Squee?

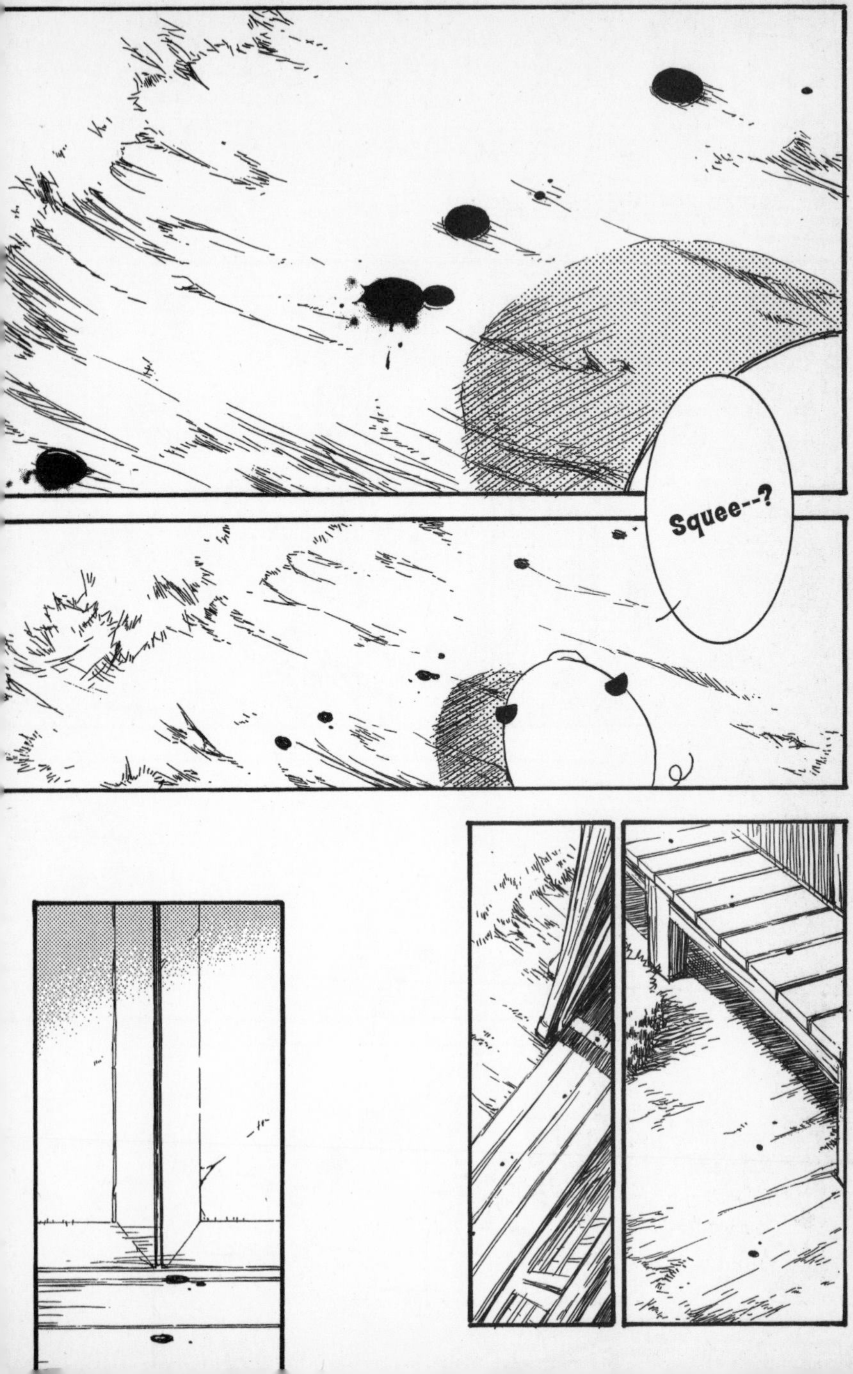
Squee--?

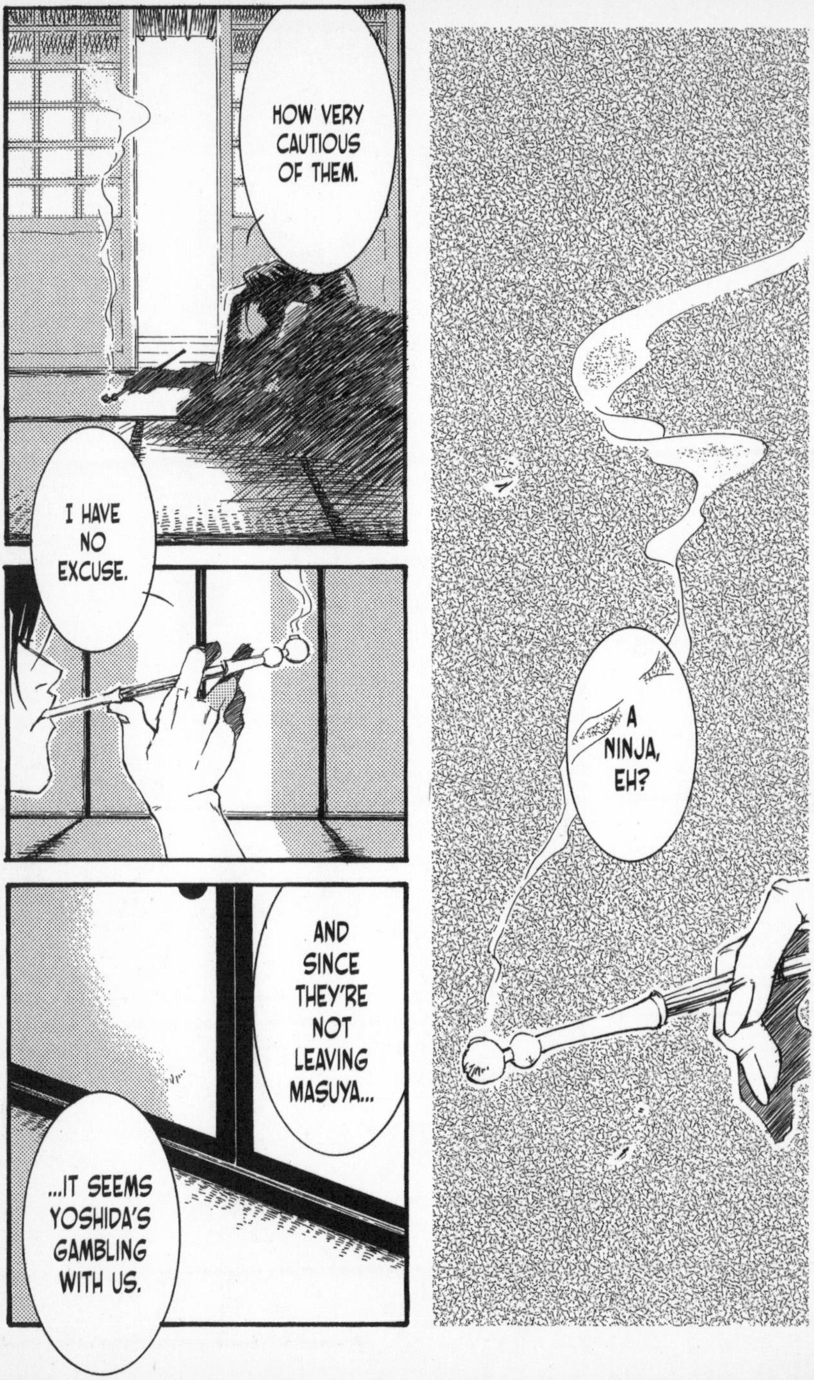
A NINJA, EH?
HOW VERY CAUTIOUS OF THEM.
I HAVE NO EXCUSE.
AND SINCE THEY'RE NOT LEAVING MASUYA...
...IT SEEMS YOSHIDA'S GAMBLING WITH US.

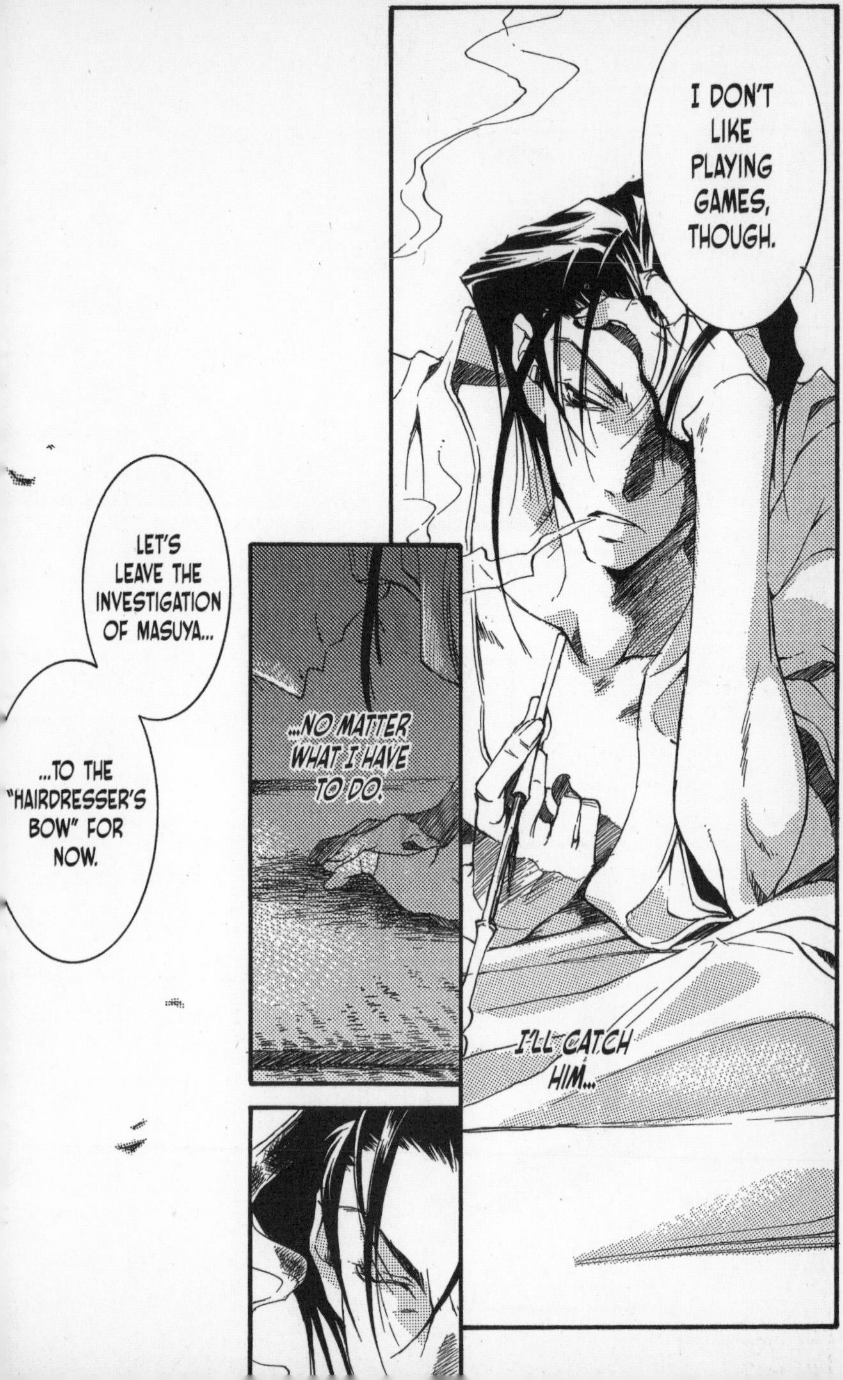
I DON'T LIKE PLAYING GAMES, THOUGH.
I'LL CATCH HIM...
...NO MATTER WHAT I HAVE TO DO.
LET'S LEAVE THE INVESTIGATION OF MASUYA...
...TO THE "HAIRDRESSER'S BOW" FOR NOW.

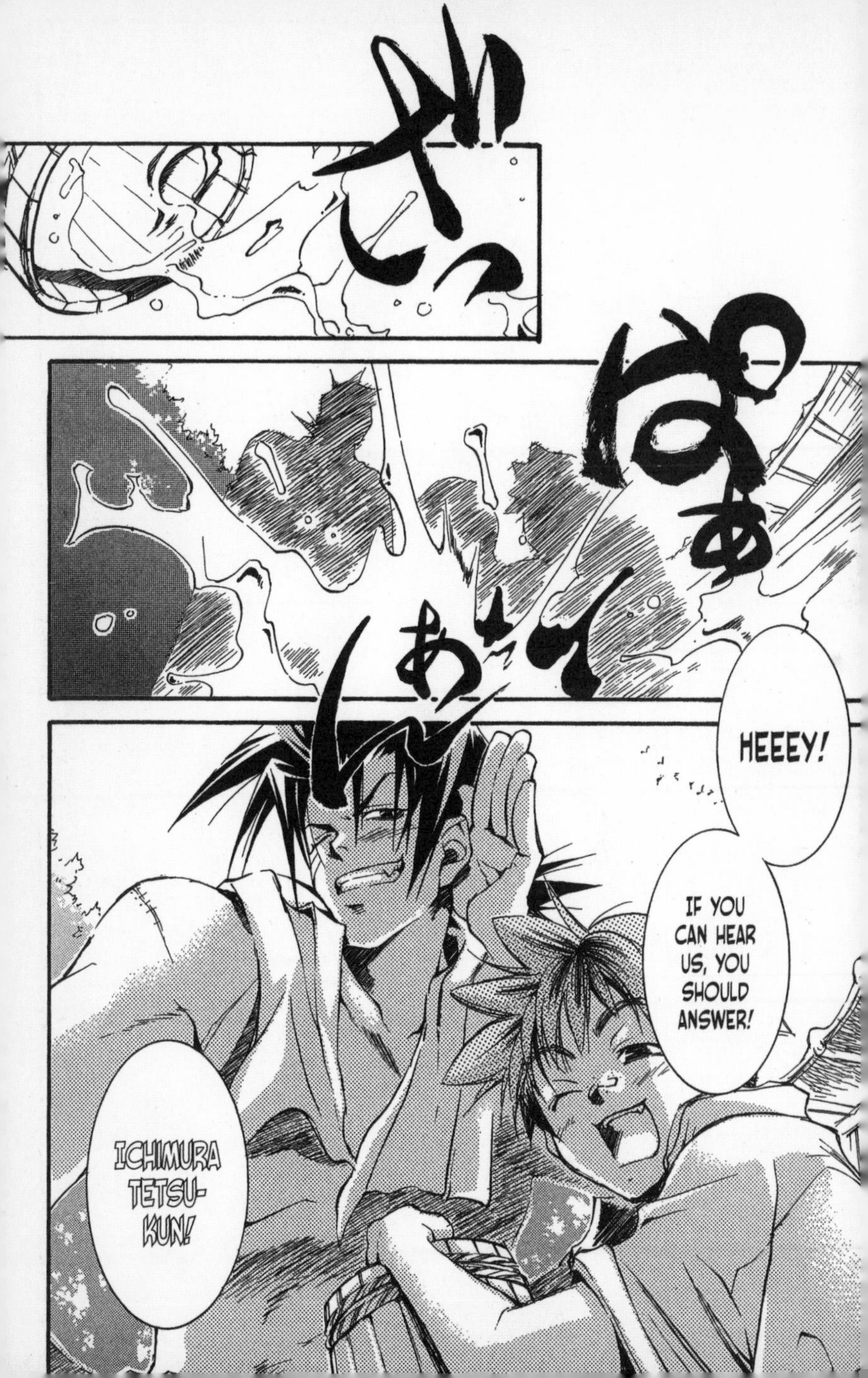

HEEEY!
IF YOU CAN HEAR US, YOU SHOULD ANSWER!
ICHIMURA TETSU-KUN!

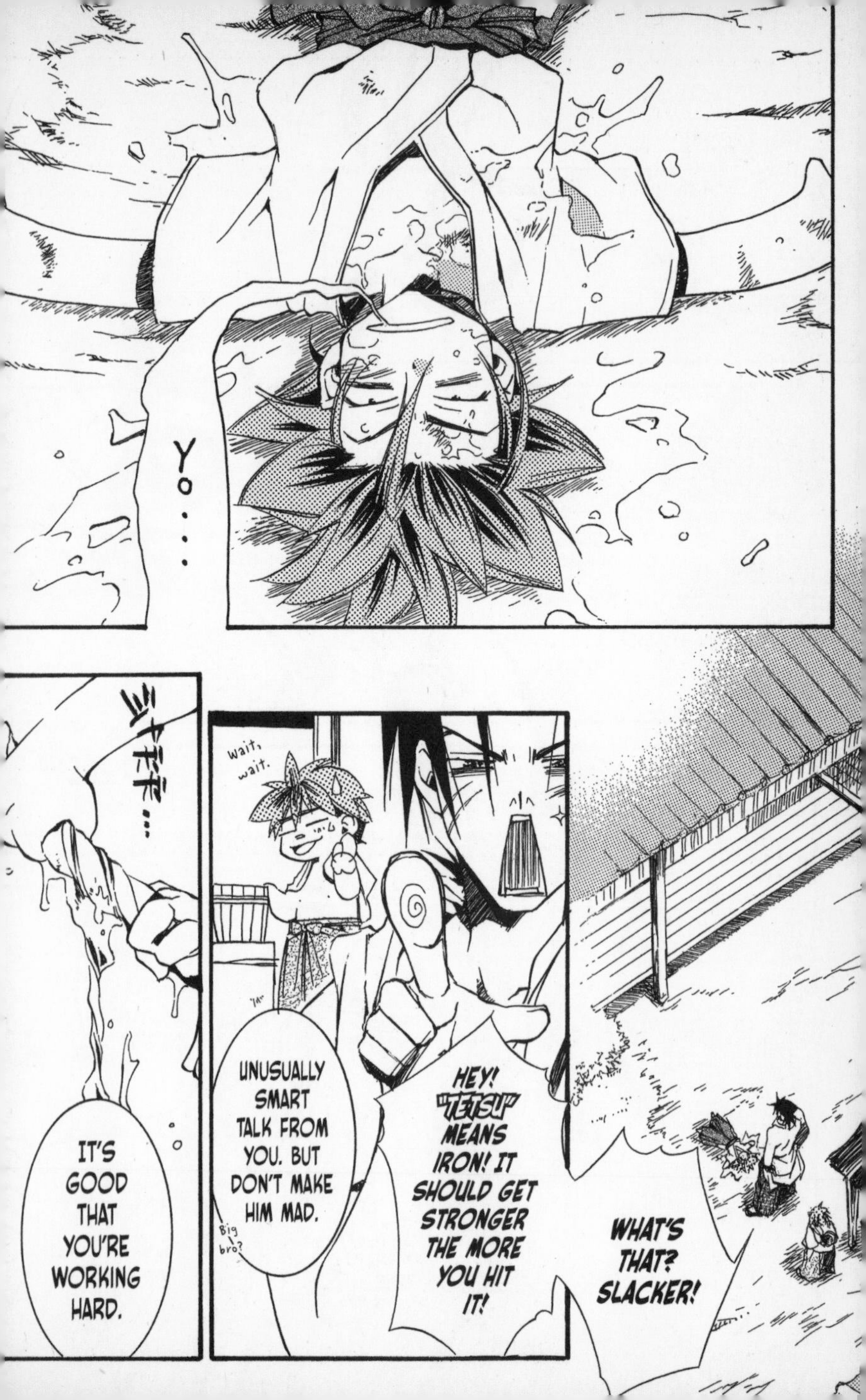

YO...
WHAT'S THAT? SLACKER!
HEY! "TETSU" MEANS IRON! IT SHOULD GET STRONGER THE MORE YOU HIT IT!
wait, wait.
UNUSUALLY SMART TALK FROM YOU. BUT DON'T MAKE HIM MAD.
Big bro?
IT'S GOOD THAT YOU'RE WORKING HARD.

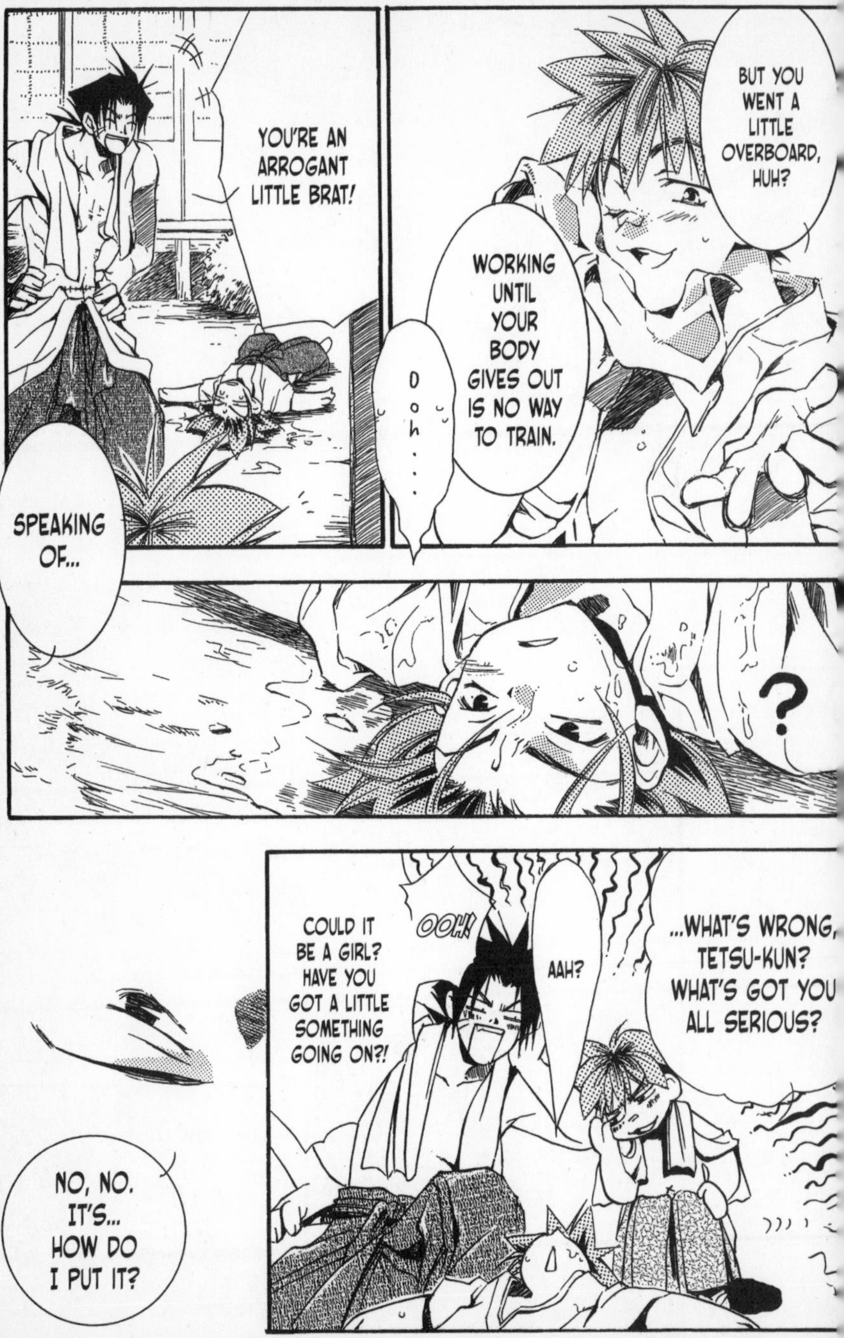
BUT YOU WENT A LITTLE OVERBOARD, HUH?
WORKING UNTIL YOUR BODY GIVES OUT IS NO WAY TO TRAIN.
Doh...
YOU'RE AN ARROGANT LITTLE BRAT!
SPEAKING OF...
?
...WHAT'S WRONG, TETSU-KUN? WHAT'S GOT YOU ALL SERIOUS?
AAH?
OOH!
COULD IT BE A GIRL? HAVE YOU GOT A LITTLE SOMETHING GOING ON?!
NO, NO. IT'S... HOW DO I PUT IT?

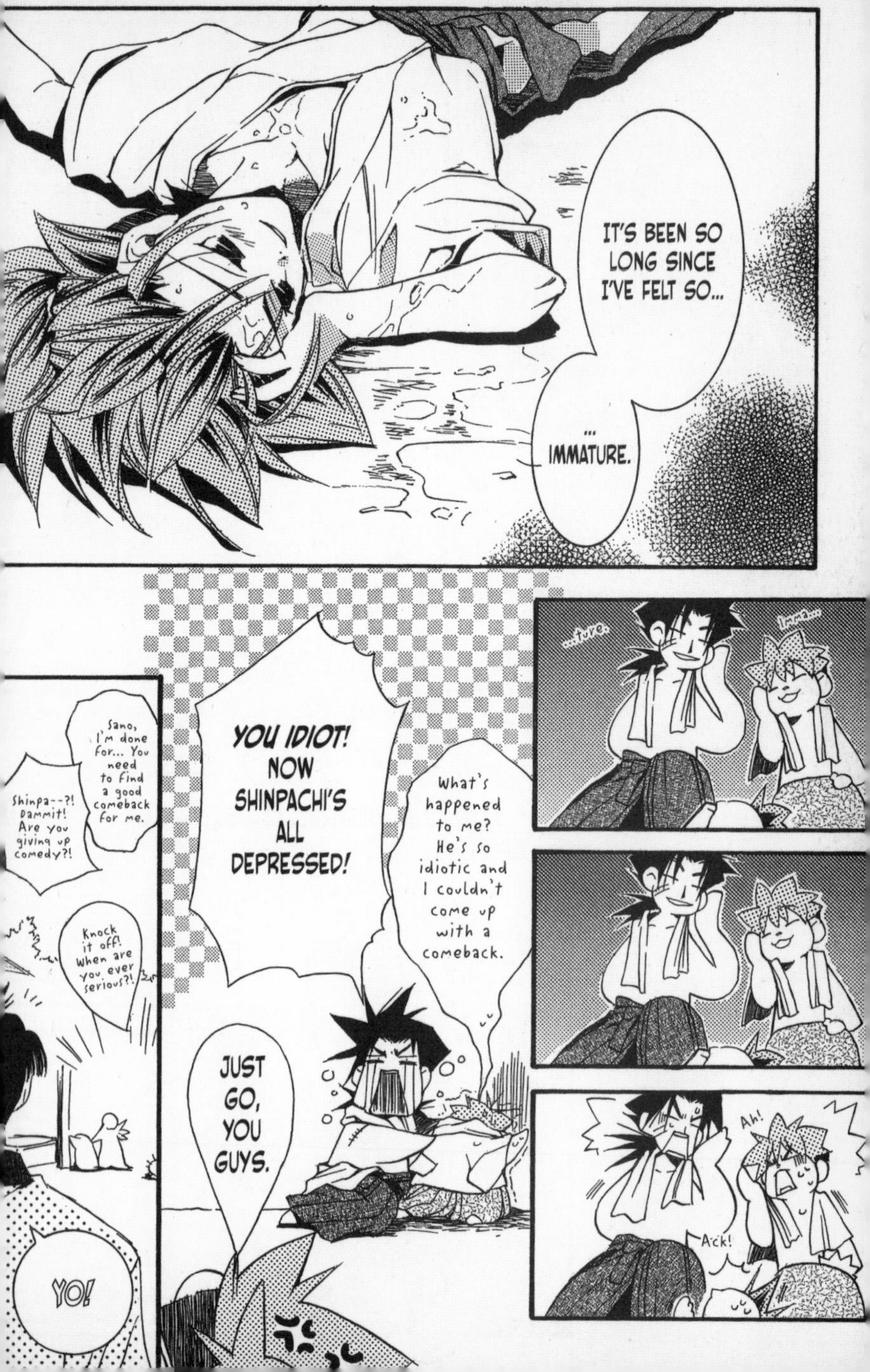
IT'S BEEN SO LONG SINCE I'VE FELT SO...
... IMMATURE.
Imma...
...ture.
Ah!
Ack!
YOU IDIOT! NOW SHINPACHI'S ALL DEPRESSED!
What's happened to me? He's so idiotic and I couldn't come up with a comeback.
JUST GO, YOU GUYS.
Sano, I'm done for... You need to find a good comeback for me.
Shinpa--?! Dammit! Are you giving up comedy?!
Knock it off! When are you ever serious?!
YO!

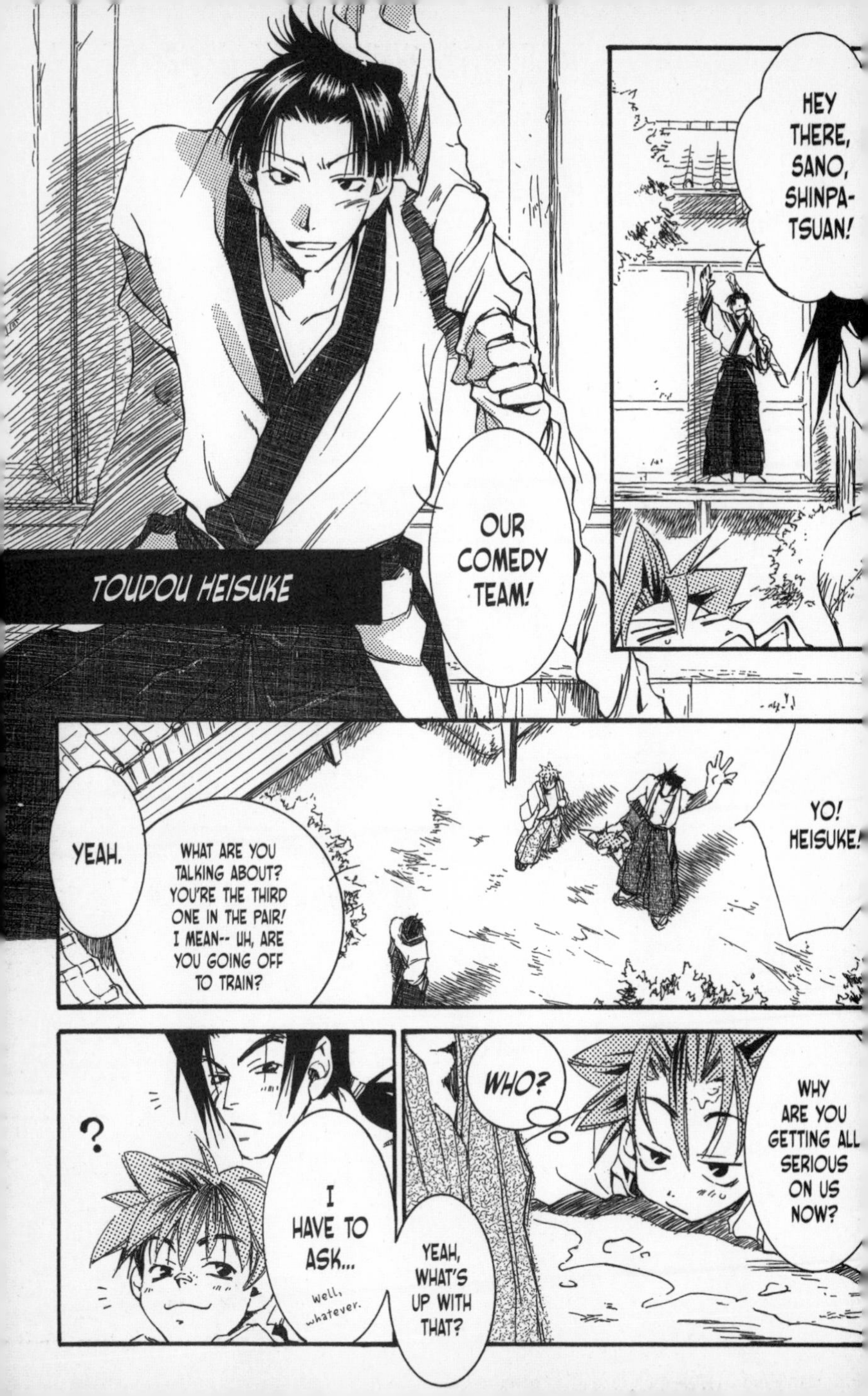
HEY THERE, SANO, SHINPATSUAN!
OUR COMEDY TEAM!
TOUDOU HEISUKE
YO! HEISUKE!
WHAT ARE YOU TALKING ABOUT? YOU'RE THE THIRD ONE IN THE PAIR! I MEAN-- UH, ARE YOU GOING OFF TO TRAIN?
YEAH.
WHY ARE YOU GETTING ALL SERIOUS ON US NOW?
WHO?
YEAH, WHAT'S UP WITH THAT?
I HAVE TO ASK...
well, whatever.
?

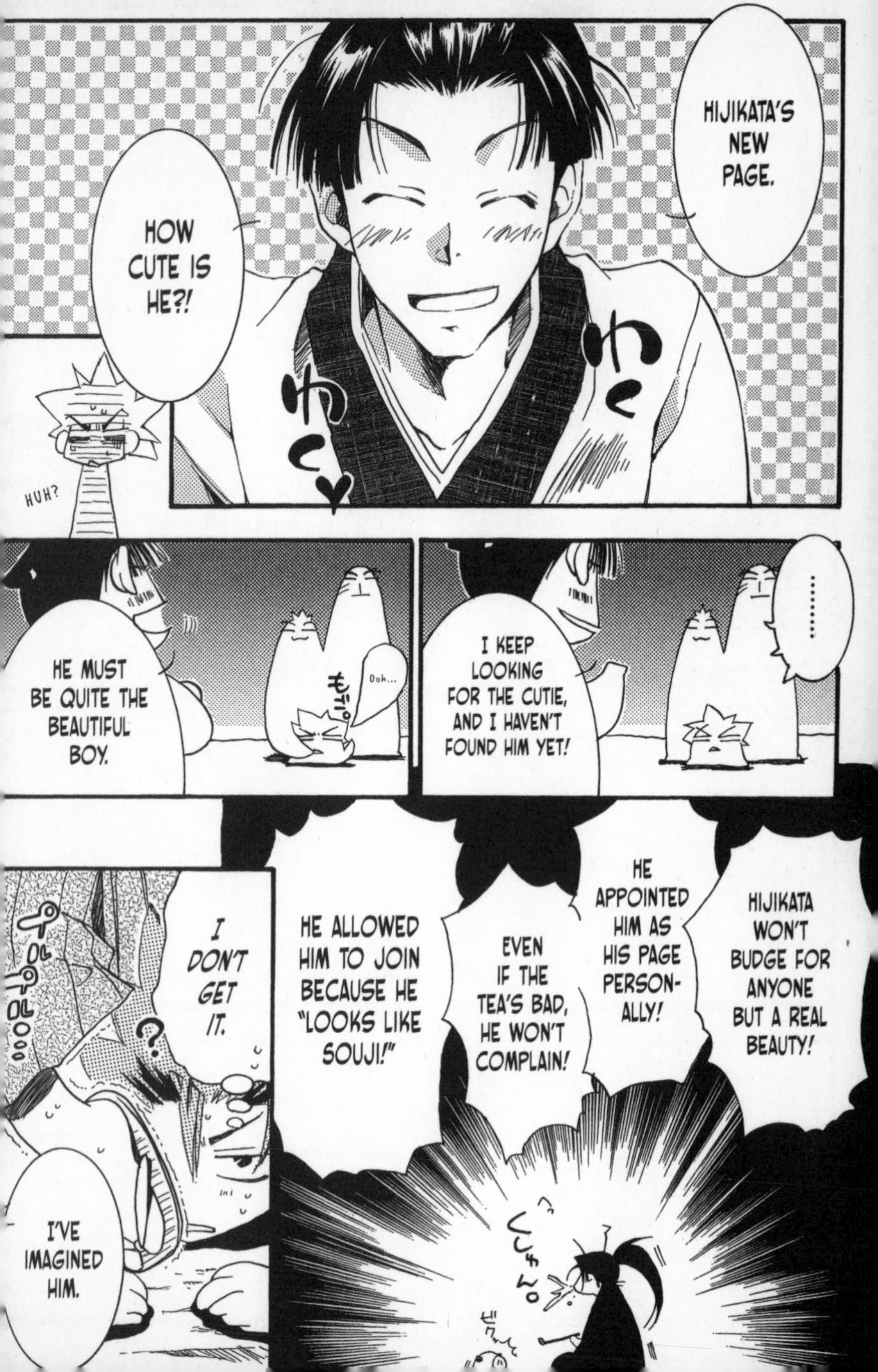
HIJIKATA'S NEW PAGE.
わく
わく♥
HOW CUTE IS HE?!
HUH?
......
I KEEP LOOKING FOR THE CUTIE, AND I HAVEN'T FOUND HIM YET!
HE MUST BE QUITE THE BEAUTIFUL BOY.
Ooh...
HIJIKATA WON'T BUDGE FOR ANYONE BUT A REAL BEAUTY!
HE APPOINTED HIM AS HIS PAGE PERSON-ALLY!
EVEN IF THE TEA'S BAD, HE WON'T COMPLAIN!
HE ALLOWED HIM TO JOIN BECAUSE HE "LOOKS LIKE SOUJI!"
I DON'T GET IT.
?
I'VE IMAGINED HIM.

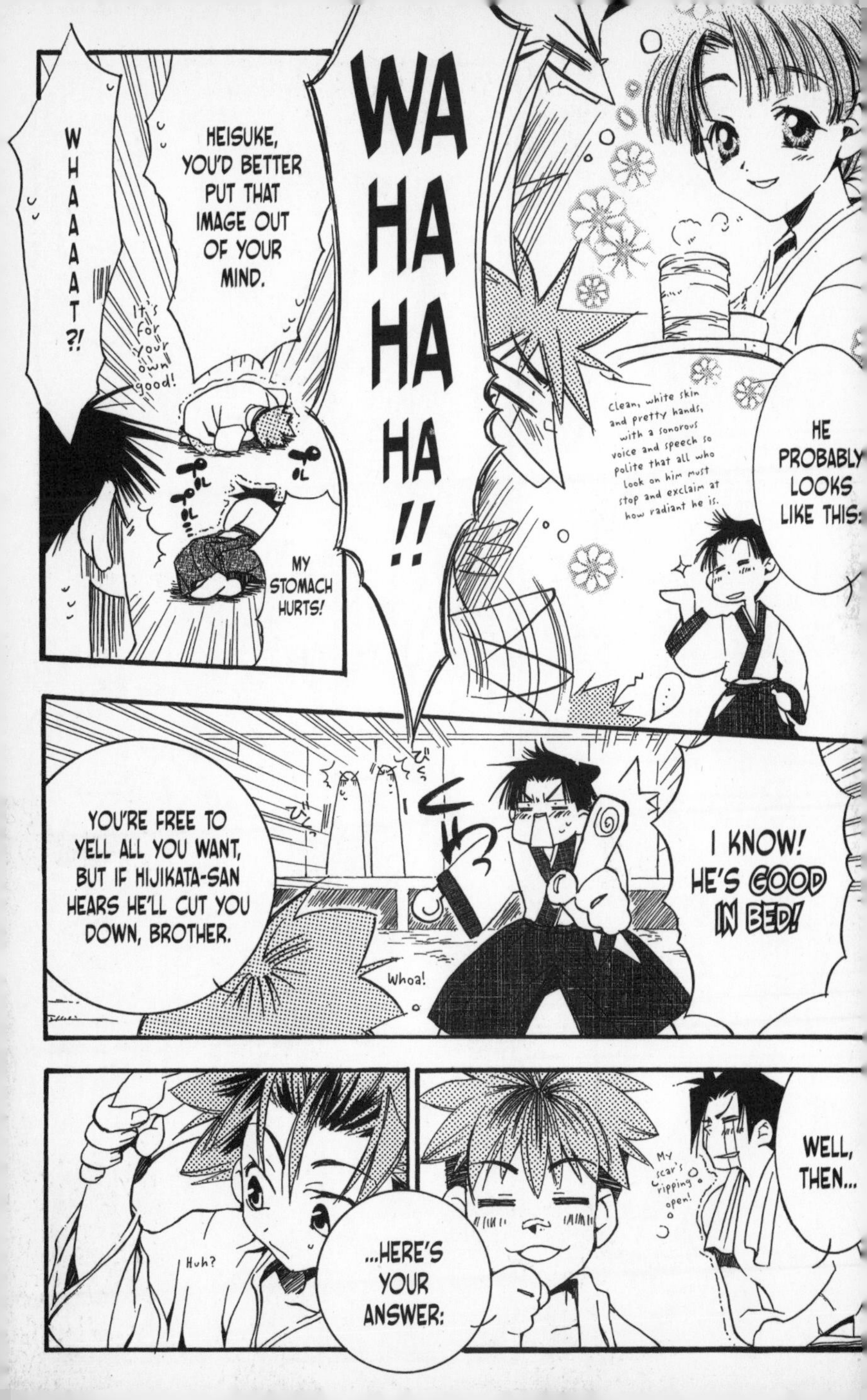
HE PROBABLY LOOKS LIKE THIS:
Clean, white skin and pretty hands, with a sonorous voice and speech so polite that all who look on him must stop and exclaim at how radiant he is.
WAHAHAHA!!
HEISUKE, YOU'D BETTER PUT THAT IMAGE OUT OF YOUR MIND.
WHAAAAAT?!
It's for your own good!
MY STOMACH HURTS!
I KNOW! HE'S GOOD IN BED!
Whoa!
YOU'RE FREE TO YELL ALL YOU WANT, BUT IF HIJIKATA-SAN HEARS HE'LL CUT YOU DOWN, BROTHER.
WELL, THEN...
My scar's ripping open!
...HERE'S YOUR ANSWER:
Huh?

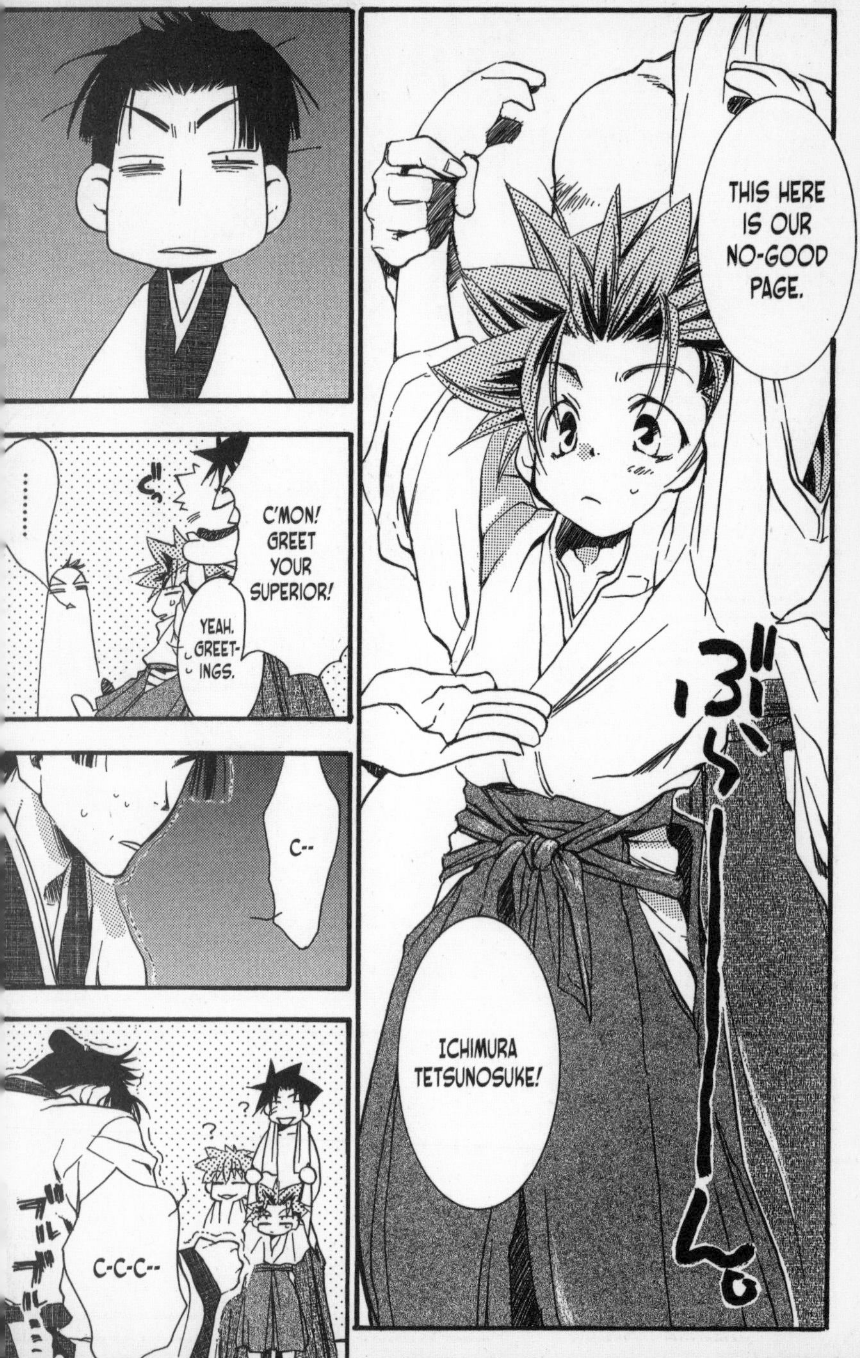
THIS HERE IS OUR NO-GOOD PAGE.
ICHIMURA TETSUNOSUKE!
C'MON! GREET YOUR SUPERIOR!
YEAH. GREET-INGS.
......
C--
C-C-C--

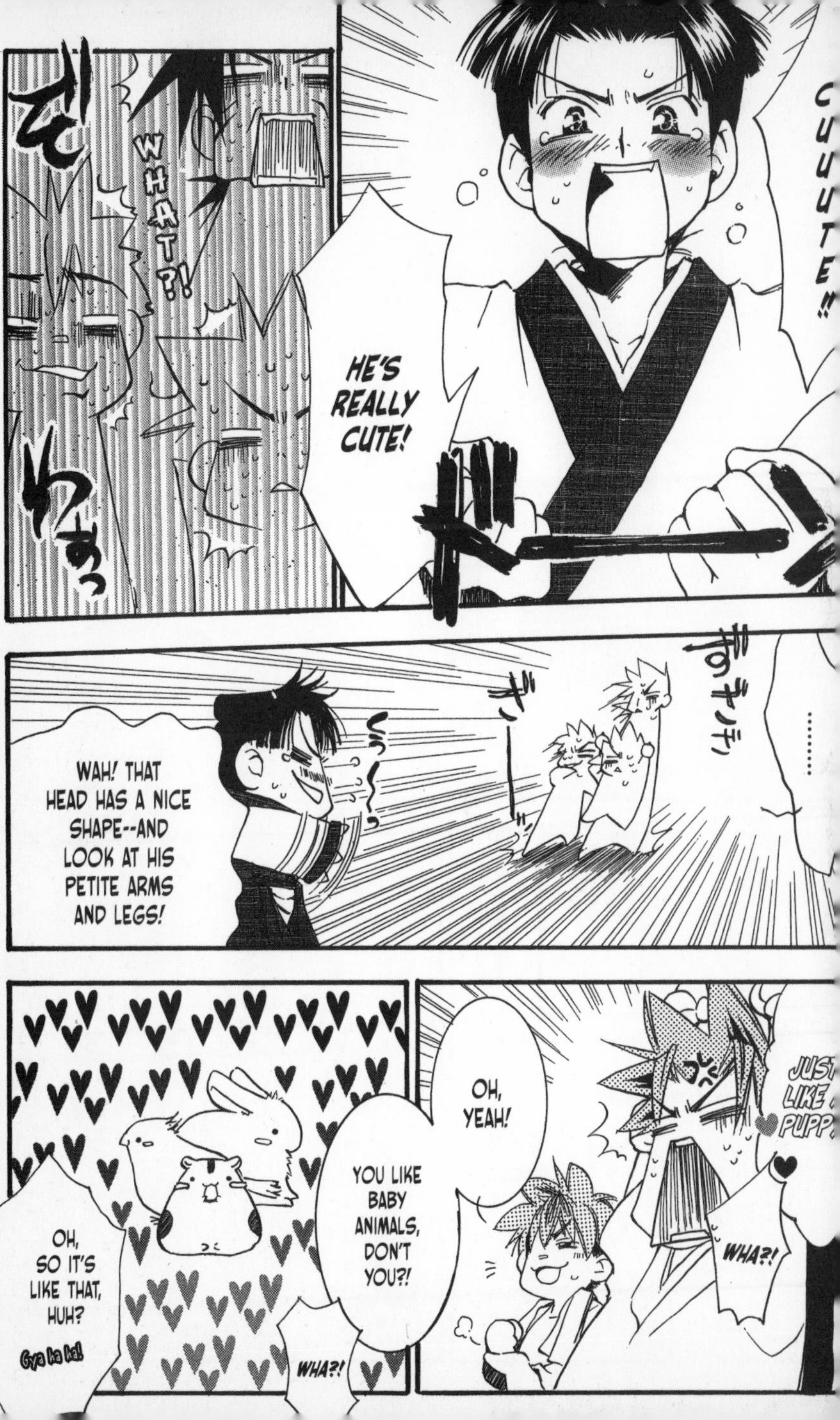
CUUUTE!!
HE'S REALLY CUTE!
WHAT?!
......
WAH! THAT HEAD HAS A NICE SHAPE--AND LOOK AT HIS PETITE ARMS AND LEGS!
WHA?!
OH, YEAH!
YOU LIKE BABY ANIMALS, DON'T YOU?!
WHA?!
OH, SO IT'S LIKE THAT, HUH?
Gya ha ha!

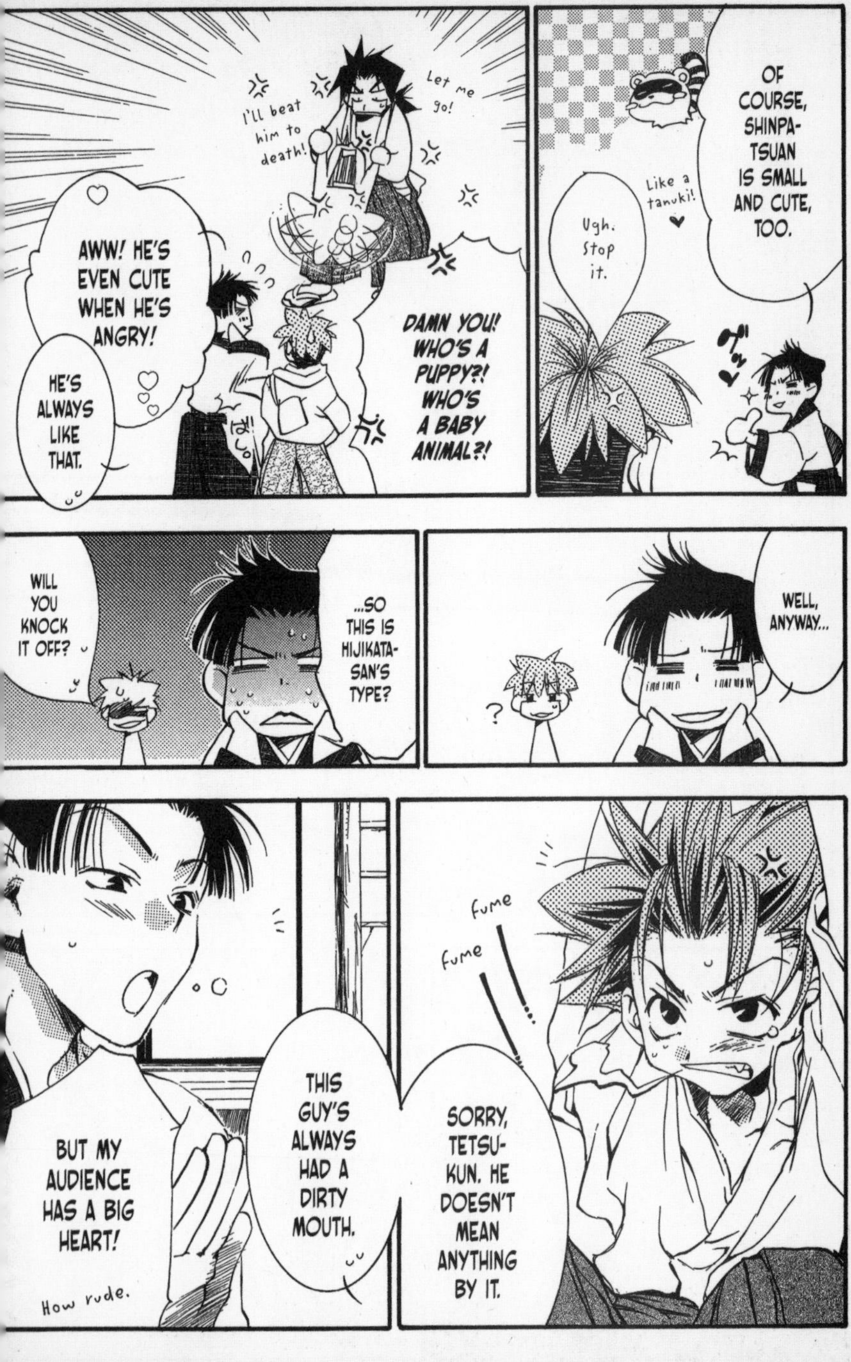
OF COURSE, SHINPA-TSUAN IS SMALL AND CUTE, TOO.
Like a tanuki! ♥
Ugh. Stop it.
Let me go!
I'll beat him to death!
DAMN YOU! WHO'S A PUPPY?! WHO'S A BABY ANIMAL?!
AWW! HE'S EVEN CUTE WHEN HE'S ANGRY!
HE'S ALWAYS LIKE THAT.
WELL, ANYWAY...
...SO THIS IS HIJIKATA-SAN'S TYPE?
WILL YOU KNOCK IT OFF?
fume
fume
SORRY, TETSU-KUN. HE DOESN'T MEAN ANYTHING BY IT.
THIS GUY'S ALWAYS HAD A DIRTY MOUTH.
BUT MY AUDIENCE HAS A BIG HEART!
How rude.

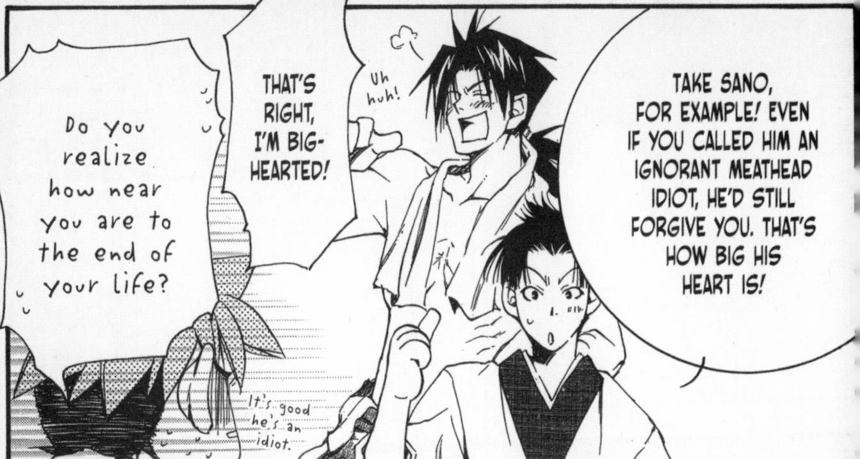
TAKE SANO, FOR EXAMPLE! EVEN IF YOU CALLED HIM AN IGNORANT MEATHEAD IDIOT, HE'D STILL FORGIVE YOU. THAT'S HOW BIG HIS HEART IS!
Uh huh!
THAT'S RIGHT, I'M BIG-HEARTED!
Do you realize how near you are to the end of your life?
It's good he's an idiot.

Shieikan: Dojo from where many prominent Shinsengumi members came

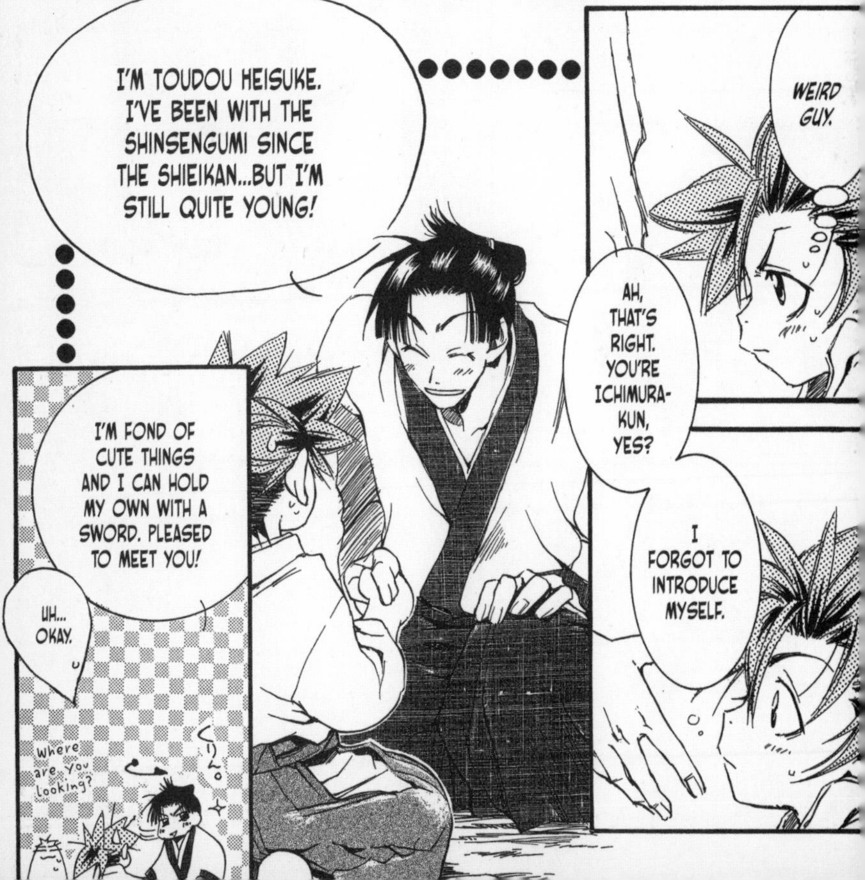
WEIRD GUY.
AH, THAT'S RIGHT. YOU'RE ICHIMURA-KUN, YES?
I FORGOT TO INTRODUCE MYSELF.
I'M TOUDOU HEISUKE. I'VE BEEN WITH THE SHINSENGUMI SINCE THE SHIEIKAN...BUT I'M STILL QUITE YOUNG!
I'M FOND OF CUTE THINGS AND I CAN HOLD MY OWN WITH A SWORD. PLEASED TO MEET YOU!
UH... OKAY.
Where are you looking?

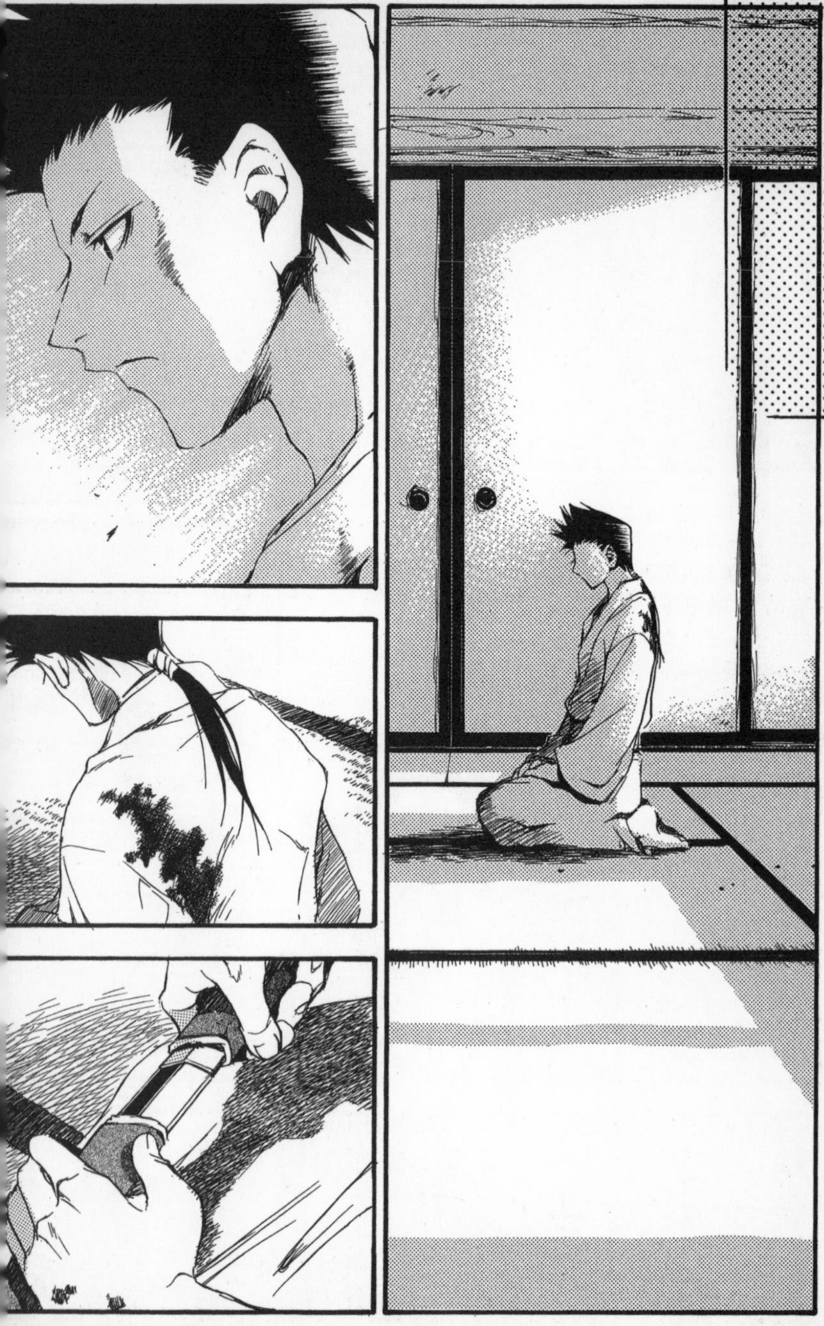

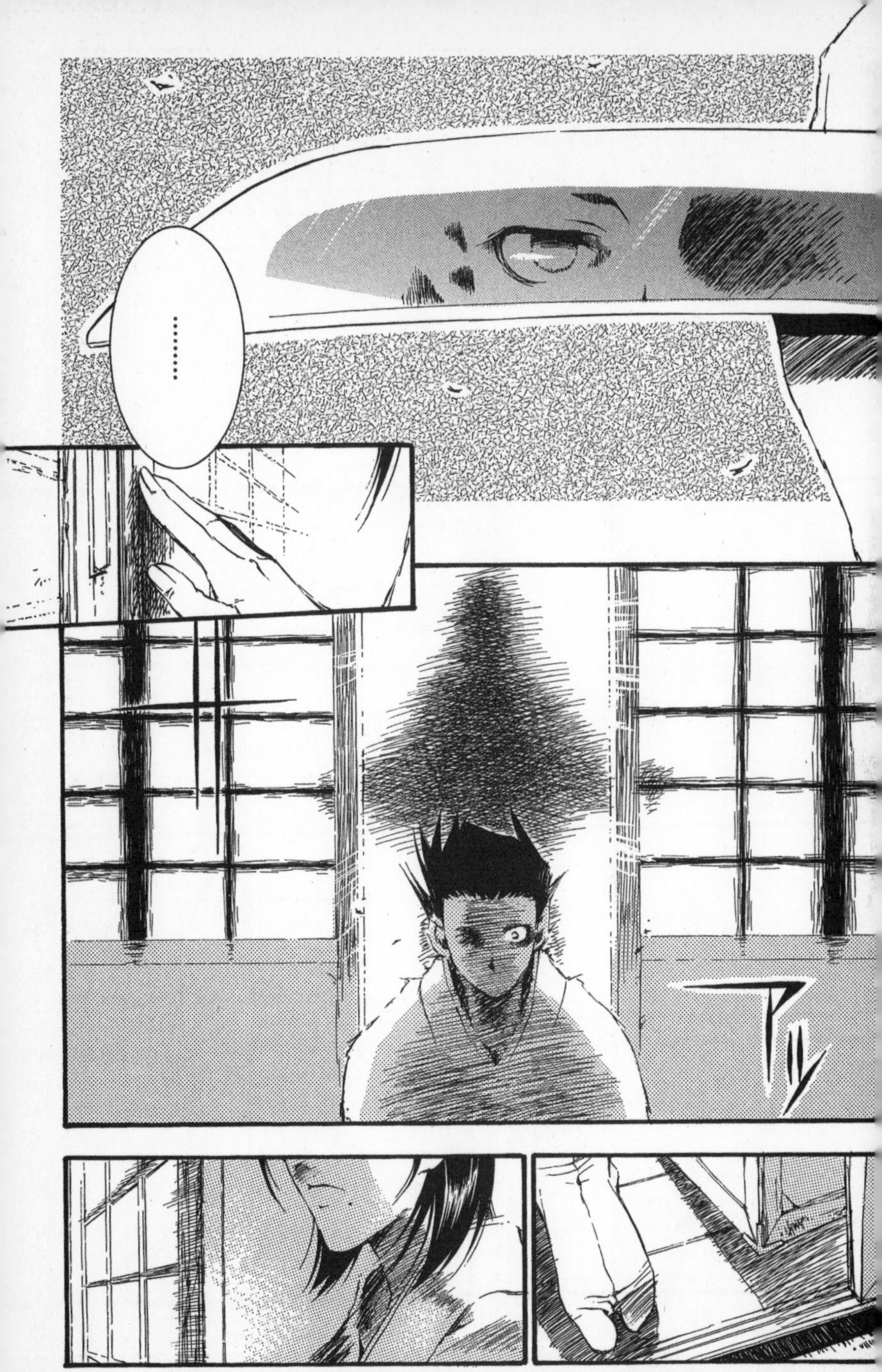
……
アッ

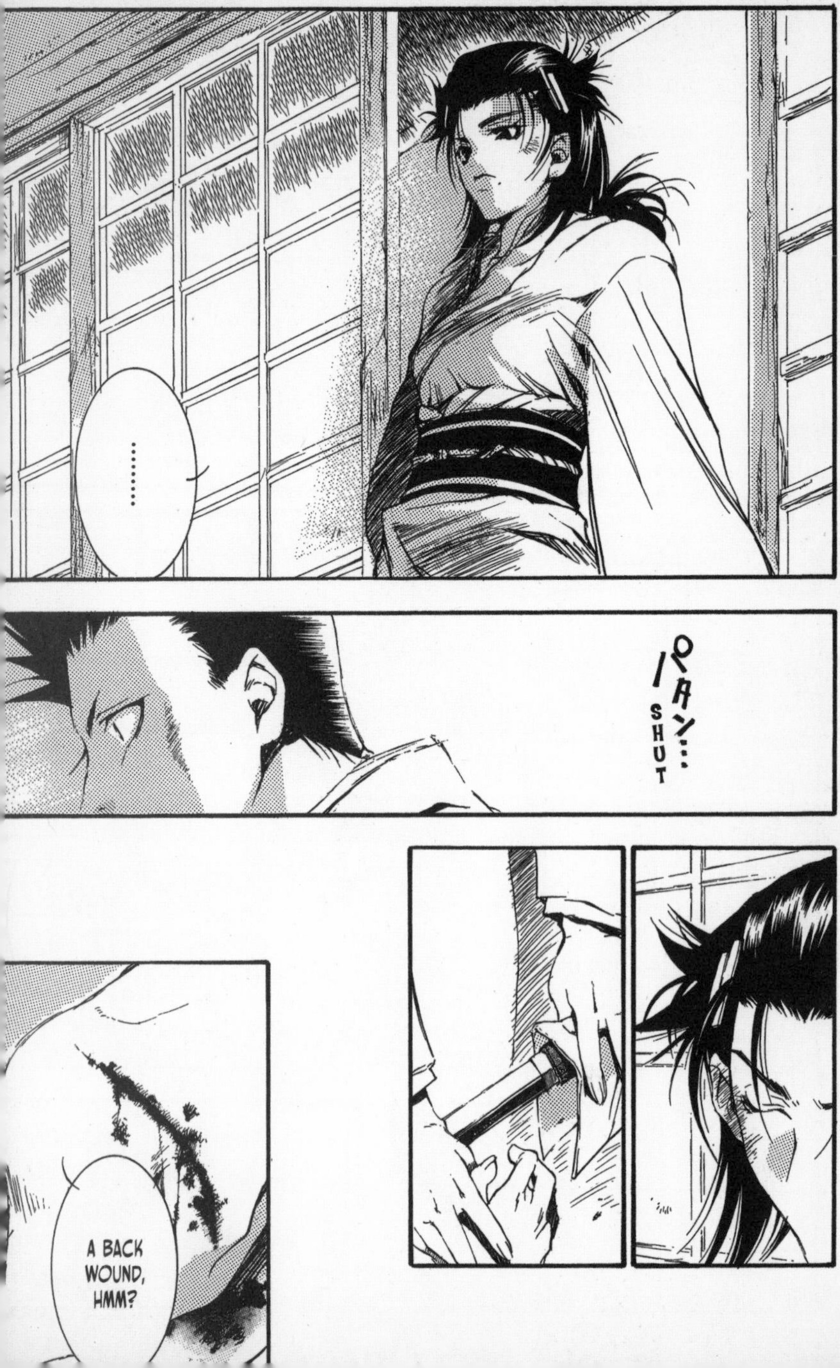
......
パタン…
SHUT
A BACK WOUND, HMM?

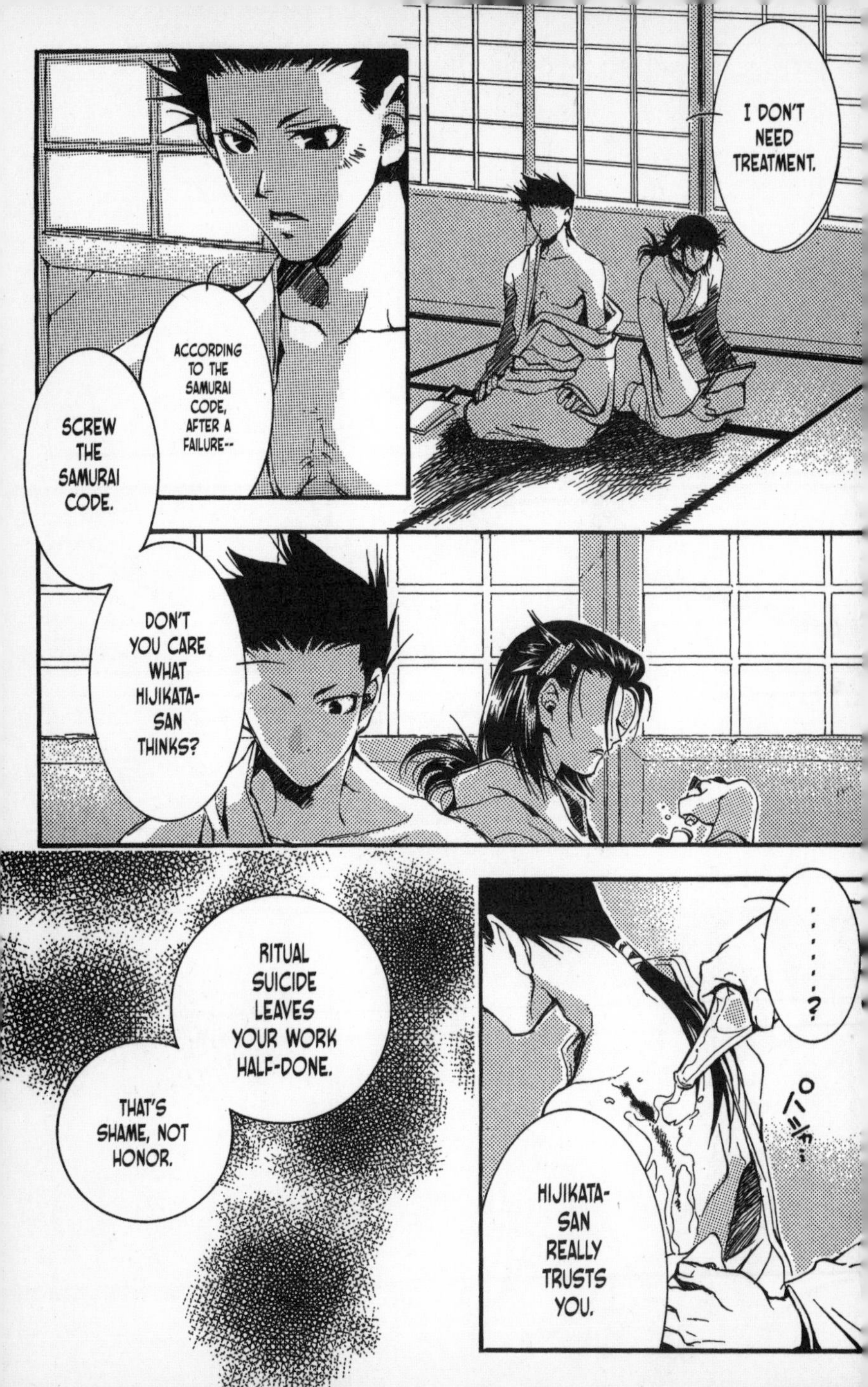
I DON'T NEED TREATMENT.
ACCORDING TO THE SAMURAI CODE, AFTER A FAILURE--
SCREW THE SAMURAI CODE.
DON'T YOU CARE WHAT HIJIKATA-SAN THINKS?
......?
HIJIKATA-SAN REALLY TRUSTS YOU.
RITUAL SUICIDE LEAVES YOUR WORK HALF-DONE.
THAT'S SHAME, NOT HONOR.

IF YOU'RE KILLED IN THE LINE OF DUTY, THAT'S ONE THING...

IF YOU DON'T DIE, YOU CAN DO 100, EVEN 200 MORE JOBS.

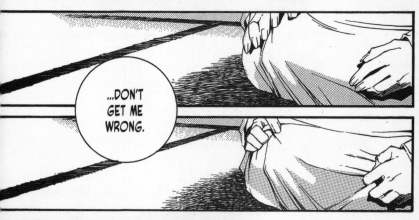

...DON'T GET ME WRONG.

BUT YOU...

...ARE NOT A SAMURAI.

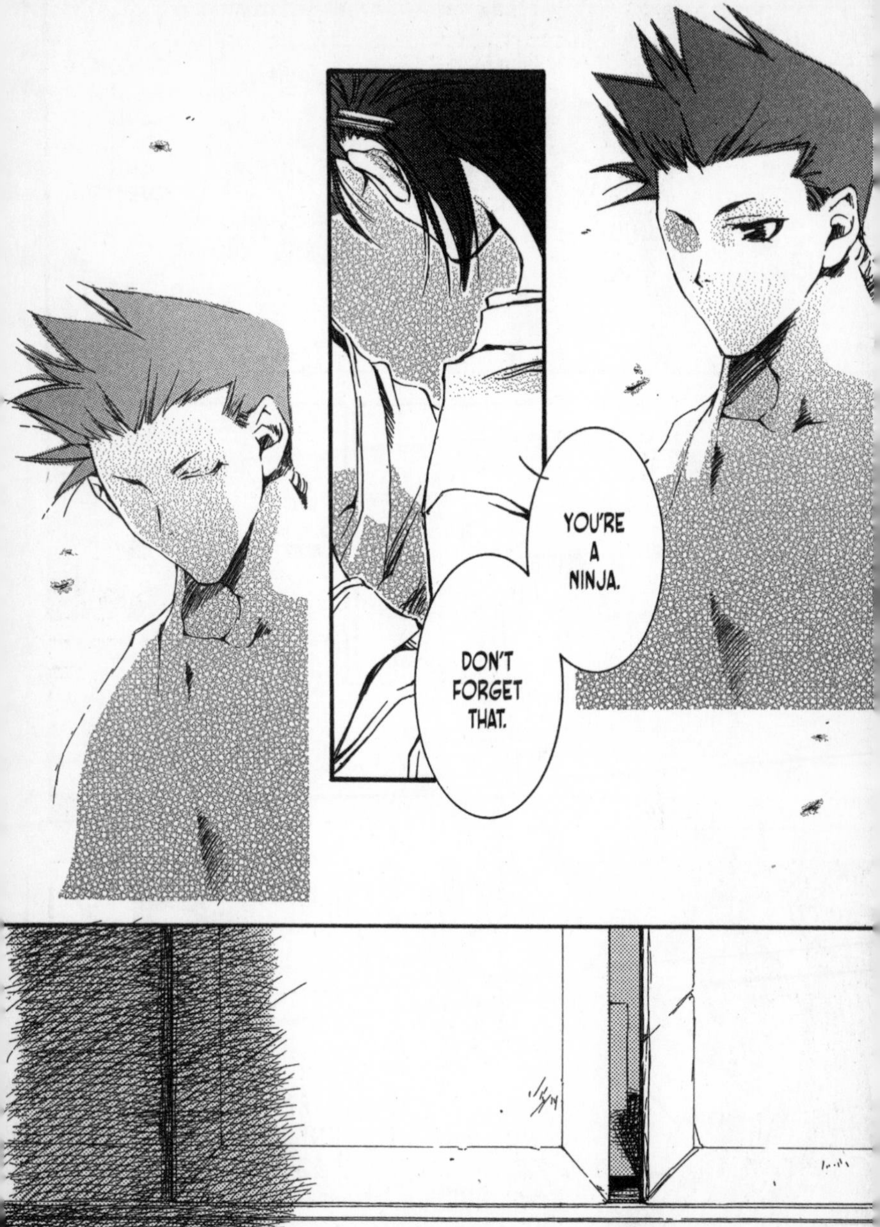
YOU'RE A NINJA.
DON'T FORGET THAT.

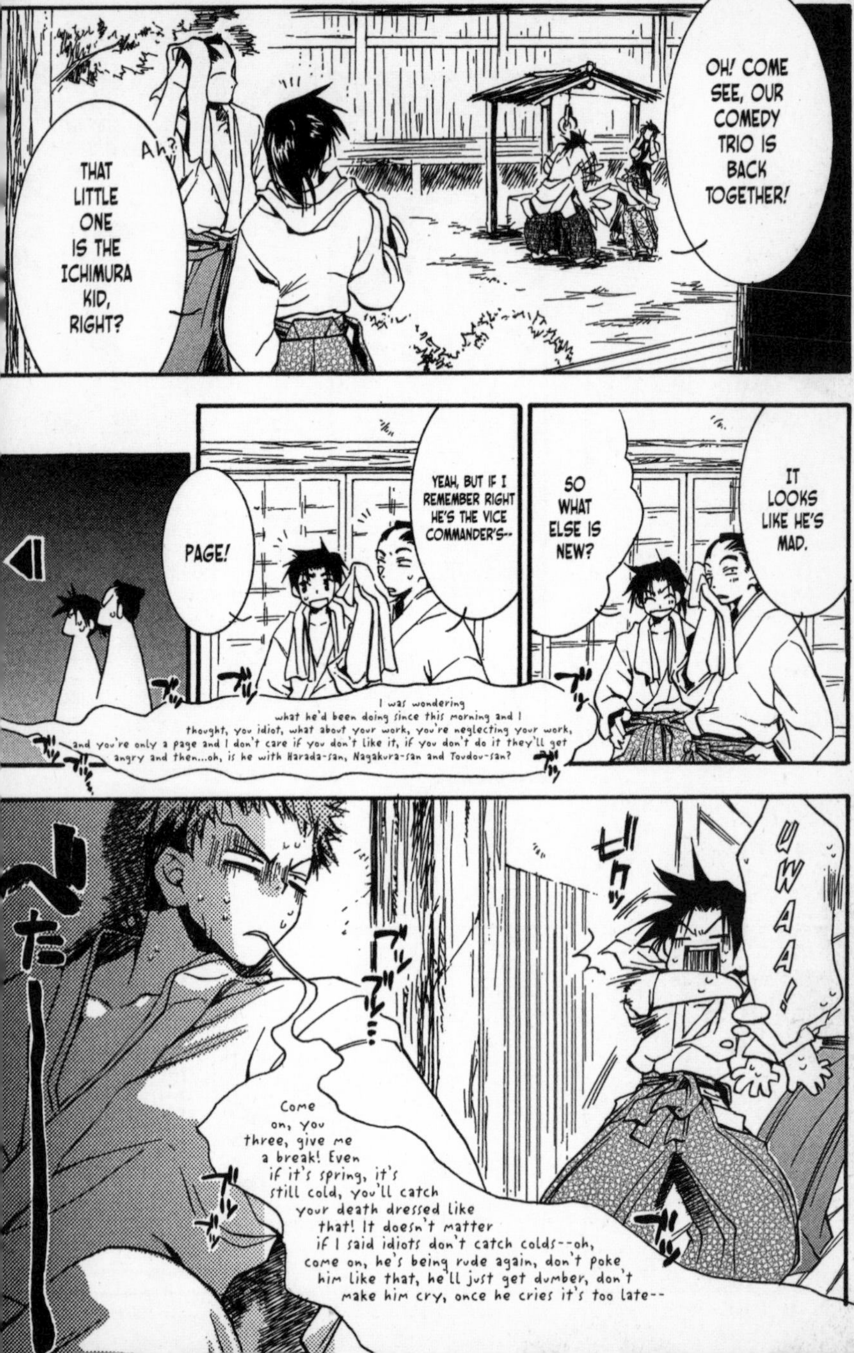
OH! COME SEE, OUR COMEDY TRIO IS BACK TOGETHER!
Ah?
THAT LITTLE ONE IS THE ICHIMURA KID, RIGHT?
IT LOOKS LIKE HE'S MAD.
SO WHAT ELSE IS NEW?
YEAH, BUT IF I REMEMBER RIGHT HE'S THE VICE COMMANDER'S--
PAGE!
I was wondering what he'd been doing since this morning and I thought, you idiot, what about your work, you're neglecting your work, and you're only a page and I don't care if you don't like it, if you don't do it they'll get angry and then...oh, is he with Harada-san, Nagakura-san and Toudou-san?
UWAAA!
Come on, you three, give me a break! Even if it's spring, it's still cold, you'll catch your death dressed like that! It doesn't matter if I said idiots don't catch colds--oh, come on, he's being rude again, don't poke him like that, he'll just get dumber, don't make him cry, once he cries it's too late--

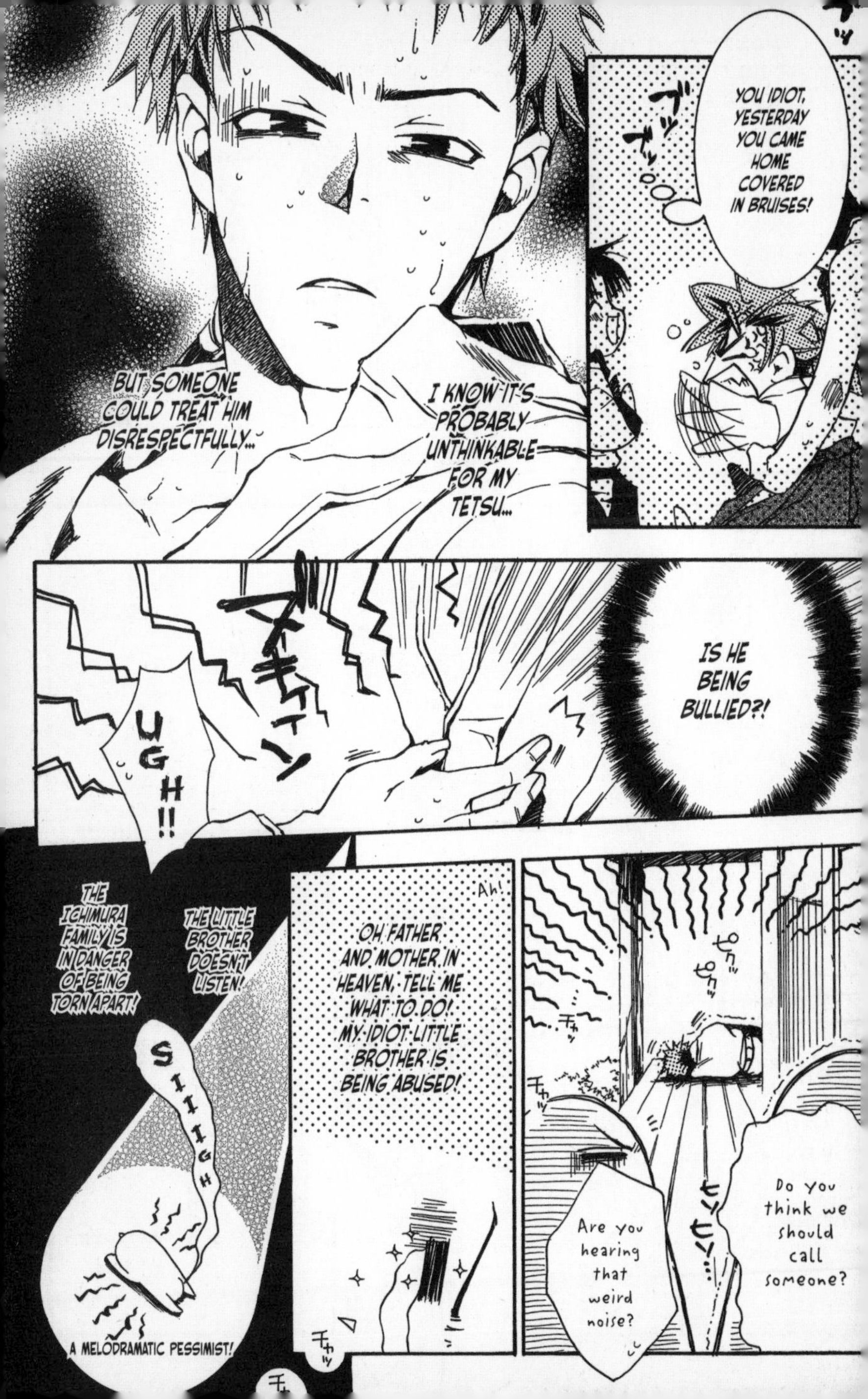
YOU IDIOT, YESTERDAY YOU CAME HOME COVERED IN BRUISES!
I KNOW IT'S PROBABLY UNTHINKABLE FOR MY TETSU...
BUT SOMEONE COULD TREAT HIM DISRESPECTFULLY...
IS HE BEING BULLIED?!
UGH!!
Do you think we should call someone?
Are you hearing that weird noise?
Ah!
OH FATHER AND MOTHER IN HEAVEN, TELL ME WHAT TO DO! MY IDIOT LITTLE BROTHER IS BEING ABUSED!
THE LITTLE BROTHER DOESN'T LISTEN!
THE ICHIMURA FAMILY IS IN DANGER OF BEING TORN APART!
SIIIGH
A MELODRAMATIC PESSIMIST!

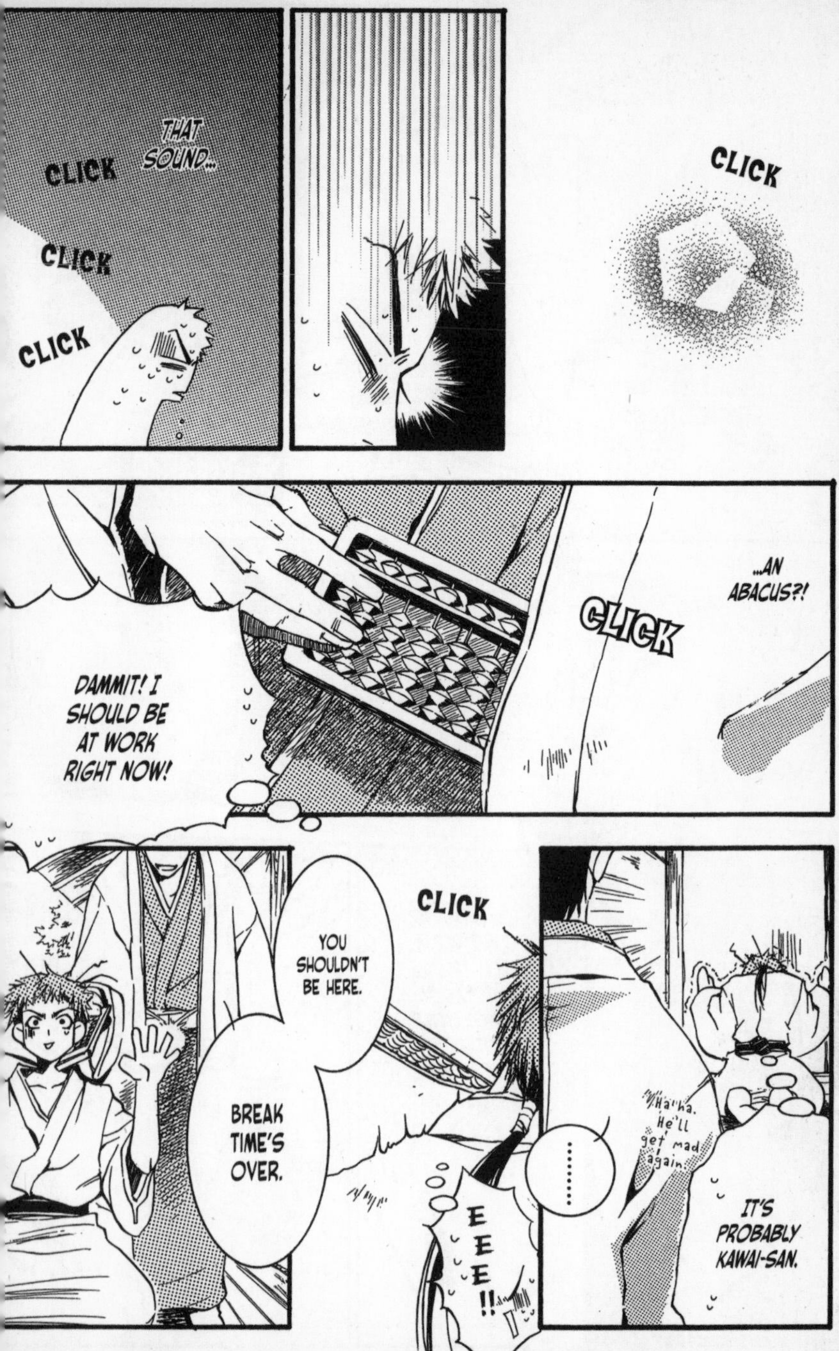
CLICK
THAT SOUND...
CLICK
CLICK
CLICK
...AN ABACUS?!
CLICK
DAMMIT! I SHOULD BE AT WORK RIGHT NOW!
IT'S PROBABLY KAWAI-SAN.
Ha ha. He'll get mad again.
......
CLICK
YOU SHOULDN'T BE HERE.
BREAK TIME'S OVER.
EEEE!!

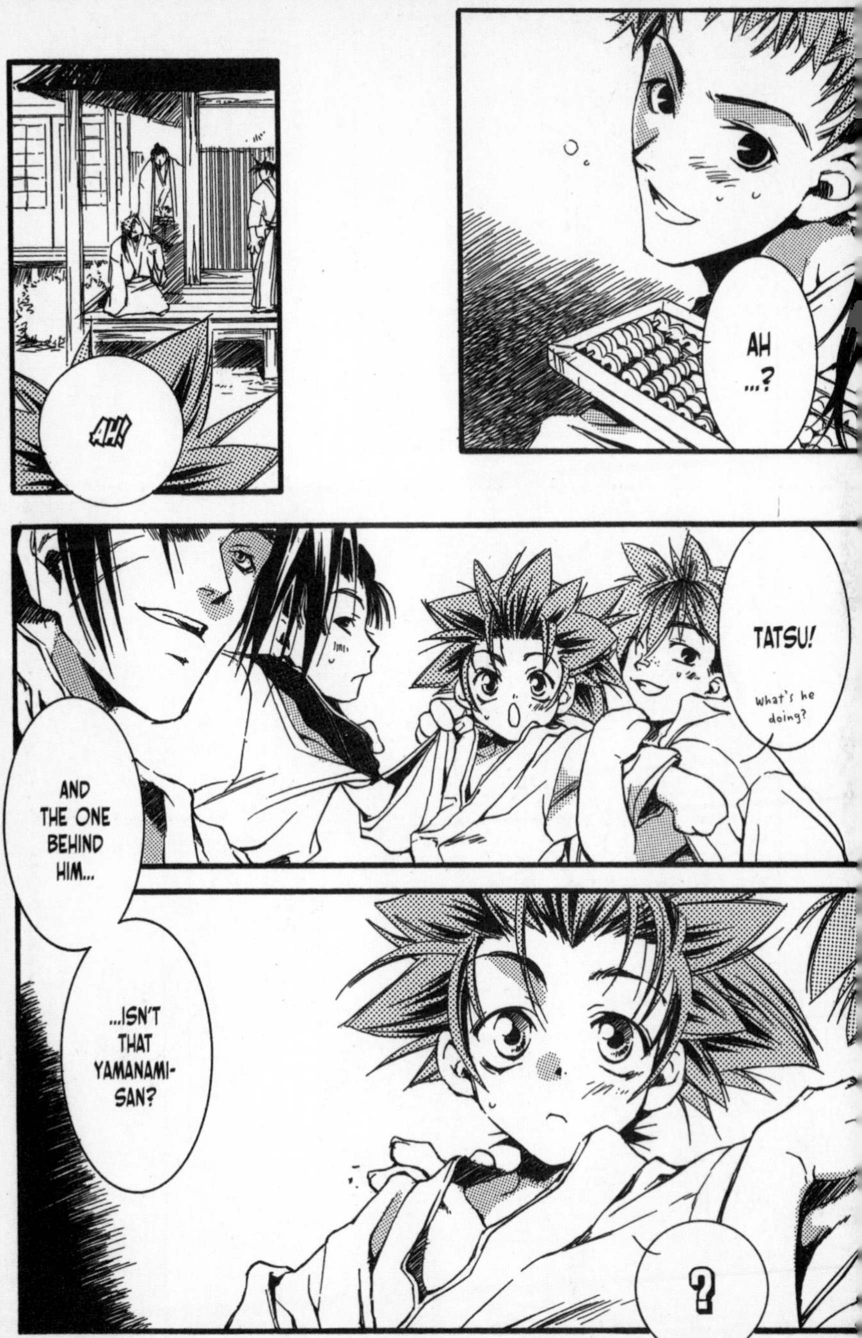
AH ...?
AH!
TATSU!
What's he doing?
AND THE ONE BEHIND HIM...
...ISN'T THAT YAMANAMI-SAN?
?

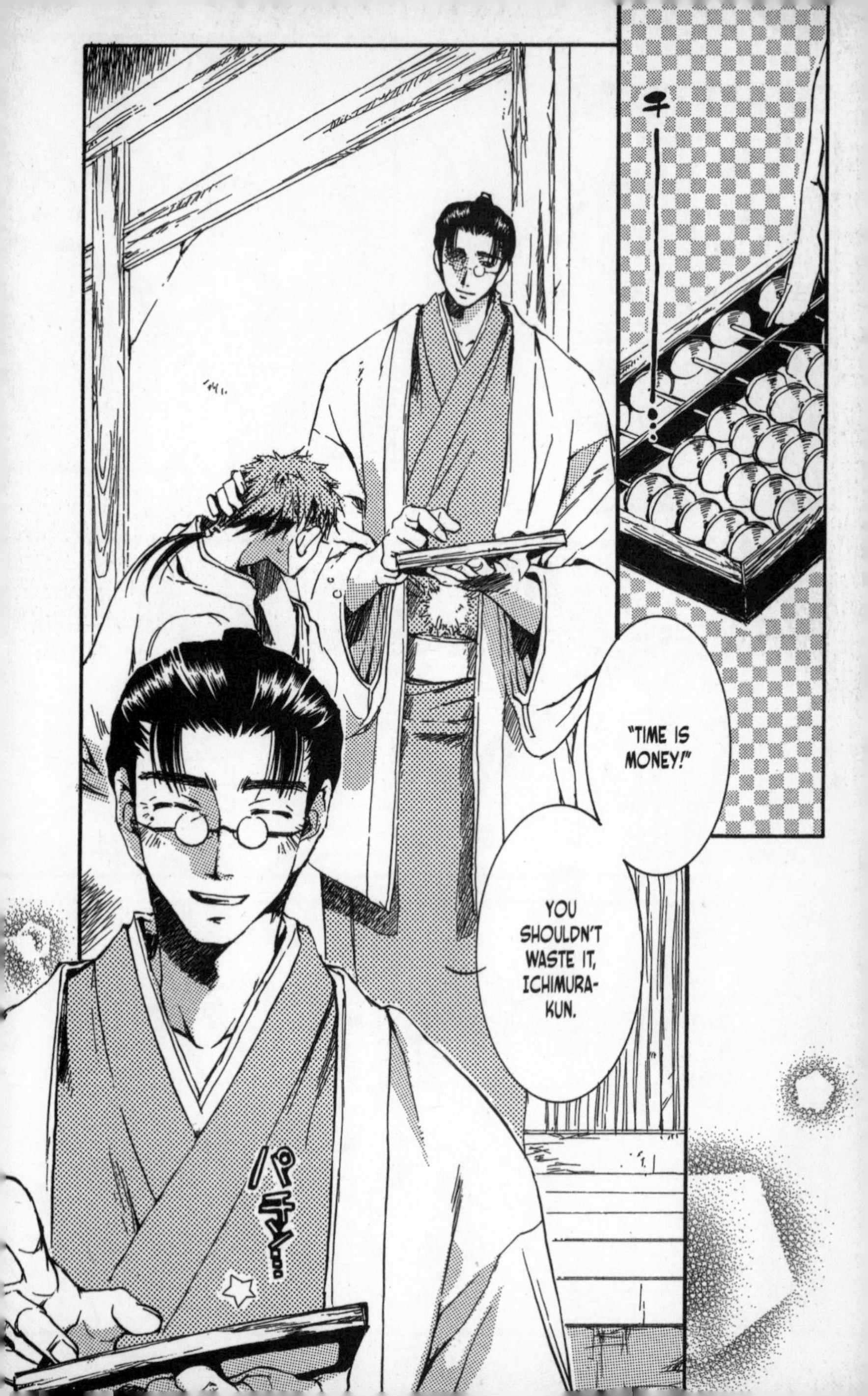
"TIME IS MONEY!"
YOU SHOULDN'T WASTE IT, ICHIMURA-KUN.
パチ
パチん

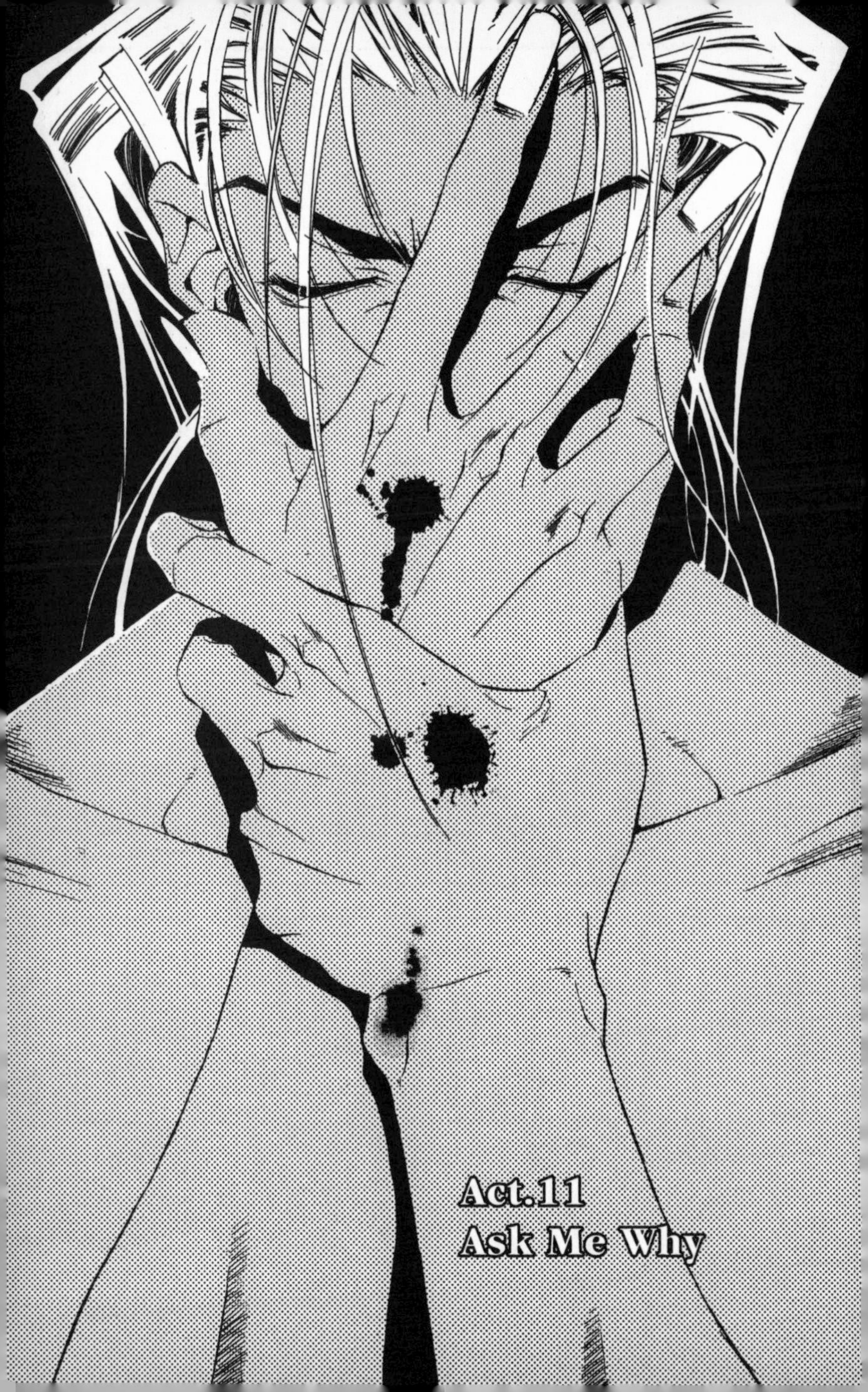
Act.11
Ask Me Why

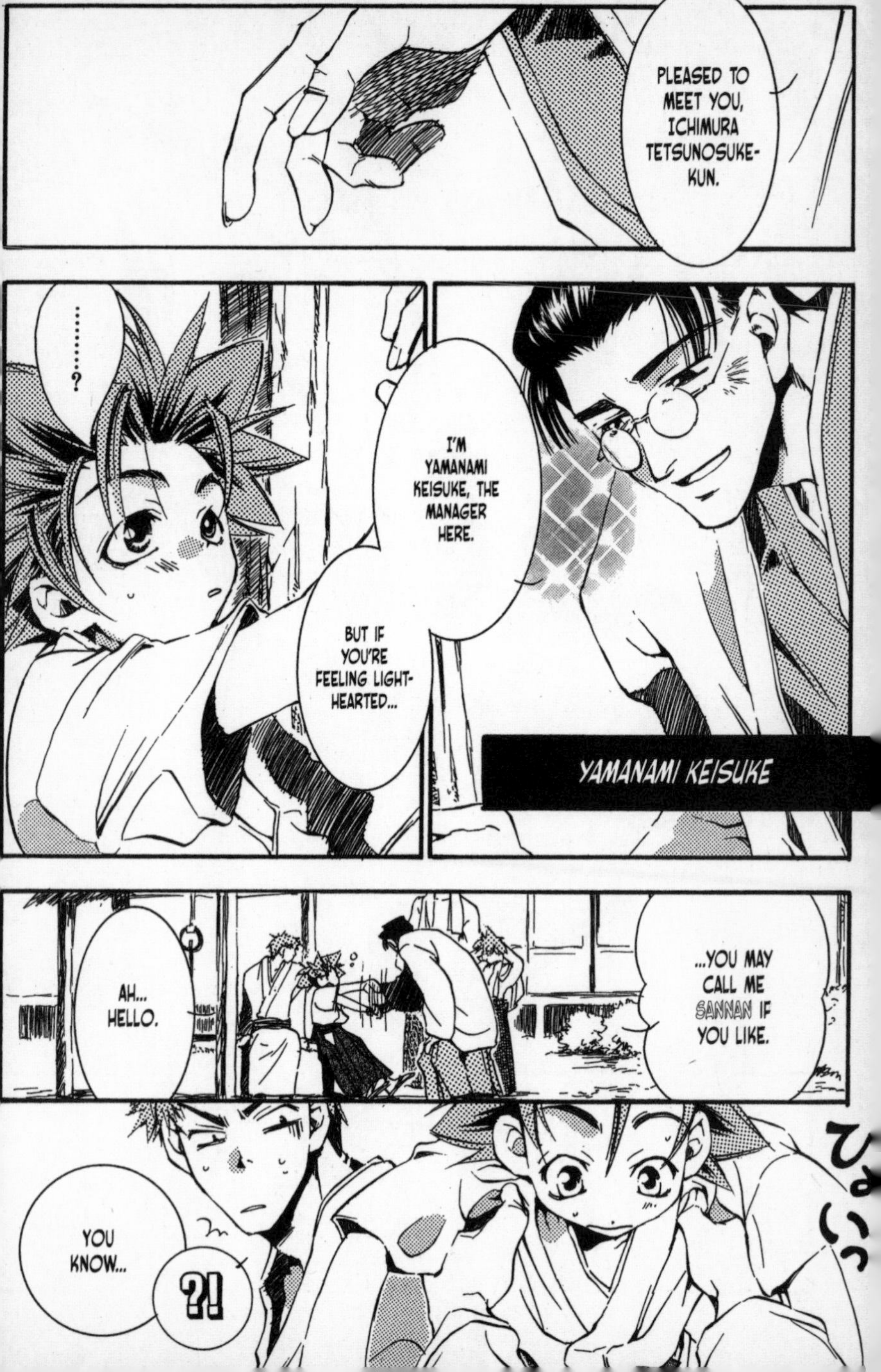
PLEASED TO MEET YOU, ICHIMURA TETSUNOSUKE-KUN.
I'M YAMANAMI KEISUKE, THE MANAGER HERE.
BUT IF YOU'RE FEELING LIGHT-HEARTED...
YAMANAMI KEISUKE
......?
...YOU MAY CALL ME SANNAN IF YOU LIKE.
AH... HELLO.
ひょいっ
YOU KNOW...
?!

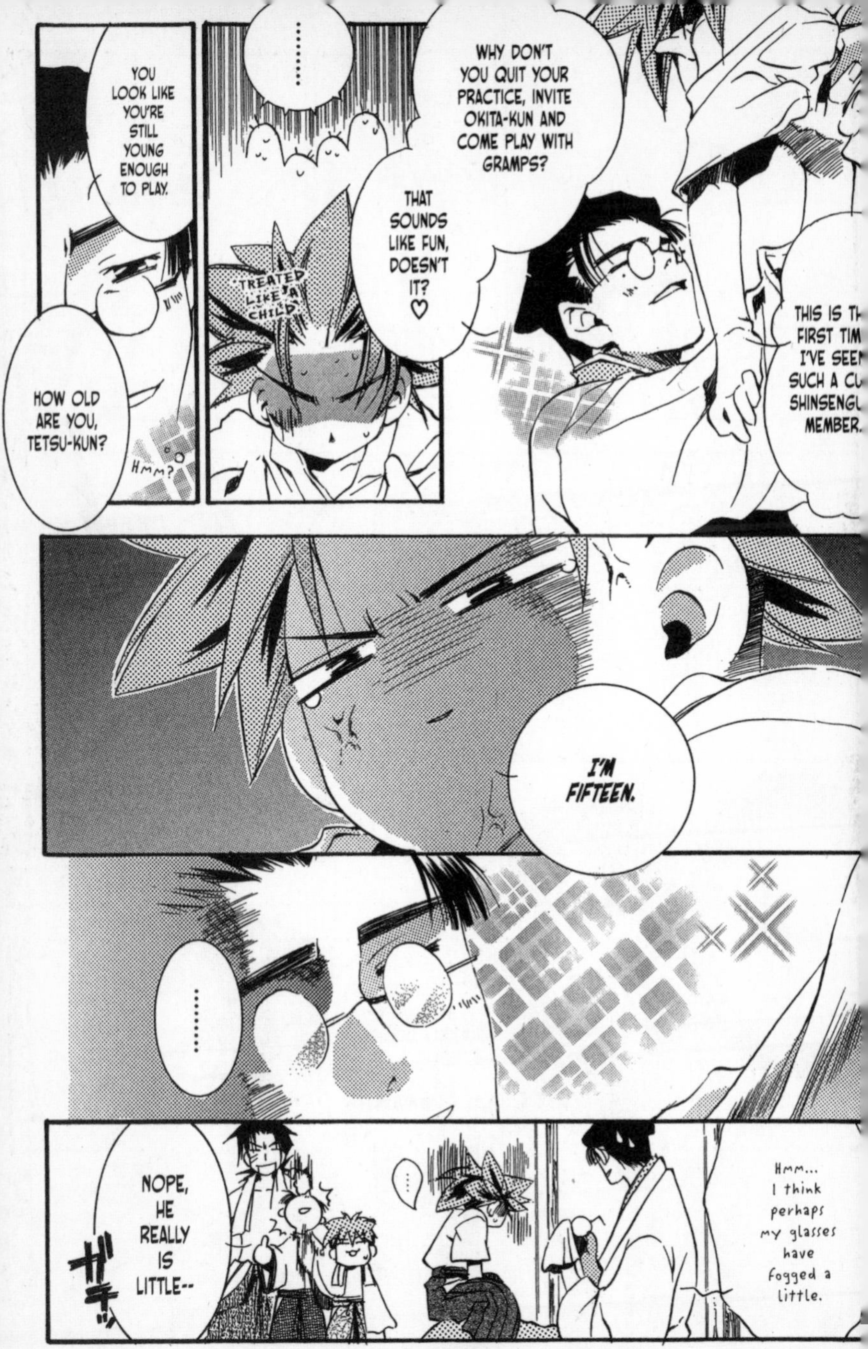
THIS IS TH FIRST TIM I'VE SEEN SUCH A CU SHINSENGU MEMBER.
WHY DON'T YOU QUIT YOUR PRACTICE, INVITE OKITA-KUN AND COME PLAY WITH GRAMPS?
THAT SOUNDS LIKE FUN, DOESN'T IT? ♡
......
TREATED LIKE A CHILD
YOU LOOK LIKE YOU'RE STILL YOUNG ENOUGH TO PLAY.
HOW OLD ARE YOU, TETSU-KUN?
HMM?
I'M FIFTEEN.
......
Hmm... I think perhaps my glasses have fogged a little.
...
NOPE, HE REALLY IS LITTLE--
In shock, for Yamanami meant well.

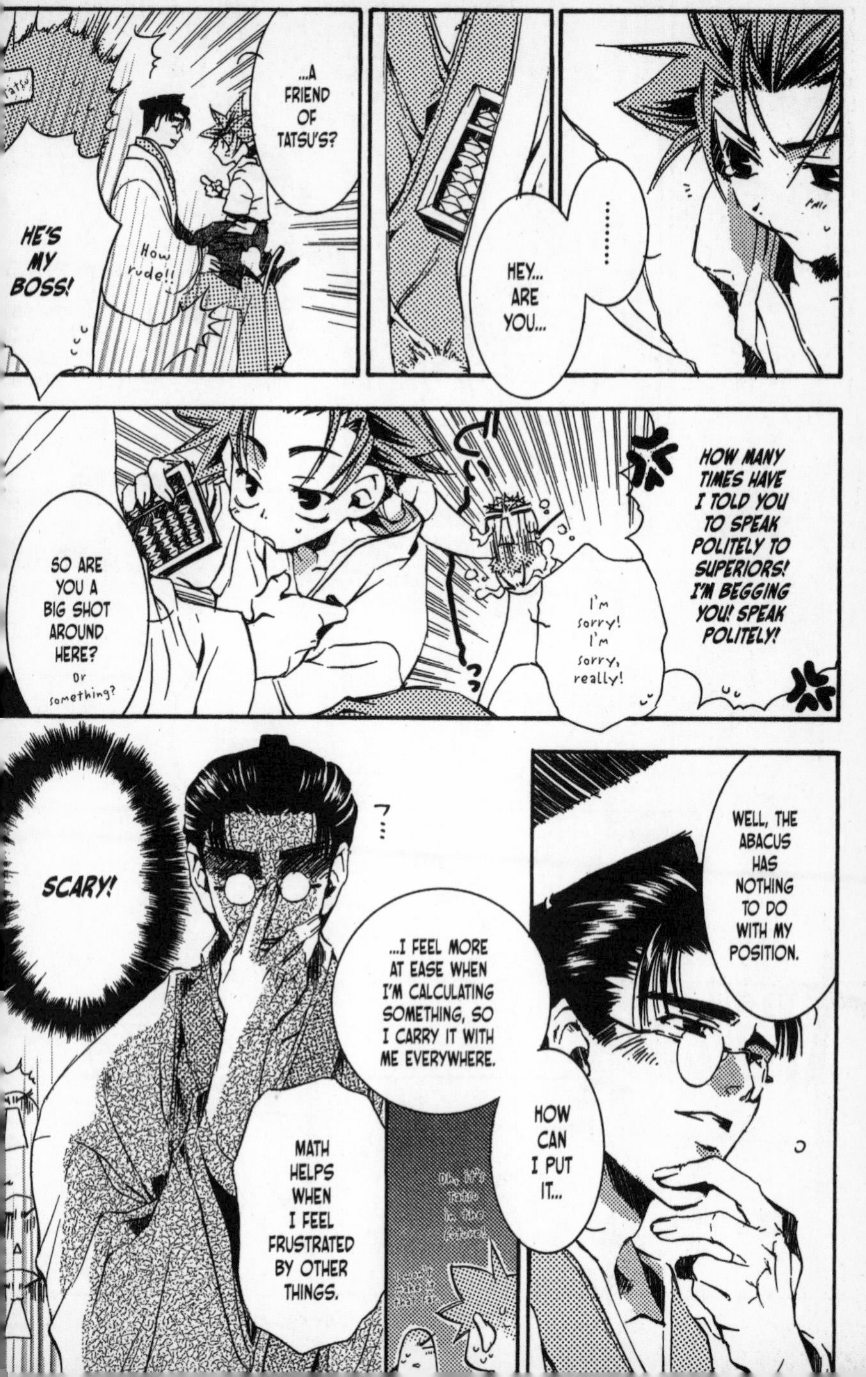
......
HEY... ARE YOU...
...A FRIEND OF TATSU'S?
Tatsu
How rude!!
HE'S MY BOSS!
HOW MANY TIMES HAVE I TOLD YOU TO SPEAK POLITELY TO SUPERIORS! I'M BEGGING YOU! SPEAK POLITELY!
I'm sorry! I'm sorry, really!
SO ARE YOU A BIG SHOT AROUND HERE? Or something?
WELL, THE ABACUS HAS NOTHING TO DO WITH MY POSITION.
HOW CAN I PUT IT...
...I FEEL MORE AT EASE WHEN I'M CALCULATING SOMETHING, SO I CARRY IT WITH ME EVERYWHERE.
MATH HELPS WHEN I FEEL FRUSTRATED BY OTHER THINGS.
SCARY!

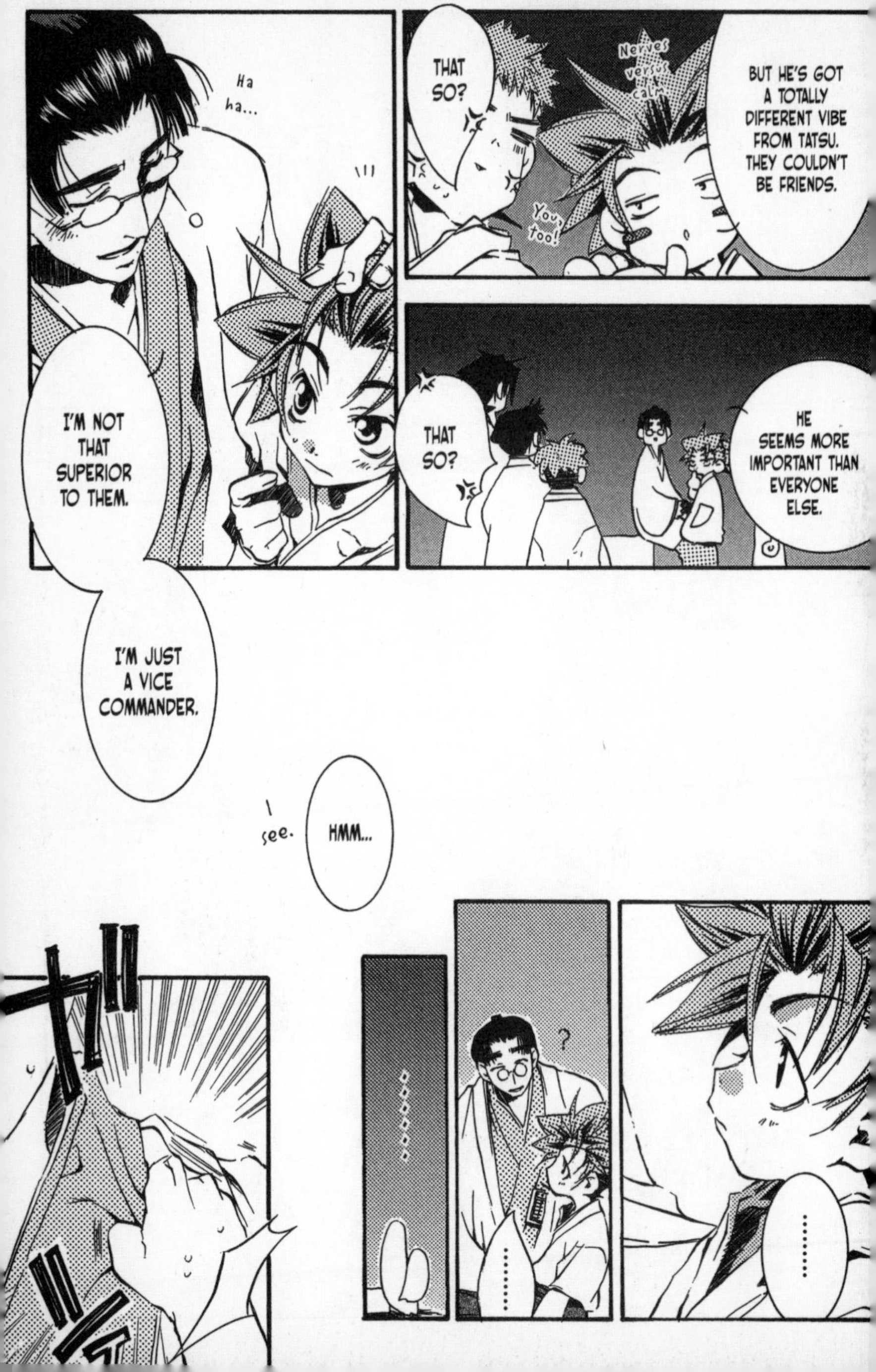
BUT HE'S GOT A TOTALLY DIFFERENT VIBE FROM TATSU. THEY COULDN'T BE FRIENDS.
Nerves versus calm
THAT SO?
You, too!
HE SEEMS MORE IMPORTANT THAN EVERYONE ELSE.
THAT SO?
Ha ha...
I'M NOT THAT SUPERIOR TO THEM.
I'M JUST A VICE COMMANDER.
HMM...
I see.
....
?
......
....

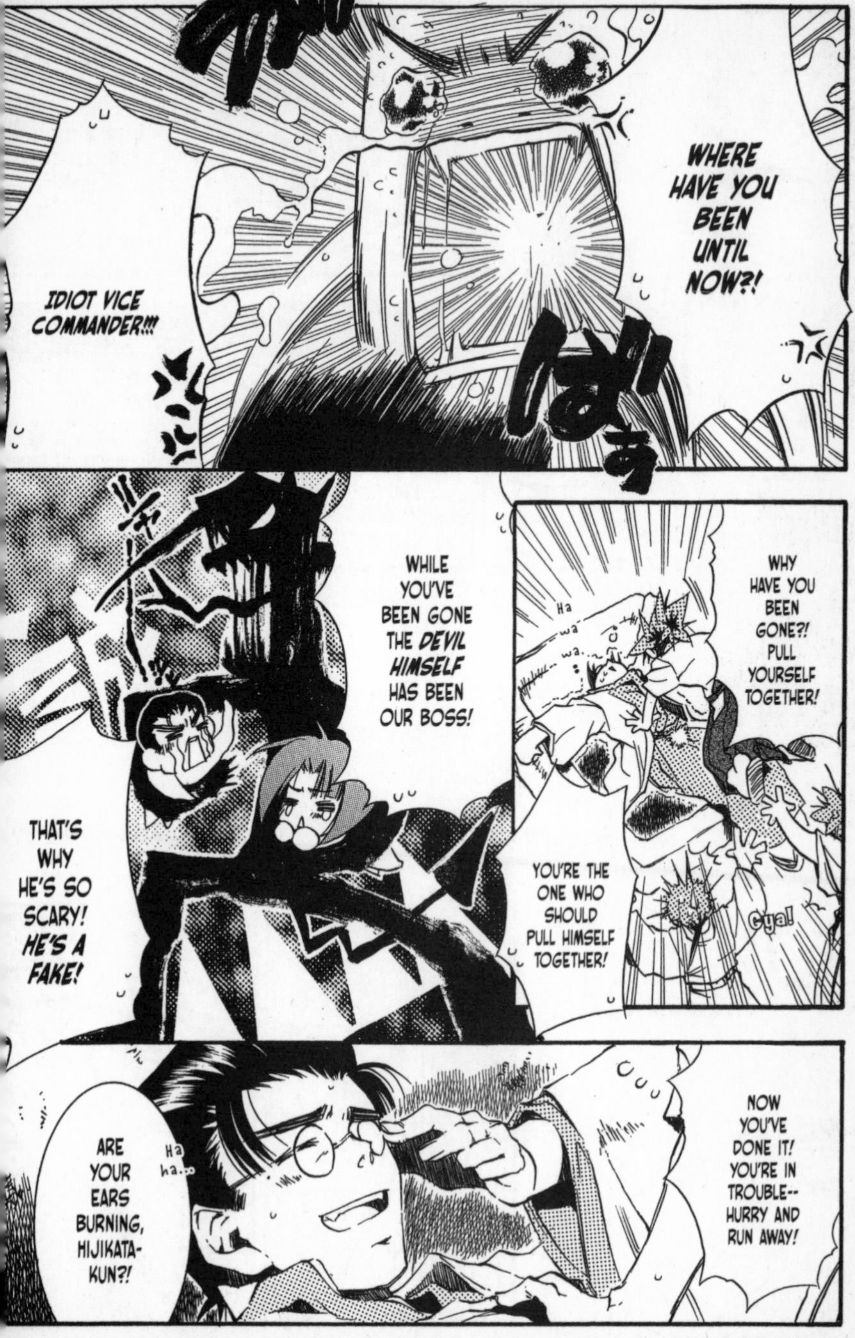
WHERE HAVE YOU BEEN UNTIL NOW?!
IDIOT VICE COMMANDER!!!
WHY HAVE YOU BEEN GONE?! PULL YOURSELF TOGETHER!
Ha wa wa...
YOU'RE THE ONE WHO SHOULD PULL HIMSELF TOGETHER!
Gya!
WHILE YOU'VE BEEN GONE THE *DEVIL HIMSELF* HAS BEEN OUR BOSS!
THAT'S WHY HE'S SO SCARY! *HE'S A FAKE!*
NOW YOU'VE DONE IT! YOU'RE IN TROUBLE-- HURRY AND RUN AWAY!
Ha ha...
ARE YOUR EARS BURNING, HIJIKATA-KUN?!

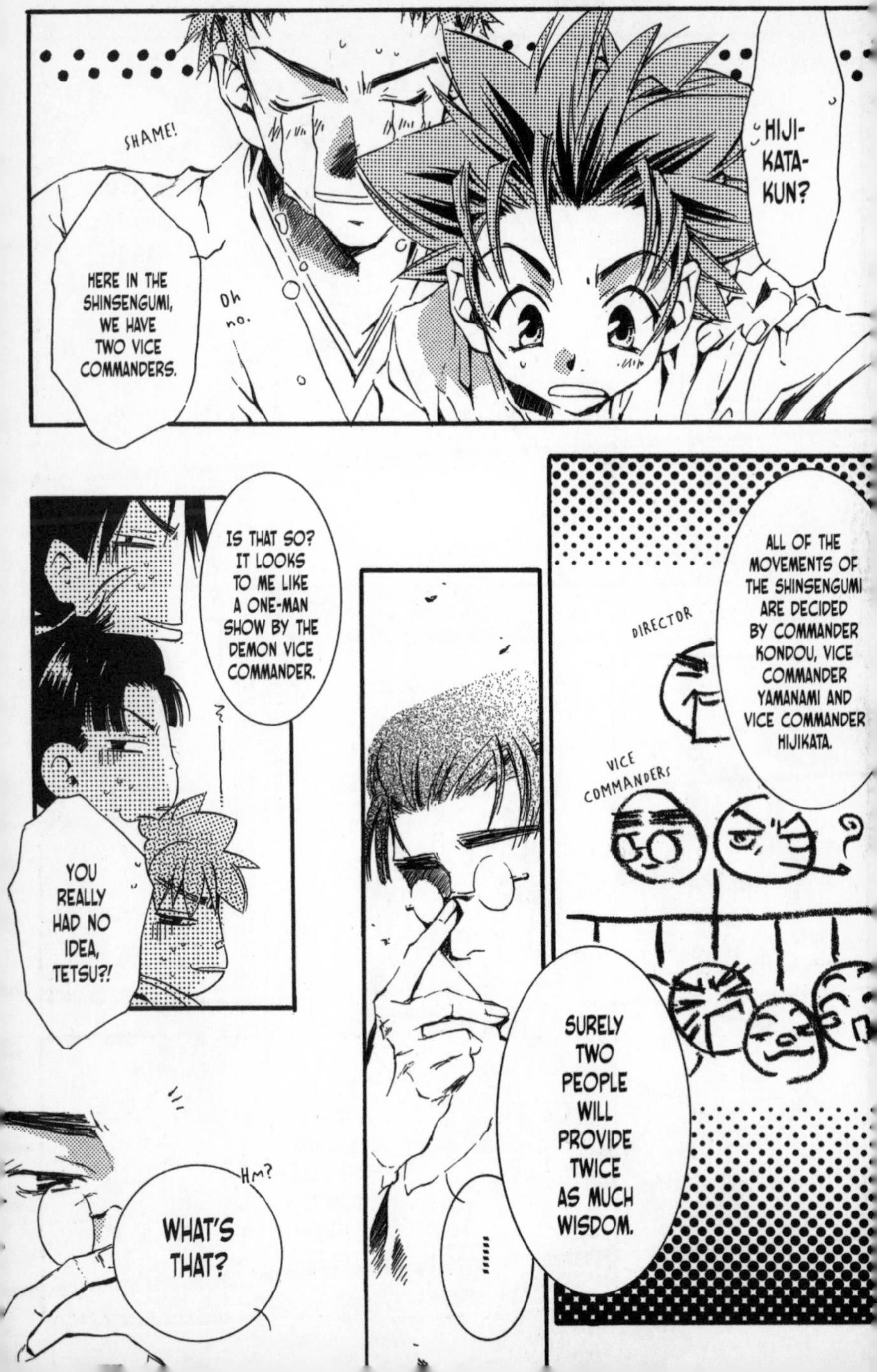
HIJI-KATA-KUN?
SHAME!
Oh no.
HERE IN THE SHINSENGUMI, WE HAVE TWO VICE COMMANDERS.
ALL OF THE MOVEMENTS OF THE SHINSENGUMI ARE DECIDED BY COMMANDER KONDOU, VICE COMMANDER YAMANAMI AND VICE COMMANDER HIJIKATA.
DIRECTOR
VICE COMMANDERS
SURELY TWO PEOPLE WILL PROVIDE TWICE AS MUCH WISDOM.
......
IS THAT SO? IT LOOKS TO ME LIKE A ONE-MAN SHOW BY THE DEMON VICE COMMANDER.
YOU REALLY HAD NO IDEA, TETSU?!
Hm?
WHAT'S THAT?

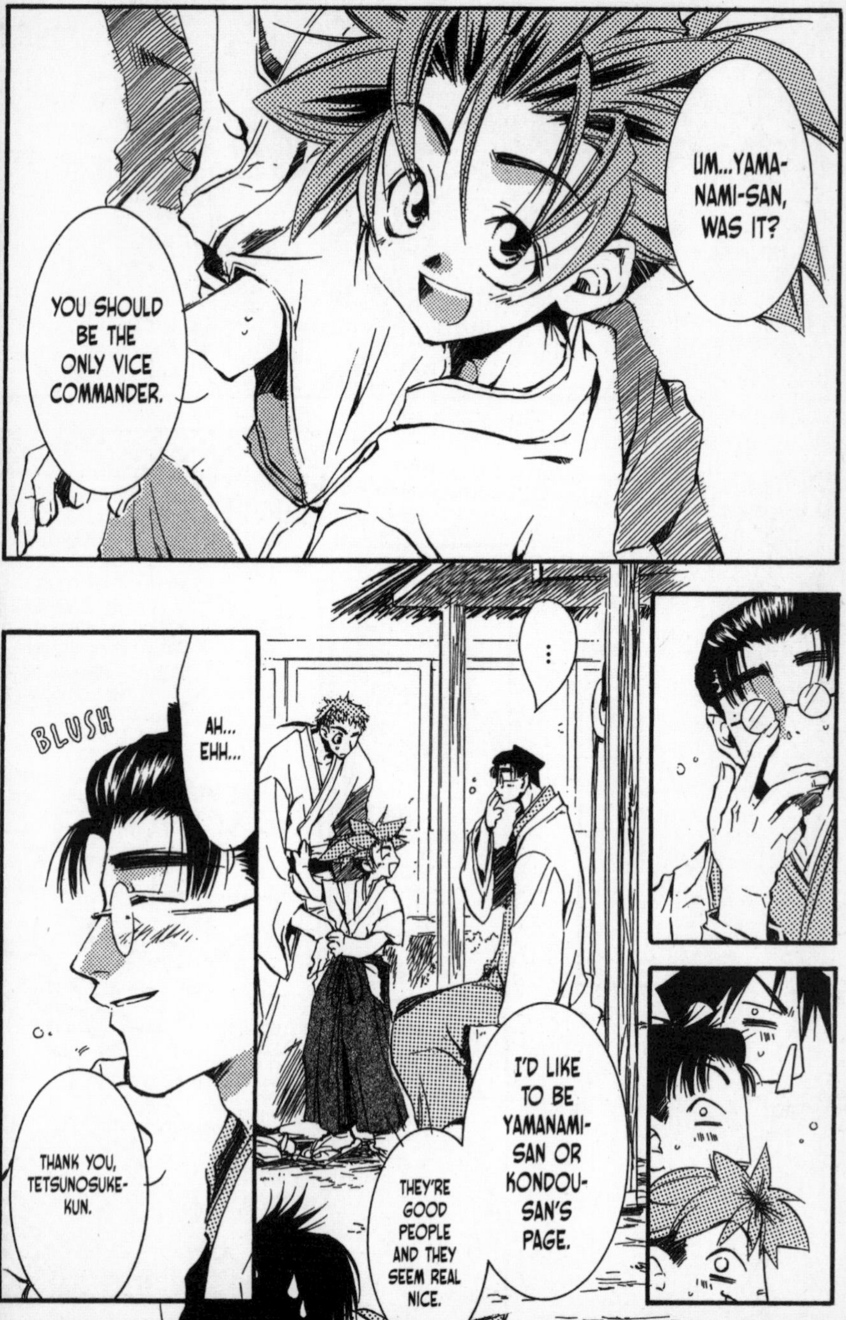
UM...YAMA-NAMI-SAN, WAS IT?
YOU SHOULD BE THE ONLY VICE COMMANDER.
...
I'D LIKE TO BE YAMANAMI-SAN OR KONDOU-SAN'S PAGE.
THEY'RE GOOD PEOPLE AND THEY SEEM REAL NICE.
AH... EHH...
BLUSH
THANK YOU, TETSUNOSUKE-KUN.

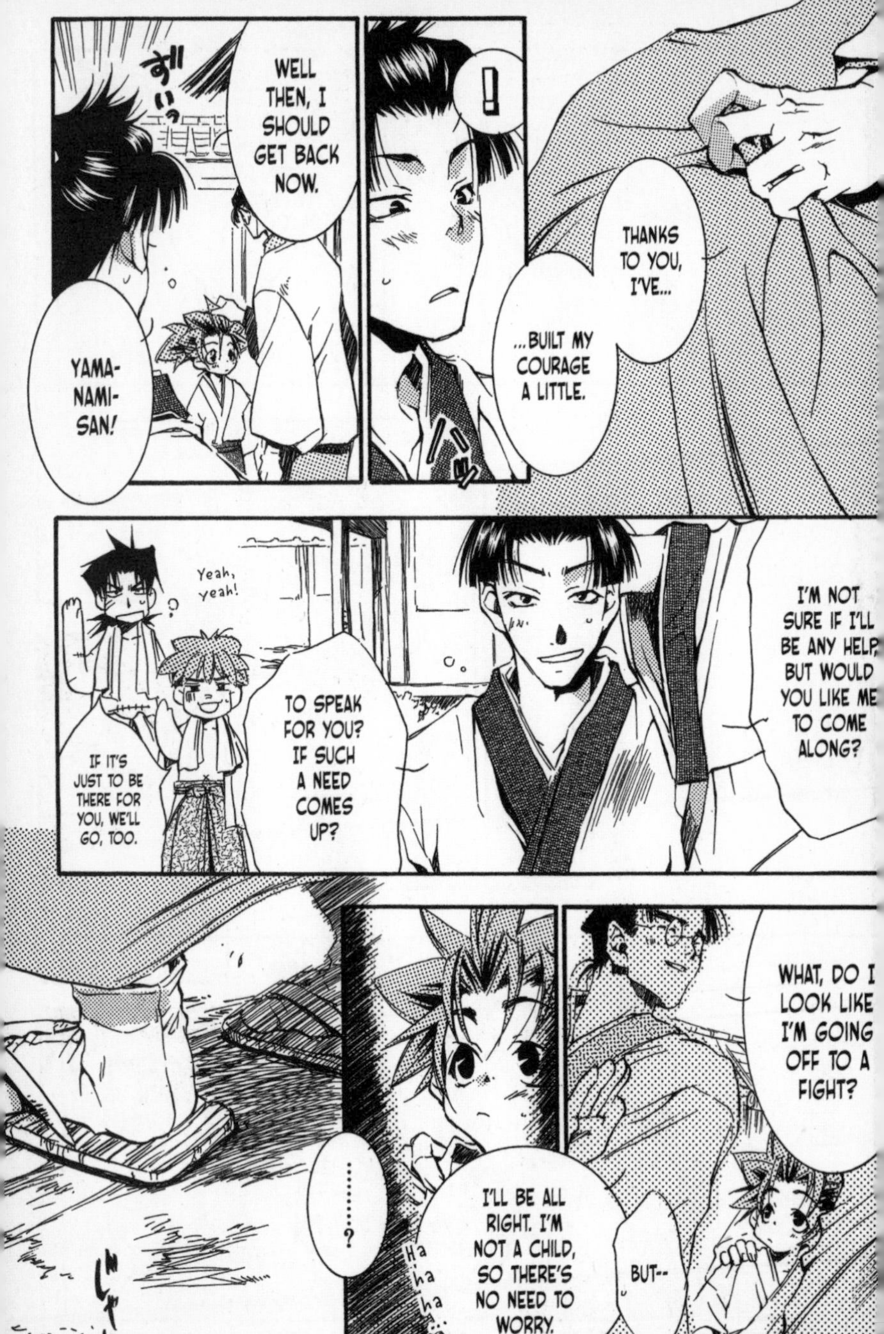
THANKS TO YOU, I'VE...
...BUILT MY COURAGE A LITTLE.
!
WELL THEN, I SHOULD GET BACK NOW.
ずいっ
YAMANAMI-SAN!
I'M NOT SURE IF I'LL BE ANY HELP, BUT WOULD YOU LIKE ME TO COME ALONG?
TO SPEAK FOR YOU? IF SUCH A NEED COMES UP?
Yeah, yeah!
IF IT'S JUST TO BE THERE FOR YOU, WE'LL GO, TOO.
WHAT, DO I LOOK LIKE I'M GOING OFF TO A FIGHT?
BUT--
I'LL BE ALL RIGHT. I'M NOT A CHILD, SO THERE'S NO NEED TO WORRY.
Ha ha ha...
......?
じゃり

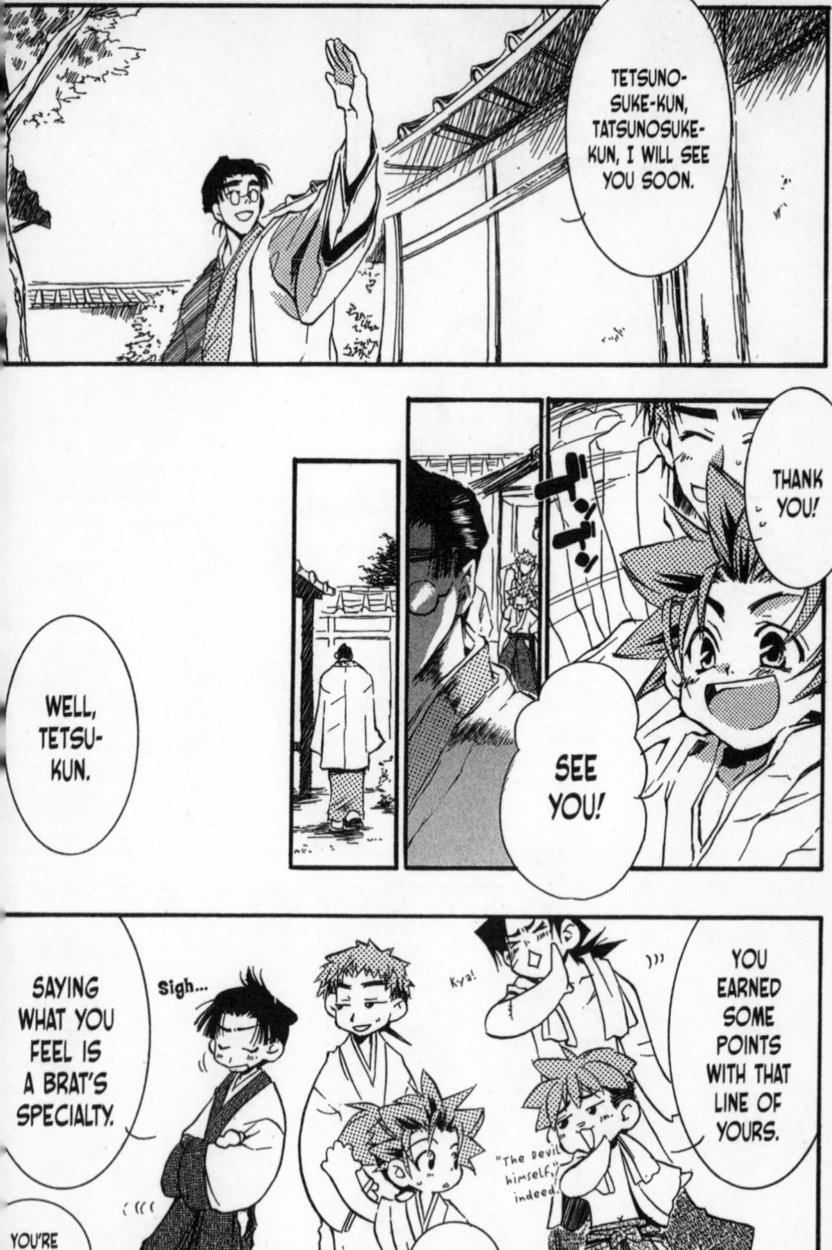
TETSUNO-SUKE-KUN, TATSUNOSUKE-KUN, I WILL SEE YOU SOON.
THANK YOU!
SEE YOU!
WELL, TETSU-KUN.
YOU EARNED SOME POINTS WITH THAT LINE OF YOURS.
Kya!
"The Devil himself," indeed.
HUH?
Sigh...
SAYING WHAT YOU FEEL IS A BRAT'S SPECIALTY.
YOU'RE ONE TO TALK.

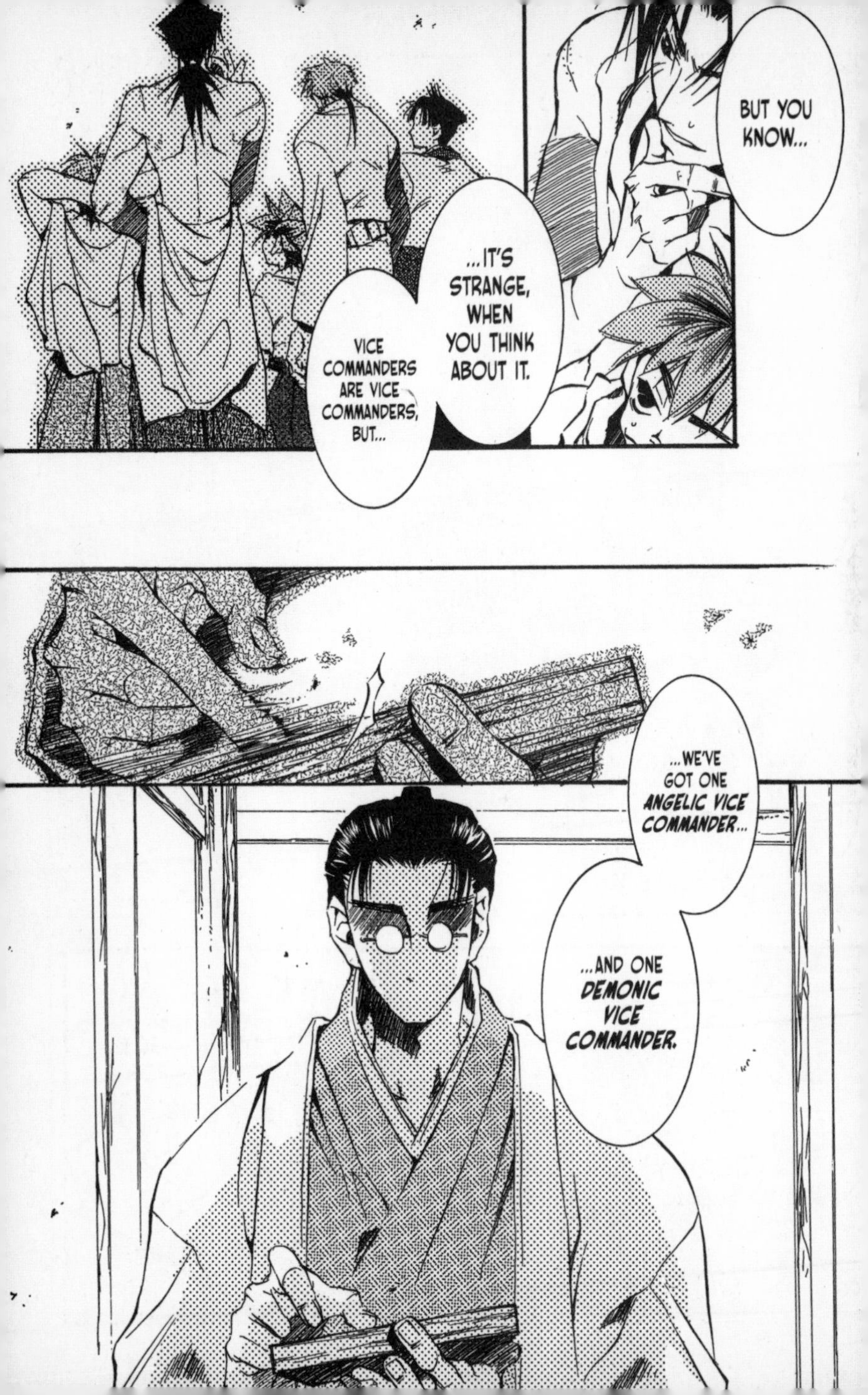
BUT YOU KNOW...
...IT'S STRANGE, WHEN YOU THINK ABOUT IT.
VICE COMMANDERS ARE VICE COMMANDERS, BUT...
...WE'VE GOT ONE *ANGELIC VICE COMMANDER*...
...AND ONE *DEMONIC VICE COMMANDER.*

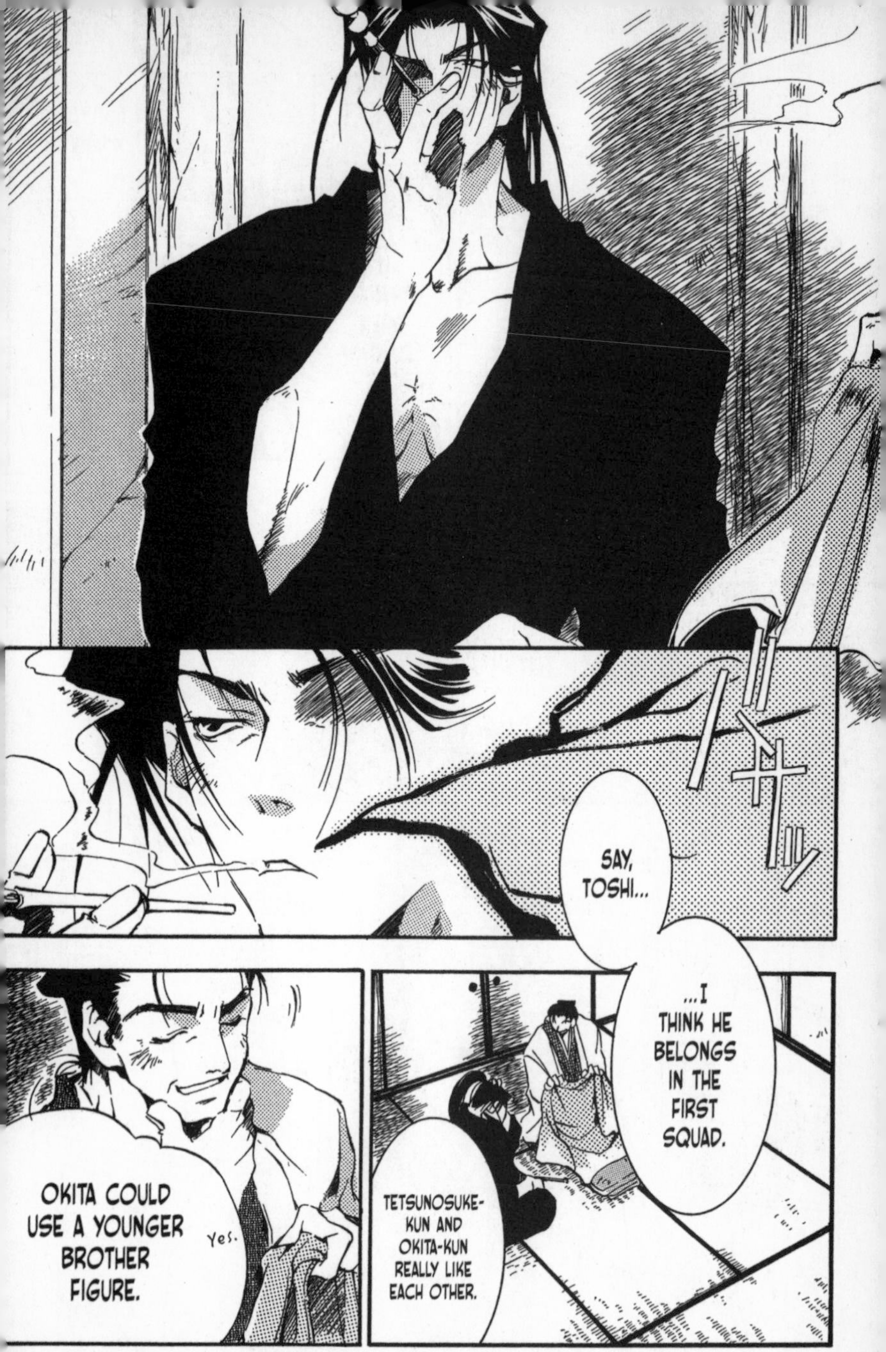
SAY, TOSHI...
...I THINK HE BELONGS IN THE FIRST SQUAD.
TETSUNOSUKE-KUN AND OKITA-KUN REALLY LIKE EACH OTHER.
Yes.
OKITA COULD USE A YOUNGER BROTHER FIGURE.

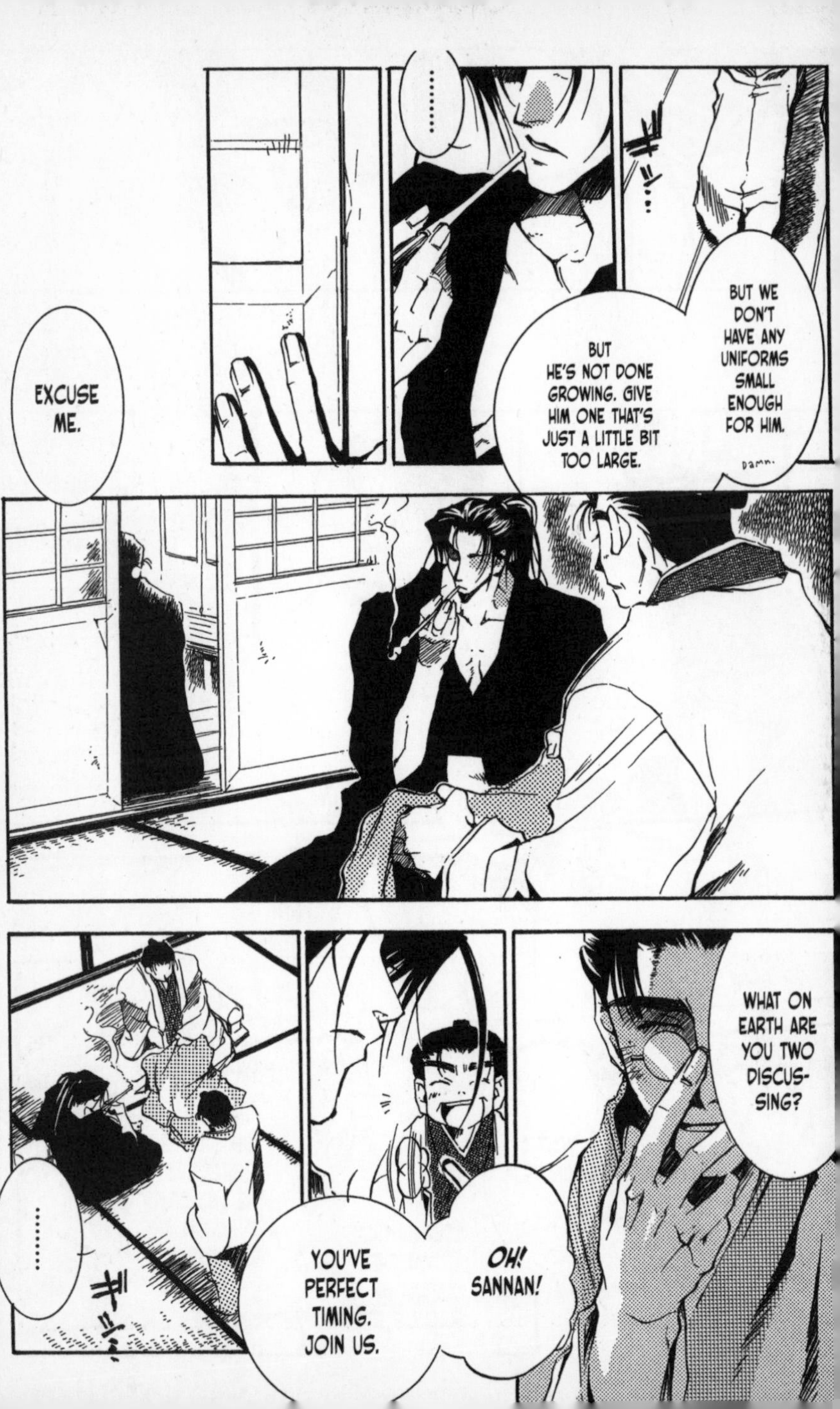
BUT WE DON'T HAVE ANY UNIFORMS SMALL ENOUGH FOR HIM.
damn.
BUT HE'S NOT DONE GROWING. GIVE HIM ONE THAT'S JUST A LITTLE BIT TOO LARGE.
......
EXCUSE ME.
WHAT ON EARTH ARE YOU TWO DISCUS-SING?
OH! SANNAN!
YOU'VE PERFECT TIMING. JOIN US.
......

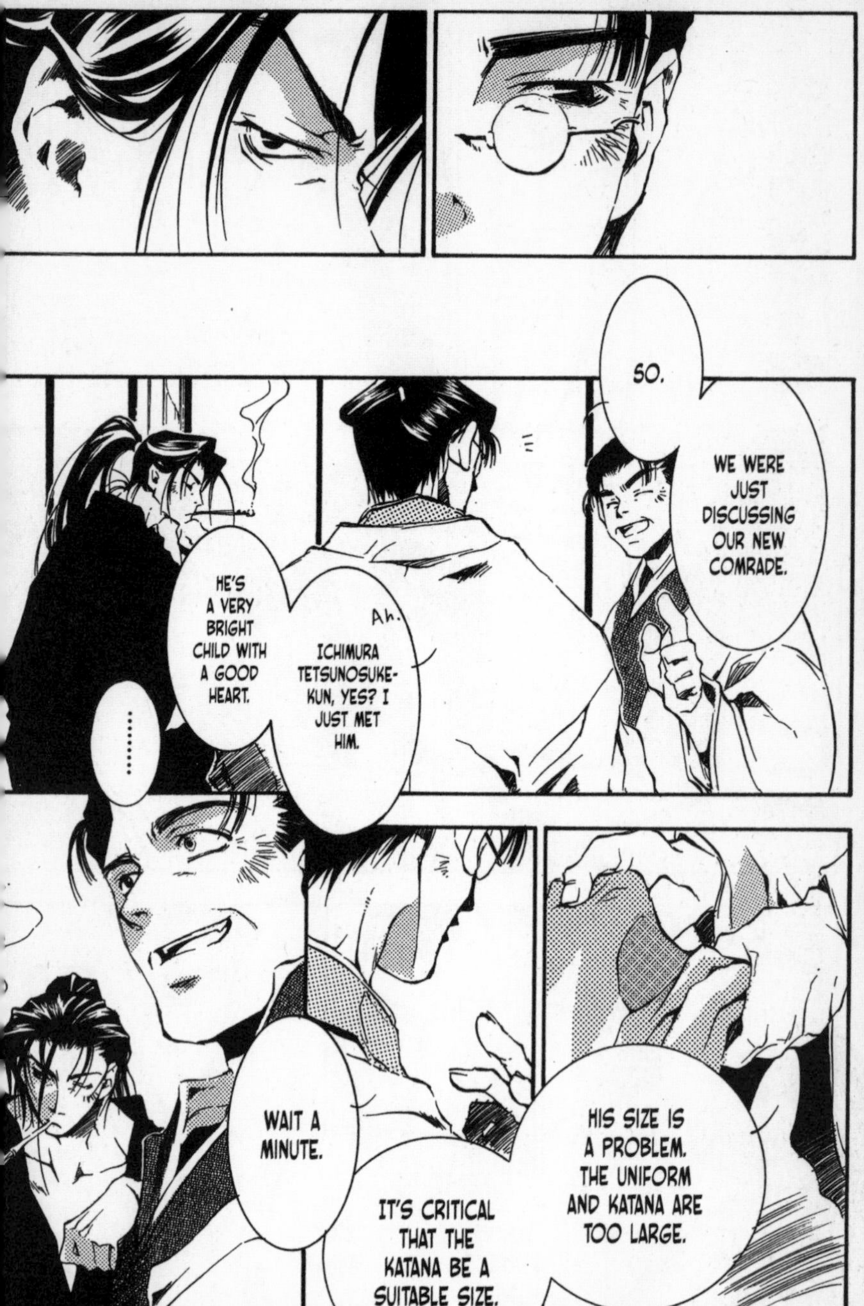
SO.
WE WERE JUST DISCUSSING OUR NEW COMRADE.
Ah.
ICHIMURA TETSUNOSUKE-KUN, YES? I JUST MET HIM.
HE'S A VERY BRIGHT CHILD WITH A GOOD HEART.
......
HIS SIZE IS A PROBLEM. THE UNIFORM AND KATANA ARE TOO LARGE.
IT'S CRITICAL THAT THE KATANA BE A SUITABLE SIZE.
WAIT A MINUTE.

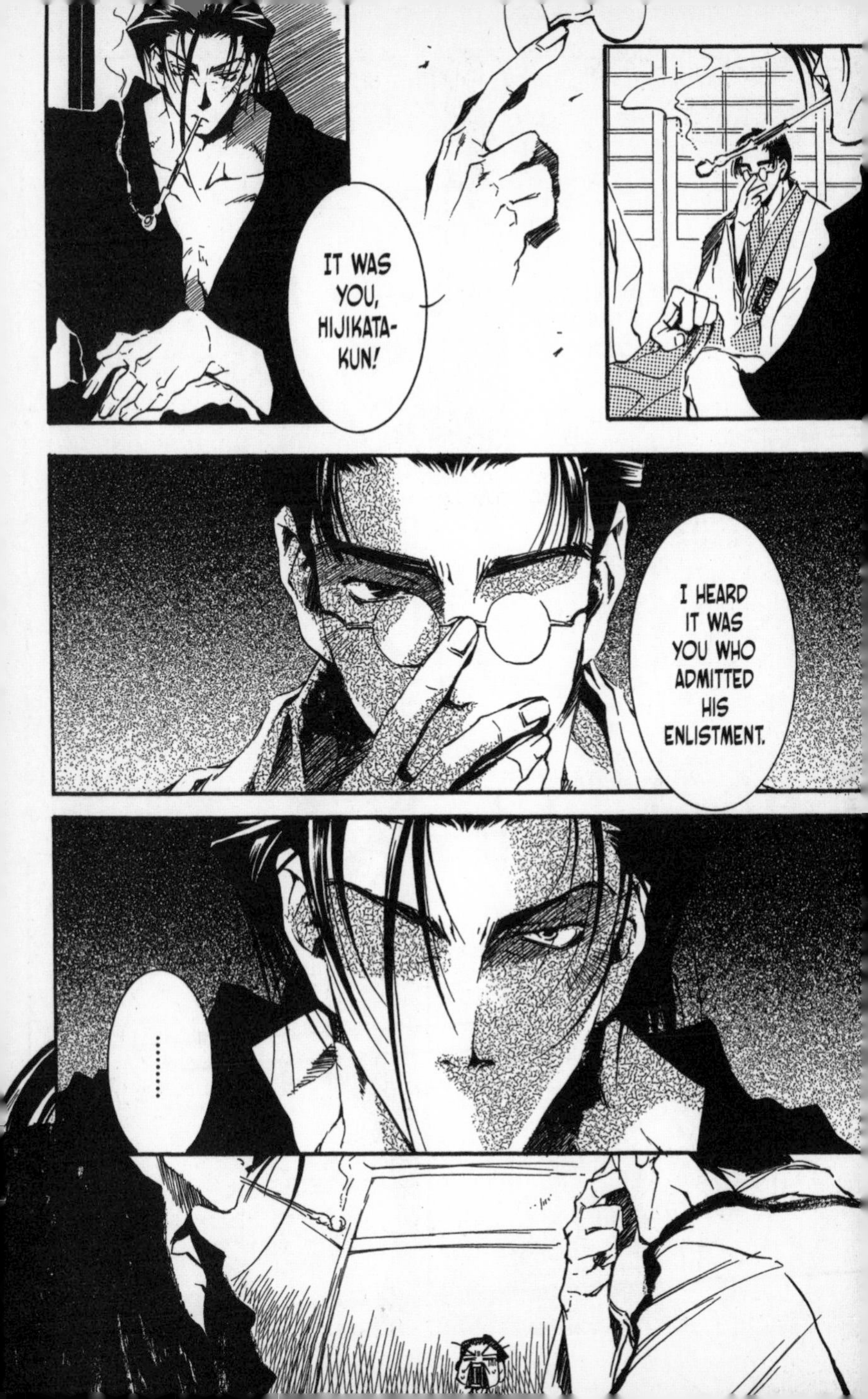

IT WAS YOU, HIJIKATA-KUN!
I HEARD IT WAS YOU WHO ADMITTED HIS ENLISTMENT.
......

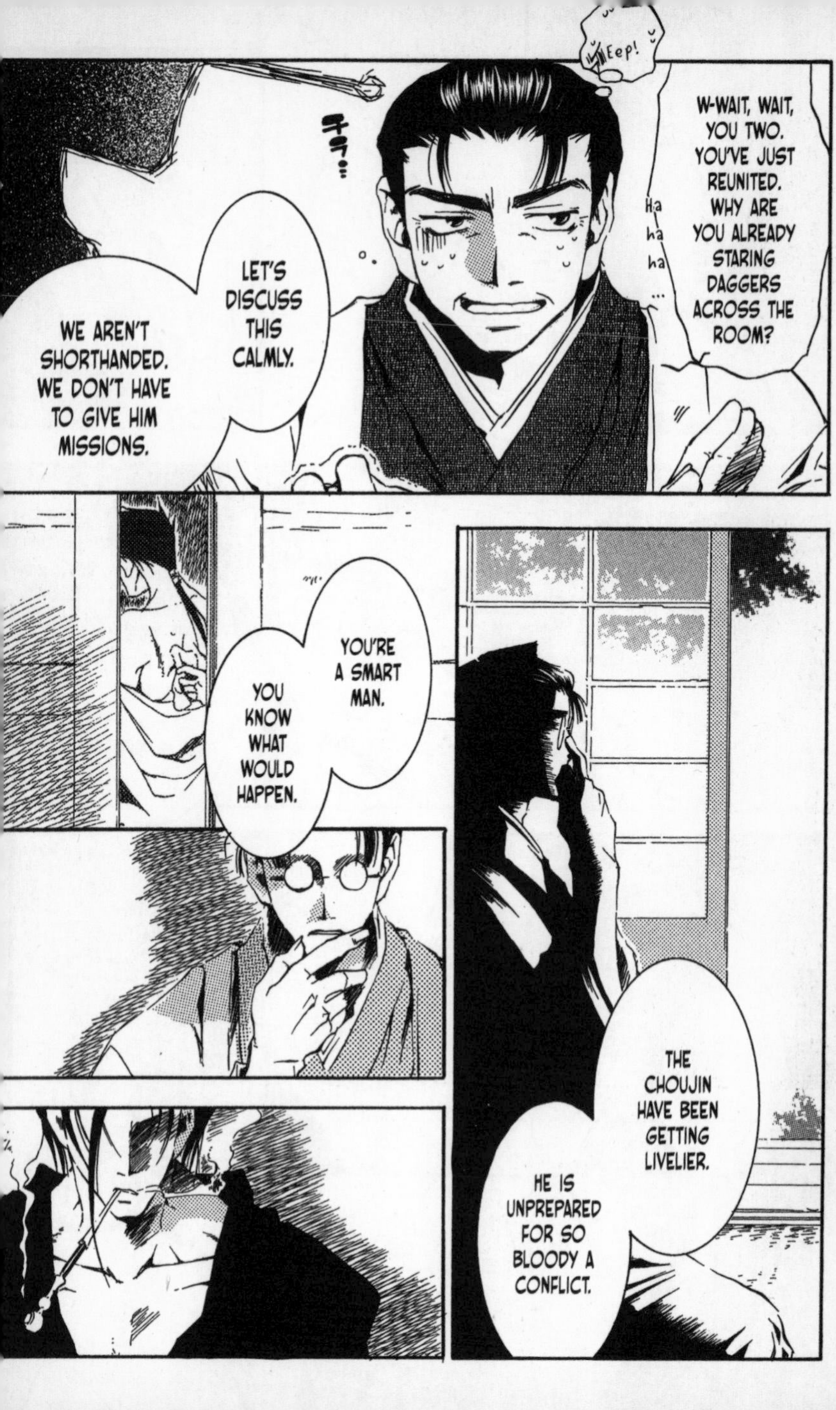
Eep!
W-WAIT, WAIT, YOU TWO. YOU'VE JUST REUNITED. WHY ARE YOU ALREADY STARING DAGGERS ACROSS THE ROOM?
Ha ha ha ...
LET'S DISCUSS THIS CALMLY.
WE AREN'T SHORTHANDED. WE DON'T HAVE TO GIVE HIM MISSIONS.
THE CHOUJIN HAVE BEEN GETTING LIVELIER.
HE IS UNPREPARED FOR SO BLOODY A CONFLICT.
YOU'RE A SMART MAN.
YOU KNOW WHAT WOULD HAPPEN.

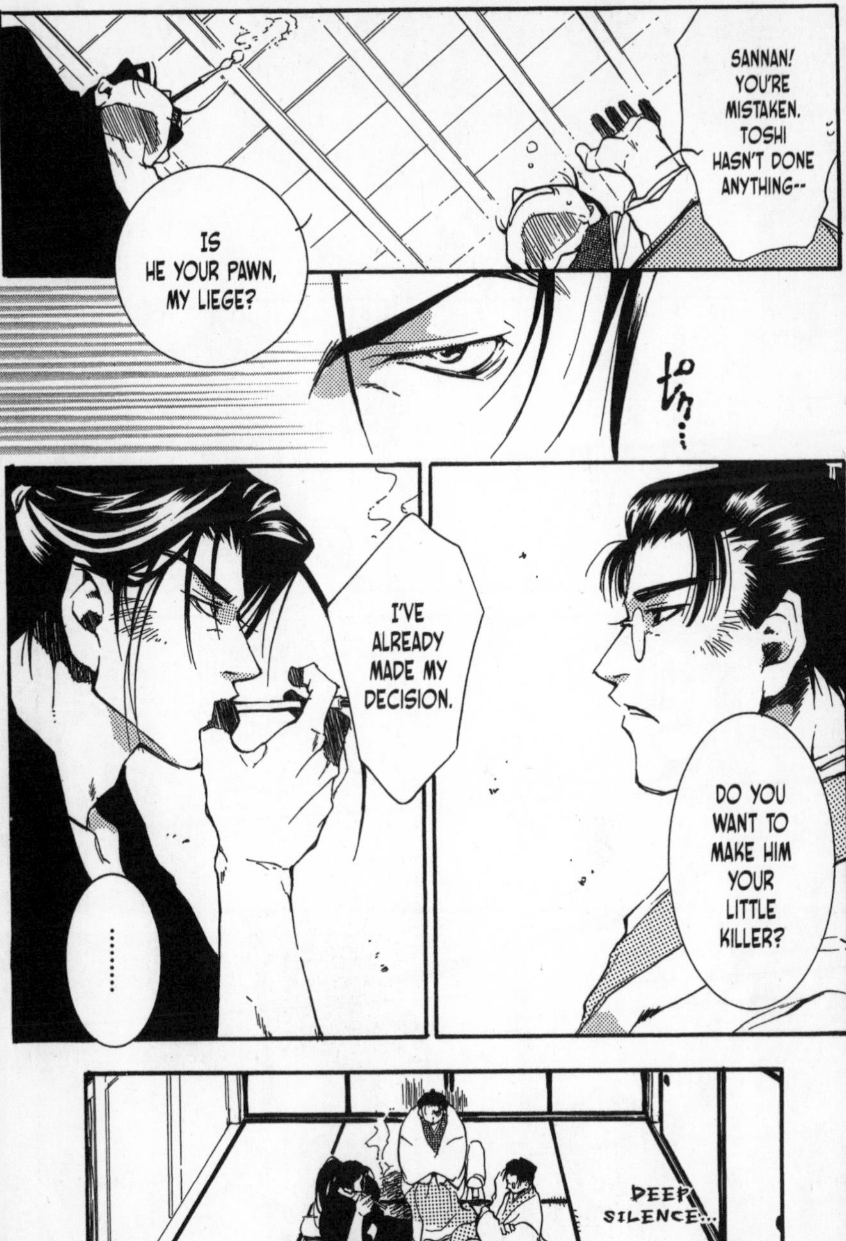
SANNAN! YOU'RE MISTAKEN. TOSHI HASN'T DONE ANYTHING--
IS HE YOUR PAWN, MY LIEGE?
DO YOU WANT TO MAKE HIM YOUR LITTLE KILLER?
I'VE ALREADY MADE MY DECISION.
....
DEEP SILENCE...

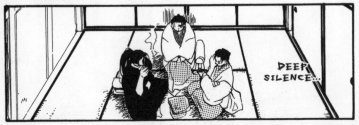

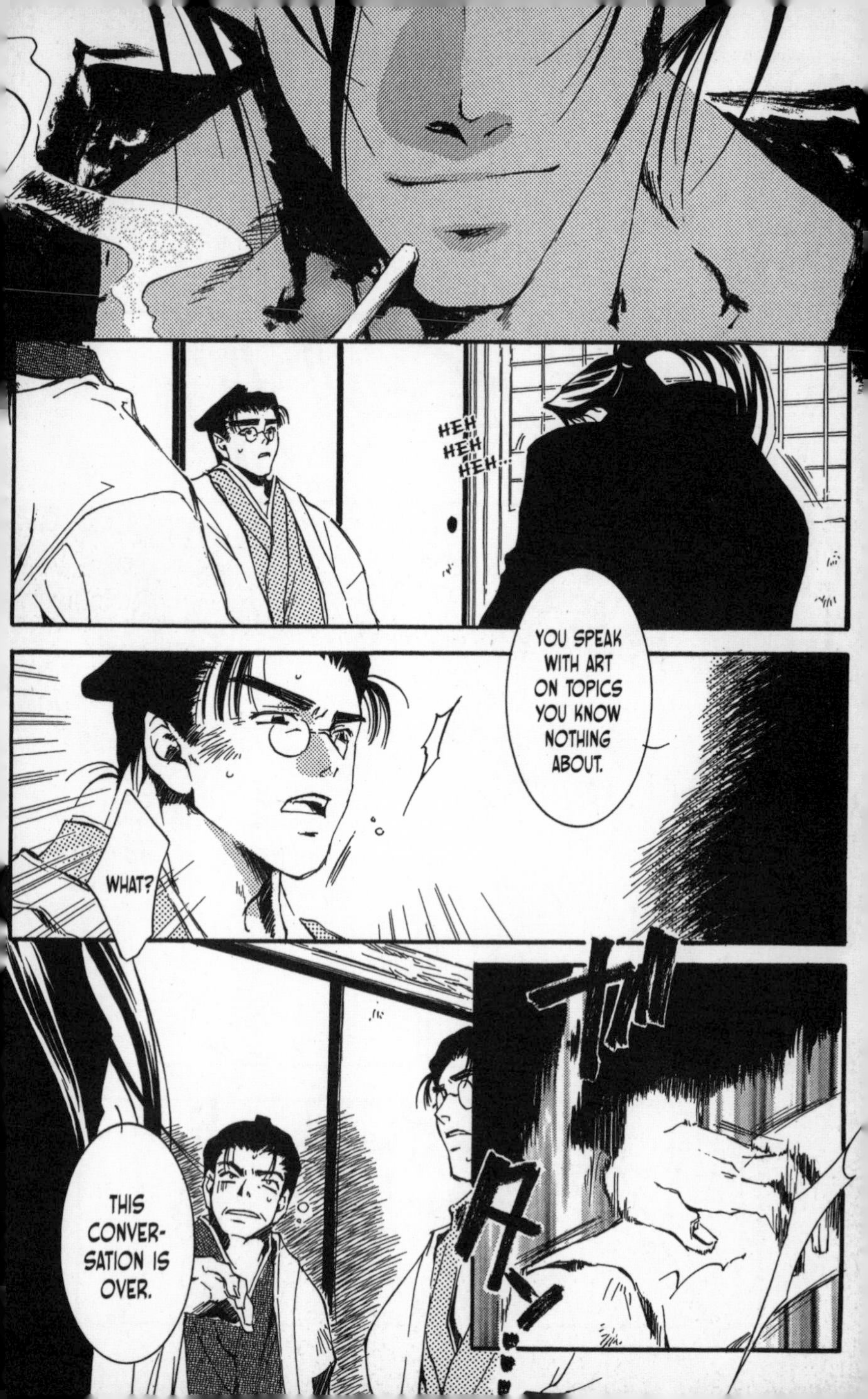
HEH HEH HEH...
YOU SPEAK WITH ART ON TOPICS YOU KNOW NOTHING ABOUT.
WHAT?
THIS CONVER-SATION IS OVER.

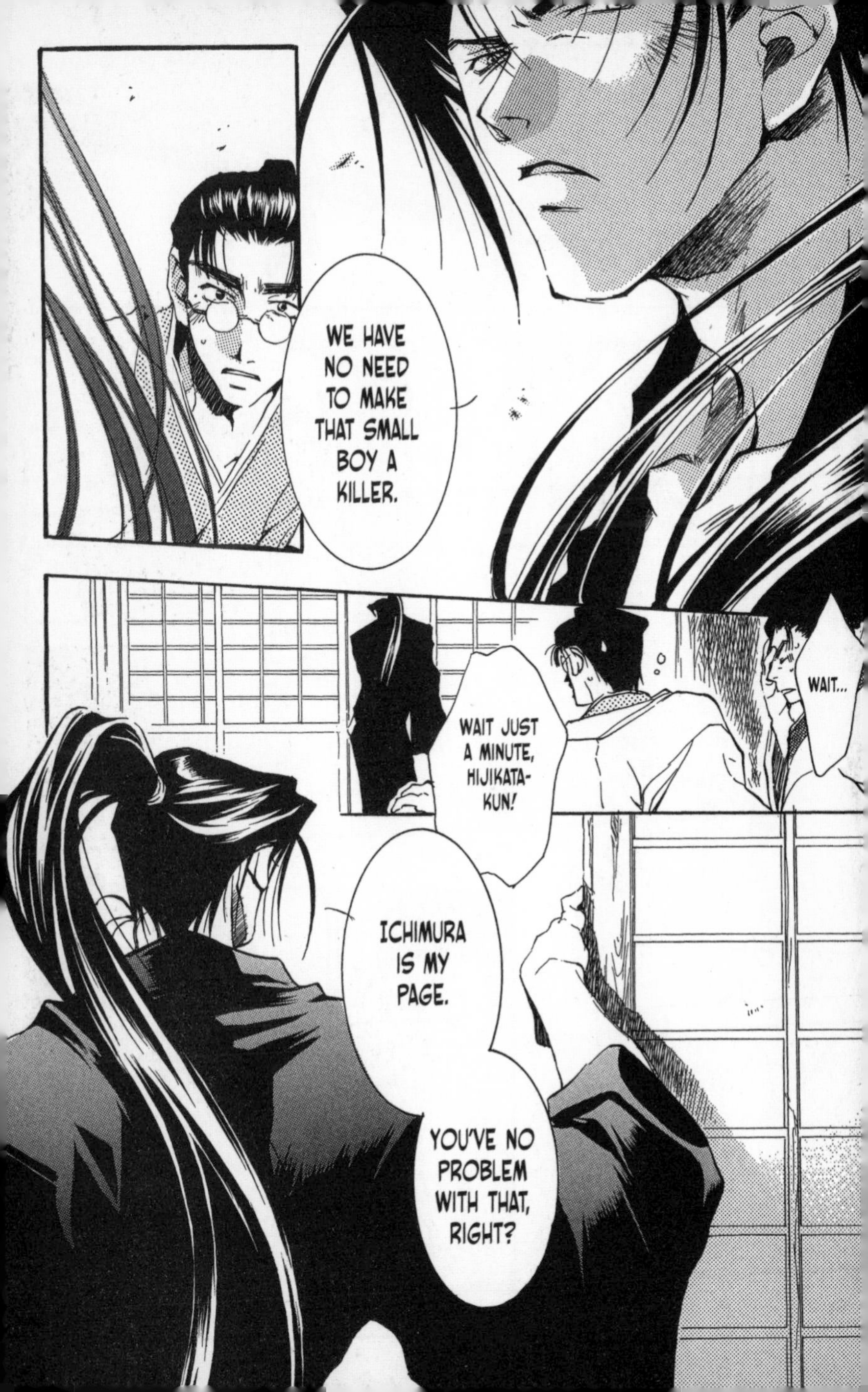
WE HAVE NO NEED TO MAKE THAT SMALL BOY A KILLER.
WAIT...
WAIT JUST A MINUTE, HIJIKATA-KUN!
ICHIMURA IS MY PAGE.
YOU'VE NO PROBLEM WITH THAT, RIGHT?

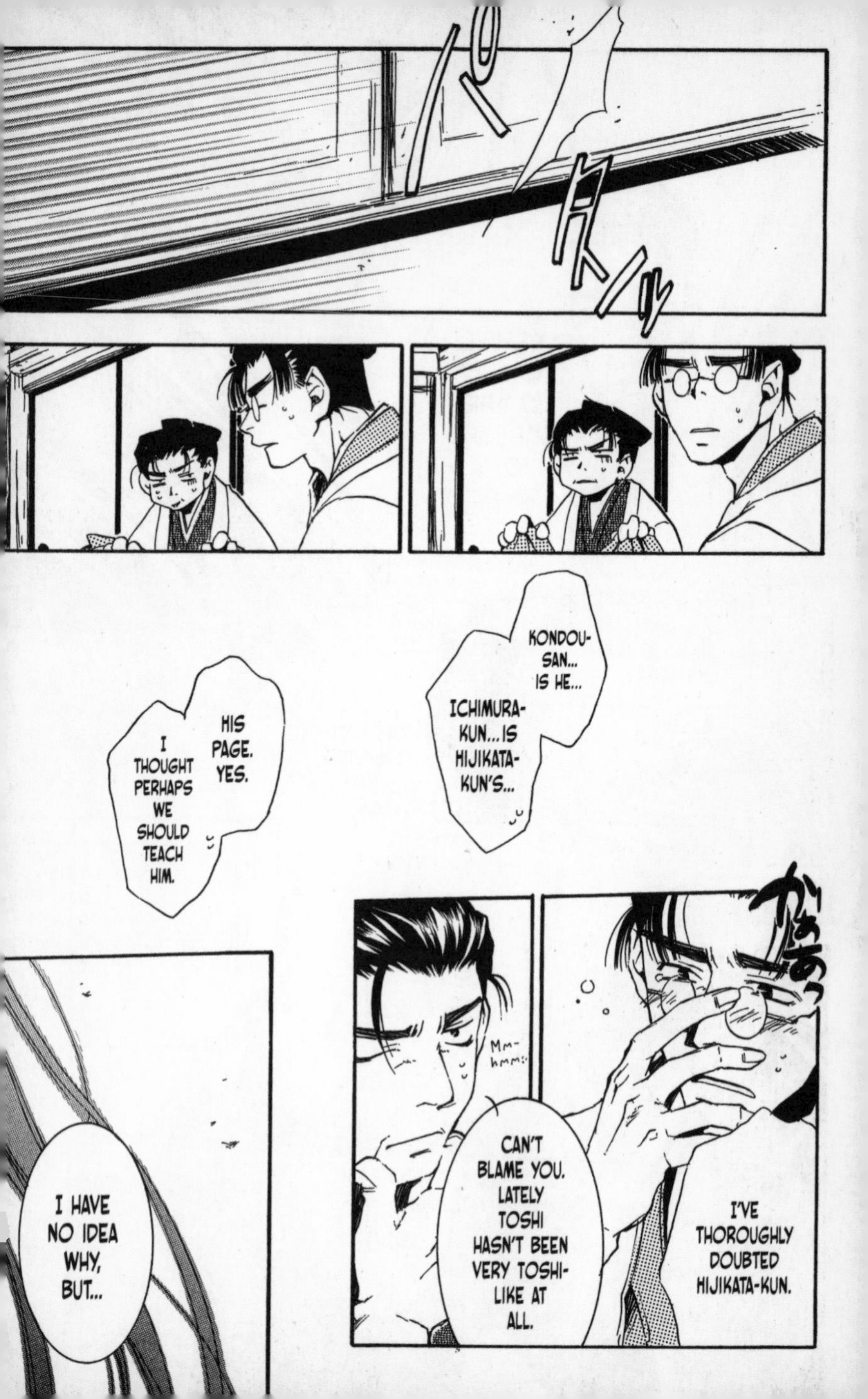
パタンッ
KONDOU-SAN... IS HE...
ICHIMURA-KUN... IS HIJIKATA-KUN'S...
HIS PAGE. YES.
I THOUGHT PERHAPS WE SHOULD TEACH HIM.
かぁあっ
I'VE THOROUGHLY DOUBTED HIJIKATA-KUN.
Mm-hmm.
CAN'T BLAME YOU. LATELY TOSHI HASN'T BEEN VERY TOSHI-LIKE AT ALL.
I HAVE NO IDEA WHY, BUT...

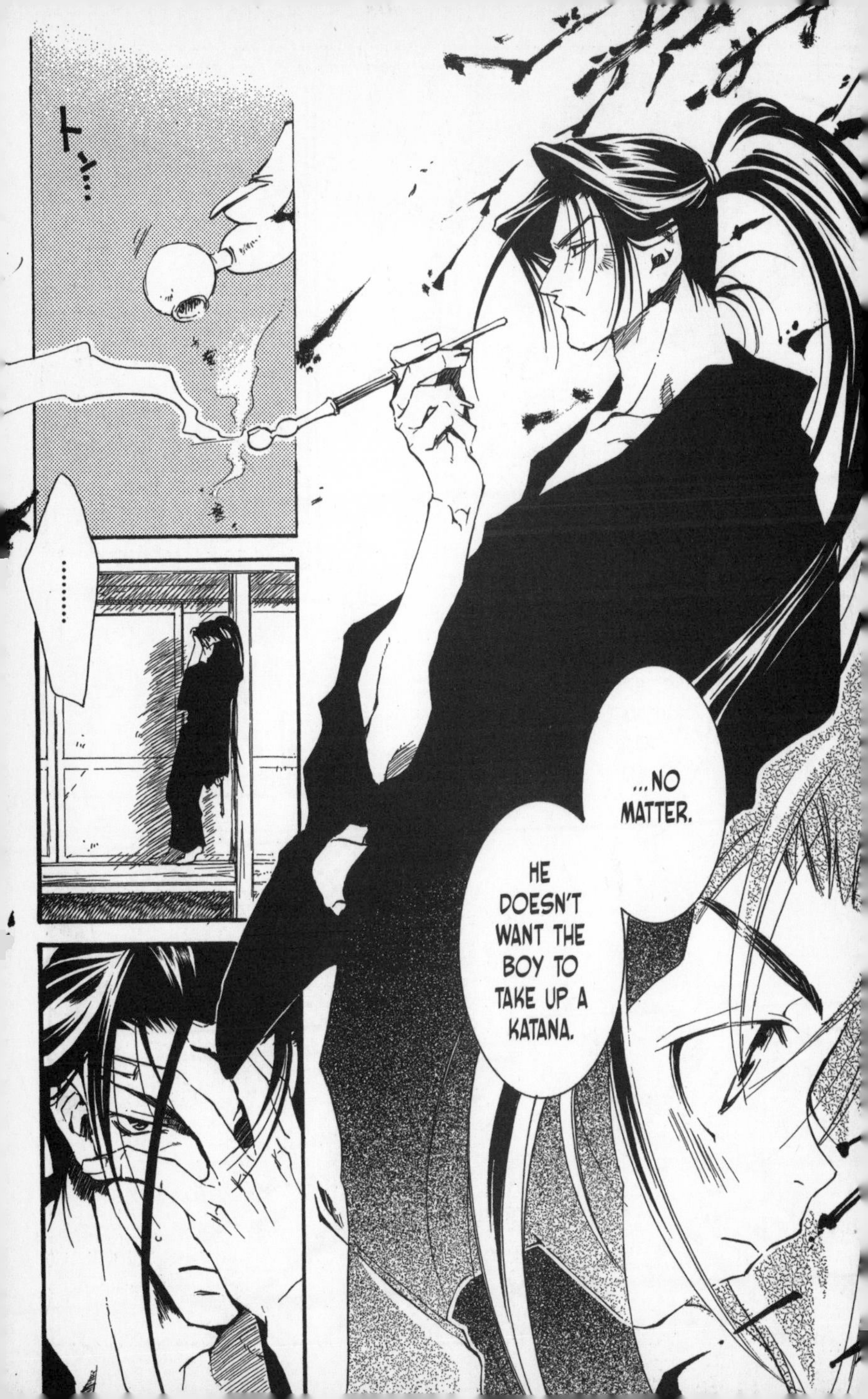

......
...NO MATTER.
HE DOESN'T WANT THE BOY TO TAKE UP A KATANA.

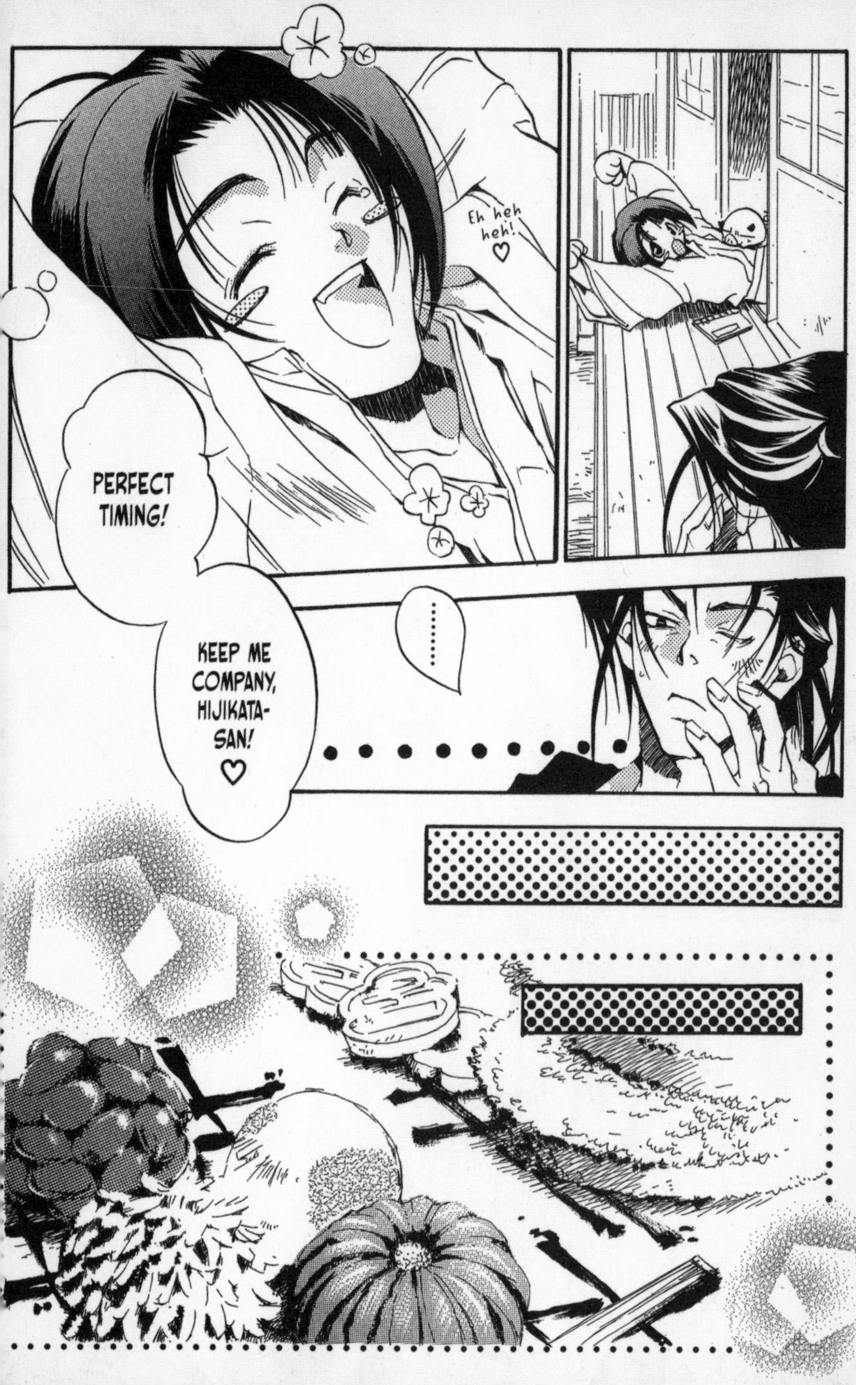
Eh heh heh! ♡
PERFECT TIMING!
KEEP ME COMPANY, HIJIKATA-SAN! ♡
......
....

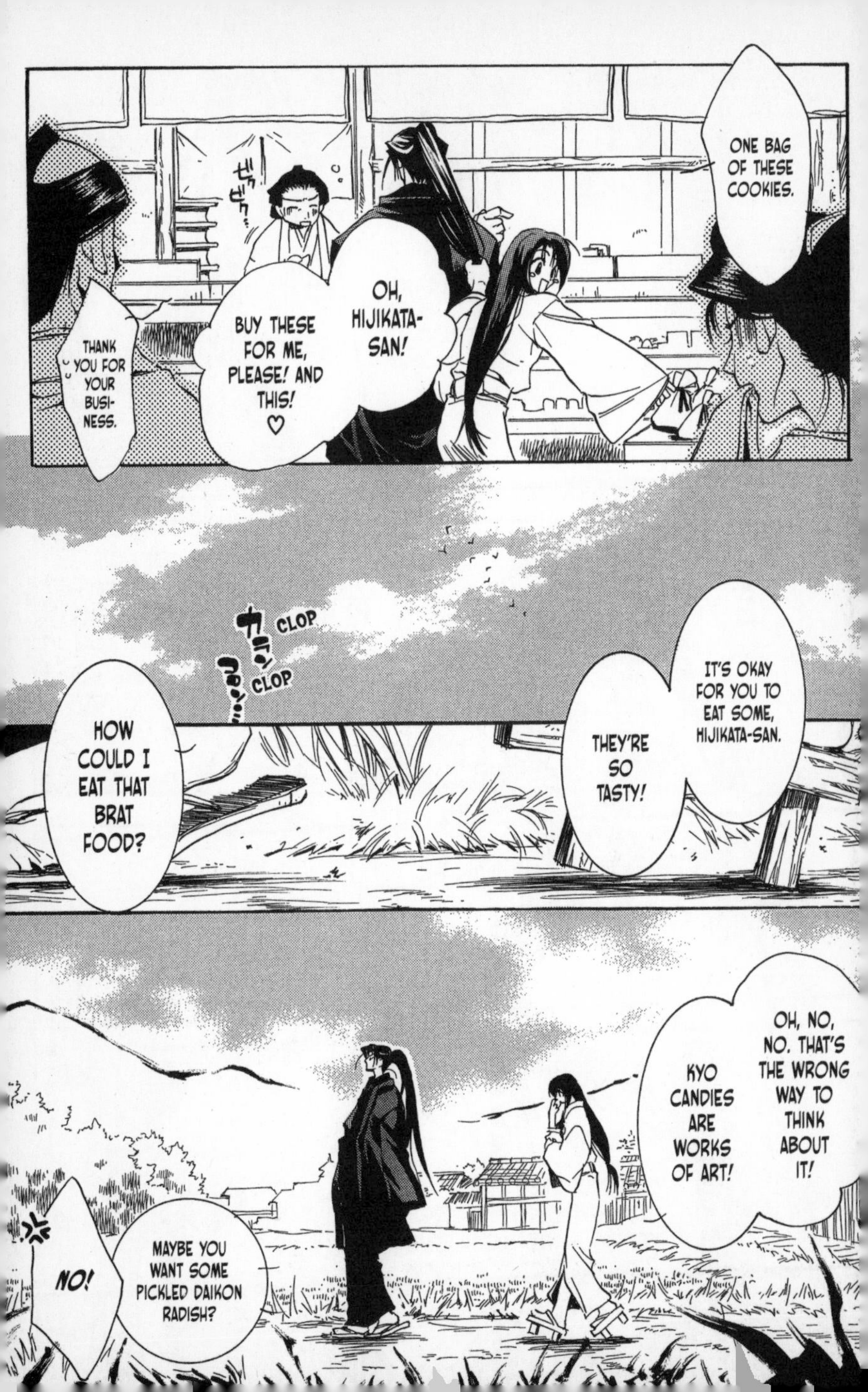
ONE BAG OF THESE COOKIES.
OH, HIJIKATA-SAN!
BUY THESE FOR ME, PLEASE! AND THIS! ♡
THANK YOU FOR YOUR BUSI-NESS.
IT'S OKAY FOR YOU TO EAT SOME, HIJIKATA-SAN.
THEY'RE SO TASTY!
CLOP
CLOP
HOW COULD I EAT THAT BRAT FOOD?
OH, NO, NO. THAT'S THE WRONG WAY TO THINK ABOUT IT!
KYO CANDIES ARE WORKS OF ART!
MAYBE YOU WANT SOME PICKLED DAIKON RADISH?
NO!

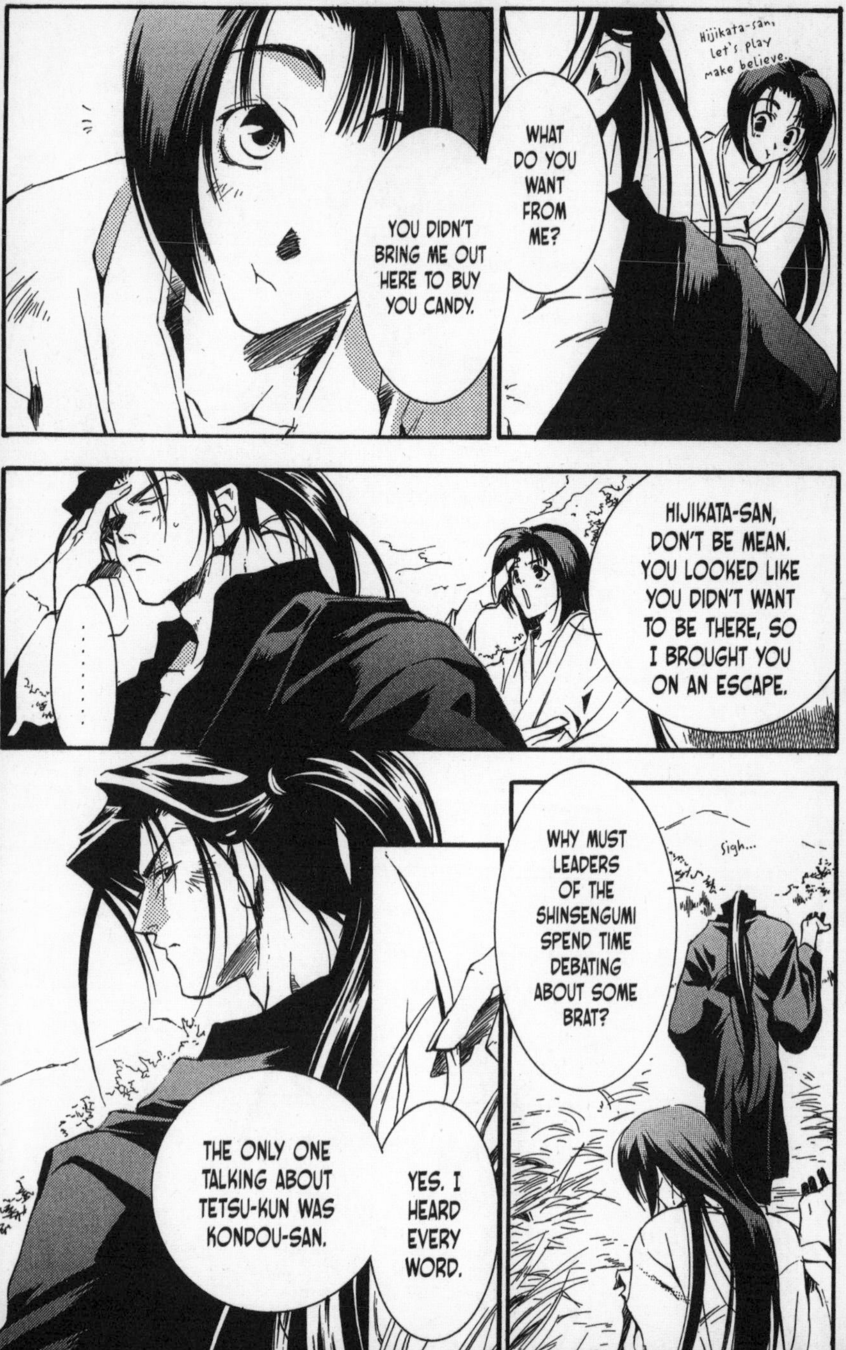
Hijikata-san, let's play make believe.
WHAT DO YOU WANT FROM ME?
YOU DIDN'T BRING ME OUT HERE TO BUY YOU CANDY.
HIJIKATA-SAN, DON'T BE MEAN. YOU LOOKED LIKE YOU DIDN'T WANT TO BE THERE, SO I BROUGHT YOU ON AN ESCAPE.
......
WHY MUST LEADERS OF THE SHINSENGUMI SPEND TIME DEBATING ABOUT SOME BRAT?
Sigh...
YES. I HEARD EVERY WORD.
THE ONLY ONE TALKING ABOUT TETSU-KUN WAS KONDOU-SAN.

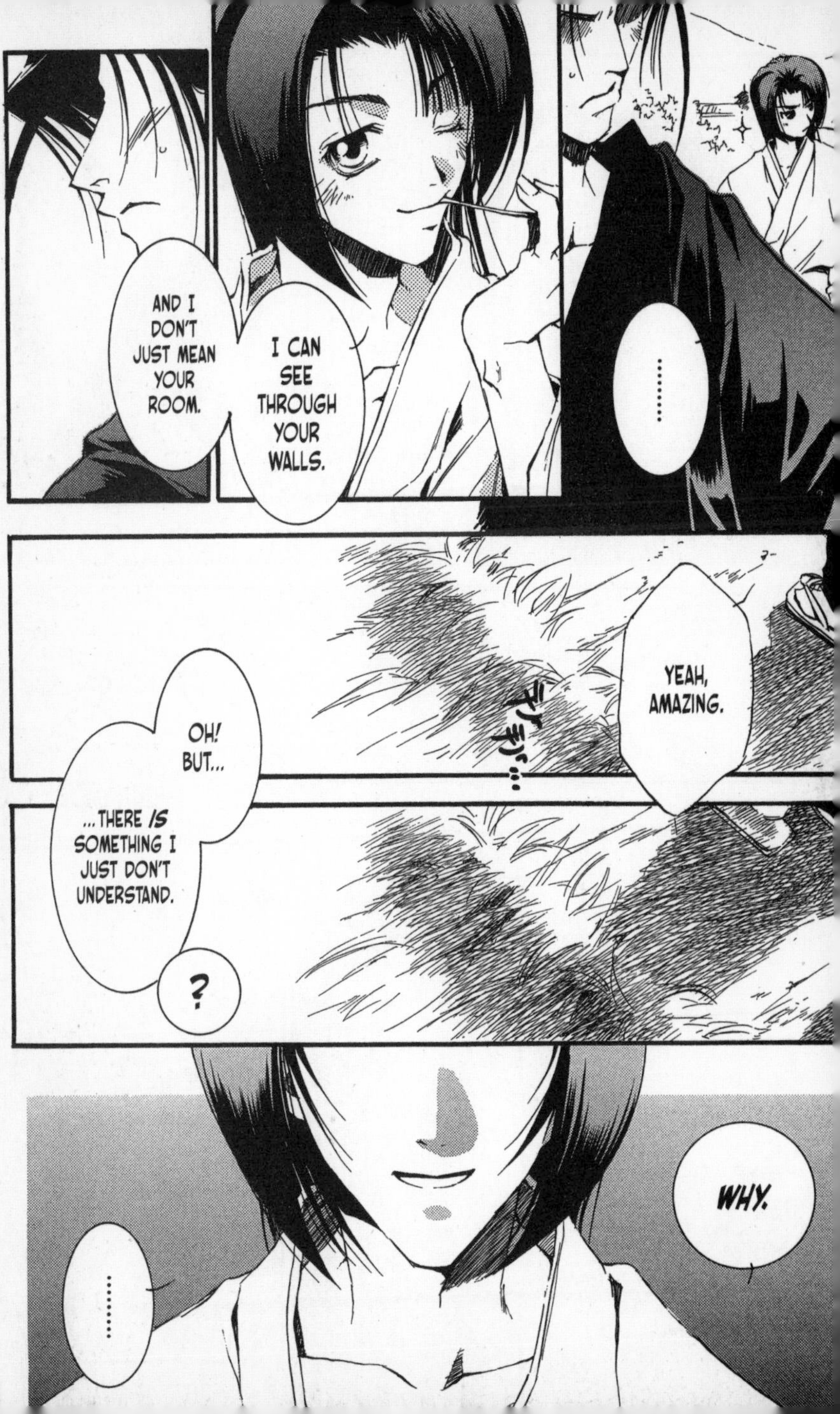
......
I CAN SEE THROUGH YOUR WALLS.
AND I DON'T JUST MEAN YOUR ROOM.
YEAH, AMAZING.
OH! BUT...
...THERE IS SOMETHING I JUST DON'T UNDERSTAND.
?
WHY.
......

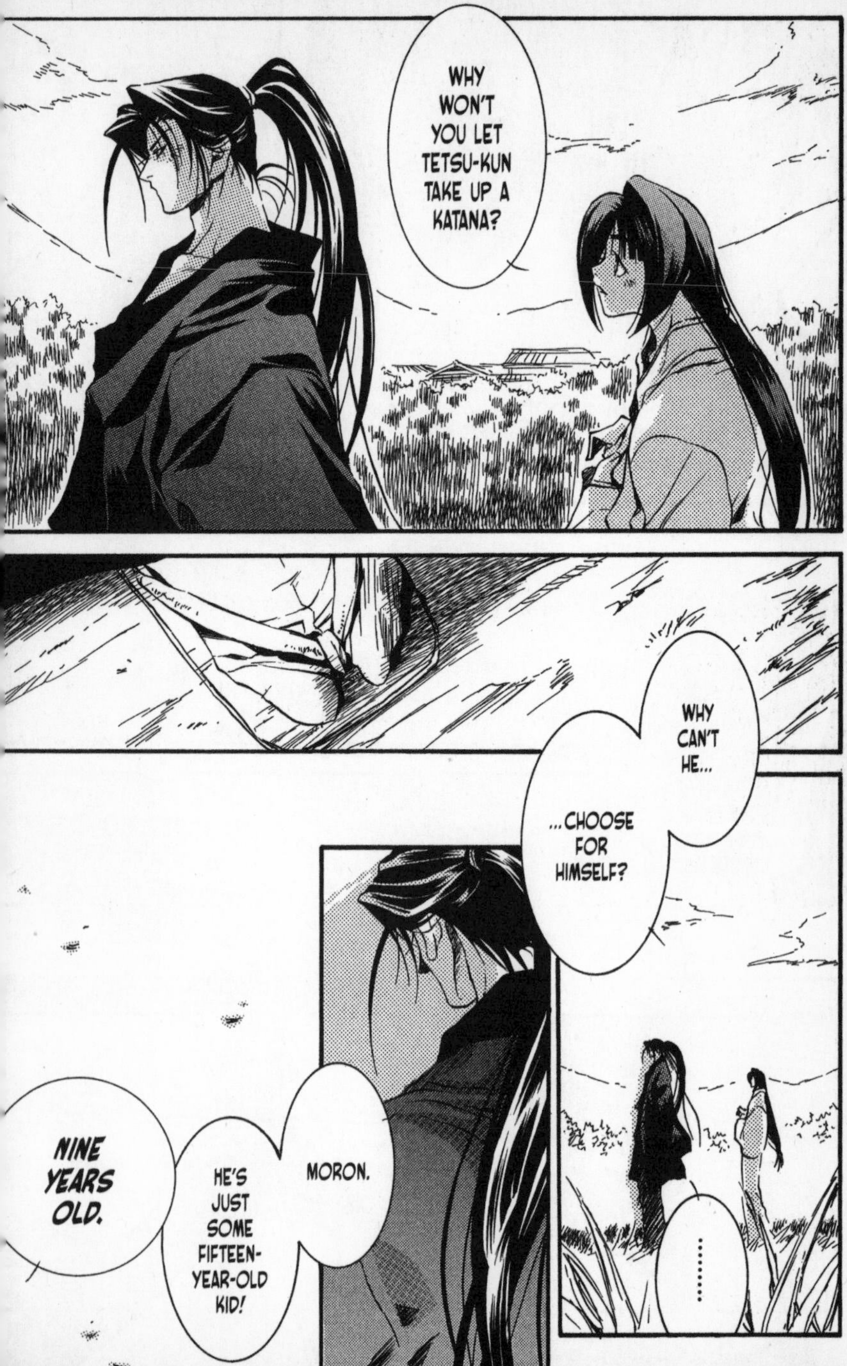
WHY WON'T YOU LET TETSU-KUN TAKE UP A KATANA?
WHY CAN'T HE...
...CHOOSE FOR HIMSELF?
....
MORON.
HE'S JUST SOME FIFTEEN-YEAR-OLD KID!
NINE YEARS OLD.

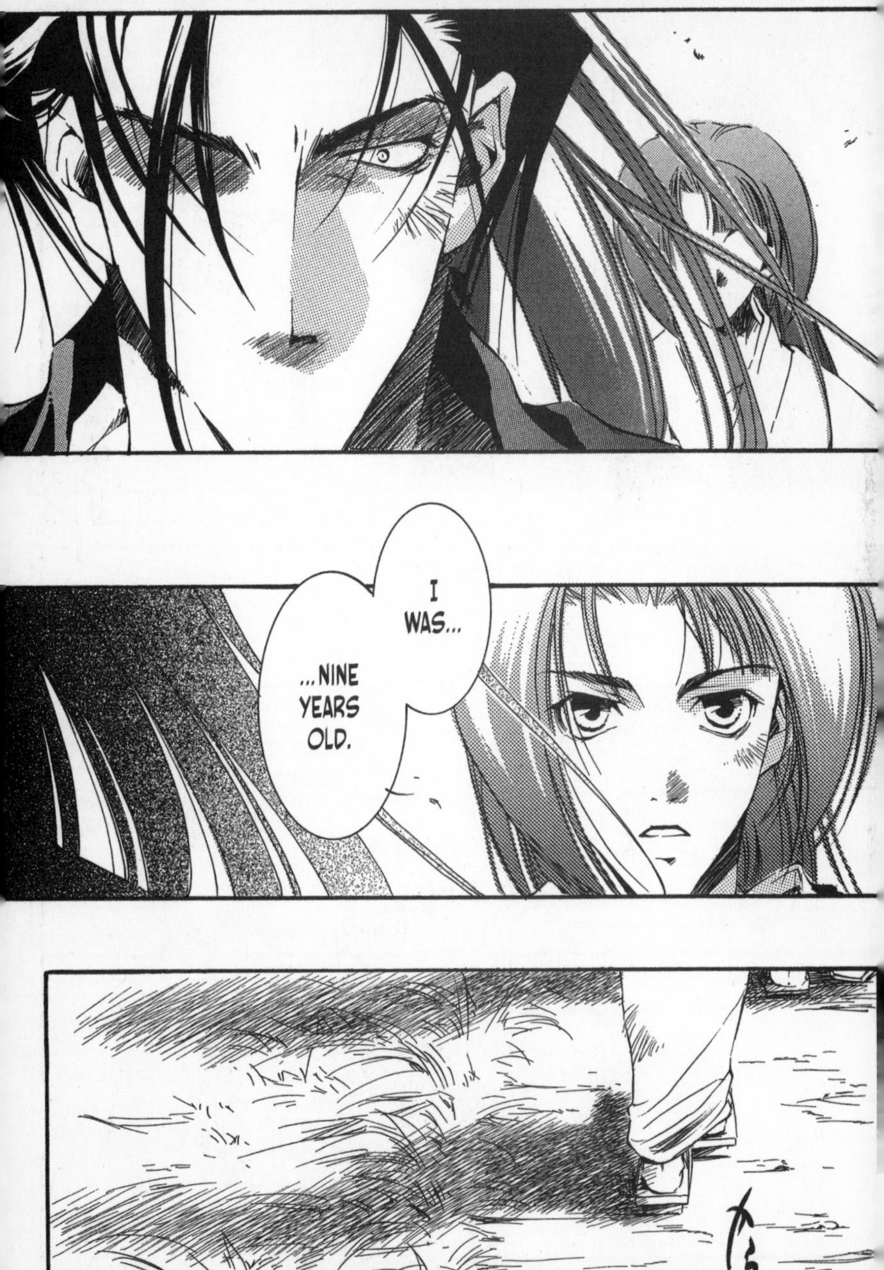
I WAS...
...NINE YEARS OLD.
からん

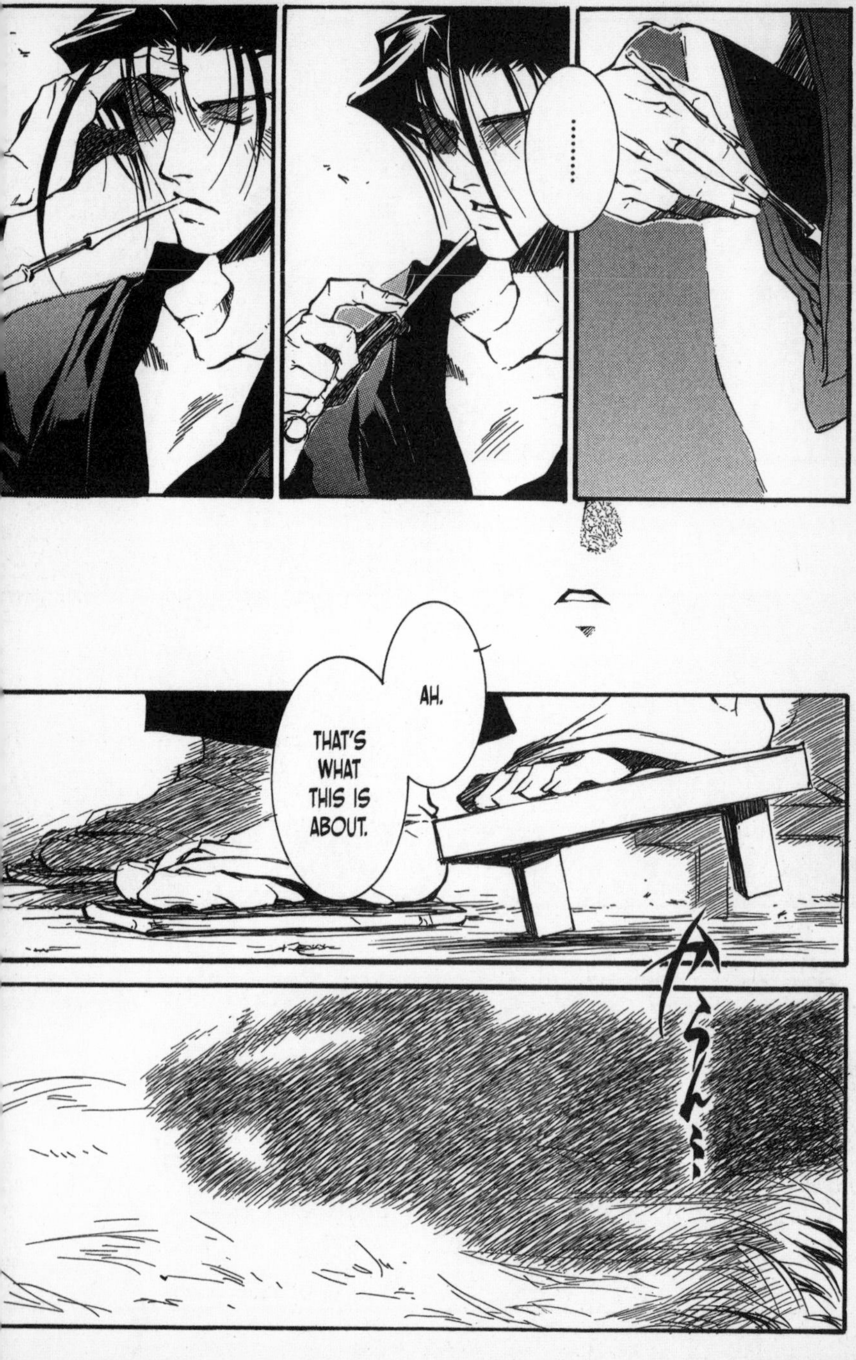
......
AH.
THAT'S WHAT THIS IS ABOUT.

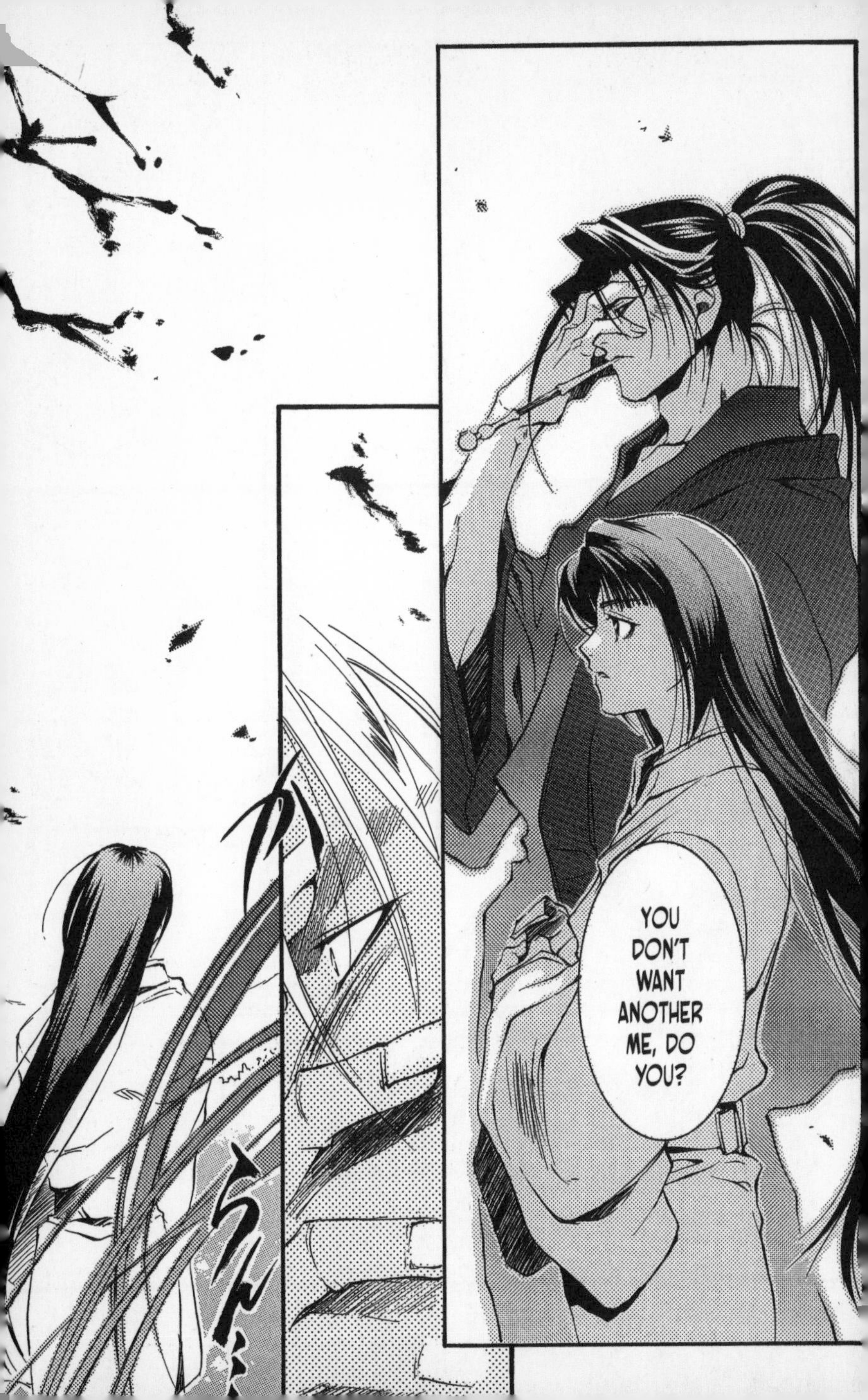
YOU DON'T WANT ANOTHER ME, DO YOU?

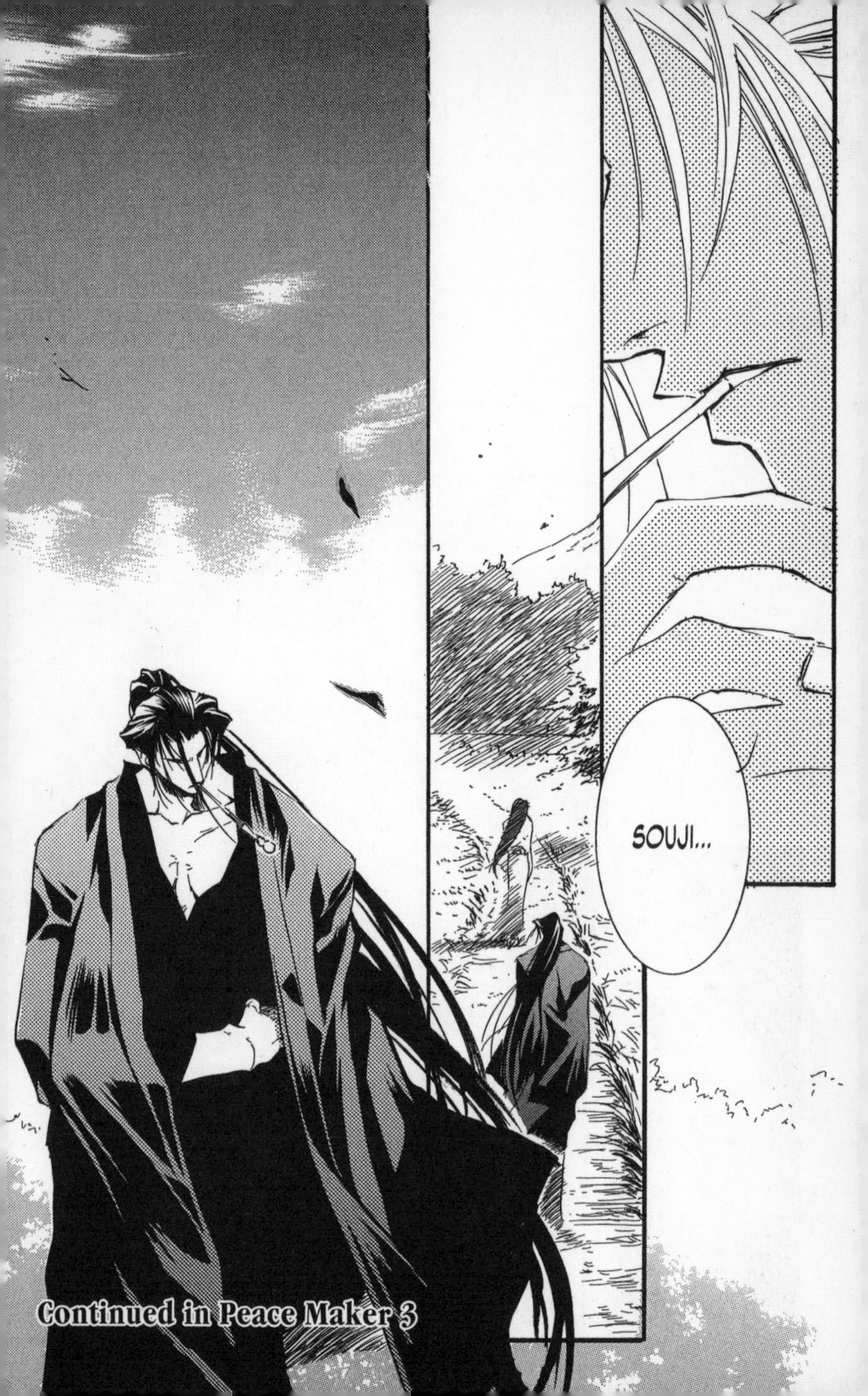
SOUJI...
Continued in Peace Maker 3

In the Next

PEACE MAKER
ピースメーカー

In a pleasure house
Enemies may meet as friends
Until the dream ends.

Coming Soon!

A GUIDE TO THE HISTORICAL ERA OF *PEACE MAKER*

THE HISTORICAL *SHINSENGUMI* WERE INCREDIBLE SWORDSMEN. THE CORE MEMBERS OF THE SHINSENGUMI--MEN LIKE OKITA SOUJI AND HIJIKATA TOSHIZOU--FORGED THEIR RAW TALENT INTO SKILL AT THE INFAMOUS SHIEIKAN DOJO IN EDO (MODERN DAY TOKYO). THE SHIEIKAN WAS THE HEAD DOJO OF THE *TENNEN RISHIN* STYLE OF *KENJUTSU* (SWORDFIGHTING). IT WOULD PROVE A MOST VALUABLE TRAINING GROUND AND FEEDER SYSTEM FOR THE SHINSENGUMI FROM THE GROUP'S INCEPTION IN 1863 UNTIL ITS DEMISE IN 1869. THE TENNEN RISHIN STYLE TAUGHT THERE BECAME WEDDED TO THE BIRTH OF THE SHINSENGUMI AND THE FATE OF JAPAN WHEN A FOURTEEN-YEAR-OLD KONDOU ISAMI BEGAN HIS TRAINING. KONDOU, THE SAME MAN WHO WOULD BECOME THE HEAD OF THE SHINSENGUMI, WAS BORN WEST OF EDO IN A RURAL FARMING COMMUNITY AS MIYAGAWA KATSUGOROU IN 1834. HIS WEALTHY FATHER WAS ABLE TO HIRE AN INSTRUCTOR TO TEACH HIS THREE SONS THE WAY OF THE SWORD, AND THE INSTRUCTOR WHO HAPPENED TO BE IN THE REGION WAS A MASTER BY THE NAME OF KONDOU SHUUSUKE. THE ELDER KONDOU WAS THE AGING MASTER OF THE SHIEIKAN DOJO IN EDO, A MINOR DOJO WHERE THE TENNEN RISHIN STYLE WAS TAUGHT. THE ELDER KONDOU WAS LOOKING FOR AN HEIR TO THE SCHOOL. YOUNG KATSUGOROU FOUND THE FIGHTING STYLE AND LIFESTYLE SUITED HIM, AND WAS FORMALLY ADOPTED BY THE ELDER, TO CONTINUE ON AS AN APPRENTICE AND EVENTUALLY TAKE OVER AS MASTER OF THE SHIEIKAN. HE WAS ADOPTED IN 1849, AND, BY 1863, WHEN THE FIRST MEMBERS OF THE SHINSENGUMI SET OUT AS A ROUSHI CORPS FROM EDO FOR KYOTO, THE CENTRAL MEMBERS OF THE SHINSENGUMI HAD BEEN TRAINED.

NANAE CHRONO MAKES EFFORTS TO INCLUDE ELEMENTS OF THE FIGHTING STYLE, TRAINING AND EQUIPMENT SO QUINTESSENTIAL TO THE LIFE OF THE SHINSENGUMI MEMBERS IN *PEACE MAKER. HIRASEIGAN* IS AN ACTUAL STANCE USED IN KENJUTSU AND KENDO, ALTHOUGH IT IS RATHER RARE NOWADAYS. IT'S UNCLEAR WHY OKITA CHOSE THIS PARTICULAR STANCE TO FIGHT THE MUCH SHORTER TETSU IN THEIR VERY FIRST FIGHT, BECAUSE THE STANCE TYPICALLY DEFENDS AGAINST SOMEONE IN *JOUDAN* (UPPER STANCE). TETSU WOULD BE TOO SHORT FOR THAT! IN HIRASEIGAN, THE *SHINAI* (BAMBOO PRACTICE SWORD) IS POINTED UP AND TO THE RIGHT TO AIM AT THE OPPONENT'S RAISED LEFT *KOTE* (WRIST). A SHORTER FIGHTER WOULD USE A STANDARD *SEIGAN* STANCE WHEN COMPETING AGAINST A TALL OPPONENT. IN KENDO, *SHOMEN* MEANS HEAD, AND *DOU* MEANS TRUNK. WHEN TETSU FIRST VISITED THE PRACTICE ROOM, THE OTHER SHINSENGUMI MEMBERS SUITED UP WITH PRACTICE ARMOR USED FOR TRAINING (NOT THE METAL ARMOR USED IN BATTLE). KENDO ARMOR CONSISTS OF FOUR PARTS: THE *MEN* (HELMET), THE DOU (CHEST PIECE), THE *TARE* (WAIST PROTECTOR), AND A PAIR OF KOTE (GLOVES).

AS IMPORTANT AS THE PHYSICAL WEAPONS AND TECHNIQUES OF FIGHTING WERE THE PSYCHOLOGICAL. THE LAWS THAT GOVERNED THE SHINSENGUMI, READ TO TETSU BY OKITA, WERE SUCH A WEAPON. THE LAWS OF THE SHINSENGUMI INVOLVED LAYING EVEN STRICTER RULES ATOP THE TRADITIONAL CODE OF THE SAMURAI, OR *BUSHIDO*. FOR THE PURPOSES OF *PEACE MAKER*, THE RULES STATE THAT MEMBERS OF THE SHINSENGUMI MUST NOT: DISOBEY THE BUSHIDO, LEAVE THE SHINSENGUMI, RAISE PRIVATE FUNDS, ENGAGE IN PRIVATE LITIGATION OR ENGAGE IN PRIVATE FIGHTS. ANY OF THOSE TRESPASSES WAS PUNISHABLE BY *SEPPUKU*, OR RITUAL SUICIDE BY DISEMBOWELMENT.

-CHRISTINE BOYLAN & HOPE DONOVAN

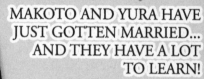

MISSING™
KAMIKAKUSHI NO MONOGATARI

2

ANYONE WHO MEETS *HER* DISAPPEARS

When Kyoichi, a.k.a. "His Majesty, Lord of Darkness," disappears, his friends in the Literature Club suspect he's been spirited away by a girl posing as his girlfriend. Their desperate investigation quickly spirals into a paranormal nightmare, where a fate worse than death waits on the "other side"...

FOR MORE INFORMATION VISIT: WWW.TOKYOPOP.COM

STOP!

This is the back of the book.
You wouldn't want to spoil a great ending!

This book is printed "manga-style," in the authentic Japanese right-to-left format. Since none of the artwork has been flipped or altered, readers get to experience the story just as the creator intended. You've been asking for it, so TOKYOPOP® delivered: authentic, hot-off-the-press, and far more fun!

DIRECTIONS

If this is your first time reading manga-style, here's a quick guide to help you understand how it works.

It's easy... just start in the top right panel and follow the numbers. Have fun, and look for more 100% authentic manga from TOKYOPOP®!